**palgrave advances in renaissance historiography**

*Palgrave Advances*

*Titles include*:

Patrick Finney (*editor*)
INTERNATIONAL HISTORY

Marnie Hughes-Warrington (*editor*)
WORLD HISTORIES

Phillip Mallett (*editor*)
THOMAS HARDY STUDIES

Lois Oppenheim (*editor*)
SAMUEL BECKETT STUDIES

Jean-Michel Rabaté (*editor*)
JAMES JOYCE STUDIES

Frederick S. Roden (*editor*)
OSCAR WILDE STUDIES

Jonathan Woolfson (*editor*)
RENAISSANCE HISTORIOGRAPHY

*Forthcoming:*

Robert Patten and John Bowen (*editors*)
CHARLES DICKENS STUDIES

Anna Snaith (*editor*)
VIRGINIA WOOLF STUDIES

Nicholas Williams (*editor*)
WILLIAM BLAKE STUDIES

Palgrave Advances
Series Standing Order ISBN 1–4039–3512–2 (Hardback) 1–4039–3513–0 (Paperback)
(*outside North America only*)

You can receive future titles in this series as they are published by placing a standing order.
Please contact your bookseller or, in the case of difficulty, write to us at the address below
with your name and address, the title of the series and the ISBN quoted above.

Customer Services Department, Macmillan Distribution Ltd, Houndmills, Basingstoke,
Hampshire RG21 6XS, England

# palgrave advances in
# renaissance historiography

edited by
## jonathan woolfson

First published 2005 by
PALGRAVE MACMILLAN
Houndmills, Basingstoke, Hampshire RG21 6XS and
175 Fifth Avenue, New York, N.Y. 10010
Companies and representatives throughout the world

PALGRAVE MACMILLAN is the global academic imprint of the
Palgrave Macmillan division of St Martin's Press LLC and of
Palgrave Macmillan Ltd.
Macmillan® is a registered trademark in the United States,
United Kingdom and other countries. Palgrave is a registered
trademark in the European Union and other countries.

ISBN 1–4039–0117–1 hardback
ISBN 1–4039–1239–4 paperback

This book is printed on paper suitable for recycling and
made from fully managed and sustained forest sources.

A catalogue record for this book is available
from the British Library.

Library of Congress Cataloging-in-Publication Data
Palgrave advances in Renaissance historiography / edited by Jonathan Woolfson.
     p. cm. — (Palgrave advances)
Includes bibliographical references and index.
ISBN 1–4039–0117–1 — ISBN 1-4039–1239–4 (pbk.)
     1. Renaissance—Historiography. 2. Renaissance. I. Woolfson, Jonathan. II. Series.

CB361.P225 2005
940.2.'1'072—dc22

                                                                                2004051408

10   9   8   7   6   5   4   3   2   1
14   13   12   11   10   09   08   07   06   05

Printed and bound in Great Britain by
Antony Rowe Ltd, Chippenham and Eastbourne

# contents

## part three

# notes on the contributors

David **Abulafia** is Professor of Mediterranean History at Cambridge University and a Fellow of Gonville and Caius College. His books have a southern Italian flavour and include *The Two Italies* (1977), *Frederick II* (1988) and *The Western Mediterranean Kingdoms, 1200–1500* (1997), all of which have also appeared in Italian. The President of Italy appointed him Commendatore dell'Ordine della Stella della Solidarietà Italiana in 2003.

Alessandro **Arcangeli** is Lecturer in Renaissance and Early Modern History at the University of Verona. He received his doctorate at the University of Pisa, has studied at the Warburg Institute, University of London (1989–90) and was a Fellow of Villa I Tatti (1998–99). His work has concentrated on the cultural history of dance (*Davide o Salomè*, 2000) and of pastimes (*Recreation in the Renaissance*, 2003; Italian translation *Passatempi rinascimentali*, 2004).

Robert **Black** is Professor of Renaissance History at the University of Leeds. His books include *Benedetto Accolti and the Florentine Renaissance* (1985) and *Humanism and Education in Medieval and Renaissance Italy: Tradition and Innovation in Latin Schools from the Twelfth to the Fifteenth Century* (2001). He has also edited *Renaissance Thought: A Reader* (2001).

Warren **Boutcher** is Senior Lecturer in the School of English and Drama, Queen Mary, University of London. He has published numerous papers on Montaigne, on Renaissance vernacular humanism and on modern intellectual history, most recently in the *Journal of the History of Ideas* (2003), in *EMF: Studies in Early Modern France* (2004), and in *Shakespeare et Montaigne: vers un nouvel humanisme*, ed. P. Kapitaniak and J. M. Maguin

(2003). His main book project is entitled *The School of Montaigne: A Cultural History of the* Essais.

**Judith C. Brown** is Vice President for Academic Affairs, Provost and Professor of History at Wesleyan University. She is the author of *In the Shadow of Florence: Provincial Society in Renaissance Pescia* (1982) and *Immodest Acts: The Life of a Lesbian Nun in Renaissance Italy* (1985), and co-editor with Robert C. Davis of *Gender and Society in Renaissance Italy* (1998). She is the author of numerous articles on women's history, the history of sexuality and the social and economic history of Renaissance Italy.

**Peter Burke** is a Fellow of Emmanuel College and was until his recent retirement Professor of Cultural History, University of Cambridge. His studies of the Renaissance include *Culture and Society in Renaissance Italy* (1972, 4th edn 1999), *The Renaissance* (1987) and *The European Renaissance* (1998).

**Riccardo Fubini** is Professor of Renaissance History at the University of Florence. He is the editor of Lorenzo de'Medici, *Lettere*, I and II (1977) and the author of *Quattrocento fiorentino. Politica, diplomazia, cultura* (1996), *L'umanesimo italiano e i suoi storici: Origini rinascimentali – critica moderna* (2001), *Humanism and Secularization, from Petrarch to Valla* (2003), and *Storiografia dell'umanesimo in Italia da Leonardo Bruni ad Annio da Viterbo* (2003).

**James Hankins** is Professor of History at Harvard University and General Editor of the I Tatti Renaissance Library. Two volumes of his collected papers, *Humanism and Platonism in the Italian Renaissance*, were published in 2003–04.

**John Jeffries Martin** is a Professor and Chair of the Department of History at Trinity University. His books include *Venice's Hidden Enemies: Italian Heretics in a Renaissance City* (1993) and *Myths of Renaissance Individualism* (2004).

**John M. Najemy** is Professor of History at Cornell University. He is the author of *Corporatism and Consensus in Florentine Electoral Politics, 1280–1400* (1982), *Between Friends: Discourses of Power and Desire in the Machiavelli–Vettori Letters of 1513–1515* (1993), and many essays on Florentine politics and Renaissance political thought. He has recently edited *Italy in the Age of the Renaissance* (2004) for the Short Oxford History of Italy series and is currently completing a history of Florence from the thirteenth to the mid-sixteenth century.

**Brian W. Ogilvie** is Associate Professor of History at the University of Massachusetts Amherst, where he teaches Renaissance and early modern European history, the history of science, and the history of religions. He has published several articles on Renaissance natural history, and his first book, *The Science of Describing: Natural History in Renaissance Europe, 1490–1620*, will appear in 2005. At present he is studying the relationships among antiquarian studies, diplomacy and polite culture in seventeenth-century Europe.

**Catherine M. Soussloff** is Professor of History of Art and Visual Culture at the University of California, Santa Cruz. She is the author of *The Absolute Artist: The Historiography of a Concept* (1997) and *The Subject in Art* (forthcoming), and the editor of *Jewish Identity in Modern Art History* (1999). She has published numerous articles and essays on the historiography of Italian art, on performance and performativity, on film, and on art theory in the European tradition.

**Jonathan Woolfson** is Adjunct Professor of Renaissance History at New York University in Florence. He is the author of *Padua and the Tudors: English Students in Italy, 1485–1603* (1998) and the editor of *Reassessing Tudor Humanism* (2002). He has published articles on the cultural and intellectual history of Tudor England and on Anglo-Italian relations in the sixteenth century.

# introduction

## jonathan woolfson

*Palgrave Advances in Renaissance Historiography* is an introduction to the main areas of debate in the study of the Renaissance today and in the last few decades. Underlying this book is a distinction between history and historiography. If history is the study of the past, historiography, in the sense which it is intended here, is the study of history. That is to say, rather than basing itself on a systematic analysis of those textual and other remains of the past that historians traditionally call 'primary sources', historiography explores the tendencies, developments and sometimes unarticulated assumptions that inform historians' writings. For the historiography of the Renaissance, 'primary sources' consist not of treatises, correspondence, institutional records, diaries or poetry dating *from* the Renaissance, but of history books and articles *about* the Renaissance. If that rather forbidding distinction means that readers turning the pages of this book will not find another general account of the Renaissance, in all its 'purple and gold',[1] there is nonetheless reason to believe that the historiographical approach to the Renaissance is a timely one. 'Renaissance' is one of the most powerful and evocative terms in the historical lexicon, but it is also one of the most contested. Yet, in spite of a tradition of scholarly articles debating the concept in several languages, there is only one modern, comprehensive treatment of the subject in English, Wallace Klippert Ferguson's much acclaimed and still essential *The Renaissance in Historical Thought*, first published in 1948. Ferguson's book, which is frequently cited in this collection, surveys the development of a concept of the Renaissance from its origins in the Renaissance itself down to his own age, including along the way consideration of the epoch-making study of Jacob Burckhardt, *The Civilization of the Renaissance in Italy*, of 1860. But the half century and more which has passed since Ferguson wrote has witnessed an unprecedented acceleration of scholarly production on the subject, and inevitably the shape of Renaissance studies has changed dramatically in that intervening period. This book does not aim at Ferguson's chronological breadth. Rather, most contributors have taken Ferguson's study itself – or that of Jacob Burckhardt – as their starting points. *Palgrave Advances in Renaissance Historiography* may thus function as an updating of Ferguson's labours, both reassessing issues on which he wrote in the light of new research, and breaking historiographical ground of which he could not be aware. In short it aims to throw the reader a compass and a lifejacket in the ocean which is today's study of the Renaissance.

One of the intellectual tendencies of our age of which Ferguson could not be aware also makes this collection timely, namely postmodernism, which has subjected the historical profession to serious, even devastating, criticism.[2] In its more radical forms the postmodern critique of history can be said to collapse the very distinction between history and historiography on which this collection depends. This critique proposes that *all* history is historiography, in the sense that historians, whether they know it or not, operate within a historiographical tradition and utilize concepts and assumptions silently inherited from their predecessors. Even total immersion in the primary sources offers no antidote to the inescapably constructed, artificial, present-oriented nature of the historical enterprise: the quest for the truth about the past is a delusion.[3] On a less radical level, however, postmodernism has encouraged historians to reflect more than before about the intellectual foundations of their work, and it is at this level that this book might be helpful to students, scholars, teachers and general readers. It does not advocate historiographical study over and above traditionally conceived historical research. On the contrary, in their essays in this volume many of the contributors combine their studies of the historiography of their subjects with a consideration of the primary materials on which they are expert. After all, it is for their work as historians that the most distinguished of them have achieved a kind of historiographical status in their own right! Nonetheless, this book argues that consideration of the historiography is vitally important in helping historians to sort historiographical assumptions, the products of later ages, from the actual subject matter of their studies.

One final reason for the importance of the historiographical approach is that, as James Hankins points out in his contribution to this volume, the historical period of the Renaissance itself lies at the origins of our modern periodization of the past and approaches to the writing of history. Even if, in its French dress, *la Renaissance* is in the main a nineteenth-century construction, it was during the fourteenth, fifteenth and sixteenth centuries that observers and innovators on the contemporary intellectual scene came to regard their own age, or aspects of it, as characterized by a rebirth, following the 'dark' Middle Ages, which in turn had followed a classical 'golden age'.[4] At the same time, historians during the Renaissance began to write about the past with a new literary and philological sophistication – and a new, more profound apprehension of historical time – which has long been located at the origins of the modern approach to the writing of history.[5] To note these different but connected ways of relating to the Renaissance today is thus to evoke a powerful modern sense of indebtedness to that age.

The scholars whose work comprises this volume testify collectively that the study of Renaissance historiography is no antiquarian endeavour. On the contrary, it seems that rumours of the Renaissance's death have been greatly exaggerated. One of the signs of such vitality is that contributors by no means always agree with each other about the significance of the Renaissance and its various historiographies, nor have they been encouraged to reach some kind of artificial consensus about matters on which they disagree. Even the significance of major individual figures in the historiography of the Renaissance, such as Jacob Burckhardt or Paul Oskar Kristeller, is much disputed: there are moments when the reader's compass might spin out of control, not least because the international flavour of the collection, with contributions from America, England and Italy, means that different authors have themselves been nurtured in different historiographical traditions. But even if the concept of the Renaissance continues to be challenged – and in her chapter Catherine Soussloff suggests that the challenge is more likely to come these days from 'early modernists' rather than from, as in the days of Ferguson, medievalists – most contributors are comfortable to continue employing the notion itself, even when they invest it with diverse meanings.

Part One of this book introduces the reader to some preliminary issues concerning when and especially where the Renaissance happened. As is indicated in the first chapter, the founding figure of modern Renaissance studies, Jacob Burckhardt, was emphatic that the Renaissance originated in Italy; he was equally insistent that it then spread to western and northern Europe, but he did not explore that process. Questions concerning the transmission of the Renaissance, from northern to southern Italy, from southern Italy to other parts of Europe, and from Europe to the rest of the world, are considered in Chapters 2 and 3. In Part Two, three of today's most important interpreters of Renaissance humanism present their contrasting views of the historiographical place of that movement in the wider Renaissance picture. And in Part Three, the historiography of the Renaissance is considered from the perspective of different modern historical disciplines. The division of chapters in this section, reflecting today's intellectual world rather than that of the Renaissance, is somewhat artificial; but readers should also bear in mind that, for the Renaissance of all subjects, boundaries are – and should be – extremely porous: it is a testimony to their importance across several disciplines that certain themes, issues and historiographical figures are referred to across different chapters of the book. That said, because of limitations of space, editorial choice, or historiographical preferences in today's academic world, not every aspect of the Renaissance has received its due. Although they are discussed in this volume, philosophy, music and economics do not have chapters to themselves.[6] Although a number of essays deal with the Renaissance outside of Italy, there can be little doubt that that country continues to be central to the modern notion of the Renaissance, and this is clearly reflected here. Furthermore, in terms of the historiography of the transmission of the Renaissance, the decision was made to introduce Anglophone readers to the less familiar areas of the Renaissance in southern Italy, Spain and Hungary (see Chapter 2), and to the Renaissance in a wider world (see Chapter 3), rather than attempt to cover the vast but much better-known story of the impact of the Italian Renaissance in northern Europe. If as a result Erasmus, the doyen of northern Renaissance humanists, and the trinity of 'Renaissance monarchs' comprising Charles V, Henry VIII and Francis I, appear on these pages less frequently than they deserve, it is hoped that most readers' perspectives on the Renaissance will be broadened as a result of that sacrifice.[7]

It remains to thank the various people who have been involved in this project: first and foremost the contributors, for their enthusiasm and commitment, and for their heroic labours in meeting pressing deadlines; Luciana O'Flaherty at Palgrave, on whose inspired combination of patience and determination I have depended; and my partner Rita Maria Comanducci, without whose superb advice, good humour and loving support this book would not exist.

## notes

1. The phrase is Johan Huizinga's, quoted in Peter Burke, *The Renaissance* (Houndmills and London, 1987), p. 1.
2. See Richard J. Evans, *In Defence of History* (London, 1997).
3. The literature is vast, but see Keith Jenkins, *Re-Thinking History* (London and New York, 1991).

4. See J. R. Hale, *The Civilization of Europe in the Renaissance* (London, 1993), pp. 585–92; M. L. McLaughlin, 'Humanist Concepts of Renaissance and Middle Ages in the Tre- and Quattrocento', *Renaissance Studies*, II (1988) 131–42; Peter Burke, *The Renaissance Sense of the Past* (London, 1969).
5. Eric Cochrane, *Historians and Historiography in the Italian Renaissance* (Chicago, 1981); Donald R. Kelley, *The Foundations of Modern Historical Scholarship: Language, Law and History in the French Renaissance* (New York, 1970); D. R. Woolf, *Reading History in Early Modern England* (Cambridge, 2001); Erwin Panofsky, *Renaissance and Renascences in Western Art* (New York, 1969), esp. pp. 42–113.
6. For philosophy see chapters by James Hankins and Riccardo Fubini; for music those of David Abulafia and James Hankins; and for economics see the chapter by Alessandro Arcangeli.
7. On these figures see Bruce Mansfield, *Erasmus in the Twentieth Century* (Toronto and London, 2003); Glenn Richardson, *Renaissance Monarchy: The Reigns of Henry VIII, Francis I and Charles V* (London, 2002); and more generally Peter Burke, *The European Renaissance: Centres and Peripheries* (Oxford, 1998); A. Goodman and A. MacKay, eds, *The Impact of Humanism on Western Europe* (London, 1990); R. Porter and M. Teich, eds, *The Renaissance in National Context* (Cambridge, 1992); Hale, *Civilization*; Robin Kirkpatrick, *The European Renaissance, 1400–1600* (Harlow, 2002); and the five-volume Open University series *The Renaissance in Europe* (New Haven and London, 2000).

# part one

# 1
# burckhardt's ambivalent renaissance

jonathan woolfson

Writing in the London *Observer* on 8 February 2004, the former Monty Python member Terry Jones explained that the main reason why he wanted to make a television series about the Middle Ages 'was to get my own back on the Renaissance':

> It's not that the Renaissance has ever done me any harm personally, you understand. It's just that I'm sick of the way people's eyes light up when they start talking about the Renaissance. I'm sick of the way art critics tend to say: 'Aaaah! The Renaissance!' with that deeply self-satisfied air of someone who is at last getting down to the Real Thing. And I'm sick to death of that ridiculous assumption that before the Renaissance human beings had no sense of individuality.

Jones' attack on the Renaissance attests to the strength of feeling about that contested concept, but also to its remarkable capacity for survival and reinvention, a 'crafty phoenix' as one scholar has recently described it.[1] For if today, as is sometimes suggested, there is a 'crisis' in Renaissance studies,[2] this has nearly always been the case. People have been arguing about what is meant by the Renaissance – about when and where it happened; about whether or not it was a good thing; about whether, in fact, it existed at all – ever since the late eighteenth century, when 'la Renaissance' was first used to describe a distinct period in history.[3] It was in the nineteenth century that French historians, above all Jules Michelet in his massive *History of France*, popularized the term so successfully that the French word 'Renaissance' has stayed with us, despite changes in its meaning.[4] And the key mediator between a French and Italian Renaissance in that period was the Swiss historian Jacob Burckhardt. Writing in German exclusively about the history of Italy, Burckhardt adopted the French version of the word in his epoch-making book of 1860, *Die Kultur der Renaissance in Italien: Ein Versuch – The Civilization of the Renaissance in Italy: An Essay* (first English edition 1878). It is not clear whether it adds prestige to their work, or is rather a liability, that many of today's Renaissance historians still identify this nineteenth-century writer as the founding father of their field. But if, as Terry Jones suggests, people still believe in the 'ridiculous assumption' that human beings had no sense of individuality before the Renaissance, this is largely due to Burckhardt's great book, with its famous section on 'The Development of the Individual'. Even if many of the central conclusions of Burckhardt's essay have long been contested, 'more powerfully and persuasively than any other historical work' – as one distinguished scholar of Renaissance Florence has recently written – 'Burckhardt's masterpiece has shaped our sense of our own past, our perception of how our culture has developed over the centuries from its classical and Christian origins to the present'.[5] We may wish to go further and suggest that the success and durability of the concept of the Renaissance has been – and continues to be – dependent on the influence of Burckhardt's *Civilization*.[6]

Elsewhere in this collection readers will find discussions of how the field of Renaissance studies currently stands in relation to Burckhardt.[7] Although some reference to recent developments will also be made here, the more modest aim of this chapter is to explore Burckhardt's idea of the Renaissance as it appears in his book. In the last few decades Burckhardt has been investigated afresh.[8] By delving into some central aspects of his *Civilization*, this chapter will suggest that his concept of the Renaissance is more interesting and relevant than the traditional image of it would suggest. In particular, it will aim to show what a doubtful and ambivalent picture of the Renaissance he created, one that may be of more use to us than the celebratory and triumphalist one to which we are perhaps more accustomed.

## jacob burckhardt

Burckhardt was born in 1818 in Basel, a city-republic belonging to the Swiss Confederation, to a respected middle-class family with deep roots in the town. His father was a Protestant pastor and this was probably the career marked out for Jacob too. Burckhardt commenced his university career in Basel with three years' study of classics and theology, but partly under the impact of the liberal theologian W. M. L. de Wette, he underwent a severe crisis of faith, shedding during the 1840s his traditional Protestant beliefs. The crisis marked him deeply and probably explains his interest as a historian in periods of religious transition such as the age of Constantine the Great and the Renaissance.[9] For his new vocation was history and the history of art, and this explains his move in 1839 to the University of Berlin, one of the great intellectual centres of the nineteenth century. Except for a spell at Bonn University in 1841, he remained there until 1843. The impact of Berlin on his formation as a historian was incalculable. He was taught there by some of the great contemporary masters of the subject including Leopold von Ranke,[10] and he absorbed there both the pioneering historical methodologies and the assumptions about the history of the state to which much of his later historical writing, *The Civilization of the Renaissance in Italy* in particular, represents a powerful critique.[11] But it was also in Berlin, under the influence of Franz Kugler, that his studies of the conventional subject matter of history were supplemented and challenged by an appreciation of the history of art. (He would stay in Berlin again in 1846–47 revising Kugler's textbook on art history.) In turn the history of art had the inevitable effect of drawing him towards Italy, where he toured frequently. (His visits there in 1846, 1848 and 1853–54 were particularly formative.) Besides an unhappy spell as the editor of the conservative Basel newspaper the *Basler Zeitung* in 1844–46, the rest of his life was dedicated to the researching and teaching of history. This was a vocation pursued with an intensity which, as he himself admitted, precluded 'a happy home life';[12] remaining a bachelor, he did not retire from lecturing until 1893, at the age of seventy-five, four years before his death. Most of his career was spent at the University of Basel. After a period of freelance lecturing in the city, he was appointed to the new Polytechnic at Zurich in 1855, but was wooed back to Basel in 1858 as Professor of History, a position which he later held concurrently with Professor of the History of Art. That he refused Ranke's prestigious Chair in History at Berlin University in 1872 is testimony to the extent to which, by that time, he had become entrenched in the life of his home-town, whose political and cultural atmosphere was increasingly seen as standing in opposition to the German nationalism emanating from Berlin and elsewhere. Shaken above all by the revolutionary events of the years 1846–52, Burckhardt shared his concerns about a strong and centralized German state with his younger friend and colleague Friedrich Nietzsche. Indeed he became a notable conservative critic of the mainstream political, cultural and intellectual tendencies of his time, and fearful of the impact of a range of developments in modern life, from centralization to industrialization and revolution. He professed himself an advocate, rather, of the cultural values of 'old Europe' (and fully shared some of the less elevated prejudices of that civilization, such as orientalism and antisemitism).[13] In many respects his cultural and intellectual values derive from the French and especially German Enlightenment as represented by such figures as Voltaire, Goethe and Herder.

Although lecturing was arguably his greatest gift, he is known today for a series of books which have impacted profoundly on modern perceptions of western history. His three most important were *The Age of Constantine the Great* (*Die Zeit Constantins des Grossen*, 1852); *The Cicerone: A Guide to the Enjoyment of Italian Art* (*Der Cicerone, eine Anleitung zum Genuss der Kunstwerke Italiens*, 1855); and *The Civilization of the Renaissance in Italy*. These were followed by *The Architecture of the Italian Renaissance* (*Geschichte der neueren Baukunst*, 1867). Other works were published posthumously, some from his lecture notes. These include *The History of Greek Civilization* (*Griechische Kulturgeschichte*, 1898–1902) and *Reflections on World History* (*Weltgeschichtliche Betrachtungen*, 1905).

## the civilization of the renaissance in italy approach, structure, method

In the opening paragraph of the *Civilization* Burckhardt writes that 'it is the most serious difficulty in the history of civilization that a great intellectual process must be broken up into single, and often into what seem arbitrary categories in order to be in any way intelligible'.[14] It is a point he insists upon: he asks his readers to judge his book as a whole, and later claims that 'The Renaissance would not have been the process of world-wide significance which it is if its elements could be so easily separated from one another.'[15] In fact one of the most remarkable achievements of the book, and one which in large part accounts for its power as a piece of historical writing, is the success with which he weaves a mass of rich and varied detail into a coherent account of the period. In Burckhardt's vision 'civilization' (*Kultur*) represents the total and authentic historical experience and character of a given time and place. In later times, when knowledge and historical specialization have expanded, he has been criticized for deriving this notion not from the materials of history itself – 'primary sources' – but, indirectly at least, from the idealist philosophy of G. W. F. Hegel (1770–1831), and for producing as a result an alarmingly static picture of three centuries, one which later researchers have inevitably argued is unsatisfactory in its documentation and interpretation.[16]

It is true that Burckhardt was extremely well read in those original sources for the history of Renaissance Italy that were available in print in his day, and it is also the case that he supplemented this reading with forays into the archives in Italy. On the other hand, his approach was also intuitive and subjective. The power of his book partly depends on his urbane, personable and unpretentious voice, and his amazing perception and eye for telling and ironic detail. In his account of the petty tyrants of Renaissance Italy, for example, Burckhardt recounts that the 'pastime in the summer months' of Pandolfo Petrucci, ruler of Siena, 'was to roll blocks of stone from the top of Monte Amiata, without caring what or whom they hit'.[17] It sums up the man and his despicable type more effectively than any extended description. On the other side, Leon Battista Alberti is taken to be emblematic of the more optimistic, and multifaceted, aspects of Renaissance culture.[18] Burckhardt liberally uses the kinds of subjective evidence drawn from poetry and other forms of imaginative literature that other historians treated – and treat – with suspicion.[19] In his search for the 'spirit' of the society, he believed that such material may reveal deeper truths than other, 'harder' kinds of evidence, associated in his time with Ranke and the German historical school.[20] Indeed entire sections of the *Civilization* are drawn from Italian poetry and *novelle*, and writers such as Boccaccio, Dante and Bandello are frequently cited.[21] Just as his Renaissance gives rise to the discovery of human subjectivity, so Burckhardt as a historian is also aware of the subjective nature of his work, and occasionally interposes his own ironic voice.[22] 'History to me is always poetry for the greater part', he wrote.[23]

Above all, it is his capacity not to miss the wood for the trees, to sustain a very small number of themes, which marks out his work as a masterpiece of historical writing.[24] The work is divided into six parts: (1) 'The State as a Work of Art', (2) 'The Development of the Individual', (3) 'The Revival of Antiquity', (4) 'The Discovery of the World and of Man', (5) 'Society and Festivals' and (6) 'Morality and Religion'; but Burckhardt ensures that a series of central themes, presented in different guises and evinced by different kinds of historical material, crop up throughout. It is worth documenting some examples of this structure. In identifying Dante, Petrarch and others as representatives of a new kind of secular, literary hero in Italy during the Renaissance, whose homes and tombs became the sites of cultural pilgrimage, Burckhardt illustrates in part 3 the secularization of life which is an explicit theme of part 6. The title of part 4, 'The Discovery of the World and of Man' is a phrase which was borrowed from Jules Michelet, who employed it to sum up the meaning of 'the amiable term *Renaissance*'. In Burckhardt's hands it is used to mean the discovery of new territories and a new appreciation, both artistic and scientific, of the natural world, as well as the discovery of human subjectivity and spirituality. All of this rests on the theme of part 2, 'the development of the individual'.

Burckhardt's major themes are not only sustained right across his book but also within individual parts of it. For example, in 'War as a Work of Art', chapter 9 of his first part, he notes that

> the development of the individual soldier found its most complete expression in those public and solemn conflicts between one or more pairs of combatants which were practised long before the famous *Challenge of Barletta* (1503). The victor was assured of the praises of poets and scholars, which were denied to the Northern warrior. The result of these combats was no longer regarded as a divine judgement, but as a triumph of personal merit, and to the minds of the spectators seemed to be both the decision of an exciting competition and a satisfaction for the honour of the army or the nation.[25]

Embedded in this account we have almost all of Burckhardt's main themes: the development of individualism, in this case of the individual soldier engaged in a competitive bout, whose fame will be ensured and merits praised if he should win; the end of a religious world view associated with the Middle Ages, for the result of the contest will *no longer* be regarded as a divine judgement; and finally Italy contrasted with elsewhere, for in northern Europe the warrior could not enjoy the praises of poets and scholars for his achievements. Burckhardt does not say here, but makes it repeatedly clear elsewhere, that Europe would later learn these modes of thought and habit from Italy, that indeed Italian civilization during the Renaissance constitutes something characteristically modern. Thus we may list Burckhardt's five central theses about the Renaissance in Italy as follows: (1) the Renaissance is a coherent period in history with a relatively clear beginning and end, which is to be contrasted with the Middle Ages in particular; (2) the growth of individualism and its various manifestations, such as the cult of fame and the equalization of classes, are defining characteristics of the Renaissance; (3) the Renaissance witnessed the rise of a secular, or possibly pagan, outlook; (4) Italian experience in the Renaissance was exceptional in European context; and (5) the Renaissance was the harbinger of modernity: through the Renaissance Italy taught Europe to be modern. We will see in the following observations on these arguments that these claims are more complicated that they might at first appear.

## periodization, religion, modernity

Burckhardt is insistent in the controversial assertion that the Renaissance was sharply differentiated from the medieval world. His most famous claim in the most famous passage of the book is that

> In the Middle Ages both sides of human consciousness – that which was turned within as that which was turned without – lay dreaming or half awake beneath a common veil. The veil was woven of faith, illusion and childish prepossession, through which the world and history were seen clad in strange hues. Man was conscious of himself only as a member of a race, people, party, family or corporation – only through some general category. In Italy this veil first melted into air; an *objective* treatment and consideration of the State and of all the things of this world became possible. The *subjective* side at the same time asserted itself with corresponding emphasis; man became a spiritual *individual*, and recognized himself as such.[26]

Some of the earliest and most well-known criticisms of his book were intended to counter this concept of a Renaissance sharply distinguished from the Middle Ages.[27] Nevertheless, it is less often noted that in his last section Burckhardt admits to important continuities with the medieval world, and on grounds that contest precisely the confident statement above, namely religion.

In fact his treatment of morality and religion in Renaissance Italy in part 6, far from suggesting a sharp break with the Middle Ages, would characterize the Renaissance as an age of transition. Here he is deeply and insistently aware of the danger of 'unqualified assumptions and rash generalisations', of his limited ability to do justice to the complexity of the topic.[28] Here he asks: 'Who can tell if the Italian before the thirteenth century possessed that flexible activitiy and certainty in his whole being – that play of power in shaping whatever subject he dealt with in word or in form – which was peculiar to him later?' and decides to refrain from 'an absolute and final verdict'.[29] Thus, side by side with ecclesiastical corruption, a growing religious scepticism, deeply felt anticlericalism, and rise of paganism, he draws attention to the spiritual revival movements fostered by great preachers such as Bernardino da Siena and Girolamo Savonarola, and the continued importance of saints, relics and worship in everyday life. Furthermore, in contrast to the Italian exceptionalism noted elsewhere in the book, he confesses that 'all that has to do with penitence and the attainment of salvation by means of good works was at much the same stage of development or corruption as in the North of Europe'.[30] Although 'in questions of this kind it is perilous to grasp too hastily at absolute results',[31] he admits that 'underneath this outward shell' of scepticism or paganism 'much genuine religion could still survive'.[32] How the painful spiritual journey of this pastor's son and former theology student feeds into this account can only be imagined.[33] A long tradition, dating back at least to the eighteenth-century Enlightenment, had seen the Renaissance as essentially secular.[34] It tells us much about Burckhardt's faithfulness to his sources, and to his scepticism – not least about his own thesis – that he is prepared to admit to a significant religious element in the society of Renaissance Italy.

Nonetheless, one of his most important and insistent claims is that the Renaissance was indeed characteristically modern. This claim has been enormously influential: it seems to promise us that the Renaissance is important, that it is fundamentally linked to later times, and that by studying it we will understand our own Europe and its predicaments (for the modernity that Burckhardt had in mind is not a parochially Italian affair but a broadly European one). But even discounting his doubts about religion, the claims to Italy's modernity and later impact on Europe are repeatedly asserted rather than proved, and remain difficult to understand.[35] If we take Burckhardt to be referring to a modern *period* in history, this, while helping to distinguish the Renaissance from the Middle Ages, in another sense works against giving the Renaissance a distinctive physiognomy of its own, for it may suggest that the Renaissance has never in fact ended, in which case it may not be a historical period at all, or at best be a transitional one. In fact in several parts of his book Burckhardt suggests that the civilization which he describes was ending in Italy during the sixteenth century. The 1520s in Rome are characterized as a period of decline,[36] and the Counter-Reformation is said to have 'annihilated the higher spiritual life of the people'.[37] The 'grave moral crisis' of the early sixteenth century, generated by the very phenomenon that defines his Renaissance, 'excessive individualism', may have led to Italy's ruination and loss of liberty.[38] This might suggest – and other of his writings tend to confirm – that although for Burckhardt characteristics of modernity are associated with a particular period in history – the modern age – his modernism is not in itself a period but rather a series of historical forces, forces which are potentially driving his own world towards ruin. Implicit, then, in Burckhardt's conception of the Renaissance is a profoundly felt critique of his own times.[39] Regarded with deep misgivings, modernity first arose in the Renaissance but has erupted again later, for example during the French Revolution and in subsequent European revolutions.[40]

It is only in this unsystematic, intuitive and undogmatic sense that, in words which have resounded through Renaissance scholarship down to our own times, Italy can be called the 'leader of modern ages' and Italians 'the first-born among the sons of modern Europe'.[41]

## individualism, antiquity, politics

That the Italian Renaissance witnessed the breakdown of corporate and communal forms of identity and traditional beliefs about morality and society; that this was combined with the growth of self-consciousness, of an awareness of the power to shape the self, are controversial claims and have been interrogated from a range of perspectives.[42] Even without taking into account the historical evidence, they are problematic at a conceptual level. Burckhardt's interest in Renaissance Italy may represent an escape from the Germanocentric historiography of his Berlin colleagues, and a characteristically Swiss, indeed Basler, sympathy for the experience of the city-state; Italy may be said to enable him to practise a kind of national history without the need for nationalism. Yet in another sense, treating Italians as a group betrays an Hegelian preoccupation with the spirit of a people as a collective entity, with the *Volksgeist*. Yet can a *Volksgeist* be characterized by individualism? Something of the tension inherent in the idea is conveyed by the evocative English translation of a line from the *Civilization*: 'At the end of the thirteenth century Italy began to swarm with individuality.' For how can individuals 'swarm'?[43]

In the context of his time, however, these claims also represent a critique of earlier, more restricted, visions of the Renaissance, which tied the term to a particular revival of literature, of the arts or the sciences.[44] Burckhardt in contrast insists 'as one of the chief propositions of this book, that it was not the revival of antiquity alone, but its union with the genius of the Italian people, which achieved the conquest of the Western world'.[45] The classical revival as represented by Renaissance humanism is still often considered one of the characteristic features of the Renaissance, but Burckhardt claims it was only a vehicle or outward manifestation of great changes in the Italian spirit.[46] It is thus revealing that, although the word 'Renaissance' is frequently associated with Burckhardt, he himself was ambivalent about it, sometimes calling it 'the so-called Renaissance' or placing the term in inverted commas. And he claims that the 'new birth' (represented by the term Renaissance) 'has one-sidedly been chosen as the name to sum up the whole period'.[47]

Burckhardt is also clear that the origins of Renaissance individualism are political, and hence he begins his book with a political survey. The vacuum of power and legitimacy created by decades of conflict between popes and emperors in the Middle Ages gave rise to illegitimate despots who shaped politics exactly as they liked, without reference to law, custom or morality. This in turn provided a model to other individuals to do as they wished, and also released them from the civic and communal obligations which would have stifled the pursuit of their self-interest:[48] 'In the character of these states, whether republics or despotisms, lies not the only but the chief reason for the early development of the Italian', he writes;[49] and 'each individual, even among the lowest of the people, felt himself inwardly emancipated from the control of the State and its police, whose title to respect was illegitimate, and itself founded on violence; and no man believed any longer in the justice of the law'.[50] Since in this radically new, agonistic society, claims to noble lineage counted for so little, a corollary of individualism is the 'equalization of classes' and, implicitly, the equality between women and men.[51]

An illustrious and influential tradition of historical thought on the Italian Renaissance, from predecessors of Burckhardt's such as Leonardo Bruni and Simonde de Sismondi, to successors such as Hans Baron, claimed that political freedom and cultural greatness go together. It is one of the most significant and controversial elements of Burckhardt's vision of cultural history (*Kulturgeschichte*) that he emphatically disputes this.[52] It is not that culture and politics have nothing to do with each other. On the contrary, in one sense Burckhardt in the *Civilization* is trying to bridge the disciplinary gap that had developed in his own time between the two,[53] and it is perhaps difficult to envisage his book having the same impact had politics been left out: his brand of cultural history attempted to encompass everything, and that necessarily included the power of the state. Yet in Burckhardt's iconoclastic, conservative and pessimistic vision, politics and culture (and, as we learn from his *Reflections on World History*, religion too) are nonetheless at odds with each other. In a line which might reflect Burckhardt's own decision to refrain from political entanglements, he notes that 'political impotence does not hinder the different tendencies and manifestations of private life from thriving in the fullest vigour and variety'.[54] And later he observes that 'by the side of profound corruption appeared human personalities of the noblest harmony, and an artistic splendour ...'[55] Although he admits that republican Florence was 'the scene of the richest development of human individuality',[56] that 'in many of their chief merits the Florentines are the pattern and the earliest type of Italians and modern Europeans generally',[57] that, in fact, Florence was 'the most important workshop of the Italian, and, indeed, of the modern European spirit',[58] Burckhardt's

Renaissance does not represent a victory of the *vita activa*. On the contrary, he dwells at more length on the princes and tyrants, and claims that the despotisms represent 'the completer and more clearly defined type' of Italian Renaissance state.[59] Perhaps with some unconscious relish (though if so it is disguised by an almost surreal calmness), Burckhardt first introduces the innocent reader of his book to the brutal and shocking abuses of power and acts of cruelty of the tyrants.[60] And he almost admits that there is a contradiction between this violent dimension of the Renaissance and that represented by cultural efflorescence. For example, commenting on the patronage of learning of Sigismondo Malatesta of Rimini, he observes that

> it is hard for us nowadays to believe that a monster like this prince felt learning and the friendship of cultivated people to be a necessity of life; and yet the man who excommunicated him, made war upon him, and burnt him in effigy, Pope Pius II, says: 'Sigismund knew history and had a great store of philosophy; he seemed born to all that he undertook'.[61]

On the other side, humanists in Burckhardt's vision readily lend their literary talents to the support of corrupt regimes and are themselves rootless, licentious and immoral.[62] Creative individuals and despots are thus linked in that both are the manifestations of individualism, and the state is compared to 'a work of art', like great art itself 'the outcome of reflection and calculation'.[63] The state is not a natural, inherently ethical or divinely ordained entity, as the German historians of his time tended to present it.[64]

In the above account I hope to have suggested that for all the marvellous coherence and detail in his book, Burckhardt's portrait of Renaissance society is not without its fissures and contradictions. He himself was aware enough of the difficulties of his task to state, in his opening passage:

> This work bears the title of an essay in the strictest sense of the word. No one is more conscious than the writer with what limited means and strength he has addressed himself to a task so arduous. And even if he could look with greater confidence on his own researches he would hardly thereby feel more assured of the approval of competent judges. To each eye, perhaps, the outlines of a given civilization presents a different picture; and in treating of a civilization which is the mother of our own, and whose influence is still at work among

us, it is unavoidable that individual judgement and feeling should tell every moment both on the writer and on the reader. In the wide ocean upon which we venture the possible ways and directions are many; and the same studies which have served for this work might easily, in other hands, not only receive a wholly different treatment and application, but lead also to essentially different conclusions. Such, indeed, is the importance of the subject that it still calls for fresh investigation, and may be studied with advantage from the most varied points of view.[65]

Later he claims that 'the gradual awakening of the soul of a people is a phenomenon which may produce a different impression on each spectator', a subject on which he admits that he 'is treading on the perilous ground of conjecture'.[66]

The limitations of Burckhardt's vision have already been pointed out. Despite the attempt to portray Renaissance society as a whole, he fails to do justice to its art;[67] his portrayal of religion, such an important measure of the modernity and distinctiveness of the Renaissance, is in fact ambivalent; politics and culture are at odds with each other; and the whole conception of the Renaissance as rooted in one time and space is both strengthened on one side and undercut on the other by its claims to kinship with modernity. The criticisms could be multiplied: in the later twentieth century, for example, in the light of new findings within the burgeoning field of social history, Burckhardt was frequently attacked for his limited treatment of social and economic themes. He himself seems to have been aware of many of the shortcomings of his book but professed himself to be deeply unphilosophical and undogmatic by nature; his liking of strangeness and contradiction might in fact be seen to lend his portrait of Italian Renaissance life some authenticity and conviction. After all, his Renaissance was an age of 'overstrained and despairing passions and forces'.[68] And then again it was characterized by cool and detached reflection and calculation.[69]

At one point Burckhardt associates the Renaissance with progress:

Freed from the countless bonds which elsewhere in Europe checked *progress*, having reached a higher degree of individual development and been schooled by the teachings of antiquity, the Italian mind now turned to the discovery of the outward universe, and to the representation of it in speech and in form.[70]

But all in all, Burckhardt's Renaissance is not in any simple sense an era of breezy confidence and optimism, though these things exist within it; nor is the history of Europe of which it forms a larger part simplistically teleological or linear.[71] Burckhardt considered the notion of progress 'that ridiculous vanity, as if the world were marching towards a perfection of mind or even morality'.[72] It is ironic, therefore, that the Renaissance which he did so much to interrogate and popularize is sometimes now taken as epitomizing a triumphalist and celebratory account of European history, 'a ubiquitous master narrative',[73] perhaps even a modernist conspiracy. Nothing could be further from Burckhardt's own vision and historiographical temperament.[74] His Renaissance is an age of tension and contradiction, an age as much of darkness as of light. His account of it is also a harshly pessimistic morality tale, a lesson in the realities of human history, in which apparent gains are always accompanied by losses, and in which the road to human happiness is unclear. 'The notion of the imperfectibility of mankind was deeply rooted in Burckhardt's consciousness', as was his sense of original sin.[75] Individualism is double-edged, and any celebration of the achievements of Renaissance culture is balanced by a clearsighted appreciation of its downside. In the light of our more recent history, cultural and political, it is perhaps no wonder that Burckhardt's ideas are undergoing a revival today as lessons in 'untimely self-understanding'.[76] Surely his ambivalent Renaissance still has something to teach us.

## notes

1. Randolph Starn, 'Renaissance Redux', *American Historical Review*, CIII (1998) 124.
2. See especially William Bouwsma, 'The Renaissance and the Drama of Western History', *American Historical Review*, LXXXIV (1979) 1–15.
3. J. B. Bullen, *The Myth of the Renaissance in Nineteenth-Century Writing* (Oxford, 1994); W. K. Ferguson, *The Renaissance in Historical Thought: Five Centuries of Interpretation* (Boston, 1948). See also H. Fraser, *The Victorians and Renaissance Italy* (Oxford, 1992); J. R. Hale, *England and the Italian Renaissance* (London, 1954); *Il Rinascimento nell'Ottocento in Italia e Germania*, ed. A. Buck and C. Vasoli (Bologna, 1989).
4. *La Renaissance*, published in 1855, was the seventh volume of Michelet's *Histoire de France* (1833–62).
5. Gene Brucker, 'The Italian Renaissance', in G. Ruggiero, ed., *A Companion to the Worlds of the Renaissance* (Oxford, 2002), p. 23.
6. J. J. Sheehan, 'The German Renaissance in America', in A. J. Grieco, M. Rocke and F. Gioffredi Superbi, eds, *The Italian Renaissance in the Twentieth Century* (Florence, 2002), p. 49.

7. See especially the contributions by James Hankins, Robert Black, Riccardo Fubini, Catherine Soussloff, Alessandro Arcangeli and John Martin. See also Ferguson, *Renaissance in Historical Thought*, esp. pp. 195–252; Lionel Gossman, 'Burckhardt in the Twentieth Century: Sketch of a *Rezeptiongeschichte*', in *Jacob Burckhardt: Storia della cultura, storia dell'arte*, ed. M. Ghelardi and M. Seidel (Venice, 2002), pp. 17–40; Sheehan, 'German Renaissance', pp. 47–64.

8. Note especially the important, and in part widely divergent, interpretations of E. H. Gombrich, *In Search of Cultural History* (Oxford, 1969); H. Trevor-Roper, 'Jacob Burckhardt', *Proceedings of the British Academy*, LXX (1984) 359–78; Lionel Gossman, *Basel in the Age of Burckhardt: A Study in Unseasonable Ideas* (Chicago and London, 2000); John Hinde, *Jacob Burckhardt and the Crisis of Modernity* (Montreal and London, 2000); and Hayden White, *Metahistory: The Historical Imagination in Nineteenth-Century Europe* (Baltimore and London, 1974), pp. 230–64.

9. See Thomas A. Howard, *Religion and the Rise of Historicism: W. M. L. de Wette, Jacob Burckhardt and the Theological Origins of Nineteenth-Century Historical Consciousness* (Cambridge, 2000).

10. On his student years see Hinde, *Jacob Burckhardt*, pp. 64–87.

11. On his relations with Ranke see especially Trevor-Roper, 'Jacob Burckhardt', 363; Felix Gilbert, *History: Politics or Culture? Reflections on Ranke and Burckhardt* (Princeton, 1990), pp. 93–105; Ferguson, *Renaissance in Historical Thought*, pp. 180–4; and Gossman, *Basel in the Age of Burckhardt*, ch. 11.

12. Quoted in Howard, *Religion*, p. 140.

13. See Gossman, 'Burckhardt in the Twentieth Century', pp. 17–18, 27–8; and Edward Said, *Orientalismo* (Milan, 1999), p. 206.

14. Burckhardt, *Civilization*, part 1, chapter 1, p. 21. In this chapter and in the rest of this book all references to Burckhardt, *Civilization*, are to the Harper and Row edition of *The Civilization of the Renaissance in Italy* of 1958, in the English translation of S. G. C. Middlemore, with an introduction by Benjamin Nelson and Charles Trinkaus. For ease of reference part and chapter numbers are supplied as well as page numbers.

15. Burckhardt, *Civilization*, 1.1, p. 21 and 3.1, p. 175.

16. Gombrich, *In Search*, esp. pp. 14–25. On the extent of Burckhardt's Hegelianism see also Hinde, *Jacob Burckhardt*, pp. 139–66; Howard, *Religion*, pp. 144–5, 159–62; Alison Brown, 'Jacob Burckhardt's Renaissance', *History Today*, XXXVIII (October 1988) 24; Ferguson, *Renaissance in Historical Thought*, pp. 185–8.

17. Burckhardt, *Civilization*, 1.4, p. 50.

18. Burckhardt, *Civilization*, 2.2, pp. 148–50.

19. A distinguished exception is Lauro Martines. See especially his 'The Italian Renaissance Tale as History', in A. Brown, ed., *Language and Images of Renaissance Italy* (Oxford, 1995), pp. 313–30; and his *An Italian Renaissance Sextet: Six Tales in Historical Context* (New York, 1994).

20. Gilbert, *History*, pp. 18–19.

21. For example Burckhardt, *Civilization*, 4.3–4, pp. 293–323; 5.4, pp. 377–81; 6.1, pp. 426–43.

22. Cf. Hinde, *Jacob Burckhardt*, pp. 139–66; see also White, *Metahistory*, pp. 230–64.

23. Cited in Brown, 'Jacob Burckhardt's Renaissance', p. 20. See Hinde, *Jacob Burckhardt*, pp. 196–7.

24. In fact in parts he does remain aware of chronological change within the Renaissance: Part 1 in particular moves from the thirteenth to the sixteenth century, and within this structure contains individual narrative accounts of Italy's ruling dynasties (cf. Ferguson, *Renaissance in Historical Thought*, p. 189), but in other parts of the book Burckhardt also attempts to make broad distinctions between developments in the fourteenth, fifteenth and sixteenth centuries.
25. Burckhardt, *Civilization*, 1.9, pp. 118–19.
26. Burckhardt, *Civilization*, 2.1, p. 143.
27. See especially Ferguson, *Renaissance in Historical Thought*, for a survey; Charles Homer Haskins, *The Renaissance of the Twelfth Century* (Cambridge, MA, 1927); R. L. Benson and G. Constable, eds, *Renaissance and Renewal in the Twelfth Century* (Oxford, 1982); Erwin Panofsky, *Renaissance and Renascences in Western Art* (New York, 1969), esp. pp. 42–113; and more recently Lee Patterson, 'On the Margin: Postmodernism, Ironic History and Medieval Studies', *Speculum*, LXV (1990) 87–108; and Randolph Starn, 'Who's Afraid of the Renaissance?', in *The Past and Future of Medieval Studies*, ed. John Van Engen (Notre Dame, IN and London, 1994) pp. 129–47.
28. Burckhardt, *Civilization*, 6.1, p. 426.
29. Burckhardt, *Civilization*, 6.1, pp. 426–7; 6.2, p. 444.
30. Burckhardt, *Civilization*, 6.2, p. 463.
31. Burckhardt, *Civilization*, 6.2, p. 464.
32. Burckhardt, *Civilization*, 6.2, p. 474. Howard, *Religion*, pp. 156–7.
33. See especially Howard, *Religion*, passim and Hinde, *Jacob Burckhardt*, pp. 64–87.
34. See especially Ferguson, *Renaissance in Historical Thought*, pp. 67–72, 78–112, and cf. pp. 192–3. For more recent evaluations of the role of religion in the life of the Renaissance see John Jeffries Martin's chapter below.
35. Cf. White, *Metahistory*, pp. 246–7. On the question of the Renaissance and modernity see Anthony Molho, 'American Historians and the Italian Renaissance: An Overview', *Schifanoia*, VIII (1989) 9–17; A. Molho, 'Burckhardtian Legacies', *Medievalia et humanistica*, XVII (1991) 133–9; A. Molho, 'The Italian Renaissance, Made in the USA', in *Imagined Histories: American Historians Interpret the Past*, ed. A. Molho and G. S. Wood (Princeton, 1998), pp. 263–94; John J. Martin, 'Introduction: The Renaissance between Myth and History', in Martin, ed., *The Renaissance: Italy and Abroad* (London and New York, 2003), pp. 1–21; Sheehan, 'German Renaissance', pp. 49–51; M. Ciliberto, *Il Rinascimento, storia di un dibattito* (Florence, 1975); Karl Dannenfeldt, ed., *The Renaissance: Medieval or Modern?* (Boston, 1959). For an attempt to divorce the Renaissance from modernity see Peter Burke, *The European Renaissance: Centres and Peripheries* (Oxford, 1998). On the Renaissance as a broadly European phenomenon see Burke, *European Renaissance*; W. Kerrigan and G. Braden, *The Idea of the Renaissance* (Baltimore and London, 1989); Ferguson, *Renaissance in Historical Thought*, pp. 253–89; J. R. Hale, *The Civilization of Europe in the Renaissance* (London, 1993); R. Porter and M. Teich, eds, *The Renaissance in National Context* (Cambridge, 1992); Robin Kirkpatrick, *The European Renaissance, 1400–1600* (Harlow, 2002); and the five-volume Open University series *The Renaissance in Europe* (New Haven and London, 2000). Cf. Johan Huizinga, *The Waning of the Middle Ages* (London, 1924).

36. Burckhardt, *Civilization*, 3.7, p. 246.
37. Burckhardt, *Civilization*, 3.3, p. 210.
38. Burckhardt, *Civilization*, 6.1, p. 427. In general history the question of the end of the Renaissance has received much less attention than its beginning, but see the recent book of William Bouwsma, *The Waning of the Renaissance, 1550–1640* (New Haven and London, 2000).
39. For biographical interpretations of Burckhardt's histories, see especially Gossman, *Basel in the Age of Burckhardt*; Howard, *Religion*; Peter Gay, *Style in History* (New York and London, 1974), pp. 139–82; and Hinde, *Jacob Burckhardt*, p. 196.
40. Cf. Sheehan, 'German Renaissance', p. 49–50; Gilbert, *History*, pp. 35; and especially Hinde, *Jacob Burckhardt*, passim.
41. Burckhardt, *Civilization*, 2.1, p. 143 and 6.5, p. 516.
42. On Renaissance individualism see Patterson, 'On the Margin', pp. 96–9; Kerrigan and Braden, *Idea of the Renaissance*; S. J. Greenblatt, *Renaissance Self-Fashioning: From More to Shakespeare* (Chicago and London, 1980); John J. Martin, 'Inventing Sincerity, Refashioning Prudence: The Discovery of the Individual in Renaissance Europe', *American Historical Review*, CII (1997) 1309–17; John J. Martin, 'The Myth of Renaissance Individualism', in Ruggiero, *Companion*, pp. 208–24; S. J. Milner, 'Partial Readings: Addressing a Renaissance Archive', *History of the Human Sciences*, XII (1999) 96–8; Starn, 'Who's Afraid of the Renaissance', pp. 143–4; S. Cohn, 'Burckhardt Revisited from Social History', in Brown, *Language and Images of Renaissance Italy*, pp. 217–34; Geoff Baldwin, 'Individual and Self in the Later Renaissance', *The Historical Journal*, XLIV (2001) 341–64; David Norbrook, 'Life and Death of Renaissance Man', *Raritan*, VIII.4 (1989) 89–110; S. J. Greenblatt, 'Friction and Friction', and N. Z. Davis, 'Boundaries of the Sense of Self in Sixteenth-Century France', both in T. C. Heller, M. Sosna and D. E. Wellbery, eds, *Reconstructing Individualism: Autonomy, Individuality and the Self in Western Thought* (Stanford, CA, 1986), pp. 30–52 and 53–63. See also Alessandro Arcangeli's comments in Chapter 8 below.
43. Cf. J. Woolfson, 'Bishop Fox's Bees and the Early English Renaissance', *Reformation and Renaissance Review*, V (2003) 7–8.
44. See Riccardo Fubini, 'Rinascimento riscoperto? Studi recenti su Jacob Burckhardt', in R. Fubini, *L'umanesimo italiano e i suoi storici: Origini rinascimentali – critica moderna* (Milan, 2001), pp. 256–64.
45. Burckhardt, *Civilization*, 3.1, p. 175.
46. Burckhardt, *Civilization*, 3.1, pp. 180–2. See also 4.4, p. 303.
47. Burckhardt, *Civilization*, 3.1, p. 175. See also Riccardo Fubini, 'Origini e significato del "Die Kultur der Renaissance in Italien" di Jacob Burckhardt', in Fubini, *L'umanesimo italiano*, pp. 213–14; and Riccardo Fubini's comments below, Chapter 6.
48. Burckhardt, *Civilization*, part 1, esp. 1.1–2.
49. Burckhardt, *Civilization*, 2.1, p. 143.
50. Burckhardt, *Civilization*, 6.1, p. 437.
51. Burckhardt, *Civilization*, 5.1, pp. 353–60; 5.4, pp. 377–81; 5.6, pp. 389–95.
52. See Baron's comments in his 'The Limits of the Notion of Renaissance Individualism: Burckhardt after a Century (1960)', in Hans Baron, *In Search of Florentine Civic Humanism: Essays in the Transition from Medieval to Modern*

*Thought* (Princeton, 1988), II, pp. 155–81, esp. pp. 168–75. On Baron and Bruni see James Hankins, 'The Baron Thesis after Forty Years', *Journal of the History of Ideas*, LVI (1995) 309–38; Riccardo Fubini, 'Renaissance Historian: The Career of Hans Baron', *Journal of Modern History*, LXIV (1992) 541–74; James Hankins, ed., *Renaissance Civic Humanism: Reappraisals and Reflections* (Cambridge, 2000) and the extensive bibliography cited therein; and E. Muir, 'The Italian Renaissance in America', *American Historical Review*, C (1995) 1110–11. On Sismondi see Bullen, *Myth of the Renaissance*, pp. 50–8; Fubini, *L'umanesimo italiano*, pp. 223–4; Norbook, 'Life and death of Renaissance Man', 97; Ferguson, *Renaissance in Historical Thought*, pp. 165–8.

53. Hinde, *Jacob Burckhardt*, pp. 167–98; Gilbert, *History*, esp. pp. 81–92. See also the essential discussion in Gossman, *Basel in the Age of Burckhardt*, ch. 11.

54. Burckhardt, *Civilization*, 2.1, p. 144; cf. Hinde, *Jacob Burckhardt*, pp. 27–8 and passim; White, *Metahistory*, pp. 230–64; J. Rüsen, 'Jacob Burckhardt: Political Standpoint and Historical Insight on the Border of Postmodernism', *History and Theory*, XXIV (1985) 235–46.

55. Burckhardt, *Civilization*, 6.1, p. 443.

56. Burckhardt, *Civilization*, 1.2, p. 31.

57. Burckhardt, *Civilization*, 1.7, p. 103.

58. Burckhardt, *Civilization*, 1.7, p. 106. See also Milner, 'Partial Readings', 89–105.

59. Burckhardt, *Civilization*, 1.1, p. 22.

60. Cf. Gay, *Style in History*, pp. 139–82.

61. Burckhardt, *Civilization*, 3.6, p. 235.

62. Burckhardt, *Civilization*, esp. 3.11, pp. 273–4.

63. Burckhardt, *Civilization*, 1.1, p. 22.

64. The role of Hegelian philosophy in Burckhardt's book is critical to an understanding of the place of politics in relation to culture: see Gombrich, *In Search*, pp. 14–25; Norbrook, 'Life and Death of Renaissance Man', 98. See also Claire Farago, 'The Status of the "State as a Work of Art": Re-Viewing Burckhardt's Renaissance from the Borderlines', in *Cultural Exchange between European Nations during the Renaissance*, ed. G. Sorelius and M. Srigley (Uppsala, 1994), pp. 16–32.

65. Burckhardt, *Civilization*, 1.1, p. 21.

66. Burckhardt, *Civilization*, 3.4, p. 303.

67. Cf. his comment on this, 1.1, p. 21. See also Hinde, *Jacob Burckhardt*, pp. 270–97; Michael Ann Holly, 'Cultural History, Connoisseurship and Melancholy', in Grieco, Rocke and Gioffredi Superbi, *Italian Renaissance in the Twentieth Century*, pp. 195–6; and M. Ghelardi, *La scoperta del Rinascimento: L'"Età di Raffaello" di Jacob Burckhardt* (Turin, 1991), passim.

68. Burckhardt, *Civilization*, 2.3, p. 162.

69. See especially Burckhardt, *Civilization*, 1.1, pp. 21–5, 1.7, pp. 82–106 and 1.8, 107–14.

70. Burckhardt, *Civilization*, 4.1, p. 279.

71. See especially Hinde, *Jacob Burckhardt*, pp. 13–14 and passim.

72. Cited in Howard, *Religion*, p. 160.

73. Patterson, 'On the Margin', p. 92. See also Bouwsma, 'The Renaissance and the Drama of Western History'; and Bouwsma, *Waning of the Renaissance*, p. viii.

74. Gossman, *Basel in the Age of Burckhardt*, ch. 11. Howard, *Religion*, pp. 153, 157–9, Hinde, *Jacob Burckhardt*, p. 27.
75. Hinde, *Jacob Burckhardt*, p. 114 and see generally his treatment of the *Civilization*, pp. 220–6.
76. Rüsen, 'Jacob Burckhardt', 245, and see Howard, *Religion*, pp. 157, 168–9.

# 2

# the diffusion of the italian renaissance: southern italy and beyond

## david abulafia

The Italian Renaissance, and the history of Italy during the late medieval and early modern periods, have traditionally been analysed with a heavy emphasis on Florence, Venice and Rome, paying attention as well to culturally significant northern principalities such as Mantua, Ferrara and Urbino, but with rather little interest in the Italian south. As will be seen, southern Italy has its own tradition of scholarship attentive to the Neapolitan Renaissance; the question is, however, whether this tradition has been successfully integrated by historians of Renaissance Italy into a wider picture of the cultural life of Italy between the fourteenth and the sixteenth centuries. One aim of this chapter is to ask how the cultural life of Renaissance southern Italy related to that of the north and centre; in addition, it is important to consider how far the south acted as a channel through which Renaissance ideas reached lands further afield, most importantly (for dynastic reasons) Spain and Hungary.

There are further reasons for insisting on the special interest of southern Italy. The presence of foreign scholars and craftsmen, including German printers (some Jewish) was a striking feature of the high culture of late medieval southern Italy, and it will be seen how links to Flanders, in particular, were fostered, with exciting consequences in the fields of painting and music. But the most important feature of the south was, quite simply, its distinctive political character, which had considerable impact on patterns of patronage. As in the north there were great princes who took an active interest in the production of manuscripts and other cultural activities: the Acquavivas, for example, in Apulia. Princely power was exercised in ways not dissimilar to that of the great northern *signori*.

But above the princes, at least notionally, there existed a king who sought to impose his will across the southern half of the Italian peninsula, and who used his scholars and courtiers as agents in the presentation of his political case.

The cultural life of southern Italy has sometimes been dismissed as the creation of hand-picked alien courtiers, whose own roots lay elsewhere (generally in the north of Italy) and whose intellectual or artistic training took place outside the borders of the kingdom. Pontano, the greatest south Italian humanist of the late fifteenth century, was, indeed, an Umbrian. However, this is to ignore the realities of patronage at this period: the Aragonese kings of Naples had created a court which was a powerful magnet for scholars of varied origins, and other courts, such as Ferrara, shared this characteristic. Moreover, it is simply not the case that southern Italy and Sicily produced no native writers and artists of exceptional calibre: Antonello da Messina and Sannazaro stand out. A second negative image of south Italian cultural life would emphasize the lateness of its efflorescence, seeing Pontano and his academy as mere successors to earlier generations who had discussed similar ethical and political issues in the Florence of Salutati and Bruni. This, again, is evidence of historians' obsession with Florence; yet the tradition of cultural patronage in southern Italy reached back through the Aragonese rulers, the Angevins and Frederick II of Hohenstaufen to the Norman rulers in the twelfth century.

Having made a case for the respectability of the study of south Italian Renaissance culture, it is now necessary to set out the context, before moving through the historiography to key figures and movements in literary culture, the fine arts and music.[1] An essential feature of the cultural identity of southern Italy was the meeting of different cultures within the kingdom (after 1282, kingdoms) of Sicily. The Norman kingdom, established in 1130, had included both southern Italy and the island of Sicily, and had been home to Greeks, Latins, Jews and Muslims.[2] Indeed, it offered a point of contact between the medieval West and the learning of the Greek and Arabic worlds, bringing to the attention of twelfth-century readers such works as Ptolemy's *Almagest* and the *Meno* and *Phaedo* of Plato. Although the Muslims were suppressed in the late twelfth and early thirteenth centuries, Greek literary culture remained alive, and the Arabic-speaking Jews continued, in some measure, to function as intermediaries between the West and the culture of Islam: the Jew Faraj of Girgenti prepared medical manuscripts for King Charles I in the late thirteenth century, while slightly earlier Frederick II had made use of Spanish and Provençal Jews, who were set to work to translate Aristotelian texts in southern Italy. Opinions differ as to the importance of Frederick's entourage – whether it was a pale shadow of the vibrant, multi-lingual Norman court or a ruler-dominated centre for the study of sciences, especially zoology.[3] On the other hand, there were interesting developments in fine art, with the imitation of classical artistic models, most notably on the great city gateway of Capua. Whereas under the Normans cultural patronage had been concentrated at the royal palaces in Palermo, there was a shift of the centre of government, and therefore of patronage, to the mainland from the time of Frederick II. Naples began to emerge as the cultural centre of the Sicilian Kingdom, especially following the endowment of a royal university there in 1224.

The significance of Naples grew when the part-German, part-Norman Hohenstaufen dynasty was displaced, following decades of warfare with the papacy, by the house of Anjou, in 1266. The Angevins brought with them from the royal court of France the 'Gothic' artistic styles seen in the great basilica of Santa Chiara in Naples. A massive revolt against Charles, the 'Sicilian Vespers' of March 1282, resulted in his loss of Sicily, which was promptly conquered by the king of Aragon.[4] Thereafter two 'Sicilies' existed; one could hardly say that they coexisted, since conflict between Anjou and Aragon continued intermittently, and forms the essential background to the French invasion of Italy in 1494. The Angevin rulers of the mainland refused to abandon the formal title 'king of Sicily'; it was thus common to call the mainland half the 'kingdom of Naples' or simply 'the Kingdom', *il Regno*.

Questions of political status were of vital importance to the exercise of cultural patronage in Angevin Naples. The king of Naples was a vassal of the pope, and, in 1311–13, he was also threatened with invasion by the German emperor, Henry VII. Out of these experiences grew a concern with the justification of the right of the king to rule as 'emperor in his own kingdom', free from external interference, whatever notional obligation might exist to a suzerain. This can be seen clearly in the legal commentaries of Andrea of Isernia and Marino da Caramanico either side of 1300. Samantha Kelly has shown how King Robert 'the Wise' (1309–43) sought to project an image of himself as a 'New Solomon', and lavished favours on Petrarch, crowning him as poet laureate.[5] Boccaccio spent his early years as a bank clerk in Naples, but in a Florentine counting house, rather than at court: his *Decameron* portrays life at all levels in mid-fourteenth-century Naples; but his Florentine friend Nicola Acciaiuoli stayed on and rose to become the first minister of the kingdom. Royal patronage of the arts was expressed in summonses to Giotto and

Cavallini, who painted frescos for the royal court. That the cultural life of Naples was not derivative, dependent on northern and central Italian models, emerges clearly from an examination of King Robert's interest in Greek culture. Roberto Weiss documented the career of Barlaam, a south Italian Greek who instructed Boccaccio, while Robert showed a continued interest in Arabic texts, mediated through Jewish scholars.[6] Significant too were the literary and artistic links between Naples and Provence, for the kings of Naples were also, from the time of Charles I, counts of Provence; Avignon, whose rule they shared with the pope in the early fourteenth century, functioned as a bridge linking Italian culture to southern France.[7]

The contrast between the cultural liveliness of the early fourteenth century and the lack of vigour in the period between the arrival of the Black Death (1347) and the death of Queen Joanna II (1435) is striking; there were severe political crises, beginning under Robert's grand-daughter Joanna I, and continuing through her murder (1382) and that of her successor Charles III of Durazzo, also king of Hungary (1386). The University of Naples experienced severe recession. At the start of the fifteenth century, King Ladislas sought to reassert the primacy of Naples in peninsular politics, campaigning in Tuscany, but the consequence seems to have been neglect of south Italian affairs. Magnificent funerary monuments for Neapolitan royalty indicate that some artistic traditions were kept alive. In southern Italy, as in Sicily, the power of the greater nobility expanded at the expense of the Crown, as the nobles supported rival claimants to the Angevin throne. The most celebrated claimant was 'Good King René' who managed to gain precarious control of southern Italy following the death of Joanna II in 1435, but was displaced by King Alfonso V of Aragon in 1442. René was a fanatical enthusiast for chivalric culture, creating the knightly Order of the Croissant, which brought together his subjects from Naples, Provence, Anjou and Lorraine, and writing the much admired *Livre du Cuer d'amour Espris*.[8] He was also a patron of the fine arts: the Florentine workshop of della Robbia magnificently fashioned his coat-of-arms out of ceramics; and he competed with his Aragonese rivals for the services of the sculptor Laurana. René should be seen as a figure raised in the north European courtly tradition but open to Italian culture. However, his impact as a patron and writer was largely confined to the French and Provençal worlds. Indeed, a more significant channel of communication between Renaissance Italy and north European culture was to be the Burgundian court in Flanders.

Alfonso's capture of Naples in 1442 saw the triumph of a self-consciously classical programme in the arts, and also in politics.[9] Alfonso projected himself as a conquering Caesar.[10] He took delight in neo-classical medallions portraying him as a victorious hero; he appears in Roman dress crowned by the Roman gods Mars and Bellona on one medallion by Cristoforo di Geremia. He took up residence in Naples until his death in 1458, transforming the appearance of the city, and rebuilding the great Castelnuovo on its western edge. Although the castle was an overt symbol of royal power, Alfonso sought to soothe the fears of the south Italian barons by taking their counsel in his parliaments, and relying on their votes of taxes.[11] Yet, though seeming to turn his back on his Iberian lands so that he could pursue ambitions in Italy, including hopes of succession to the duchy of Milan, Alfonso also presented himself as a Spanish Roman emperor, in the tradition of Trajan, and drew on Spanish Roman culture, epitomized by Seneca, in attempts to project images of himself as a just and magnanimous ruler.[12] In this he succeeded, insofar as he acquired the sobriquet 'the Magnanimous'. His network of allies in northern Italy grew, in tribute to his remarkable diplomatic skills: he had real charm. Federico da Montefeltro, duke of Urbino, was happy to record his appointment as Alfonso's captain in the inscription surrounding the ceiling of his *studiolo* in Urbino.[13] Political and dynastic ties to Milan and Ferrara were fostered, despite an earlier history of rivalry with the Sforzas of Milan. He gained éclat from his adherence, a little late, to the Peace of Lodi established in 1454 by the principal Italian states: this effectively confirmed the legitimacy of his rule over Naples.

As will be clear, his conquest of Naples was the first of a series of political transformations that gave shape to the development of humanistic culture in Naples. Under Alfonso, humanists such as Beccadelli sought to justify Alfonso's claim to rule, to describe what it was to rule well, and to support the claim that monarchy itself was desirable. Attention to these issues remained intense under Ferrante (reigned 1458–94), whose claim to the throne was compromised both by the fact that he was Alfonso's bastard son (the other Aragonese territories, not being Alfonso's private possessions as Naples was, were passed to Alfonso's brother John of Navarre), and by the continuing resentment of pro-Angevin barons in the provinces, who sought the restoration of King René. Baronial rebellion was suppressed in 1465, though it flared up again twenty years later, and the division of the baronage into 'Angevins' and 'Aragonese' long continued. The victory of Ferrante over his enemies at Troia (1462) was recorded in the six spectacular door panels of the triumphal arch in Naples, a heroic epic cast in bronze.[14] The rebellion indicated that

Alfonso's conciliatory policies towards the greater barons had failed, and Ferrante, with his own son Alfonso duke of Calabria (King Alfonso II, 1494) sought support in the cities, showing suspicion of the nobility, who rebelled again in 1485. It is this rebellion, and its brutal suppression, that was recorded by the late sixteenth-century Neapolitan author Camillo Porzio, in his famous tract on the *Congiura dei Baroni*.[15] True or false, stories of tortures and massacres unleashed on the Neapolitan nobility by an enraged Ferrante and Alfonso helped create the very negative image of these kings which subsequent rulers, French and Spanish, saw no reason to play down.

Charles VIII, king of France, marched into Naples in 1494–95, as heir to the Angevin title; and the shock of the French invasion of Italy was not lessened by Charles' failure to hold Naples; the Aragonese dynasty was in severe disarray, as king succeeded king (Alfonso II, Ferrante II, Federigo), and as it became plainer than ever that the loyalty of the barons and of the cities was in constant flux.[16] Charles carried away from Naples precious works of art and fine books.[17] Guicciardini famously lamented the end of an era of relative peace and the opening of a new era in which Italy became the plaything of great powers, with Ferrante's Spanish cousin Ferdinand of Aragon rapidly contesting the claims of Charles VIII and then Louis XII of France to rule over Naples. The last in the series of political shocks to be delivered to the south Italian humanists was the Spanish conquest of the kingdom of Naples by Ferdinand of Aragon in 1503, as a result of a brilliant campaign by his general Fernando González de Córdoba; but the war was fought against the French, and the Neapolitans had become, to all intents, bystanders.[18] The kingdom of Naples remained a personal possession of the king of Aragon, ruled by viceroys, but clearly the intellectual climate had changed decisively: there was no longer a call to defend the active exercise of monarchy on the soil of Italy, since Ferdinand spent only a few months in Naples. Still, in many respects what he had achieved, and was able to pass to his successor Charles of Habsburg, was the re-creation of Alfonso the Magnanimous' western Mediterranean empire.

Throughout the Aragonese period Naples had been a major actor on the Italian political stage, involved in such crises as the War of Ferrara and the Pazzi conspiracy in Florence, enjoying for several decades a close alliance with Milan, and later with the Florence of Lorenzo de'Medici. The political significance of Naples in wider Italian politics is never denied, though rather little studied. But it will be necessary in what follows to investigate whether the cultural significance of the south has been underestimated.

The roots of the historiography of the southern Renaissance can be traced back to Jacob Burckhardt's insistence on the importance of the court of Emperor Frederick II of Hohenstaufen as a precocious precursor of the courts of the Italian 'despots', exercising cultural patronage, but following the political and cultural model of oriental sultans rather than of contemporary European kings.[19] This image of the oriental despot was redeployed when Burckhardt looked at Ferrante I of Naples, whom he saw in a sense as a replica of Frederick, translated to the fifteenth century, and unable to control his vicious impulses. A similar approach to Ferrante and Alfonso II was adopted by John Addington Symonds.[20] Their analysis of Ferrante thus turned on his political conduct, seen in the hostile light of the French and Spanish sources; his reign was not taken to be of great cultural significance, since scholars were slaves to the king's caprices. It was the achievement of a pupil of Burckhardt, Eberhard Gothein (who himself taught Ernst Kantorowicz, the famous, or notorious, biographer of Frederick II) to demonstrate the cultural vitality of southern Italy in the fifteenth century in his highly innovative book *Die Culturentwicklung Süditaliens* of 1886, part of which was translated into Italian as *Il Rinascimento nell'Italia meridionale* in 1915.[21] Gothein was a prolific economic and social historian, famous for his determination, in the face of more conservative historians such as Dietrich Schäfer, to write broad social history (which is what he meant by *Kulturgeschichte*), in a manner that anticipated the approaches of the French *Annales* school.[22] His work was as much a social anthropology of fifteenth-century Naples as an appreciation of its role in Renaissance culture; thus he emphasized the significance of the *seggi*, the political and regional groupings within Naples.

Still greater was the impact of a long-lived south Italian historian and philosopher who addressed fundamental political, aesthetic and ethical questions while maintaining a fascination with the life of the kingdom of Naples at all levels, from the backstreets to the royal and viceregal courts: Benedetto Croce. In three areas he made a particular mark on the study of southern Italy during the Renaissance. One was his understanding of the relationship between political events and the culture of the south, visible in his *La Spagna nella vita italiana durante la Rinascenza*, which asked whether the Aragonese monarchy and Spanish viceroyalty saw the cultural life of southern Italy fall under Iberian influence.[23] A second issue was how far political treatises justifying the conduct of rulers such

as Ferrante of Naples 'prefigured' Machiavelli's *Prince* in their insistence
that harsh acts may be the necessary means to achieve desirable political
ends: in *Prima del Machiavelli* he examined a tract written in defence of
King Ferrante following the second baronial rebellion.[24] A third area was
Croce's insistence on the distinctive political character of the Neapolitan
kingdom, on the lack of common political purpose and identity; his
famous *History of the Kingdom of Naples* sought to explain its apparent
decay and disorder.[25]

Croce expressed a liberal stance in his historical and philosophical
work. A very different political perspective was offered by the Spanish
legal scholar Francisco Elías de Tejada, who encompassed the literary
and philosophical achievements of Naples between 1442 and 1665 in
the five volumes of his *Nápoles hispánico*; this work was published in
Spain from 1958 onwards by the reactionary Carlist movement.[26] The
central argument was that Spanish culture had a distinctive character of
its own, formed in the long struggles to establish a Spanish state; it was
not a European culture, but something *sui generis*, and Catholic. Elías de
Tejada asked, however, where Naples under Spanish rule fitted into this
understanding of Spanish identity. He sought to demonstrate that the
south of Italy did have the privilege of being taken into this separate
world following its conquest by Alfonso in 1442 and by Ferdinand in
1503: it was a real part of Spain. His first volume was dedicated to the
period between the two conquests, a period in which he assumed that the
'Spanish' identity of southern Italy was fast established; and his second
volume looked at the next half-century. The underlying themes were the
defence of king, faith and fatherland, with considerable emphasis on the
role of southern Italy in the defence of Christendom against the Turkish
menace. But his work is something more than a highly tendentious
curiosity representing the thinking of an extreme group from the Franco
era. He accumulated vast amounts of raw information, so that he offers
what is virtually an index of Neapolitan authors and their works, and he
provided evidence of the extraordinary richness of literary production,
and of the prominence of debates about the ethical dimension to
political conduct, continuing beyond 1500. Moreover, interest in his
work has revived, with the appearance of Italian translations of the first
two volumes, admittedly from the far-right publisher Controcorrente,
and of the acts of a conference seeking to elucidate his ideas (again,
sympathetically rather than critically).[27]

In fact, the study of south Italian humanism has advanced by leaps
and bounds as a result of the close analysis of texts and the parallel
publication of works of synthesis by more balanced scholars as Santoro

and Tateo. What emerges is a sense that south Italian humanists engaged with fundamental ethical questions concerning the nature of the virtues (and the vices). Mario Santoro's work on attitudes to the theme of fortune in Renaissance Italy commenced with Giovanni Pontano, and looked closely as well at Tristano Caracciolo and Galateo, two other very significant southern humanists (the latter of whom had Greek as his mother tongue).[28] His work raises again fundamental questions about the extent to which ideas associated with Machiavelli and other Tuscan writers can be identified earlier in the writers of the *Regno* such as Pontano, even if that is not necessarily to presume influence from the southern writers on those in the north. Santoro provided a helpful short survey in English of humanism in Naples, concentrating on the period from 1442 to 1501.[29] He emphasized how the coming of Alfonso to Naples in 1442 marked a decisive break with existing cultural traditions. He stressed the importance of political shocks, such as the baronial rebellions and the French invasion of 1494, on the political thinking of Pontano and his contemporaries. But he was also careful to address critically the question whether southern humanism was, while court-based, also 'provincial', a mere offshoot of northern tendencies, and whether its personnel was to a large extent not even Neapolitan. Associated with this is the question whether humanist culture was exclusively court-based. He insisted that Alfonso's own approach to cultural patronage was a perfect example of the image of the princely patron favoured by contemporary humanists. He presented Alfonso as an active figure in the promotion of culture, as a humanist in his own right, a role expressed in the 'hour of the book', time spent every day in his library after dinner with his entourage of scholars. The king himself is Maecenas. This is not to suggest, however, that literary culture at the Neapolitan court was forced into a single mould: the famous disputes of Facio, Valla and Manetti suggest a delight in invective among the courtiers themselves. Santoro underlined the significance of the revival of the University of Naples, under royal patronage, and its role as a centre for the study of Aristotelian and Latin texts. Here it was King Ferrante who showed more enthusiasm, which reflects the shift under Ferrante of some humanistic activities away from the court. Further evidence that the southern Renaissance was not simply an offshoot of the north is provided by the responsiveness of figures such as Pontano to the events of 1494, in which the philosopher statesman played a significant role, apparently changing sides when he formally welcomed the French king into Naples. For Santoro and other Italian scholars, the political changes of the period 1442 to 1503 did not undermine, but in fact recharged, the humanist culture of southern Italy.

This emphasis on the significance of Pontano, particularly his ethical treatises, is also found in the distinguished work of Francesco Tateo. In addition to many closely focused studies such as an edition of Pontano's *De magnanimitate*, he provided an overview of key aspects of south Italian humanism in his contributions to the multi-volume *Letteratura Italiana Laterza*, addressing Latin culture and writing in the vernacular.[30] Here, he divided his attention between Pontano, seen as the 'innovative personality' of southern humanism, Jacopo Sannazaro, the influential author of the *Arcadia* (among other works), and a group of writers in Italian whose works are taken as proof of the individuality of the southern Renaissance. This is not to deny that Pontano built on foundations laid by, among others, Antonio Beccadelli, also known as 'Il Panormita', secretary to Alfonso and Ferrante, whose youthful extravaganza the *Hermaphroditus* provided a model, if a scandalous one, for the writing of epigrammatic verse. Tateo also addressed the work of those who continued the Pontanian tradition: members of Pontano's academy such as the publisher Pietro Summonte, celebrated for his account of the famous tournament of Barletta between Spanish and French troops in February 1503.[31] Tateo stressed the importance of political changes in the work of Tristano Caracciolo (d. 1517), who wrote vigorously against Ferdinand the Catholic's ill-judged plans to introduce the Inquisition into Naples, and also addressed such themes as fortune and nobility, continuing to raise the ethical issues that Pontano had examined in his own writings.[32] He underlined, too, the loyalty of Sannazaro to the Neapolitan house of Aragon; Sannazaro returned from France to Naples in 1505 after briefly sharing the exile there of King Federigo. Tateo, based in Bari, not unnaturally revealed a predilection for Apulian humanists, notably Antonio de Ferrariis, 'il Galateo' (1440–1516). Tateo showed how Galateo's Greek background helped render him indifferent to the cult of Latin rhetoric. Yet he was not simply a provincial physician; he had spent time at court, and he was a very well-read author who boldly examined fundamental ethical issues, in the light of his deep Christian faith, and adopted a distinctive approach to writing about geography and archaeology. For Tateo, he was attempting to write a science of the human condition that can be set against the rhetorical history-writing of his contemporaries. He certainly did not idealize the Spanish conquerors of 1503: *utinam haec litora hispanae nunquam tetegissent nostra carinae*, 'if only the Spanish ships had never touched our shores' was the view he forcefully expressed in his *De educatione*. This book was intended for the young Ferdinand, duke of Calabria, living in permanent exile in Valencia; and it was a passage that caused some difficulty to Elías de

Tejada when he sought to show that Galateo too was really an admirer of things Spanish.

Galateo was one of those who switched between Latin and the vernacular. The place of vernacular culture in the southern Renaissance emerges from Tateo's study of such authors as Loise de Rosa, author of a celebrated chronicle in Neapolitan dialect that seems remote from the concerns of courtly philosophers such as Beccadelli. But Masuccio Salernitano, the author of a collection of fifty *Novelle* in the mould of Boccaccio, was shown by Tateo to occupy an interesting position on the edge of courtly society; he dedicated his stories to the duchess of Calabria, wife of the future King Alfonso II of Naples; a central part of his work was attention to a moral message, which, in the final version, was spelled out at the end of each tale. This emphasis on moral messages also appears in the popular edition of Aesop's fables produced by the illustrious Neapolitan printer Francesco del Tuppo: a spectacularly produced *Esopo volgare* was first printed in 1485.

The Italian tradition of close study of southern humanists has remained active. New editions or analyses of texts by Pontano, such as his account of the first baronial rebellion against Ferrante, have enlarged understanding of key figures.[33] Bruno Figliuolo has emphasized the importance of figures active at the court and University of Naples from the outer fringes of the Regno: Matteo dell'Aquila (d. 1475), a philosopher from the Abruzzi; Angelo Catone, from the papal enclave of Benevento (d. 1496), who was also interested in medicine; Pietro Ranzano (d. 1492/93), a theologian from Sicily, later active in Hungary.[34] Such figures combined traditional learning with an awareness of newer cultural trends, and exercised influence in the universities of Tuscany, Umbria and northern Italy. Such studies of second-rank figures are important in ensuring that hard lines are not drawn between humanistic culture and the intellectual world of the universities, any more than between Latin culture and the vernacular.

The links, so often intimate, between the Neapolitan writers and the royal house were explored from another angle by Jerry Bentley. His *Politics and Culture in Renaissance Naples* placed Aragonese Naples firmly on the map of Renaissance humanist culture.[35] Bentley emphasized the relationship between that culture and the political interests of the Crown. His humanists, like those of Sforza Milan described by Ianziti, were engaged in a collaborative enterprise to justify monarchy, and, beyond that, the claims of the Aragonese dynasty to rule in southern Italy.[36] This involved a significant transformation in the humanist message. Themes discussed in a Florentine republican setting had to be re-assessed in a monarchic one. For Bentley the real 'halcyon days' were the reign of Alfonso the Magnanimous, and he saw his son as more 'utilitarian' in his cultural patronage, while recognizing that contemporaries well beyond Naples (not least in Florence) remained enthusiastic about Ferrante. Alfonso had the charm and resources to attract to his court a galaxy of scholars who were not merely well acquainted with humanists elsewhere in Italy, but influential as well. Bentley's sense that the Neapolitan humanists must not be isolated from the wider Italian setting is worth stressing. In his interpretation, Naples did indeed become, in the mid to late fifteenth century, a focal point of Renaissance patronage and production. The supreme example of the wider influence of Alfonso's court is Lorenzo Valla, whose exposé of the politically-charged Donation of Constantine as a forgery strengthened Alfonso in his relations with the papacy, and whose history of the career of Alfonso's father Ferdinand of Antequera, king of Aragon, enhanced the image of the Aragonese dynasty.[37] Valla had spent time at the papal court, and this was also home for a time to other humanists active in Naples: Bartolomeo Facio, from near Genoa, a great enemy of Valla; and the Florentine Giannozzo Manetti, who arrived in Naples after the death of his patron Pope Nicholas V (1455); his willingness to defend monarchic rule contrasts oddly with his earlier denunciations of Alfonso as a tyrant, during the war of Piombino (1448). This interplay between Neapolitan and Roman humanism deserves further study.

Bentley's attention to political dimensions also allowed him to examine several vernacular authors. Diomede Carafa (d. 1487) was an intensely loyal servant of the Crown, a member of an illustrious family, and author of a series of *Memoriali* in which he set out his idea of the perfect courtier (*Dello optimo cortesano*) and, in his *I doveri del principe*, his understanding of how a prince should aim to please his subjects.[38] For Bentley, Carafa 'projected a practical realism foreign to earlier theorists', and possessed 'stunning insights' into economic matters, encouraging the Crown to invest in trade, industry and agriculture in order to promote the well-being not just of the treasury but of the king's subjects, for, Carafa insists, 'when the lord has rich subjects, he himself cannot be poor'.[39] And yet, as Bentley recognized, there also existed a sort of dualism in the life of these humanists. At one level they conducted sophisticated and elegant discussions of virtuous ethical conduct, especially among princes; but at another level, as royal secretaries, they were the servants of hard-nosed rulers who expected them to devote a significant amount of time to the promotion of their ruler's political interests. Thus (in common with humanists elsewhere) they were propagandists who used their rhetorical skills to present the ruler's actions in the best possible light; the violence of Ferrante was the result of provocation, not of wilful malevolence. Bentley saw Pontano as the last and most sophisticated voice in an ethical debate that began with Beccadelli: of course it was desirable to apply classical and Christian ethics to the conduct of one's life, but sometimes high principles had to be sacrificed in order to attain internal peace, an attitude which can obviously be compared to that of Machiavelli. What is still needed, however, is an assessment of Pontano's wider influence; all his major works were readily available in print by 1518–19, and some had been printed in Naples from 1481 onwards by the printer Moravus.

The Neapolitan Renaissance thus cannot qualify as a simple continuation of Florentine 'civic humanism', for its political concerns were quite different to those of the Florentines; but it appears as something more than a mere literary movement, a cult of courtly entertainment. Still, it is important not to ignore the distinguished Latin poetry of the Aragonese court of Naples. To understand the poetic traditions cultivated in Naples, one can turn to another writer in English, Carol Kidwell. In three narrative accounts of the careers of leading Neapolitan cultural figures, Marullus, Pontano and Sannazaro, she has demonstrated the close interweaving of their political and literary careers.[40] Marullus, a soldier poet of Balkan origin, emerges as a particularly fine practitioner of Latin verse in the classical mould. Pontano, 'poet and prime minister', earned international esteem for his own verse. But the most influential of all three was Sannazaro, unlike the others a south Italian by birth, and a figure whose greatest creation (in Italian) was the *Arcadia*, an idealization of pastoral life with exceptional influence throughout sixteenth-century Europe, an influence easily visible, for example, in Sir Philip Sidney's *Arcadia*.[41] William Kennedy has analysed Sannazaro's highly successful combination of vernacular prose and poetry and his creative use of classical models.[42]

Other aspects of south Italian cultural life have received close attention. The superb royal library, and especially the books preserved today in the Biblioteca del Universitat de Vàlencia and in Paris, were studied by Tammaro de Marinis and later scholars.[43] De Marinis' massive and beautiful catalogue also pays close attention to the books that Ferrante received in 1486 from the confiscated property of rebel barons, evidence in some cases of a real interest in humanistic culture among the nobility too. Antonio Petrucci was notable for his large collection of Greek texts. The royal library contained a wide range of texts, including finely illuminated breviaries and other religious texts which, despite their traditional contents, are eloquent testimony to the marriage of Flemish and Italian artistic motifs, of which more later; but also fundamental classical texts by Pliny the Elder, Livy, Caesar, Plutarch and an old intellectual mentor, Seneca, often illuminated in very self-consciously classical styles with monumental lettering, and carrying texts in very elegant humanist hands. Some of these handsome volumes were imported (for instance as gifts from Cosimo de'Medici), but the royal court also contained skilled calligraphers such as Cinico, an ardent anthologist of morally invigorating extracts from ancient history, and scholar librarians such as the rhetorician Brancati. The delight of Alfonso the Magnanimous in classical history is well documented. Of course, these fine books were kept out of sight of the vast majority of the king's subjects, and in that sense they formed part of a closed, court-centred system of patronage; but, as will be seen, monumental art was also used to convey a sense of the dynasty's grandeur to the wider Neapolitan public.

In addition, Naples, under Francesco del Tuppo, who has already been encountered, and his German colleague Sixtus Rießinger, stood at the centre of a vibrant printing industry from 1475, which was strongly encouraged by King Ferrante.[44] Rießinger's edition of Frederick II's *Liber Augustalis* of 1231 (1475) reflected the strong interest in legal scholarship of both the king and the renascent University of Naples.[45] Arnaldus of Brussels printed the *Epistolae familiares* of Beccadelli as early as 1473. In addition to luxury codices printed on parchment and illuminated for the royal court, there was a real book industry, with texts being carried by merchants across the kingdom and beyond its borders. Particularly important among the Neapolitan printers were the Jews, native and German, who benefited from the strong protection of the king, and who showed a general preference for editions of the books of the Bible and for Bible commentaries.[46] This Hebrew scholarship had rather few resonances at court, where no Hebrew books seem to have been kept; but at least one courtier, Isaac Abravanel, a Jew who was deeply learned in the classical philosophical texts, had access to Latin scholarship (he seems to have shared the interest in Seneca of his contemporaries at the Neapolitan court). During his years in Naples (1492–94) he expressed a very negative view of kingship in his commentary on *Kings I* and *II*: 'the existence of a king is not at all essential for the people', so it may have been an advantage that he was writing in a language very few at court understood. He later resided in Monopoli, a Venetian port in Apulia, and his heirs served the viceroys of Naples until 1541. The attention to the full range of biblical texts in Hebrew shown by Abravanel and the Jewish printers mirrored the close interest among Christian authors in ancient texts, and the need to study them philologically as well as for their content, moral and historical. This is an area that has begun to repay further study: Roth's *The Jews in the Renaissance* is dated and deals thinly with the south, while the account of Abravanel's work by Netanyahu is very flawed; but thoughtful monographs by Eric Lawee and Seymour Feldman have started the process of reassessment.[47]

So far the emphasis has lain on literary production, which has dominated the historiography of the southern Renaissance, and which has been the main prop of the claim that late fifteenth-century Naples was home to a vibrant humanistic culture. But the performance of music was intimately related to the world of letters. Its principal historian has been Allan Atlas.[48] Recordings of music from the court of Naples have now become staple elements in the early music repertoire, including the important Montecassino manuscript 871.[49] Ferrante had a passion for music and dance; the dancing master Guglielmo Ebreo from Pesaro, a converted Jew and the author of a celebrated tract, worked for him.[50] But the passion for music began with Alfonso the Magnanimous, whose chapel choir was the envy of Europe (the Sforzas of Milan regularly tried to steal away his musicians); the repertoire included victory psalms written in honour of the king. The chapel choir was used as a diplomatic tool, and was sent in 1451 to Florence, while the fact that a chapel choir was founded in Ferrara in 1454 *more regio*, 'in the royal manner', suggests that the influence of Neapolitan music in northern Italy had already become very powerful. However, the predominant influence under Alfonso remained the music of the Spanish courts from which his family hailed. Links to Flanders became more important under his successor; Ferrante earned great prestige through his patronage of the Walloon composer and musicologist Johannes Tinctoris, active at court between the early 1470s and the early 1490s; he even sent him back to Burgundian lands and to the court of Charles VIII of France, his future enemy, to recruit star musicians. His musical establishment was, therefore, determinedly international: Ferrante sought the best, and his taste was also eclectic, although later he relied more on home-grown talent. Clearly the musical culture of Naples owed its vivacity to the royal court; indeed, political themes were not always far from sight and sound, as is shown by the stirring song *Viva el Rey Ferrando!*

This close interaction with the culture of the Burgundian Netherlands is also visible in the fine arts. The courts of the dukes of Burgundy and the kings of Naples had a number of striking similarities, notably the love of magnificence and the sense that this magnificence could be used to paper over any problems of political legitimacy. Painting and sculpture in Naples owed much to Flanders, as also to Italian trends.[51] Yet it is important to remember the influence of Catalan late Gothic models, such as the painter Lluis Dalmau, a favourite of Alfonso the Magnanimous, who was sent to Flanders to study the work of Jan van Eyck and Rogier van der Weyden. In addition, the great Catalan architect Guillem Sagrera helped rebuild the Castelnuovo in Naples, which combined Gothic and classical features. Direct cultural influence from Flanders can be identified in the work of the important Neapolitan court painter Niccolò Colantonio, active from the 1440s to the 1460s; his familiarity with Flemish techniques led him to imitate the use of oil emulsions in painting, a method he passed on to his star pupil, Antonello da Messina, renowned for his sensitive portraits.[52]

Sculptural works show a similar eclecticism. The decoration of the triumphal arch in Naples combines Arthurian themes, with Alfonso portrayed as the new Galahad, and imagery securely based in classical models and framed by classical architecture. As George Hersey showed, this highly influential monument, imitated widely in later centuries, was also a loud political statement accessible to all the king's subjects, and insisting on the legitimacy of Alfonso's conquest of Naples.[53] The court artist Francesco Laurana sculpted a series of ethereal busts of members of the royal family in an individualistic style, as well as helping to design the arch. But no one matched the energy and detail of Guido Mazzoni at the end of the fifteenth century: his terracotta sculpture was moulded with relentless realism, visible most famously in his 'Lamentation over the Dead Christ', a life-sized tableau preserved in the church of Monteoliveto in Naples; the figures themselves are portraits of members of the royal court, including Alfonso II. In the realms of architecture, the building of a palace at Poggioreale, now vanished, was an echo of the Medicean villa at Poggio a Caiano outside Florence; but even more ambitious was a scheme supported by Alfonso II for what Hersey has called 'the artistic renewal of Naples', involving the rebuilding of large areas of the city to create wide avenues punctuated by flowing fountains and grand piazzas; political strife ensured that these plans came to nothing until Pedro de Toledo, the Spanish viceroy, extended the western flanks of Naples in the sixteenth century.[54]

The Florentine connection was the basis of Roberto Pane's approach to the artistic history of southern Italy between the arrival of Alfonso V and the early sixteenth century.[55] His insistence that 'the southern Renaissance signifies above all "Florence in Naples"' was qualified in some areas: he recognized the importance of Flemish models in painting, describing Colantonio as 'a Fleming by adoption'; and he admitted that smaller, transportable works of art such as tapestries and panel paintings had been carried off by French conquerors, so that the evidence from southern Italy itself is dominated by the works of sculptors and architects whose work was immovable. Donatello, della Robbia and other Tuscans were attracted to the court, but were only birds of passage, looking for generous patrons. This, of course, is precisely the view that Santoro, in the world of letters, sought to challenge, and that this chapter also doubts. When late Gothic motifs appeared in the art of Aragonese Naples, they were, for Pane, a testament to the 'tenacious survival of the feudal spirit', rather than an eclecticism that saw Catalans working alongside Italians as builders and designers. Pane also insisted that the southern Renaissance was short-lived because it revolved around a court whose patronage peaked before the French invasions, a point of view that does seem to be qualified by the evidence cited earlier for princely patronage of letters and the arts in other parts of the Mezzogiorno. Pane's views were heavily influenced by a letter by Pietro Summonte, written in 1534, which stressed the debt to Florence and, in lesser measure to Flanders, of the artists working in Aragonese Naples.[56] Although Pane's views now seem overstated, his meticulous work on a large number of Neapolitan monuments serves as a reminder that, even in emphasizing the eclecticism of the Aragonese court, cultural links to Tuscany must be given close attention.

The south Italian Renaissance was not a dead end. Its diffusion can be measured in two areas: Hungary and Spain. In the first case we observe what was mainly a one-way process, with ideas and motifs arriving from Italy and being adopted at the Hungarian court, from where, in fact, they radiated further north, into Jagiellonian Poland. In the latter case there was a two-way interaction, and complex borrowings were made in both directions. To begin with Hungary, there is a wealth of artistic, literary and codicological evidence illustrating the influence of Italy, and especially Naples, at the court of Matthias Corvinus, who reigned until 1490. The link was founded both on intimate dynastic ties and on the recognition by Matthias, who aspired to the crown of the Holy Roman Empire, that magnificence in the classical mould would suit his political objectives. Naples, indeed, provided a convenient model. Yet the attraction of Italian culture was not simply pragmatic. Marianna Birnbaum has examined a number of key figures with links to Italy.[57] János Vitéz (d. 1472), archbishop of Esztergom, built up a large library and sent his protégés to study in Italy; he also acted as an intermediary between Matthias' father John Hunyadi and Alfonso the Magnanimous. Janus Pannonius, a lively poet famous for his epigrams, sometimes erotic, served Matthias as secretary until 1471, having studied in Ferrara. But, as Rósza Feuer-Tóth showed, there were also Italians at the Hungarian court who were instrumental in the development of a self-consciously classical architectural style, still visible in the remains of the royal villa at Visegrád.[58] Here the Neapolitan connection is very striking: Antonio Bonfini from the Italian Marches had close contact with Ferrante's son Giovanni, archbishop of Esztergom from 1483; he became Matthias' court historian. A figure close to Corvinus, mentioned already, was Pietro Ranzano, a Dominican friar from Palermo who had helped Valla translate Thucydides, and who wrote an *Epitome Rerum Hungaricarum* in 1488. Francesco Arrigoni spent eight years at the Hungarian court, serving as reader to the Neapolitan princess Beatrice, daughter of Ferrante and spouse of Matthias; he then returned to Italy to perform similar services for the Neapolitan princes. Francesco Bandini, a member of an important Florentine family, became a loyal servant of Ferrante, writing of Naples: 'if you want to know about the liberal arts, they have reached perfection here'. But, sent to Ferrara to help Beatrice, he found himself before long in Hungary in her company, spending thirteen years there. He advised Matthias Corvinus on Renaissance building styles. But the influence of modern styles was visible also in the spectacular library Matthias created. Comparable in its breadth and beauty to the royal library in Naples, the Bibliotheca Corviniana also acquired books actually penned and illuminated by Neapolitan courtiers, most notably Cinico. Of course it also drew on many other sources, especially Florence, but the shape and function of the collection is strongly reminiscent of the Neapolitan exemplar.[59]

Still further afield, as Harold Segel showed, the community of humanist scholars embraced the renascent Polish kingdom; the Jagiellonian University in Cracow was an important centre of Latin scholarship, much favoured, in fact, by Hungarian students.[60] Filippo Buonaccorsi (Callimachus) from Tuscany settled in Poland but was also a great admirer of Matthias Corvinus, seeing in him an exemplar of the perfect prince. But links between southern Italy and Poland were not simply mediated through Hungary. In 1518 Bona Sforza, duchess of Bari and grand-daughter of Alfonso II of Naples, married King Sigismund of Poland, following negotiations by the Petrarchan poet Cristoforo Colonna, secretary to the duke of Calabria, whose nostalgic poems about Italians in exile as far afield as Vilnius charmed the Polish-Lithuanian court. A Polish Latinist, Andrzej Krzycki (Cricius), hailed Colonna as 'a swift emissary of golden tongue, the glory of the bards of the kingdom of Sirena [Naples]'. He eventually grew critical of Bona Sforza, a figure of great influence in Polish political life. Clearly, the Polish Renaissance, like that in Hungary, drew on many sources of inspiration (the German humanist Conrad Celtis had considerable impact in Poland). Yet southern Italy was an important source of inspiration in late fifteenth-century Hungary and in early sixteenth-century Poland-Lithuania. So too the Latin culture of southern Italy percolated into Albania, where the deeds of Pyrrhus appear to have been known at the court of the close ally of the Aragonese kings of Naples, George Kastriota Scanderbeg; and Dalmatia, exposed to both south Italian and Venetian culture, was also the seat of serious study of Latin literature.[61]

This 'Pannonian Renaissance' in Hungary and the Polish Renaissance had significant features in common with the Neapolitan Renaissance: the role of the royal court in both cases, the role of the university in the latter case. In Spain, scholars even beyond the boundaries of the Crown of Aragon showed awareness of intellectual developments at the court of Naples. Ottavio di Camillo mentioned three figures with interesting south Italian connections.[62] Fernando de Córdoba was a child prodigy with a photographic memory who sought employment, unsuccessfully, at Alfonso V's court in Naples. His patron was Lorenzo Valla, who presented him to the king, while admitting that his Latin left much to be desired; later Fernando sided with the Florentine Poggio Bracciolini when Poggio accused Valla of heresy. A more important figure was Juan de Lucena, who was in Italy in the 1450s and translated, revised and appropriated to his authorship Facio's *De vitae felicitate*, which Facio had written as a denunciation of Valla's supposedly Epicurean views in *De vero bono*. Alfonso Ortiz was more positively influenced by Valla, seeing pleasure not as an impediment to virtue but as something that enhances it. Thus the lively debates in Naples resonated across Europe. Moreover, scholars from Sicily inserted themselves into the cultural life of Spain: Lucio Marineo, early in the sixteenth century, wrote extensively on the history and geography of Spain, and more particularly of Aragon, and was one of the first scholars to pay attention to the Basque language. Even so, Neapolitan scholars took some glee in contrasting their high culture with a supposed indifference to the arts among Spanish nobles and hidalgos, praising King Alfonso for his ability to distance himself from his fellow-Spaniards in this respect. Panormita reports that he inserted an open book in the royal coat of arms in order to make plain his dislike of such Philistinism (to use a modern word).[63]

Lacking a royal court, Aragonese Sicily depended more on local initiatives for cultural patronage. Messina became a particularly active centre of writing and scholarship, but Catania and Palermo also played their part, and indeed Santi Correnti has waged a vigorous and partisan campaign to defend the primacy of Catania.[64] Humanists from the island of Sicily were active both at home and abroad. Giovanni Aurispa from Noto (d. 1459) was a pioneer who taught Greek in Bologna, Florence and Ferrara. Antonio Beccadelli of Palermo, 'il Panormita', was, with the painter Antonello da Messina, the most influential Sicilian cultural figure of the Quattrocento. Both have been encountered already in a Neapolitan setting. Sicily attracted foreign artists in its own right: the sculptors Francesco Laurana and, in particular, Domenico Gagini, were active there. Andrea Romano has demonstrated the vitality of legal learning on the island, and the establishment of a royal university at Catania in 1445 gave further impetus to the study of law, philosophy, medicine and other disciplines; the Dominican friars were conspicuous among the teachers there and in other cultural centres. Many Sicilian humanists had studied in the universities of northern and central Italy, or in the kingdom of Naples. Concetta Bianca underlined the importance of Messina as a centre of printing in the last decades of the Quattrocento (it is no surprise to find a German printer, Heinrich Alding, among the early typographers).[65] Henri Bresc, from the perspective of an economic and social historian, examined the circulation of Latin books on the island, such as texts of Vergil.[66] Latin culture was accompanied by a vigorous vernacular culture, both in demotic Sicilian and in a highly Tuscanized Italian that looked back to Petrarch. Even the Sicilian dependency of Malta seems to reveal similar cultural trends, to judge from the vernacular *Cantilena* of the notary Pietro Caxaro (d. 1485), the first document in Maltese; and there is some evidence that there were competent Latinists in this outpost.[67]

Finally, it is important to return briefly to the question whether the French invasion of 1494 led to the diffusion of Italian Renaissance ideas and motifs in France. It was not simply panel paintings, silver and gold plate and tapestries that travelled north with the departing French armies. (Maybe the Italian allies tried to stop Charles at the battle of Fornovo in 1495 partly in order to recover looted goods; Charles self-righteously complained that some favourite books were lost then.) The master of terracotta, Guido Mazzoni, went to France, where he designed the now lost tomb of Charles VIII, who quite possibly had been deeply moved by the 'Lamentation' in Naples. But the influences from Italy seem to have consisted of a pot-pourri of themes, from garden design to architectural detail, some drawn from the north rather than the briefly conquered south. Large items packaged and sent north included bronze doors and glazed windows from Naples, and it is possible that Poggioreale, the royal villa itself based on a Medicean model, had some influence on the design of Charles' great château at Amboise. Even so, Antonovics' view is that the cultural effects of the invasion of 1494 were quite limited.[68]

As in the days of Giotto and Cavallini, the success of the Neapolitan court as a centre of artistic patronage was greatly enhanced by the king's ability to attract the services of artists and men of letters from Flanders and northern Italy as well as Spain. Yet this in itself proves that it was far from being a 'provincial' court, but was, rather, one of the cultural centres that set the tone of late fifteenth-century Italy – a comment that applies not merely to the fine arts but to the whole range of cultural patronage evinced in Aragonese Naples. Naples' identity as a kingdom did not mean that it stood outside the Italian norm, was alien, the seat of violent baronial passions typified by those expressed in the partly verifiable tale of the duchess of Malfi.[69] For it was also, as has been seen, a region from which, through dynastic links or proximity, Italian culture radiated into eastern Europe and the Mediterranean. Bearing in mind the links between Naples and Flanders, it is also possible to see in the Neapolitan Renaissance one of the channels through which contact was maintained between the 'northern' and the Italian Renaissance. Indeed, the experience of Naples suggests how false it is to assume that Renaissance Italy was somehow separate from the wider cultural world of late medieval and early modern Europe.

## notes

1.  For an outline of the political history of southern Italy, see David Abulafia, *The Western Mediterranean Kingdoms, 1200–1500: The Struggle for Dominion* (London, 1997).
2.  David Abulafia, 'The Italian Other: Greeks, Muslims and Jews', in David Abulafia, ed., *Italy in the Central Middle Ages* (Oxford, 2004), pp. 215–36.
3.  David Abulafia, *Frederick II: A Medieval Emperor*, 3rd edn (London, 2002), pp. 251–89.
4.  Steven Runciman, *The Sicilian Vespers: A History of the Mediterranean World in the Thirteenth Century* (Cambridge, 1958); Jean Dunbabin, *Charles I of Anjou: Power, Kingship and State-Making in Thirteenth-Century Europe* (London, 1998).
5.  Samantha Kelly, *The New Solomon: Robert of Naples (1309–43) and Fourteenth-Century Kingship* (Leiden, 2003).
6.  Roberto Weiss, *Medieval and Humanist Greek* (Padua, 1977), passim.
7.  M. Pade, H.R. Jensen and L. Waage Petersen, eds, *Avignon and Naples: Italy in France, France in Italy in the Fourteenth Century*, Analecta Romana Instituti Danici, Supplementum XXV (Rome, 1997).

8.  F. Robin, *La cour d'Anjou-Provence: la vie artistique sous le règne de René* (Paris, 1985); C. de Mérindol, *Le roi René et la seconde maison d'Anjou: emblématique, art, histoire* (Paris, 1987); René of Anjou, *The Book of the Love-Smitten Heart*, ed. and trans. Stephanie Viereck Gibbs and Kathryn Karczewska (New York, 2001).
9.  Alan Ryder, *Alfonso the Magnanimous, King of Aragon, Naples and Sicily 1396–1458* (Oxford, 1990).
10. George Hersey, *The Aragonese Arch at Naples, 1443–75* (New Haven, CT, 1973).
11. Alan Ryder, *The Kingdom of Naples under Alfonso the Magnanimous* (Oxford, 1975).
12. Peter Stacey, 'Imperial Rome and the Legitimation of Political Authority in Renaissance Naples', Ph.D. thesis (University of Cambridge, 2000).
13. Cecil Clough, 'Federico da Montefeltro and the Kings of Naples: A Study in Fifteenth-Century Survival', *Renaissance Studies*, VI (1992) 113–72.
14. *Le porte di Castelnuovo: il restauro* (Naples, 1997).
15. Camillo Porzio, *La Congiura dei Baroni* (various editions since 1586, for example Naples, 1964; Milan, 1965; Venosa, 1989).
16. David Abulafia, ed., *The French Descent into Renaissance Italy 1494–95: Antecedents and Effects* (Aldershot, 1995).
17. A.V. Antonovics, '"Il semble que ce soit là un vrai Paradis terrestre": Charles VIII's Conquest of Naples and the French Renaissance', in Abulafia, *French Descent*, pp. 311–25.
18. Carlos-José Hernando Sánchez, *El reino de Nápoles en el imperio de Carlos V: la consolidación de la conquista* (Madrid, 2001); José-Enrique Ruiz-Domènec, *El Gran Capitán: retrato de una época* (Barcelona, 2002).
19. Jacob Burckhardt, *Civilization of the Renaissance in Italy* (New York, 1958), 1.1, pp. 22–5.
20. John Addington Symonds, *Renaissance in Italy: The Age of the Despots* (London, 1875), pp. 115–16.
21. Eberhard Gothein, *Die Culturentwicklung Süditaliens in Einzel-Darstellungen* (Breslau, 1886); *Il Rinascimento nell'Italia meridionale*, ed. T. Persico (Florence, 1915).
22. Felix Gilbert, *History: Politics or Culture? Reflections on Ranke and Burckhardt* (Princeton, 1990), pp. 81–2.
23. Benedetto Croce, *La Spagna nella vita italiana durante la Rinascenza* (Bari, 1917).
24. Benedetto Croce, *Prima del Machiavelli: una difesa di Re Ferrante I di Napoli per il violato trattato di pace del 1486 col papa* (Bari, 1944).
25. Benedetto Croce, *History of the Kingdom of Naples*, ed. H. Stuart Hughes (Chicago, 1970).
26. Francisco Elías de Tejada Spínola, *Nápoles hispánico*, 5 vols (Madrid, 1958–64): I: *La etapa aragonesa, 1442–1503*; II: *Las decadas imperiales, 1503–1554*; III: *Las Españas aureas, 1554–1598*; IV: *Las Españas argentas, 1598–1621*; V: *Las Españas rotas, 1621–1665*.
27. Francisco Elías de Tejada, *Napoli spagnuola*, ed. Silvio Vitale (Naples, 1999–2002), I: *La tappa aragonese*; II: *Le decadi imperiali*. See also *Napoli e le Spagne. Atti del Convegno Francisco Elías de Tejada: Realismo giuridico e Istituzioni ispano-napoletane* (Naples, 1999).

28.  Mario Santoro, *Fortuna, ragione e prudenza nella civiltà letteraria del Cinquecento*, 2nd edn (Naples, 1978).
29.  Mario Santoro, 'Humanism in Naples', in Albert Rabil, ed., *Renaissance Humanism: Foundations, Forms and Legacy*, 3 vols (Philadelphia, 1988), I: *Humanism in Italy*, pp. 296–331. For Alfonso V cf. Avelino Sotelo Álvarez, *Alfonso V de Aragón y I de Nápoles y el humanismo italiano* (Torrevieja, 1996).
30.  Francesco Tateo, ed., *Ioannis Ioviani Pontani de magnanimitate* (Florence, 1969); *L'umanesimo meridionale*, Letteratura italiana Laterza XVI (Bari, 1972).
31.  Giuliano Procacci, *La disfida di Barletta tra storia e romanzo* (Milan, 2001).
32.  Cf. Avelino Sotelo Álvarez, *Tristano Caracciolo, un noble humanista en el reino de Nápoles: vida, obra y pensamiento* (Torrevieja, 1998).
33.  Liliana Monti Sabia, *Pontano e la storia: dal de bello neapolitano all'*Actius (Rome, 1995); Liliana Monti Sabia, ed., *Ioannis Ioviani Pontani de immanitate liber* (Naples, 1970).
34.  Bruno Figliuolo, *La cultura a Napoli nel secondo Quattrocento: ritratti di protagonisti* (Udine, 1997).
35.  Jerry Bentley, *Politics and Culture in Renaissance Naples* (Princeton, 1987).
36.  Gary Ianziti, *Humanistic Historiography under the Sforzas: Politics and Propaganda in Fifteenth-Century Milan* (Oxford, 1988).
37.  On Valla: Jerry Bentley, *New Testament Scholarship in the Renaissance* (Princeton, 1983); Maristella Lorsch, 'Lorenzo Valla', in Rabil, *Renaissance Humanism*, I, pp. 332–49.
38.  Gioacchino Paparelli, ed., *Dello optimo cortesano* (Salerno, 1971); Franca Petrucci Nardelli, ed., *Diomede Carafa: Memoriali* (Rome, 1988).
39.  David Abulafia, 'The Crown and the Economy under Ferrante I of Naples (1458–94)', in T. Dean and C. Wickham, eds, *City and Countryside in Late Medieval and Early Renaissance Italy: Studies Presented to Philip Jones* (London, 1990), pp. 125–46, reprinted in David Abulafia, *Commerce and Conquest in the Mediterranean, 1100–1500* (Aldershot, 1993).
40.  Carol Kidwell, *Marullus: Soldier Poet of the Renaissance* (London, 1989); *Pontano: Poet and Prime Minister* (London, 1991); *Sannazaro and Arcadia* (London, 1993).
41.  Sir Philip Sidney, *The Old Arcadia*, ed. Katherine Duncan-Jones (Oxford, 1994).
42.  William Kennedy, *Jacopo Sannazaro and the Uses of Arcadia* (Hanover, NH, 1983).
43.  Tammaro de Marinis, *La biblioteca napoletana dei re d'Aragona*, 4 vols (Milan, 1947–52), and *Supplemento*, 2 vols (Verona, 1969); Gennaro Toscano and Cabeza Sánchez-Alornoz, *La Biblioteca Reial de Nàpols: d'Alfons el Magnànim al Duc de Calabria, 1442–1550* (Valencia and Naples, 1999); José Alcina Franch, *La biblioteca de Alfonso V de Aragón en Nápoles*, 2 vols (Valencia, 2000).
44.  Mariano Fava and Giovanni Bresciano, *La stampa a Napoli nel XV secolo*, 2 vols (Leipzig, 1911–13); Mario Santoro, *La stampa a Napoli nel Quattrocento* (Naples, 1984).
45.  Hermann Dilcher, ed., *Constitutiones regni Siciliae. 'Liber Augustalis'. Neapel 1475: Faksimiledruck* (Glashütten and Taunus, 1973).
46.  David Abulafia, 'The Role of the Jews in the Cultural Life of the Aragonese Kingdom of Naples', in *Gli Ebrei in Sicilia dal tardo Antico al Medioevo: studi in onore di Mons. Benedetto Rocco*, ed. N. Bucaria (Palermo, 1998), pp. 35–53,

reprinted in David Abulafia, *Mediterranean Encounters, Economic, Religious, Political, 1100–1550* (Aldershot, 2000).

47. Cecil Roth, *The Jews in the Renaissance* (Philadelphia, 5720/1959); Benzion Netanyahu, *Don Isaac Abravanel, Statesman and Philosopher*, 5th edn (Ithaca, NY, 1998); Eric Lawee, *Isaac Abarbanel's Stance toward Tradition: Defense, Dissent and Dialogue* (Albany, NY, 2001); Seymour Feldman, *Philosophy in a Time of Crisis: Don Isaac Abravanel, Defender of the Faith* (London, 2003).

48. Allan Atlas, *Music at the Aragonese court of Naples* (Cambridge, 1985); Allan Atlas, 'Aragonese Naples', in Iain Fenlon, ed., *The Renaissance*, Man and Music II (London, 1989), pp. 156–73.

49. Jordi Savall and La Capella Reial de Catalunya, *Alfons V el Magnànim 1396–1458, El Canconiero de Montecassino* (Alia Vox, 2001); Marcello Serafini and the Florilegia Ensemble, *O tempo bono: Music at the Aragonese Court of Naples, MS Montecassino 871, sec. XV* (Symphonia, 2001); Jordi Savall and Hespérion XX, *Viva el Rey Ferrando: Renaissance Music from the Neapolitan Court 1442–1556* (EMI, 1984; Virgin Classics, 1995; reissued as part of *Music for the Spanish Kings*, Virgin Classics, 2001); cf. Isabel Pope and Masakata Kanazawa, *The Musical Manuscript Montecassino 871: A Neapolitan Repertory of Sacred and Secular Music of the Late Fifteenth Century* (Oxford, 1978).

50. Guglielmo Ebreo of Pesaro, *De pratica seu arte tripudii: On the Practice or Art of Dancing*, ed. Barbara Sparti (Oxford, 1995).

51. Till Borchert, ed., *The Age of van Eyck: The Mediterranean World and Early Netherlandish Painting, 1430–1530* (London, 2002), in particular the essay by Andreas Beyer on Naples and Flanders.

52. Luciana Arbace, *Antonello da Messina, catalogo completo*, I Gigli dell'arte XXIX (Florence, 1993); Salvatore Tramontana, *Antonello e la sua città* (Palermo, 1981); Dominique Thiébaut, *Le Christ à la colonne d'Antonello de Messine* (Paris, 1993).

53. Hersey, *Aragonese Arch.*

54. George Hersey, *Alfonso II and the Artistic Renewal of Naples, 1485–1495* (New Haven, CT, 1969).

55. Roberto Pane, *Il Rinascimento nell'Italia meridionale*, 2 vols (Milan, 1975–77).

56. Text in Pane, *Rinascimento*, I, pp. 63–71.

57. Marianna Birnbaum, 'Humanism in Hungary', in Rabil, *Renaissance Humanism*, II, pp. 292–334.

58. Rósza Feuer-Tóth, *Art and Humanism in Hungary in the Age of Matthias Corvinus*, Studia Humanitatis VIII (Budapest, 1990).

59. For MSS still in Hungary: Ilona Berkovits, *Illuminated Manuscripts from the Library of Matthias Corvinus* (Budapest, 1964); for MSS now outside Hungary: C. Csapodi and K. Csapodi-Gárdonyi, eds, *Bibliotheca Corviniana: The Library of King Matthias Corvinus of Hungary* (Shannon, 1969); for scribes, cf. Otto Mazal, *Königliche Bücherliebe: die Bibliothek des Matthias Corvinus* (Graz, 1990).

60. Harold Segel, *Renaissance Culture in Poland: The Rise of Humanism, 1470–1543* (Ithaca, NY, 1989).

61. David Abulafia, 'Scanderbeg: A Hero and his Reputation', in Harry Hodgkinson, *Scanderbeg* (London, 1999), pp. ix–xv.

62. Ottavio di Camillo, 'Humanism in Spain', in Rabil, *Renaissance Humanism*, III, pp. 55–108.

63. Pane, *Rinascimento*, I, p. 29.

64. Santi Correnti, *Sicilia del Quattrocento: l'umanesimo mediterraneo* (Catania, 1992).
65. Concetta Bianca, *Stampa e cultura a Messina alla fine del Quattrocento*, 2 vols (Palermo, 1988).
66. Henri Bresc, *Livre et société en Sicile* (Palermo, 1971).
67. Godfrey Wettinger and Michael Fsadni, *Peter Caxaro's Cantilena: A Poem in Medieval Maltese* (Malta, 1968).
68. Antonovics, '"Il semble que ce soit là un vrai Paradis terrestre"', in Abulafia, *French Descent*, pp. 311–25.
69. Barbara Banks Amendola, *The Mystery of the Duchess of Malfi* (Stroud, 2002).

# 3

# renaissance europe and the world

## peter burke

In a recent essay the Italian scholar Salvatore Settis asked himself and his readers about the future of classical studies in a globalizing, multicultural world, and suggested that a global framework was not inappropriate for the study of ancient Greek and Roman culture. A similar point could and should be made about the Renaissance, which has often been studied as an Italian or sometimes as a European event or process. It is only relatively recently that scholars have tried to place it – or rather, to replace it – in a global context. To be more exact, we should speak of a gap or better still, of a time-lag between two groups of scholars.

On one side, specialists on different parts of the world beyond Europe have long been concerned with the impact of European culture in the sixteenth century in their different regions. Many of these specialists do not use the term 'Renaissance', although this practice is gradually spreading.[1]

On the other side, specialists on the Renaissance have generally been slow to look beyond Europe. As the citations to this chapter show, the idea of viewing the Renaissance in a global context did not appeal to many scholars before the beginning of the 1980s.

There are of course exceptions to this rule. Friedrich Sarre's article on Michelangelo's invitation to work in the Ottoman Empire goes back to 1909, Gilbert Chimard's book on 'exotic' America and the French Renaissance to 1911, Josef Strzygowski's attempt to derive Bramante's St Peter's from Armenian churches to 1919, Jean Seznec's study of Renaissance images of Asian and American gods to 1931, Geoffroy Atkinson's book on the 'new horizons' of the French Renaissance to 1935, Silvio Zavala's study of Thomas More in New Spain to 1937 and Leonardo Olschki's article on exoticism in Renaissance art to 1944. We should not forget these or other pioneers.

All the same, the rise of scholarly interest in the topic in the last generation will be obvious enough, like its link to attempts to 'reframe' or 'decenter' the Renaissance, to detach it from a triumphalist 'grand narrative' of the progress of western civilization.[2] The shift in approach might be symbolized by an exhibition mounted in Washington in 1992 and designed to commemorate rather than celebrate the five hundredth anniversary of Columbus' landfall. The exhibition and the accompanying volume, *Circa 1492*, took a bird's eye view of the world at that time and offered a striking example of the way in which cultural globalization is affecting the domain of scholarship.[3]

A few recent studies place great stress on non-European elements in the Renaissance. In *The Renaissance Bazaar* (2002), for instance, Jerry Brotton describes the view of the Renaissance as a purely European movement as a 'myth which is moribund'. By contrast his own emphasis on 'Muslim Spain, Mamluk Egypt, Ottoman Turkey, Persia, and the Silk Road between China and Europe' runs the risk of exaggeration in the opposite direction. It also runs the risk of confusion, between the Renaissance as a movement and the Renaissance as a period and also between the spread of the movement beyond Europe and the contributions to the movement made by non-European artists and scholars. In discussing this broad topic, distinctions are necessary.

It may therefore be helpful to begin by distinguishing four approaches to 'Renaissance Europe and the world', that will be discussed in order. In the first place, Renaissance interest in other cultures, oriental, pre-Columbian or African. In the second place, contributions to the Renaissance that originated beyond western Europe, notably the contributions of Byzantines and Muslims. Thirdly, what might be called for convenience the 'export' of the Renaissance and the varied reception of the movement from China to Peru. Fourth and last, a comparative approach to 'renaissances' in the plural.

All four sections will be focused on the Renaissance as movement rather than the Renaissance as period. They will also be selective rather than exhaustive, using examples of recent work in order to discuss general problems.

## the humanists and the world

In the 1950s, the American historian Karl Dannenfeldt was already arguing that 'far from considering Greece as the original home of civilization, wisdom and the arts, the humanists recognized and gave credit to the earlier contributions of the pre-classical civilizations of the ancient orient'. He was thinking of ancient Egypt in particular. Since that time a good deal of work has been done on Renaissance Egyptology, including representations of Egypt in art as well as the humanist interpretations of hieroglyphs studied by Erik Iversen. [4]

Some scholars traced connexions between ancient Egypt and the New World. As Jean Seznec noted, Lorenzo Pignoria, the humanist who added a 'Discourse on the Gods of the Indies' (that is, the divinities of Mexico, India and Japan) to the 1615 edition of Vincenzo Cartari's *Images of the Gods*, claimed that the Egyptians had conquered Mexico and introduced their deities there.[5]

The humanists were also interested in the world beyond Europe in more recent times. To be more exact, some humanists expressed such interests – not Petrarch or Leonardo Bruni, Erasmus or Lipsius, but Poggio, Giovio and a certain number of lesser figures. The humanist geographers of the Renaissance have been mapped by Numa Broc.[6] Studies of humanist histories of Asia, Africa, America or the world in general are gradually becoming more frequent.[7] Many humanists appear in Donald Lach's encyclopaedic survey of European knowledge of Asia in the sixteenth century.[8]

Again, historians of literature such as Stephen Greenblatt are paying increasing attention to the impact of other continents on the imagination of writers such as Montaigne, Ronsard, Shakespeare and Camões.[9] Historians of art have been studying Renaissance representations of other cultures. Linguists have been paying attention to the study of non-European languages at this time, notably Arabic, learned with the hope of converting the Muslims to Christianity.[10]

Two new fields of cultural history which have been intensely cultivated in the last generation, the history of travel and the history of collections, reveal a combination of an interest in the Renaissance with one in the world beyond Europe on the part of some princes, artists and scholars.[11]

Let us examine these studies in more detail region by region, beginning with the Middle East and ending with the New World.

The fear that the Ottoman Empire would expand and swallow up its neighbours underlay the increasing interest taken in it in this period, especially by scholars in the eastern half of Europe, from Venice to Vienna. Recent studies of this interest include work on Paolo Giovio and Francesco Sansovino (both of whom wrote about the Turks without leaving Italy) as well as a monograph on Ogier Ghiselin de Busbecq, the Habsburg ambassador to the Porte, whose Latin letters were one of the main sources of information about the Ottoman Empire in the sixteenth century.[12] By contrast, the work of Johan Leunclavius, who knew Turkish and translated Ottoman histories into Latin, remains relatively neglected. It would be interesting to know how much assistance he received from scholars in the Ottoman Empire such as the Hungarian renegade dragoman Murad.

Turning to material culture, the fashion in Italy and elsewhere for collecting Turkish objects, including carpets from Anatolia and pottery from Iznik, has been studied by Rosamond Mack and others, revealing very clearly that the Ottoman Empire was a source of attraction as well as anxiety.[13]

In the case of India, it was the expansion of the Portuguese seaborne empire that led to the rise of European interest in the sub-continent. In this domain King João III of Portugal (reigned 1521–57) was a key figure who has been surprisingly little studied, a patron of the Renaissance at home as well as expansion abroad. In his time artefacts from India began to appear in European collections. It was soon after her marriage to João III in 1525, as Annemarie Jordan Gschwend has recently shown, that Catherine of Austria, the sister of Charles V, began collecting orientalia. Viceroys of India presented her with objects for her collection, including an elephant of rock crystal that was displayed in the *C.1492* exhibition.[14] It was also at this time that João de Barros, the administrator of the Portuguese Casa de India and a man of humanist interests, wrote his *Décadas de Ásia* (1552–53), a history of Portuguese expansion that has not received the attention it deserves from students of the history of historical writing.[15]

Barros included China in his history, buying a slave who could read Chinese to help him with his work. However, most of the information about East Asia that reached Europe at this time came from missionaries (Matteo Ricci on China, for instance, or Francis Xavier on Japan), who have generally been studied by historians of the Counter-Reformation rather than historians of the Renaissance. Although the great age of *chinoiserie* was still centuries away, some artefacts from East Asia were known in Europe at this time. Lorenzo de'Medici received a piece of Chinese porcelain as a present in 1487, while some blue and white Chinese bowls are represented in Bellini's *Feast of the Gods*.

Little was known about Africa at this time, especially before the publication in 1550 of the *Description of Africa* by 'Leo Africanus' (Hasan al-Wazzân), a North African who lived for a time at the court of Leo X.[16] It might therefore seem that Africa had nothing to do with the Renaissance. However, a few people who played prominent roles in the Renaissance, from Albrecht Dürer to Grand Duke Cosimo de'Medici, owned objects from Africa, salt-cellars in the first case and ivory horns in the second, even though Dürer described his salt-cellars as coming 'from Calicut'.[17]

In the mountain of studies on the discovery of the New World, a few items stand out for their relevance to the Renaissance movement. Detlev Heikamp and others have studied the circulation of Mexican artefacts from mosaic masks to pictographic codices in Renaissance circles such as that of the Medici, while Anthony Pagden and Frank Lestringant have studied figures who, if not exactly humanists, at least demonstrated interest in the humanist movement.[18]

Pagden devoted a chapter of his *Fall of Natural Man* to José de Acosta, the Jesuit missionary who wrote the natural and moral history of the Indies, noting his frequent references to Aristotle and his classification of 'barbarians' or non-westerners into three types, more or less 'humane' or 'civilized' (*humanus*) in the humanist sense of the term. For his part, Lestringant has written two books about the cosmographer André Thevet, looking in particular at what he wrote about the Indians of Brazil and emphasizing his use of the book on the history of inventors by the Italian humanist Polydore Vergil.

To sum up so far. Much has been written about the European interest in other cultures in the age of the Renaissance, but relatively few attempts have been made to link this interest to the Renaissance movement. One of the most serious of these attempts was made recently by Joan-Pau Rubiés, whose book on travellers to south India between 1250 and 1625 includes a discussion of humanism. However, his travellers, such as Ludovico Varthema and Antonio Pigafetta, were located on the edge of humanism. Mainstream humanists, such as Poggio, Pietro Martire d'Anghiera and Ramusio, stayed at home and wrote up or edited the information that the travellers provided, sometimes distorting it in the process. Thus Poggio wrote a description of Indian customs on the basis of information from the traveller Niccolò Conti.[19]

The closest link between studies of the Renaissance and studies of European expansion seems to be at the level of classical models or schemata. Gonzalo Fernández Oviedo and José de Acosta, for instance, followed the model of Pliny in their natural histories of the Indies. Pietro Martire and João de Barros both called their histories 'Decades' in homage to Livy, implicitly comparing the rising Spanish and Portuguese empires with that of Rome. The grammars of non-European languages – Nahuatl, Quechua, or Tupí – produced by missionaries with a humanist training, followed the model of Latin grammars, despite the structural differences between those languages and Latin.

Turning to the less conscious schemata studied by Aby Warburg and his followers, John Friedman and others have noted that the so-called 'monstrous races', derived from Pliny and others, were relocated in the New World from Columbus onwards.[20] Partha Mitter (whose doctoral thesis was supervised by E. H. Gombrich at the Warburg Institute), has shown that Indian gods were perceived by Varthema and other travellers as devils or monsters.[21] 'Barbarian' was another unfavourable stereotype derived from the classical tradition and widely employed to describe non-European cultures. Neutral or favourable classical stereotypes such as 'Amazons' or 'the Golden Age' were also projected on to the New World in this period and later.

## origins of the renaissance

With the major exception of the world of Islam, there is little to say about the influence of other cultures on Renaissance art, literature or thought (excluding Byzantium on the grounds that it was not a foreign but a 'sibling' culture).[22] Nicole Dacos has studied some possible cases of Mexican influence on the decoration of the *loggia* at the Vatican by Raphael and his workshop, for instance, or on the capitals of the palace of the prince-bishops at Liège, but only to conclude that Aztec art was too alien to assimilate.[23]

Again, studies of the so-called 'Manueline' architecture of early sixteenth-century Portugal have noted the oriental, and more specifically the Indian or African sources of some of its ornaments, including monkeys, crocodiles, elephants and slaves.[24]

The debt to Islam requires a lengthier discussion. Scholars concerned with the classical tradition in the Middle Ages have long been aware of the importance of the Islamic world, especially the Muslims of southern Italy and Spain, in the transmission of Greek learning to the West; research on Arab translations of Greek thinkers continues.[25]

It took rather longer for westerners to notice the fact that the striped churches of medieval Siena and elsewhere imitate the decoration of mosques in the Middle East. In her recent study of Venice, Deborah Howard suggests, for instance, that Piazza San Marco was inspired by the courtyard of the Great Mosque at Damascus, while the Palazzo Ducale alludes to Mamluk architecture, and the *fondachi* in which foreigners (Germans, Turks) were segregated are like the *funduqs* that were familiar to Venetian merchants in Aleppo and elsewhere.[26]

In contrast to studies of the Middle Ages, discussions of the Renaissance have relatively little to say about contributions from the world of Islam.

In the domain of intellectual history we have been offered fascinating fragments of information. We know for example that the commentary on Aristotle's *Poetics* by Averroes (Ibn Rushd) was published in Latin translation in Venice in 1481; that Regiomontanus transcribed the *Algebra* of al-Khowarizmi; that Peurbach and Copernicus knew the work of the ninth-century Arab astronomer al-Battani; and that Avicenna (Ibn Sina) was studied in the Renaissance as he had been in the later Middle Ages.[27] The nearest approach to a synthesis has been offered by Charles Burnett.[28]

The situation is a similar one for architecture. It has been pointed out, for instance, that the hospitals of Florence and Milan in the fifteenth century followed the design of those of Damascus and Cairo.[29] In the case of Rome, André Chastel went so far as to suggest that Bramante's St Peter's might be viewed as a reply to the recently-completed mosque of Bayezid in Istanbul.[30] In the case of Venice, Ennio Concina and Deborah Howard have noted eastern motifs on Renaissance buildings. The palace of Ca' Zen, for instance, built between c.1533 and 1553, has oriental arches on the façade, alluding to the economic and political involvement of the Zen family in the affairs of the Middle East.[31]

All the same, much of what Renaissance artists learned from the Islamic world remained virtually invisible until quite recently. One reason for this invisibility is probably the fact that these artists learned especially from the so-called 'applied arts', the study of which used to be relatively neglected. Italian Renaissance majolica, for instance, developed from the Hispano-Moresque tradition of ceramics, was introduced to Italy by Catalan merchants from Majorca (hence the name 'majolica'). Again, representations of ceramics from Iznik and carpets from Anatolia can be found in a number of Renaissance paintings, from van Eyck to Crivelli, attesting to familiarity with these artefacts in the milieu of merchants as well as princes.[32]

Perhaps the biggest debt of Renaissance artists to the East concerns the decorative motifs we still know as 'arabesques'. The typographer Stanley Morison pointed out that after Gentile Bellini returned from Istanbul, 'the arabesque took hold of the decorative craftsmen practising in Venice', especially in the case of printed ornaments and bindings. Cellini's interest in Turkish daggers with arabesques which he tried to emulate and surpass is well known. From Italy, these designs spread to other parts of Europe. In France, the printer Jean de Tournes of Lyon used arabesque ornaments. Knowledge of these ornaments was spread via pattern-books such as Peter Flötner's *Maureskenbuch* (1549) or Jacques Androuet de Cerceau's *Grandes arabesques* (1582).[33]

In the case of the visual arts, at least, a provisional conclusion from the examples discussed in this section might be that western culture had been more open to exotic influences in the Middle Ages than it was in the Renaissance, when the ideal of classicism was an obstacle to this kind of borrowing and hybridization. Only in the domain of decoration was eclecticism still permitted, witness not only arabesques but also the decorative details on manueline architecture and the Afro-Portuguese ivories mentioned above.

What is still lacking is a sustained attempt to weave together the strands of knowledge described in the last few paragraphs in order to produce a general picture. Such a general picture would have to go beyond mathematics, the sciences and architecture to include a discussion of the importance of Islamic influence on Renaissance culture in general. Spain is an obvious focus for this kind of investigation, given the importance of the Morisco community there until the early seventeenth century. Did St Teresa, for instance, owe anything to the Sufi tradition, at least indirectly? What exactly should we make of the reference to 'Cide Hamete Benengeli, Arabic historian' in *Don Quixote*?[34]

## the renaissance outside europe

The third question to be addressed in this chapter is the question of reception. To what extent did the Renaissance, its ideas and its artefacts, spread beyond Europe?

There is most to say about the Americas. Both local and foreign scholars have emphasized the introduction of humanism to the New World and especially to New Spain. After the Spanish conquest of Mexico, Latin schools were established in Mexico City, in Michoacán, and most famous of all, in Tlatelolco, where the college of Santiago was founded in 1536 by the bishop, fray Juan de Zumárraga, and endowed with a library including such classical authors as Cicero, Juvenal, Livy, Plutarch, Seneca and Virgil.[35] The University of Mexico was inaugurated in 1553 with a speech in Latin by Professor Francisco Cervantes de Salazar (c.1518–1575), a new arrival from Spain. His commentaries on the Spanish humanist Juan Luis Vives, including three dialogues set in Mexico (1554), were used as a Latin textbook. Universities were also founded in Lima and Santo Domingo.

More than half a century ago Irving Leonard and Silvio Zavala showed that some of the masterpieces of Renaissance literature, notably *Utopia* and *Don Quixote*, were well known in the New World.[36] Vasco de Quiroga, who was bishop of Michoacán from 1537 to 1565, not only studied More's

*Utopia* but tried to put it into practice.[37] Copies of Castiglione's *Courtier* were also to be found in libraries in Mexico and Peru.[38]

Contributions to Renaissance literature came from the New World. In Lima, the Academia Antártica was a centre of versification in the style of Petrarch. The Spanish poet Alonso de Ercilla wrote his famous epic the *Araucana* in South America, describing the resistance to the Spaniards by the indigenous people of Chile (then a remote part of the viceroyalty of Peru) and presenting this resistance in a heroic style inspired by both classical epic and Ariosto.[39] Bernardo de Balbuena, who arrived in Mexico in 1584 and became bishop of Puerto Rico, wrote a poem about Mexico and a pastoral novel, *Siglo de oro en las selvas de Erífile* (1608). A particular focus of recent study is the *mestizo* Garcilaso de la Vega, known as 'the Inca', who settled in Spain and there wrote a history of Peru in a humanist manner.[40]

In the case of architecture, most buildings of the period have been destroyed, especially by earthquakes, but enough remains to show that in this domain too Spaniards wanted to bring the Renaissance to the New World, following the designs of Serlio, for instance, or decorating the façade of a palace with medallions and grotesques. Indeed, it has been argued by Valerie Fraser that the classical style of architecture was particularly important in Spanish America because it both represented and reinforced the sense of cultural superiority.[41] It has also been pointed out by the Latin American critic Angel Rama and others that new cities in the Americas followed the regular grid plan recommended in Renaissance treatises on architecture but difficult to achieve in the old cities of Europe.[42]

In the case of painting and sculpture, what Gruzinski calls 'the invasion of European images' was a by-product of missionary endeavours to convert the Indians and to sustain their devotion. The process has been studied intensively by students of the Renaissance and the Counter-Reformation alike and it has been divided into three stages: the import of European religious prints, the arrival of European painters, and finally the rise of local artists.[43] Particular attention has been given to the Franciscan Diego de Valadés, who was active in Mexico as a missionary, a print-maker and the author of the *Rhetorica Christiana*.[44]

The three 'gunpowder empires', Ottoman, Safavid and Mughal, may be considered together. Anna Contadini has noted that while Europe's debt to Islam has been examined in some detail, studies of Islam's debt to Europe are sparse.[45] Little has been said about Safavid Persia. All the same it is fascinating to learn from recent research that the artist Bihzad copied Costanzo da Ferrara's drawing of a seated scribe, turning him into an artist in the process.[46] The traveller Pietro Della Valle recorded seeing Italian paintings for sale in the city of Isfahan.[47] The seventeenth-century painter Muhammad-Zaman ibn Haji Yusuf of Kum made use of Renaissance prints.[48]

In the case of the Ottoman Empire, half in and half out of Europe, the evidence is much richer and it has been studied intensively. Thanks to the work of Franz Babinger, Julian Raby and Jerry Brotton, we know that Sultan Mehmed II was not only the conqueror of Constantinople but also a patron of Italian artists such as Costanzo da Ferrara, who made a portrait medal of the sultan, and Gentile Bellini, who painted his portrait in oils. The Greek humanist George of Trebizond and the Florentine humanist Francesco Berlinghieri were among those who dedicated books to Mehmed, who showed interest in some classical texts, among them Ptolemy's geography and the histories written by Herodotus, Livy and Curtius.[49]

Mehmed's successors were less oriented towards Italy, but Bayezid (to whom Leonardo offered his services) invited Michelangelo to Istanbul, while Suleiman the Magnificent, encouraged by Ibrahim Pasha (grand vizier 1523–36), was a patron of Renaissance artists, at least in the earlier part of his reign. A number of scholars, notably Gülru Necipoglu, have focused on the splendid crowned helmet that Suleiman commissioned from the Caorlini workshop in Venice together with a sceptre and a throne, displayed during the Ottoman advance on Vienna and apparently intended to tell the West that the sultan was a true emperor.[50] Others have studied the *baldacchino* designed for the sultan by Jacopo Sansovino or the tapestries that were made for him by Flemish weavers who came to Istanbul for the purpose.[51]

Mughal India was the furthest from Europe of the three gunpowder empires but it was also the one with the most intensive cultural contacts with Renaissance Europe, especially in the time of the emperor Akbar, as Michael Beach, Gauvin Bailey and others have made clear in a number of studies. Jesuits gave Akbar paintings and engravings, and Akbar ordered his artists to copy them. They coloured the prints and employed elements from them in their own work. For example, the miniature painter Basawan, Akbar's favourite, adapted prints by Dürer.[52]

The Jesuits also introduced Renaissance architecture into India, where Serlio enjoyed an 'afterlife'.[53] There are even traces of humanism to be found there. In 1586, for instance, a Florentine merchant in 'Cochin' found a copy of Castiglione's *Courtier* for sale there.[54]

In East Asia, it was once again the Jesuits who brought the Renaissance along with the Counter-Reformation. The many studies of the Italian missionary Matteo Ricci make it abundantly clear that he introduced Chinese mandarins to Renaissance rhetoric, astronomy, geography and the art of memory as well as to ancient philosophy.[55] As in Mexico and Peru, the Jesuits imported religious prints into China and, as art historians such as Michael Sullivan and James Cahill have pointed out, these prints made a considerable impact on Chinese art, on landscape painting in particular. Chinese landscape painters did not imitate western models, but awareness of an alternative to their own tradition helped them to innovate.[56]

In Japan, the penetration of both Christianity and Renaissance culture was deeper than in China. The Jesuit Francis Xavier brought religious paintings and noted that they helped awaken interest in Christianity. Another Jesuit, the Italian Antonio Valignano, founded colleges at Azuchi and Arima. Latin was taught in these colleges, using local editions of classical texts, including Cicero. Painting and engraving were also taught there. Some secular as well as religious paintings followed the models provided by European prints, including a screen with battle scene based on a print of Lepanto. The Japanese 'embassy' of young samurai brought paintings – and possibly a copy of Castiglione's *Courtier* as well – when they returned from their long visit to Europe in the late sixteenth century.[57]

By contrast, until quite recently it was assumed that there was nothing to say about the Renaissance in Africa. Ezio Bassani and William Fagg have put the subject on the map, drawing attention to what they call 'Afro-Portuguese' ivories with European subjects such as centaurs or coats of arms as well as local elephants and so on. The decoration, beaded and braided, resembles Manueline architecture. Bassani and Fagg suggest that these ivories are an early example of art made for export. For instance, an inventory of Cosimo de'Medici's possessions made in 1553 mentions two Afro-Portuguese ivory horns, while in 1560 his wife Eleonora de Toledo owned five Afro-Portuguese ivory spoons. Hence African craftsmen might be said to have participated in the Renaissance without knowing that they were doing so.[58] An overview of the relations between Africa and the Renaissance is promised in a forthcoming collection of essays edited by Kate Lowe and Tom Earle.[59]

Distinctions naturally need to be drawn between the impact or influence of the Renaissance in Africa, Asia and America. For example, the relative importance of the Renaissance in Spanish America owed a good deal to the Spanish expatriates who were trying to reproduce their home culture in their new home. All the same, several important general themes emerge from this survey. One such theme is the role of missionaries in introducing the Renaissance as well as Christianity to the world beyond Europe. They brought religious images because of their content, but these images provoked interest on account of their style. The medium was part of the message. Another recurrent theme is the important role of prints, which were easy to export in large numbers, in spreading the knowledge of Renaissance art.

A third major theme is that of the effects of these cultural encounters, notably cultural mixing or hybridization, discussed in particular detail by Bailey in the case of India and by Gruzinski in that of Mexico (as their coinage of the term 'Afro-Portuguese' suggests, Bassani and Fagg are also concerned with this theme).[60]

Kesu Das, for instance, was a Hindu painter who worked from prints to produce Christian images such as St Jerome, combining them with 'Persian-style rock formations'. Turning from artists to patrons, Bailey asks why the Mughal court was interested in Christian art, noting that 'they did not necessarily perceive the imagery as Christian'. On the contrary, images of Christian saints and angels were used 'to proclaim a message based on Islamic sufi and Hindu symbolism and linked with Persian poetic metaphor'.[61]

Following a series of studies of the culture of colonial Mexico, the French historian Serge Gruzinski has devoted an essay to the process of cultural hybridization or *métissage*, in which he discusses general themes, such as the importance of Ovid's *Metamorphoses*, themselves metamorphosed or mexicanized, in the culture of New Spain, and also specific examples, like the house of the Dean of Puebla in the late sixteenth century, decorated with monkeys and female centaurs that referred simultaneously to classical and local traditions.[62]

The question whether decorations like these, like the façades of churches from Arequipa to Goa, represent conscious artistic syncretism, or whether they are the unintended consequence of asking local craftsmen to follow European models that were unfamiliar to them, remains open.

## renaissance and renascences

Despite important precedents, from Max Weber to Marc Bloch, the study of comparative history is still treated with suspicion by many scholars, just as it is often reduced to the search for similarities, at the expense of contrasts and of what might be called 'functional equivalents'.

In the case of the Renaissance, two kinds of comparison suggest themselves and have been pursued by a few scholars: comparisons with other periods and comparisons with other parts of the globe.

In an essay on 'Renaissance Europe and the World', it is the second theme that needs to be privileged, though without forgetting Erwin Panofsky's important study, *Renaissance and Renascences in Western Art*. Many scholars have been content to assume the originality of 'the' Renaissance, but Panofsky tried to define it by means of systematic comparison with other movements, notably the Carolingian Renaissance and the Renaissance of the Twelfth Century.[63]

In the case of humanism, George Makdisi, Benjamin Elman and others have pointed out that ideas that we often take to be typically 'humanist', notably the idea of the dignity of humankind, can be found in non-western cultures. In the Islamic world, the central ethical concept of *adab* might be rendered by the Latin *humanitas* as well as by the English term 'civilization'.[64] In traditional China, intellectuals were much concerned with the ideal man, *ch'ün tzu*, as they were with the cultivation of the self, *hsiu-shen*. They also resembled Renaissance humanists in their concern with philology as well as philosophy.[65]

Characteristically, Arnold Toynbee was already concerning himself with 'Renaissances' in the plural at much the same time as Panofsky, over half a century ago, as part of his vast *Study of History*. The use of the term 'Renaissance' to describe cultural movements in the world outside Europe goes back earlier than Toynbee. At the beginning of the twentieth century, the Arabs and the Chinese both described contemporary debates and experiments in the arts as renaissances, but only in the general sense of cultural revival.[66]

Toynbee, on the other hand, was explicitly comparative. In his study of 'contacts between civilizations in time' he dismissed the idea of 'the' Renaissance as an ethnocentric illusion, pointing out that 'there had been other Renaissances of Hellenism' as well as other 'dead' cultures and going on to discuss renaissances in philosophy, religion, language and so on.

There is a whole series of examples of revivals of the classical tradition that were independent of the Italian Renaissance. In the case of literature and learning, one thinks of the different Byzantine renaissances identified by scholars in the field.[67] In the case of architecture one might turn to the Ottoman Empire, for instance, where the late classical tradition exemplified in the church of Santa Sophia was followed in a series of mosques built in Istanbul, Edirne and elsewhere.

Turning to renaissances of non-classical traditions, a famous example is the Confucian revival in the age of Chu Hsi. Just as Pico and Ficino are known as 'neoplatonist' philosophers, Chu Hsi might be described as a 'neo-confucian'.[68]

In Chinese painting too enthusiasm for tradition led to revivals of past styles as well as to forgeries of the work of past masters. The interest in connoisseurship and the collecting of works of art that developed in Renaissance Italy had its parallel in early modern China, as Joseph Alsop, Craig Clunas and others have pointed out. [69] As Clunas puts it with characteristic forcefulness, 'There can be little or no justification for seeing what was happening in Europe as a dynamic "rebirth"', while refusing the same description to 'what was happening at Suzhou at the same time'.[70]

In some ways the cultural history of Japan offers even closer parallels to some aspects of the Italian Renaissance. In the first place, as David Pollack and others have noted, the relation between Japan and Chinese culture resembles that between Italy and ancient Greek and Roman culture, close in some respects but distant in others, inspiring emulation in the sense of both imitation and competition.[71]

In the second place, as I suggested more than thirty years ago, the Genroku era in Japanese cultural history (1688–1703) witnessed a cluster of cultural achievements and innovations some of which have often been described, like their counterparts in Renaissance Italy, in terms of secularization, realism and individualism.[72]

Needless to say these views are controversial. The distinguished Italian historian Adriano Prosperi once criticized my essay *The Renaissance* (1987) for denying the specificity of the Italian movement by referring positively to Toynbee and referring to 'renaissances' in the plural. Toynbee did indeed commit himself to the view that the Italian Renaissance was not 'a unique occurrence' but 'no more than one particular instance of a recurrent historical phenomenon'.[73]

My own point was not to deny the specificity of the Italian Renaissance or of any other movement of cultural revival, or indeed to assume that all revivals are equally important – they are not, and their relative importance is a matter for empirical investigation. What I do want to say, though, like Toynbee, is that movements to revive some of the ideas, forms or practices of the past have certain family resemblances and are therefore worth studying comparatively, giving attention to both the similarities and the differences between them.

## globalizing the renaissance

We have seen that the project of placing or replacing the European Renaissance in a global context is a relatively new one, though it necessarily draws on old as well as new research. The cultural and political situation has become favourable for such a project, indeed it might be said to have become too favourable, so that we may expect to see more references to the contribution of Islam for reasons of political correctness as well as from intellectual conviction. The danger today is not the neglect of non-western contributions but the exaggeration of their importance, as in the claim that eastern objects 'provided the inspiration' for Alberti, Bellini, Dürer and van Eyck.[74] In order to achieve a balanced verdict what we need is a real synthesis of the work done so far on the Renaissance in world context, paying due attention to processes of hybridization. A synthesis of this kind is an ambitious and difficult task but not an impossible one.

## notes

1. Guillermo Tovar de Teresa, *Pintura y Escultura del Renacimiento en México* (Mexico City, 1979).
2. Claire Farago, ed., *Reframing the Renaissance* (New Haven, 1995); Germaine Warkentin and Carolyn Podruchny, eds, *Decentring the Renaissance: Canada and Europe in Multidisciplinary Perspective, 1500–1700* (Toronto, 2001); Stephen Milner, ed., *At the Margins: Minority Groups in Pre-Modern Italy* (forthcoming, Minneapolis and London, 2005).
3. Jay A. Levenson, ed., *Circa 1492: Art in the Age of Exploration* (New Haven and Washington, DC, 1991).
4. K. H. Dannenfeldt, 'The Renaissance and Pre-Classical Civilizations', *Journal of the History of Ideas*, XIII (1952) 435–49; Erik Iversen, *The Myth of Egypt*, 2nd edn (Princeton, 1993).
5. Jean Seznec, 'Un essai de mythologie comparée au début du 17e siècle', *Mélanges d'archéologie et d'histoire*, XLVIII (1931) 268–81.
6. Numa Broc, *La géographie de la Renaissance* (Paris, 1980).
7. Charles Boxer, 'Some Aspects of Western Historical Writing on the Far East, 1500–1800', in W. G. Beasley and E. G. Pulleyblank, eds, *Historians of China and Japan* (London, 1961), pp. 307–21; J. B. Harrison, 'Five Portuguese Historians', in C. H. Philips, ed., *Historians of India* (London, 1961), pp. 155–69; V. J. Parry, 'Renaissance Historical Literature in Relation to the Near and Middle East (with Special Reference to Paolo Giovio)', in Bernard Lewis and P. M. Holt, eds, *Historians of the Middle East* (London, 1962), pp. 277–89; David Brading, 'The Incas and the Renaissance: The Royal Commentaries of Inca Garcilaso de la Vega', *Journal of Latin American Studies* XVIII (1986) 1–23; Margarita Zamora, *Language, Authority and Indigenous History in the Comentarios reales* (Cambridge, 1988).
8. Donald Lach, *Asia in the Making of Europe* (Chicago, 1965).
9. C. Maurice Bowra, 'Camões and the Epic of Portugal', in his *From Virgil to Milton* (Oxford 1945), pp. 86–138; Stephen Greenblatt, *Marvelous Possessions: The Wonder of the New World* (Oxford, 1991); David Quint, *Epic and Empire* (Princeton, 1993).

10. K. H. Dannenfeldt, 'The Renaissance Humanists and the Knowledge of Arabic', *Studies in the Renaissance*, II (1955) 96–117; J. Fück, *Die arabischen Studien in Europa bis in den Anfang des 20. Jahrhunderts* (Leipzig, 1955); John Robert Jones, *Learning Arabic in Renaissance Europe, 1505–1624* (London, 1988); G. J. Toomer, *Eastern Wisedome and Learning: The Study of Arabic in Seventeenth-Century England* (Oxford, 1996).

11. Joan-Pau Rubiés, *Travel and Ethnology in the Renaissance* (Cambridge, 2000); Detlef Heikamp, *Mexico and the Medici* (Florence, 1972); Alan A. Shelton, 'Cabinets of Transgression: Renaissance Collections and the Incorporation of the New World', in John Elsner and Roger Cardinal, eds, *The Cultures of Collecting* (London, 1994), pp. 175–203; Annemarie Jordan Gschwend, 'Curiosities and Exotica in the Kunsthammer of Catherine of Austria', *Bulletin of the Society for Renaissance Studies*, XIII (1995) 1–9.

12. Parry, 'Renaissance Historical Literature'; Eric Cochrane, *Historians and Historiography in the Italian Renaissance* (Chicago, 1981), pp. 324–37; Stéphane Yerasimos, 'De la collection des voyages à l'histoire universelle: la *Historia universale de'Turchi* de Francesco Sansovino', *Turcica*, XX (1988) 19–41; Zweder R. W. M. von Martels, *Augerius Gislenius Busbecquius: Leven en werk van de Keizerlijke gezant aan het hof van Süleyman de Grote* (Groningen, 1989).

13. Rosamond E. Mack, *Bazaar to Piazza: Islamic Trade and Italian Art, 1300–1600* (Berkeley, 2002).

14. Levenson, *Circa 1492*, catalogue n.14. Cf. Jordan Gschwend, 'Curiosities and Exotica'.

15. Boxer, 'Some Aspects of Western Historical Writing'.

16. Oumelbanine Zhiri, *L'Afrique au miroir de l'Europe* (Geneva, 1991).

17. Ezio Bassani and William B. Fagg, *Africa and the Renaissance: Art in Ivory* (New York, 1988), p. 53.

18. Heikamp, *Mexico and the Medici*; Shelton, 'Cabinets of Transgression'; Eloise Quiñones Keber, 'Collecting Cultures: A Mexican MS in the Vatican Library', in Farago, *Reframing the Renaissance*, pp. 229–42; Anthony Pagden, *The Fall of Natural Man* (Cambridge, 1982); Frank Lestringant, *L'atelier du cosmographe* (Paris, 1991).

19. Rubiés, *Travel*, pp. 88, 143, 301.

20. John B. Friedman, *The Monstrous Races in Medieval Art and Thought* (Cambridge, MA, 1981), pp. 197–207.

21. Partha Mitter, *Much Maligned Monsters* (Oxford, 1977), pp. 16–20.

22. Keith Setton, 'The Byzantine Background to the Italian Renaissance', *Proceedings of the American Philosophical Society*, C (1956) 1–56; Deno J. Geanakoplos, *Interaction of the Sibling Byzantine and Western Cultures* (New Haven, 1976).

23. Nicole Dacos, 'Présents américains à la Renaissance: l'assimilation de l'exotisme', *Gazette des Beaux-Arts*, LXXIII (1969) 57–62.

24. Paulo Pereira, 'A simbólica manuelina', in P. Pereira, ed., *História da Arte Portuguesa*, II (Lisbon, 1995), pp. 115–55.

25. Fritz Rosenthal, ed., *The Classical Heritage and Islam* (London, 1975); Dimitri Gutas, *Greek Thought in Arabic Culture* (London, 1998).

26. Deborah Howard, *Venice and the East* (New Haven, 2000), pp. 104, 120, 178.

27. Paul L. Rose, *The Italian Renaissance of Mathematics* (Geneva, 1975), p. 93; Charles B. Schmitt, 'Renaissance Averroism Studied through the Venetian

Editions of Aristotle-Averroes', in C. B. Schmitt, *The Aristotelian Tradition and Renaissance Universities* (London, 1984), ch. 8; Nancy G. Siraisi, *Avicenna in Renaissance Italy* (Princeton, 1987).

28. Charles Burnett, 'The Second Revelation of Arabic Philosophy and Science: 1492–1562', in C. Burnett and Anna Contadini, eds, *Islam and the Italian Renaissance* (London, 1999), pp. 185–98.

29. Ralph Quadflieg, 'Zur Rezeption islamischer Krankenhaus architektur in der italienischen Frührenaissance', in E. Liskar, ed., *Europa und die Kunst des Islam* (Vienna, 1985), pp. 73–81.

30. André Chastel, 'La Renaissance italienne et les ottomans', in Agostino Pertusi, ed., *Venezia e l'Oriente fra tardo medioevo e rinascimento* (Florence, 1966), p. 527; a milder statement in A. Chastel, *The Golden Age of the Renaissance* (London, 1965), pp. 24, 315.

31. Ennio Concina, *Arabesco* (Venice, 1994), p. 74; Howard, *Venice and the East.*

32. Chastel, *Golden Age*, pp. 13–24; Lisa Jardine, *Worldly Goods* (London, 1996) p. 9; Anna Contadini, 'Artistic Contacts: Current Scholarship and Future Tasks', in Burnett and Contadini, *Islam and the Italian Renaissance*, pp. 1–16.

33. Stanley Morison, *Venice and the Arabesque* (London, 1955); J. Michael Rogers, 'Ornament Prints, Patterns and Designs', in Burnett and Contadini, *Islam and the Italian Renaissance*, pp. 133–65.

34. Americo Castro, *The Structure of Spanish History*, trans. Edmund L. King (Princeton, 1954).

35. Miguel Mathes, *Santa Cruz de Tlatelolco: la primera biblioteca académica de las Américas* (Mexico City, 1982); Dianne M. Bono, *The Cultural Diffusion of Spanish Humanism in New Spain* (New York, 1991), pp. 41–9; Serge Gruzinski, *Painting the Conquest: The Mexican Indians and the European Renaissance* (Paris, 1992), pp. 150–3.

36. Irving Leonard, *Books of the Brave* (Cambridge, MA, 1949).

37. Silvio Zavala, *La 'Utopia' de Tomás Moro en la Nueva España* (Mexico City, 1937); Zavala, *Sir Thomas More in New Spain: A Utopian Adventure of the Renaissance* (London, 1955).

38. Peter Burke, *The Fortunes of the Courtier* (Cambridge, 1995).

39. Quint, *Epic and Empire.*

40. Brading, 'Incas and the Renaissance'; Zamora, *Language.*

41. Valerie Fraser, 'Architecture and Imperialism in Sixteenth-Century Spanish America', *Art History*, IX (1986) 325–35; V. Fraser, *The Art of Conquest* (Cambridge, 1990).

42. Angel Rama, *La ciudad letrada* (Hanover, NH, 1984); Mario Sartor, *Arquitectura y urbanismo en Nueva España* (Mexico City, 1992).

43. Jorge Alberto Manrique, 'La estampa como fuente del arte en la Nueva España', in Henri Zerner, ed., *Le stampe e la diffusione delle immagini e degli stili* (Bologna, 1983), pp. 67–72; Jorge Alberto Manrique, *Manierismo en Nueva España* (Mexico City, 1993); Serge Gruzinski, *La guerre des images* (Paris, 1990); Tovar de Teresa, *Pintura y Escultura*, p. 61.

44. Thomas Cummins, 'From Lies to Truth: Colonial Ekphrasis and the Act of Crosscultural Translation', in Farago, *Reframing the Renaissance*, pp. 152–74.

45. Contadini, 'Artistic Contacts'.

46. Jerry Brotton, *The Renaissance Bazaar* (Oxford, 2002), p. 138.

47. Peter Burke, *The European Renaissance: Centre and Peripheries* (Oxford, 1998), p. 107.

48. Eleanor Sims, 'The European Print Sources of Paintings by the Seventeenth-Century Persian Painter Muhammad-Zaman ibn Haji Yusuf of Kum', in Zerner, *Le stampe*, pp. 73–83.

49. Franz Babinger, *Mehmed the Conqueror and his Time*, English trans. (Princeton, 1978); Julian Raby, 'Cyriacus of Ancona and the Ottoman Sultan Mehmed II', *Journal of the Warburg and Courtauld Institutes*, XLIII (1980) 242–6; J. Raby, *Venice, Dürer and the Oriental Mode* (London, 1982); J. Raby, 'East and West in Mehmed the Conqueror's Library', *Bulletin du bibliophile* (1987) 297–321; Jerry Brotton, *Trading Territories: Mapping the Early Modern World* (London, 1997), pp. 87–118.

50. Gülru Necipoglu, 'Süleiman the Magnificent and the Representation of Power in the Context of Ottoman–Habsburg Rivalry', *Art Bulletin*, LXXI (1989) 401–27. On the helmet, cf. Otto Kurz, 'The Golden Helmet', in his *Decorative Arts of Europe and the Islamic East* (London, 1977), pp. 249–58; Concina, *Arabesco*, pp. 57–76.

51. Lisa Jardine and Jerry Brotton, *Global Interests: Renaissance Art between East and West* (Ithaca, NY, 2000), pp. 63–131.

52. Michael Beach, *Mughal and Rajput Painting* (Cambridge, 1992); Gauvin A. Bailey, *The Jesuits and the Great Mogul: Renaissance Art at the Imperial Court of India, 1580–1630* (Washington, DC, 1998); G. A. Bailey, 'Jesuit Catechism and the Arts in Mughal India', in John O'Malley et al., eds, *The Jesuits* (Toronto, 1999), pp. 380–401; G. A. Bailey, *Art on the Jesuit Missions in Asia and Latin America, 1542–1773* (Toronto, 1999).

53. David M. Kowal, 'The Jesuit Contribution to Architectural Development in Portuguese India', in O'Malley, *The Jesuits*, pp. 480–504.

54. Burke, *Fortunes of the Courtier*.

55. Jonathan Spence, *The Memory Palace of Matteo Ricci* (London, 1984), pp. 116, 141–2, 251 and passim.

56. Michael Sullivan, *Symbols of Eternity: The Art of Landscape Painting in China* (Oxford, 1979); James F. Cahill, *The Compelling Image: Nature and Style in Seventeenth-Century Chinese Painting* (Cambridge, MA, 1982); Bailey, *Art on the Jesuit Missions*, pp. 82–111.

57. Michael Cooper, ed., *The Southern Barbarians: The First Europeans in Japan* (Tokyo, 1971); Léon Bourdon, *La compagnie de Jésus et le Japon, 1547–70* (Paris, 1993); Burke, *Fortunes of the Courtier*; Bailey, *Art on the Jesuit Missions*, pp. 52–81.

58. Bassani and Fagg, *Africa and the Renaissance*.

59. *Black Africans in Renaissance Europe* (Cambridge, forthcoming, 2005).

60. Serge Gruzinski, *La pensée métisse* (Paris, 1999); Rolena Adorno, *Guaman Poma: Writing and Resistance in Colonial Peru* (Austin, 1986).

61. Bailey, *Jesuits and the Great Mogul*, p. 35.

62. Gruzinski, *La pensée métisse*, pp. 127–51, 112–16; cf. Erwin W. Palm, 'El sincretismo emblemático de los Triunfos de la Casa del Deán en Puebla', *Comunicaciones*, VIII (1973) 57–62.

63. Erwin Panofsky, *Renaissance and Renascences in Western Art* (New York, 1969).

64. George Makdisi, *The Rise of Humanism in Classical Islam and the Christian West* (Edinburgh, 1990), pp. 89–93.
65. Benjamin A. Elman, *From Philosophy to Philology: Intellectual and Social Aspects of Change in Late Imperial China* (Cambridge, MA, 1984).
66. J. B. Grieder, *Hu Shih and the Chinese Renaissance* (Cambridge, MA, 1970).
67. Steven Runciman, *The Last Byzantine Renaissance* (Cambridge, 1970).
68. Daniel K. Gardner, *Chu Hsi and the Ta-hsueh* (Cambridge, MA, 1986).
69. Joseph Alsop, *The Rare Art Traditions* (London, 1982); Craig Clunas, *Superfluous Things* (Cambridge, 1991). Craig Clunas, Evelyn Welch and others are engaged in a project comparing Renaissance Italy with Ming China.
70. Clunas, *Superfluous Things*, p. 92.
71. David Pollack, *The Fracture of Meaning: Japan's Synthesis of China from the 8th through 18th Centuries* (Princeton, 1986).
72. Peter Burke, *The Italian Renaissance: Culture and Society in Italy*, revised edn (Cambridge, 1999), pp. 252–6.
73. Arnold J. Toynbee, *A Study of History*, IX (London, 1954), p. 4.
74. Brotton, *Renaissance Bazaar*, p. 1.

# part two

# 4
# renaissance humanism
# and historiography today
## james hankins

Since the Second World War the problem of defining the Renaissance
has seemed to many historians tightly linked – indeed almost identical
– with the problem of defining the humanist movement. It is easy to see
why this is the case. If the splendour of Renaissance art makes the period
attractive, it is humanism that makes it articulate. The literature and
philosophy of the period, it is reasoned, is our best guide to understanding
what the Renaissance was all about. If all the cultural products of an age
are expressions of a common *Weltanschauung*, as scholars influenced by
historicism still assume, the ideals of the humanists must be the ideals
of the Renaissance.

Yet the virtual identification of humanism with the Renaissance is
a relatively recent phenomenon, at least in northern Europe. In the
half century following the publication of Jacob Burckhardt's *Civilization
of the Renaissance in Italy* (1860) the tendency was in fact to demote
or even dismiss the importance of the movement. The true engine of
Renaissance culture for Burckhardt was the spirit of individualism, and
of this spirit the humanists' activities were effects rather than causes.
Burckhardt in fact admired the philological accomplishments of the
humanists, but had strong reservations about them as personalities,
and his work in general tended to decentre the 'Revival of Classical
Antiquity' as the keynote of the age. Whatever their merits as scholars
and transmitters of antiquity, the profligate, conceited, scurrilous and
irreligious characters of the humanists could not be admired. Unlike
many of his contemporaries, Burckhardt would not dismiss Neo-Latin
literature out of hand as uninspired pastiche, servile imitation, confected
from the dusty remains of a dead language, but even he admitted that the

aesthetic of Neo-Latin stood at the opposite pole from the taste of his own Romantic period. Others were even sharper critics of humanist literature. 'Having nothing to say, they said it interminably', Philippe Monnier wrote, devastatingly.[1] The humanists were seen as frivolous courtiers and rootless *littérateurs* whose main interest was acquiring glory for themselves by promoting a fashion for the antique. They were characteristic products of the Renaissance, but not its leading spirits.

Burckhardt's view of humanism, dominant in northern Europe, was far less influential in Italy. Italian students of the Renaissance, living in the nationalistic afterglow of the Risorgimento, were much more inclined to magnify the humanists' accomplishments. Italian scholarship in the decades around 1900, led by Remigio Sabbadini (1850–1934), celebrated the humanists' recovery of classical literature, their role in reviving classical education, and their innovative methods as philologists and pedagogues. Even more influential for the future were the Italian philosophers of the period, such as Bertrando Spaventa (1817–1883), Francesco Fiorentino (1834–1884) and later Benedetto Croce (1866–1952) and Giovanni Gentile (1875–1944), who began to study the thought of the humanists seriously for the first time. For these men philosophers such as Marsilio Ficino, Giovanni Pico della Mirandola, Francesco Patrizi and Giordano Bruno – even professional scholastics such as Pietro Pomponazzi – were seen as part of the humanist movement and their works understood as pure theoretical elaborations of the humanist spirit. With nationalistic fervour this school embraced the view that Ficino, Pico, Pomponazzi and Bruno were pioneers of modern philosophy and that a straight line could be drawn from their ideas to German idealism, the dominant philosophy of the time. At the handbook level, *l'Umanesimo* became a period in the history of philosophy, between *la Scolastica* and *la Rivoluzione Scientifica*.

Outside of Italy the understanding of humanism as a philosophical movement was slower to make headway. A major impetus in this direction came from the German Neo-Kantian Ernst Cassirer, who in his *Individuum und Kosmos in der Philosophie der Renaissance* (1927) was prepared to give Italian philosophers of the Renaissance credit for taking important steps towards modernity. Naturally, it was the German Renaissance philosopher Nicolaus Cusanus who was the true pioneer of modern thought: he was the first philosopher to foreground the problem of knowledge and the first to adumbrate the scientific function of mathematics and the Infinite. For Neo-Kantians, this was the very definition of modernity. But the Italian philosophers had also moved in the direction of modernity in their understandings of Freedom and Necessity and the relation of subject and object. They had begun the long transition in western thought from transcendence to immanence and from a belief in the givenness of nature to the modern consciousness of human freedom, a transition that would have its term (for Cassirer) in Hegel and existentialism. In the end, Cassirer drew back from asserting that the Renaissance as a whole was the first modern period of philosophy – that honour he still reserved to the seventeenth century of Descartes and Leibniz. But the tendency of his analysis is to show how Renaissance thinkers 'determined the problem' of the divine and the Infinite, '[handing] it down in a new form to the following centuries, the centuries of exact science and systematic philosophy'.

Thus by the middle of the twentieth century, the two broad tendencies discernible in the contemporary historiography of humanism were already in evidence: the view that humanism was primarily a literary and educational movement, devoted to the revival of antiquity, and the understanding of humanism as a philosophy of man. These tendencies were deepened and elaborated after the Second World War by three leading interpreters of humanism, Eugenio Garin, Hans Baron and Paul Oskar Kristeller.

Garin, at one time a protégé of the fascist philosopher Giovanni Gentile, in the aftermath of the war sought to detach humanism from the idealist perspective of the Italian historiographical tradition while at the same time preserving its tendency to see humanism as a proto-Enlightenment philosophy, a precursor of modernity. Garin had an unusual intellectual development for a student of the Renaissance. Starting with a classical and positivist training, he moved from youthful studies of early modern British moral philosophy back to the Italian Renaissance. After an idealist phase in his early career,[2] Garin set out during the 1950s to reinterpret the history of Italian philosophy, disengaging it from the Hegelian perspective in which it had been seen before the war, and reintegrating it into what is sometimes called a 'neo-historicist' orientation.[3] For someone still very much in the Italian tradition, however, this meant finding a way in which Italian humanism could yet be said to be genetically linked with modern philosophy. But in the post-war period, idealism in Italy had been discredited by its association with Gentile and the fascist *ventennio*; modern philosophy on the continent came to be identified with French existentialism and Marxism.

A major resource in Garin's rethinking of humanism was the writings of Antonio Gramsci, the leading representative of Marxist humanism in Italy.[4] Though Garin himself never became a Marxist or a communist, he did much to popularize Gramsci's thought in Italy in the post-war period, and his scholarship is explicitly an attempt to apply Gramscian methods and cultural imperatives to historical research. Gramsci's distinction between traditional and organic intellectuals and his notion of 'cultural hegemony' are clearly behind Garin's famous characterization of the fifteenth century as a period that saw an evolution from active participation of humanists like Leonardo Bruni in civic life to a politically quietist culture under the *egemonia medicea*, dominated by metaphysics, religion and Platonic 'villa intellectuals'. And it is difficult not to see Gramsci's anti-dogmatic Marxism behind Garin's account of the humanist rejection of scholasticism, or behind his description of Valla's historical criticism an admiration for the 'organic intellectual' taking on the hegemonic belief-system of the Church. It was in fact Garin who largely established the popular modern image of the humanist as critical intellectual, the forerunner of the Enlightenment *philosophe*, and therefore of the modern humanist. The intellectual style of Garin's humanists is to undertake 'open-ended research', in contrast to the scholastics' closed world of foregone conclusions. This made them sensitive to the historicity of human culture and made them perceive the intelligible order of nature, *logos*, as products of *Menschenwerke*. Garin thus established a deep ideological connection between Italian humanism and the more radical forms of modern humanism coming out of Marxism and existentialism.[5] In books like *Dal Rinascimento all'Illuminismo* (1970) he worked hard to document the conclusion that the two movements were connected genetically, and not just united by a common mentality.[6]

Garin's post-war embrace of a Gramscian philosophy that validated itself by practical commitments in the realms of ethics and politics had a further effect on his studies. It was really only in the post-war period that the study of Renaissance thought broadened out beyond speculative philosophy into the realms of politics, language, and social thought, and this was largely a result of Garin's new orientation. To study the role of intellectuals in a Gramscian mode meant to study the sources of their cultural power. Garin's interest in the concrete functions of intellectuals in society and politics, in how humanists created their own *verità effettuale*, nourished his existing interest in the biographical and contextual approach to the interpretation of humanists, best seen in his famous series of *ritratti*.[7] He was thus also predisposed to welcome the concept of 'civic humanism' when Hans Baron popularized it in the mid-1950s.[8] Garin was the main proponent in Italy of Baron's vision of early Renaissance Florence as a modernizing culture that empowered active citizen intellectuals.[9]

Baron's own intellectual roots lay in Weimar Germany, in the Berlin of Meinecke, Troeltsch, and other epigoni of Dilthey's *Geistesgeschichte*.[10] His view that Renaissance humanism in its purest manifestation was a republican movement and had given birth to modern democratic culture had an extraordinary success in the third quarter of the last century.[11] It represented a powerful challenge to Burckhardt's view of humanists as rootless literary aesthetes, wandering from court to court, flogging their precious antiquarian wares to style-conscious aristocrats. Baron's civic humanists were republican statesmen, deeply patriotic, who revived ancient Roman culture in the service of their cities. Baron argued that there was a strong symbiosis between the republican traditions of city-states like Florence and Venice and the revival of antiquity sponsored by the humanist movement. Thanks to this symbiosis, the humanists acquired the ideological resources to reject 'medieval' Christian values such as hierarchy, lordship, apostolic poverty, humility, monasticism, otherworldliness and holy virginity. In their place, the humanists promoted a set of civic values whose aim was to achieve the happiness and success of their own, earthly cities. Hence they praised the acquisition of wealth, the maintenance of families and family patrimonies, a spirit of equality and freedom, the active life of participation in civic and military affairs, military virtue, and in general an ethic of self-sacrifice and love for the common good. The study of classical literature was a way to inculcate these more secular values. Baron saw this broad shift as a move away from medieval social and political values in the direction of modern ones. So for Baron, too, humanism was a modernizing movement, but the modernity in this case was political modernity, identified with the republicanism of western Europe and America.

Baron's understanding of humanism emerged from a larger contemporary debate about what the social and political effects of humanism had been and should be. The subject was given particular urgency in the period of Nazism and the Second World War by the upsurge of genocidal barbarism in a land which only shortly before had been considered the homeland of modern humanism. The challenge of Marxism also raised in acute form the question whether political commitment was appropriate for scholars and literary figures. Whereas Marxists themselves usually answered this question with a resounding yes, not everyone was convinced that ideologically-committed scholarship, in the fifteenth or the twentieth century, could escape the distortions of a political agenda. Practically every major philosopher of the time participated in the debates on humanism and intellectual engagement, including figures like Gramsci, Sartre, Heidegger, Jaspers, Hannah Arendt and the Catholic existentialist Jacques Maritain.[12] It was in the midst of this philosophical reflection on the meaning of humanism that Paul Oskar Kristeller, in his mid-thirties, began to formulate his own definition of Renaissance humanism.[13]

Kristeller's response to the war years was rather different from that of continental intellectuals who had mostly lived quietly through the war (apart from some fervent participation in the 'resistance des années cinquantes'). Kristeller's parents had been victims of Nazi death camps, and he himself had seen his career derailed by the politicization of scholarship under the Nazi regime. In his youth Kristeller had been attracted to the Neo-Kantianism of the Marburg school; he saw Kantianism as a modernized form of Platonism and hence as part of a *philosophia perennis*, a philosophical tradition of permanent value for humanity.[14] After a brief flirtation with existentialism in the late 1920s – and after his teacher Heidegger aligned himself with the Nazis – Kristeller returned to the Neo-Kantian fold, where he remained for the rest of his long and productive life.[15] In his scholarly methodology Kristeller was much impressed by the writings of the Neo-Kantian Heinrich Rickert. Rickert had rejected the Diltheyan model of *Verstehen* and the idea of *Geisteswissenschaften*, arguing instead that historical and social explanation ultimately conformed to the same cognitive model as other domains of empirical inquiry. Kristeller, too, insisted that humanistic research was a science; he always regretted that English lacked a word correlative to *Wissenschaft* in German, which permits the assimilation of humanistic to scientific research. This orientation made him resistant to the ideal of the engaged intellectual. And Kristeller's 'scientific' attitude to scholarship helps account for the overwhelmingly descriptive character of his historical writings, his tendency to think in terms of long traditions and his almost complete lack of interest in causal explanation.[16]

In any case, when Kristeller took up the subject of humanism in the early 1940s, his Kantian ideal of a *Wissenschaft* completely independent of contemporary history and of a purely rational scholarly subject who abstained from value judgements flowed together with his hatred of politicized scholarship to produce a radically historicized interpretation of Renaissance humanism. Kristeller was determined to establish a clear distinction between the philological, literary and rhetorical humanism he saw in the Renaissance and the unhistorical and often politicized interpretations of humanism he saw multiplying around him in the 1940s.[17] Kristeller was particularly hostile to the contemporary American definition of humanism as a generalized affirmation of this-worldly, materialistic human values and the rejection of religion and all values claiming to have spiritual and transcendental sources. Much of what became Kristeller's famous definition of humanism in fact emerged from his patient efforts to explain to his American colleagues why the humanism he studied was different from the kind practised in Humanist Associations and Ethical Culture Societies. An American humanist who picked up *The Renaissance Philosophy of Man* when it was first published in 1948, hoping to find out about his spiritual ancestors, would have been instructed in no uncertain terms that Renaissance humanists were *not* philosophers but literary men learned in Greek and Latin, and that they certainly had nothing to do with that 'rather vague and imprecise' philosophy masquerading as humanism in these decayed modern times.[18] In later essays, Kristeller continued his implied polemic against modern American humanism.[19] He made a sharp distinction between literary humanists and professional philosophers like Ficino and Pico (a distinction which is still not only rejected, but perfectly unintelligible in Italy). Every American humanist knew that Pietro Pomponazzi had been the first humanist philosopher to reject the immortality of soul; Kristeller taught that humanists in general believed and defended the immortality of the soul, and that in any case Pomponazzi was not a humanist but a late scholastic. Nor were the humanists atheists, secret or otherwise; almost all of them were Christian believers. Indeed, many of them, as Kristeller showed in a famous article, were actually members of Catholic religious orders.[20] They did not struggle with a benighted scholasticism to establish human autonomy and intellectual freedom; in fact, the struggle between humanism and scholasticism (a central episode in the history of thought for European historians of philosophy) was for Kristeller no more than a series of 'interdepartmental rivalries'.

Even if a modern American humanist, hoping to find his spiritual ancestors, turned from Renaissance humanists, as defined by Kristeller, to Renaissance philosophers, he would find no comfort in Kristeller's writings. He would be told that the Renaissance philosopher's belief in the dignity of man was compatible with religious belief and indeed largely derived from a metaphysical interpretation of Christian theology. Renaissance philosophers, in contrast with modern humanists, also believed in the immortality of the soul and the unity of truth. Both doctrines were based on a philosophical tradition that stretched back to the ancient Greeks and had continued 'undiminished in its essence' through the Christian period. The renaissance of Platonism was 'a link in the golden chain of Platonic metaphysics', a revival of eternal truths, which connected antiquity and modernity via Kant. It was not a modernizing movement aimed at undermining scholasticism; its great guru, Marsilio Ficino, had even had a scholastic education, as Kristeller discovered, and had continued to use concepts and categories of medieval scholasticism in his mature writings.[21]

Kristeller's historicization of humanism constitutes probably the most important revolution in post-war scholarship on Renaissance thought; and, though resisted by Garin and Italian scholarship in general,[22] it has led to a series of historicist and empirical assaults on what might be called the Modernist Paradigm of Renaissance thought: that is, the Whiggish tendency, beginning with Pierre Bayle and the Enlightenment, to read the intellectual history of the Renaissance teleologically, to trace elements of modern thought to Renaissance roots.[23] It is clear that the Paradigm had a number of blind spots which left it exposed to empirical criticism in the changed ideological environment of the later 1960s and 1970s, with its 'antihumanist' trends.[24] One was its tendency to take what were in fact deeply-rooted themes in western thought and present them as proto-modern inventions of the Renaissance. What was thought to be Pico's 'modern' affirmation of human freedom and the human power of autopoesis turned out on closer inspection to be near-quotations from Boethius and the Cappadocian Fathers. Ficino's emphasis on the 'divinization of human nature', at one time thought to prefigure Hegelian theology, was in fact a restatement of the old Stoic and neoplatonic theme of *homoiosis theô*. The central place of soul in the Ficinian cosmos, once held to reflect a peculiarly 'Renaissance' sense of the dignity of man, was shown by Michael Allen to be a borrowing from Proclus.[25] The Paradigm tended to underestimate the diversity and dynamism of Renaissance Aristotelianism and its central role in shaping Renaissance and modern scientific thought, and it ignored, too, the power and originality of Renaissance humanist theologies before the Reformation. It was uninterested in the humanists' attempt to revive Christian antiquity and in their determined attempts to make paganism safe for Christendom. Scholars in the grip of the Paradigm generally refused to see in Catholic Christianity any impulses toward modernism or positive intellectual change of any kind. Since, in line with Hegelian principles, it regarded national self-determination and political hegemony as preconditions of cultural flourishing, it tended to dismiss the late Renaissance in Italy on *a priori* grounds as a period of decline.[26] In its interpretation of political thought the Modern Paradigm was blind to the political conservatism of the overwhelming majority of Renaissance intellectuals, to the traditional character of pre-Machiavellian political thought, and to the complicity of early Renaissance republican thinkers in oligarchy and imperialism.

All of these blind spots have been explored actively since the 1950s, often by associates, students and followers of Kristeller. Whether they add up to a new paradigm is difficult to say. Certainly the net effect is to emphasize the pre-modern or traditional character of much Renaissance thought; to smooth out the transitions from medieval to modern thought; and to demolish the idea that the period, if it is a period, displayed any unitary *Geist*. Kristeller's view, for all its merits as an empirical description of the literary evidence, is also, like that of Burckhardt and Garin, plainly a static one: we are given little sense of the genesis and development of the movement over time. 'Only that can be defined which has no history', says Nietzsche, and the post-war generation's preoccupation with questions of definition tended to obscure the dynamic element in humanism's history. Another weakness in humanist historiography during the thirty years after the war was its failure to appreciate how the character of humanism changed according to city and region. But both of these shortcomings have been increasingly addressed by students of humanism since the 1980s.

A dynamic portrait of humanism was attempted as long ago as 1875, when John Addington Symonds' *Renaissance in Italy* followed the progress of Neo-Latin literature through four periods from Petrarch to Pietro Bembo.[27] Symonds' four periods, 'to a certain extent arbitrary', ran from Petrarch's age of 'inspiration and discovery, when the enthusiasm for antiquity was generated', to a second period of 'arrangement and translation' in the early fifteenth century, to a third 'age of academies', to a final period of purism, typified by the work of Pietro Bembo, which spelt the end of true erudition and saw the transfer of genuine learning across the Alps. Aside from Symonds, it is difficult to think of other detailed attempts to divide the humanist movement into stages or periods, especially on internal, developmental criteria. Since the Second World War, and largely under the influence of Hans Baron, historians have been more inclined to periodize humanism on the basis of external historical conditions and crises. Thus, in addition to Baron's 'crisis' of 1402, separating 'quietist' or unengaged humanism of the fourteenth century from the civic humanism of the Quattrocento, we have Garin's well-known division of the Florentine Quattrocento into a period of civic humanism in the first part of the century, followed by a period of political quietism consequent on the Medici ascendancy, which encouraged otherworldly philosophies such as Platonism and pure scholarship of the type exemplified by Poliziano.[28] In a similar spirit, William J. Bouwsma saw the emergence of a Venetian civic humanism in the late sixteenth century as a response to external challenges to Venice's independence, while more recently, Kenneth Gouwens has argued that the Sack of Rome formed a watershed in the history of Roman humanism.[29] Internalist analyses of diachronic change have come mostly in the context of local studies, such as Margaret King's discussion of the stages of Venetian humanism, or of particular aspects of the humanist revival, such as the present writer's account of the Platonic revival of the fifteenth century.[30] The most important contribution to a diachronic understanding of the humanist movement as a whole, which takes account of both the internal development of the movement and its response to changing historical circumstances, is Ronald G. Witt's recent 'In the Footsteps of the Ancients': The Origins of Humanism from Lovato to Bruni, which covers the early stages of the movement from the second half of the thirteenth through the beginning of the fifteenth century.[31] A similar synthetic work that would continue the story from Bruni through the sixteenth century is still wanting.

In the 1980s historians of humanism began to analyse the humanist movement in terms of space as well as of time. The study of humanism, like that of the Renaissance in general, has long been skewed by an excessive focus on Florence, and Baron's republican interpretation of humanism in particular seemed to expose itself to revisionism, given that the majority of humanists active throughout the period worked for non-republican regimes. Papal Rome offered an especially striking contrast with Florence, for though heavily influenced by Florentine humanism in the early Quattrocento, after 1450 Rome developed its own distinctive style of humanism which quickly became a rival to the Florentine school. Roman humanists celebrated papal monarchy as the successor of imperial Rome and renewed the idea of a Roman cultural empire, particularly Rome's role as the arbiter of correct Latinity, artistic excellence and Christian orthodoxy. John W. O'Malley, Egmont Lee, John F. D'Amico and Charles Stinger have all written studies illuminating the special characteristics and concerns of Roman humanism and the Associazione 'Roma nel Rinascimento' in Rome since 1984 has provided a focus for ongoing research and the publication of texts.[32] Other studies have illuminated distinctive styles of humanism in Naples, Milan, Ferrara and the Veneto, where virtue, loyalty to the state, the positive value of family, wealth and civic participation, and sacrifice of private interest to the common good all turn out to be themes compatible with adherence to a monarchical principle.[33] The most important work in English on Venetian humanism, Margaret King's Venetian Humanism in an Age of Patrician Dominance, reveals a humanism that is republican in orientation, yet much more conservative than that of the Florentine civic humanists.[34] Venetian humanists lacked the critical edge of their Florentine contemporaries, tending instead to celebrate the stable and consensual character of Venetian patrician rule. Venetians saw themselves as heirs of the virtuous Romans of antiquity; their praise of virtue aimed to strengthen patrician claims to power and empire, whereas in Florence the praise of virtue was often a way of privileging ability and moral integrity over lineage and ascribed status. In Venice, philological criticism was the friend, not the enemy, of cherished civic myths. In general the study of regional humanisms in Italy has undermined Baronian claims about the centrality of Florentine republican humanism in the history of the movement.

The study of humanisms outside of Italy has similarly tended to add breadth and nuance to the understanding of the movement's character. For Italians the cultural and political life of ancient Rome was always their unquestioned cynosure, but the same cannot be said for the nations of northern Europe. German humanists cited Tacitus to assert the superiority of their primitive vigour and uncorrupted morals over the effete peoples of the Mediterranean, while French humanists celebrated the glories of their medieval traditions of crusading. French, German, Spanish and English humanists all liked to trace their national origins back to Greek or Trojan ancestors, thus short-circuiting their debts to Rome (and by extension to the modern Italians). Humanists working for Mehmed II invented a Trojan ancestry for the Ottomans, justifying their conquest of Constantinople in 1453 as revenge for the fall of Troy. Hungarian humanists even found a vocabulary to exalt the 'barbarian tradition' founded by Attila the Hun, thus reversing one of the fundamental dichotomies of Italian humanism from the time of Petrarch.[35]

Recent research on humanism has thus paid more attention to its chameleonic transformations over time and space, but some studies have also begun to focus on its spread down the social pyramid as well. New research has highlighted the role of humanism in shaping non-élite culture, particularly through public ritual, public rhetoric, spectacle and visual symbolism, as well as through humanist writing in the vernacular.[36] Humanism is usually taken to be (and sometimes dismissed as) an élite movement affecting only persons wealthy enough to enjoy an education in the classics. But recent studies disclose the ambition of humanists to influence a broader social spectrum and to cross gender lines by making available the works of classical authors and contemporary humanists in vernacular languages. Leonardo Bruni in particular seems to have organized a programme of vernacular translation of his Latin works and to have composed his own vernacular writings in order to spread the ideals of his civic humanism, and some of his historical writings were as popular in Italian as they were in Latin. For instance his *First Punic War*, a compilation based on Polybius, was given five separate Italian translations in the fifteenth century, survives in 120 vernacular manuscripts, and before 1600 was printed twelve times in Italian, four times in French and once in German – seventeen vernacular editions in all, as compared with only five Latin editions.[37] Marsilio Ficino took similar pains to spread his Platonic religious reform in the vulgar tongue, and we know that some of these translations were explicitly undertaken to make his writings available to female readers.[38] Much recent research has emphasized the symbiotic relationship of Latin and *volgare* in the early and high Renaissance, challenging the old canard, going back to Romantic nationalism of the nineteenth century, that Latin humanism was 'culturally regressive, élitist, unoriginal and predominantly didactic. … Poets were replaced by scholars who gave themselves over to imitating a dead literature instead of carrying forwards the newly founded and vigorous one in their own spoken mother tongue.'[39] Scholars like Carlo Dionisotti, Gianfranco Folena, Mario Martelli, and Rossella Bessi have understood, by contrast, that contemporaries regarded the Latin language and Latin literature as an indispensable resource for the reform and enrichment of the Italian tongue.[40]

The study of humanism's footprint in vernacular literary culture has also strengthened the argument that humanist culture was not so much imposed 'from above', by powerful patrons and political élites, as it was the outcome of a complex cultural negotiation between the middling ranks of society, the *popolo*, and the ruling classes. Ronald Witt's *In the Footsteps of the Ancients*, already cited, shows that the lively Trecento tradition in Florence of making vernacular translations of the classics prepared that city to become the leader of the humanist movement at the end of the fourteenth century. The translations of Cicero, Seneca, Livy, Sallust and Aristotle by men like Brunetto Latini, Giambono da Bona, and Bartolomeo da San Concordia – all representatives of the popular classes – established an interest in and an identification with ancient Roman republicanism among Florentines, and provided an alternative to the culture of chivalry and courtly love coming from high medieval France. Since the mid-thirteenth century, chivalric culture had been associated with the magnates and other would-be aristocrats, but professional humanists – almost all of them from the middle ranks of society – who emerged on the scene in the late Trecento made possible a new kind of culture that could be shared between the middling and upper classes of city-states.[41] Indeed, the presence of the Latin classics and humanistic literature in vernacular dress was an indispensable precondition for the spread of neo-Roman culture among the ruling élites of Italy. In some court environments, such as the court of Filippo Maria Visconti, Duke of Milan, classical and humanistic writings were far more likely to be read in the vernacular than in Latin.

The new classical culture of the Italian upper classes was popularized thanks to the spread of the humanist school during the first half of the Quattrocento, and the character and originality of humanistic education has become a topic of intense debate in recent decades. Two broad lines of revisionism have been proposed. In 1982 Lisa Jardine and Anthony Grafton challenged Garin's portrait of humanist education as an indoctrination into critical historical and philological skills, 'open-ended research', civic virtue, and human flourishing. The basis of their critique is a study of commentaries and notes from the school of Guarino which seems to disclose a gap between the prescriptive theoretical writings of the humanists and actual classroom practice. While the humanists' educational treatises call for an education in eloquence and virtue, classroom practice appears to emphasize close reading of texts, with a focus on grammar and the acquisition of information about the classical world. Grafton and Jardine compare humanist education unfavourably with scholasticism, which they credit with 'training men for employment in powerful and lucrative occupations'; scholastic scientific and legal writings were 'no sterile indoctrination in the authoritative messages of a few selected texts', but generated 'vast, unsuspected views of insight and speculation'. Humanist education emphasized rote learning over logical analysis and memorization over argument; hence it was an admirable training for future bureaucrats who were expected passively to administer the policies of their betters. It 'fitted the needs of the new Europe that was taking shape, with its closed governing élites, hereditary offices and strenuous efforts to close off debate on vital political and social questions'. It 'fostered in all its initiates a properly docile attitude to authority'.[42]

Grafton and Jardine's negative view of humanist education, an artefact of New Left radicalism in America, has hardly gone unchallenged,[43] but it might be pointed out that among those subjected to this putatively stultifying educational regime were Leonardo Bruni, Lorenzo Valla, Marsilio Ficino, Pico della Mirandola, Machiavelli, Angelo Poliziano, Erasmus, Thomas More, Rabelais, and Montaigne – not exactly a list of intellectual conformists. But a much weightier critique of traditional views on humanist education has been launched by Robert Black, who has massively documented the essential continuity between the methods and texts used by medieval grammarians and those used by humanist educators.[44] Black admits that the canon of texts read did broaden somewhat in the Quattrocento, and the introduction of Greek and rhetorical training constituted new elements. He also recognizes that the clientele of educators changed towards the end of the fifteenth century: medieval grammarians were providing pre-professional training while Renaissance humanists sought to form a social élite. The latter shift is perhaps responsible for the new ideological dress of humanist education in the Quattrocento. Membership in a social and political élite was now justified by mastery of a set of texts held to transmit models of virtue and wisdom. Black's work is the first serious, empirically-based study of the practices of the humanist school, and its picture of the methodological conservatism of humanist grammarians carries conviction. Yet we are still left with the question of how it happened, if indeed there was really little or no change in teaching methods between 1200 and 1500, that a very large number of fifteenth-century humanists in fact succeeded in writing much better Latin prose and verse than their medieval predecessors.

The study of humanist educational practice can be seen as part of a wider trend in recent historiography to understand the routines and practices of humanists in their professional lives. Most humanists were either teachers at schools and universities, private tutors, private secretaries, state officials, chancellors or diplomats – the professions where a knowledge of literature and eloquence would count as qualifications. In addition to some valuable studies of individual humanist educators,[45] we now have a much better sense of the day-to-day activities of humanist chancellors, and the role of humanist studies in their professional activities, thanks to a number of biographical studies.[46] A recent study by Marcello Simonetta gives a more synoptic view of the 'world of the secretary', with the emphasis on the humanist as a political actor, while from a literary point of view Douglas Biow has explored the effects of the humanists' *deformazione professionale* on their writings.[47] And there is of course a large and growing literature on the professional roles – or lack of them – available to women humanists.[48]

While humanist thought and literature was undeniably influenced by their daily professional routines, it is also the case that humanists themselves were pioneers in new skills of criticism and textual analysis. The recovery of Graeco-Roman antiquity implies a project of research into the classical past, and the humanist movement from the beginning made classical scholarship a central activity. The modern study of humanist philology, which has its roots in the work of Remigio Sabbadini, J. E. Sandys, Rudolf Pfeiffer, Sebastiano Timpanaro and other classical scholars of the early twentieth century, has in recent decades been one of the

richest fields of humanistic research, a field in which Italian scholars
have continued to play the leading role. Led by Giuseppe Billanovich,
Alessandro Perosa, Augusto Campana and Gianvito Resta in the post-war
period, the modern study of humanist philology has traced back to the
Renaissance the origins of modern methods of translation, palaeography,
text editing, lexicography, and commentary, as well as critical research
in the field of Greco-Roman history and antiquities.[49]

Of course a research programme oriented towards finding the roots
of modern historical and philological disciplines runs the risk of
Whiggism and other forms of anachronism, and there has been a strong
countervailing tendency in recent scholarship to emphasize the many
differences in aim and context between modern scholarly disciplines
and their Renaissance ancestors. The work of Anthony Grafton has been
of particular importance in recovering the coeval context and aims of
Renaissance scholarship. In addition to his two-volume intellectual
biography of Joseph Scaliger, which in effect contains histories of
Renaissance textual criticism and historical chronology, Grafton has
written important studies of the sixteenth-century doctor and polymath
Girolamo Cardano and of the humanist and artist-engineer Leon Battista
Alberti. Among his more interesting contributions is *Forgers and Critics*, a
book which argues *inter alia* that humanists did not so much invent a new
philology as revive ancient critical techniques, and that the humanists
did not revive these techniques in the interests of pure research, but
rather in pursuit of their own political and cultural agendas. Grafton
even goes so far as to claim that the revived techniques of historical and
textual analysis often served purposes antithetical to the aims of modern
scholarly research, for instance forgery or the creation of more plausible
myths and invented historical traditions.[50] The study of the reception of
the classical authors in the Renaissance has similarly acted as an antidote
to anachronism in the history of classical scholarship.[51]

The historical writing of the humanists has often been considered
their most innovative and enduring contribution to literature and
scholarship.[52] It was the humanist historians, after all, who invented
the myth of the Renaissance itself and the tripartite division of history
into ancient, medieval and modern that is still in use today.[53] Ancient
Christian and medieval historians, following their biblical sources, had
seen world history as a succession of empires culminating in the Roman
Empire and the Incarnation of Christ. It was the *pax romana* established
by Augustus, under the guidance of Divine Providence, that had made
possible the spread of Christianity and its ultimate establishment as

the state religion under the fourth-century emperors from Constantine to Theodosius. The Roman Republic was regarded as little more than a disorderly prelude to the grand period of imperial and Christian triumph. The armature around which the subsequent history of the western world was built was the twin histories of Christianity (inevitably triumphalist) and of the Roman Empire (inevitably a story of decline).

In the early fifteenth century the historians Leonardo Bruni (1370–1444) and Biondo Flavio (1392–1463), taking into account such developments as the emergence of the Italian city-states, recent Italian supremacy in arms, and the flourishing of arts and letters, decided that Italy and the West was experiencing a rebirth. Biondo invented the concept of the fall of the Roman Empire in his *Historiarum ab inclinatione Romanorum libri* (1437–42), and in his *Italia illustrata* (1453) he described a rebirth of ancient literature in fourteenth-century Italy.[54] In Bruni's case the idea that a Renaissance of the classical world was taking place subserved an ideological commitment to republican government. For him, the Roman republic before the domination of Caesar had been antiquity's Golden Age, destroyed by the tyrannical rule of the emperors. Now that imperial rule had faded in Italy and was being replaced by a confederation of free republics under Florentine leadership, the historical circumstances for the renewal of the Golden Age were present, Bruni felt; and the Florentines' recovery of ancient Latin literature and the ancient arts of painting, sculpture and architecture were visible signs that the city was on the verge of becoming the new Rome.[55] Italy and the western world had entered a third age after the height of republican Rome and the trough of an imperial middle age.

But the topos of rebirth, of a revival of antique norms after an intervening Middle Age, was not confined to republican thinkers like Bruni. It was too useful for that. It quickly became popular among humanist writers of all ideological stripes, who found it especially useful when praising their patrons or themselves. Thus Bartolomeo Platina (1421–1481), writing the life of Pope Nicholas V (reigned 1447–55), praises the pontiff for his patronage of letters. He describes how Nicholas had encouraged public lectures on the classics, original compositions in Latin and translations from Greek to Latin, 'so that Greek and Latin letters, which had lain in the dark and dust for the previous six hundred years, finally acquired a certain splendor'. With a fine disregard of chronology Platina goes on to give credit to Nicholas for sending Poggio around Europe to recover from the barbarians lost works of Latin literature, and praises the pope for rebuilding the Rome of the Caesars and the early Church.[56]

The topos of age-old neglect (lasting anywhere from six hundred to a thousand years) coming to an end, literature and the arts restored, ancient virtue and military skill revived, was repeated endlessly in the Renaissance and was soon appropriated by historians of music, the fine arts, religion and war. It is a staple constructive device in Vasari's *Lives of the Artists* as in Johannes Tinctoris' and Heinrich Glarean's overviews of recent musical history. Often a single figure is identified as the heroic innovator who corrects the abuses of the past and puts an art on the road to recovering its antique glory: Petrarch in literature, Giotto in painting, Donatello in sculpture, John Dunstable or Josquin Desprez in music. Modern historians of literature and the arts have been understandably reluctant to accept such judgements at face value. Most scholars now trace the origins of humanism, *all'antica* sculpture and naturalistic painting to the mid-thirteenth century, while other scholars emphasize the continuity of medieval patterns of thought and style in the works of Renaissance artists and writers.[57] Musicologists have come to see the idea of a musical Renaissance beginning around 1430 as a kind of 'historiographical accident', a misconception traceable to the fact that early music historians lacked reliable information about medieval music.[58] Yet the idea of the Renaissance itself, as a period beginning roughly in the mid-fourteenth century and stretching into the seventeenth century, remains firmly cemented into the western historiographical traditions. It survives, at least in part, because historians of later periods and schools – Reformation, Enlightenment, liberal, historicist, Marxist, and postmodern – have mostly shared with the humanists the same underlying ideological orientation, namely hostility to dogmatic religion and to the ecclesiastical and educational structures inherited from the Middle Ages that sustain it.

It is of course true that many humanists of the Renaissance were pious Catholics and churchmen, and many more benefited gratefully from ecclesiastical patronage. It is also true that an important aim of many Italian and northern humanists was the reform of religion, which in a Renaissance context naturally meant returning Christianity to its ancient roots. This process begins in the early Quattrocento with a revival of the Church Fathers and is radicalized in the sixteenth century by Protestant humanists and reformers who aimed to refound Christianity on an evangelical model. Among the most important revisions to the history of humanism in the last three decades has been the discovery of serious movements of religious and theological reform among the Italian humanists of the early and high Renaissance.[59] It was these movements, not just linguistic purism, that gave humanism its critical edge in opposing scholasticism. Humanists wrinkled their noses at scholastic Latin and denounced scholastic texts as corrupt – as untrue to the pure ancient traditions of law and theology that were for them the only rightful basis of authoritative teaching. But as recent studies show, their real opposition to scholasticism went much deeper, and reflected fundamental differences in the understanding of language, history, and the nature of religion. Humanism implied a historicizing of texts and doctrines and humanists were in general much more open to 'alien wisdom' from paganism and other religious traditions than was typical of contemporary scholasticism. At the same time the humanists provided tools for dismantling the ideological infrastructure of the medieval church. Lorenzo Valla's demolition of the Donation of Constantine and its claims about papal political authority is only the most famous and explicit example. There were many others. The humanists also replaced universal histories in which the progress of Christianity was the central theme and Divine Providence the guiding force with city-state and royal histories where liberty, human virtue and military glory were the chief concerns. Humanists popularized the study of Greek and Hebrew which opened western eyes to Orthodox and Jewish traditions and threw received interpretations of authoritative texts into doubt. Their study of the early Church Fathers revealed a world where there existed a much wider range of theological and ecclesiological opinion, and this had a similarly destabilizing influence on settled beliefs and practices.

Thus as the traditions of medieval Christianity gradually began to be included in the humanist critique of modernity – a critique always implied in their privileging of ancient culture – the radical possibilities of humanism as cultural movement stood revealed. It is no accident that all of the classical reformers of the Reformation had had a humanist training, even if many humanists of the time remained loyal to the Roman Church.[60] It was the humanist vision of history – of an uncorrupted Golden Age of evangelical Christianity to which it was imperative to return – that fired the early reformers, just as it was the humanist vision of classical antiquity that had inspired the Renaissance movement. The humanists, one might say, backed into the Reformation as they had backed into the Renaissance. Bernd Moeller's famous formulation, *Ohne Humanismus keine Reformation* – no Reformation without humanism – applies above all to the humanist sense of the past. That sense was a necessary if not sufficient condition for the European movement of spiritual and ecclesiological reform that drove the transformation of the medieval into the modern world.[61] It is possible to interpret humanism as a revival of antiquity or as an elaboration of medieval cultural practices,

but to ignore the dynamic, forward-looking elements of the movement
is to risk a serious underestimate of its historical significance.

## notes

1. P. Monnier, *Le Quattrocento, Essai sur l'histoire littéraire du XVe siècle italien*
   (Paris, 1910, 1924), I, p. 228.
2. See M. Capati, *Cantimori, Contini, Garin: Crisi di una cultura idealistica* (Bologna,
   1997). For the controversy that arose in the late 1990s about Garin's career
   under fascism, see the account, with Garin's eloquent self-defence, in E. Garin,
   *Intervista sull' intellectuale*, ed. M. Ajello (Rome and Bari, 1997), and *Colloqui
   con Eugenio Garin: Un intellectuale del Novecento*, ed. R. Cassigoli (Florence,
   2000); both works provide much autobiographical detail.
3. See *Tra scienza e storia: Percorsi del neostoricismo italiano: Eugenio Garin, Paolo
   Rossi, Sergio Moravia*, ed. F. Cambi (Milano, 1992).
4. See E. Garin, *La filosofia come sapere storico con un saggi autobiografico* (Rome
   and Bari, 1959, new edn with the 'saggio autobiografico', 1990), and E. Garin,
   *Con Gramsci* (Rome, 1997).
5. Garin, *La filosofia come sapere storico*, p. 139.
6. E. Garin, *Dal Rinascimento all'Illuminismo. Studi e ricerche* (Pisa, 1970).
7. E. Garin, *Ritratti di umanisti* (Florence, 1967).
8. Garin claimed to have anticipated Baron, or to have developed the same
   results independently of Baron; see Garin, *La filosofia come sapere storico*,
   p. 140.
9. E. Garin, *Italian Humanism: Philosophy and Civic Life in the Renaissance*, trans.
   P. Munz (New York, 1965, repr. 1975), first published in 1947 (see note 12,
   below).
10. On Baron see the detailed studies of R. Fubini, 'Renaissance Historian: The
    Career of Hans Baron', *Journal of Modern History*, LXIV (1992) 541–74; and K.
    Schiller, *Gelehrte Gegenwelten: über humanistische Leitbilder im 20. Jahrhundert*
    (Frankfurt am Main, 2000).
11. See the introduction to *Renaissance Civic Humanism: Reappraisals and Reflections*,
    ed. J. Hankins (Cambridge, 2000), pp. 1–13.
12. Garin points out that his famous book on Italian humanism first appeared
    in the same series as Heidegger's *Letter on Humanism*; the series was edited by
    Ernesto Grassi, who had served the Nazi regime during the 1930s as a kind
    of apostle of Heideggerianism to the Italians. See E. Garin, *Der italienische
    Humanismus*, trans. G. Zamboni, Sammlung Überlieferung und Auftrag, Reihe
    Schriften V (Bern, 1947).
13. On Kristeller's intellectual sources see now J. Monfasani, 'Toward the Genesis
    of the Kristeller Thesis of Renaissance Humanism: Four Bibliographical Notes',
    *Renaissance Quarterly*, LIII (2000) 1156–68.
14. At the end of his *Marsilio Ficino and His Work after Five Hundred Years* (Florence,
    1987), p. 18, Kristeller writes, 'In my opinion ... Ficino's ... greatest significance
    as a thinker (and also as a scholar) rests on the fact that he constitutes an
    important member and link ... in that golden chain which is the tradition
    of rational metaphysics that leads from the Presocratics and Plato to Kant,
    Hegel and beyond. In my long career as a scholar, and in the midst of hard,

difficult and often disastrous times, this tradition has been for me a rock of intellectual and moral support, much stronger than the numerous fashionable theories and ideologies that have come and gone in rapid succession over the years.' See also the comments of Riccardo Fubini in Chapter 6 below.

15. What follows is in part based on personal recollections of the author, but one may also consult Margaret L. King, 'Iter Kristellerianum: The European Journey (1905–1939)', *Renaissance Quarterly*, XLVII (1994) 907–29; the memoir quoted *in extenso* there is a version of a longer document entitled 'Recollections of My Life', a manuscript privately circulated by Kristeller among his friends; a copy may be found at New York, Columbia University, Rare Book and Manuscript Room, Kristeller Collection, box 23.

16. On this aspect of Kristeller's intellectual formation, see Schiller, *Gelehrte Gegenwelten*, pp. 144–9.

17. Even Jaeger's 'Third Humanism' Kristeller and friends like Panofsky privately considered suspect for its mixing of cognitive and normative thought, and even for containing crypto-Nazi thinking disguised as Greek *Paideia*; see Schiller, *Gelehrte Gegenwelten*, p. 149, and cf. Riccardo Fubini's comments in Chapter 6 below.

18. *The Renaissance Philosophy of Man*, ed. E. Cassirer, P. O. Kristeller, and J. H. Randall, Jr (Chicago, 1948). This collection remained the standard 'reader' in America on Renaissance humanism for nearly half a century, and is still in print.

19. See P. O. Kristeller, *Renaissance Thought and its Sources* (New York, 1979), for an overview of Kristeller's interpretation of Renaissance humanism and philosophy.

20. P. O. Kristeller, *Medieval Aspects of Renaissance Learning*, ed. E. P. Mahoney, 2nd edn (New York, 1992).

21. P. O. Kristeller, 'The Scholastic Background of Marsilio Ficino', first published in *Traditio*, II (1944) 257–318, reprinted in Kristeller's *Studies in Renaissance Thought and Letters* (Rome, 1956) pp. 35–98.

22. For Garin's polite disagreements with his long-time friend, Kristeller, see Garin, *La filosofia come sapere storico*, pp. 146–7.

23. See my article 'Renaissance Philosophy between God and the Devil', in A. J. Grieco, M. Rocke, F. Gioffredi Superbi, eds, *The Italian Renaissance in the Twentieth Century* (Florence, 2002), pp. 269–93.

24. See L. Ferry and A. Renaut, *French Philosophy of the Sixties: An Essay on Antihumanism*, trans. M. H. S. Cattani (Amherst, MA, 1990).

25. M. J. B. Allen, 'Ficino's Theory of the Five Substances and the Neoplatonists' *Parmenides*', *The Journal of Medieval and Renaissance Studies*, XII (1982) 19–44, reprinted in Allen's *Plato's Third Eye: Studies in Marsilio Ficino's Metaphysics and its Sources* (Aldershot, 1995), essay 8.

26. On this mistake see E. Cochrane, *The Late Italian Renaissance, 1525–1630* (New York, 1970), pp. 1–18.

27. J. A. Symonds, *Renaissance in Italy*, I: *The Revival of Learning* (London, 1877), chapters 2–7.

28. See especially E. Garin, *L'età nuova: ricerche di storia della cultura dal XII al XVI secolo* (Naples, 1969), p. 283, and 'Poliziano e il suo ambiente', in his *Ritratti di umanisti*, pp. 131–62.

29. W. J. Bouwsma, *Venice and the Defense of Republican Liberty: Renaissance Values in the Age of the Counter-Reformation* (Berkeley, 1968); K. Gouwens, *Remembering the Renaissance: Humanist Narratives of the Sack of Rome* (Leiden, 1998).

30. M. L. King, *Venetian Humanism in an Age of Patrician Dominance* (Princeton, 1986); J. Hankins, *Plato in the Italian Renaissance*, 2 vols (Leiden, 1990).

31. (Leiden, 2000).

32. J. W. O'Malley, *Praise and Blame in Renaissance Rome: Rhetoric, Doctrine and Reform in the Sacred Orators of the Papal Court* (Durham, NC, 1979); J. W. O'Malley, *Rome and the Renaissance: Studies in Culture and Religion* (London, 1981); Egmont Lee, *Sixtus IV and Men of Letters* (Rome, 1978); J. F. D'Amico, *Renaissance Humanism in Papal Rome: Humanists and Churchmen on the Eve of the Reformation* (Baltimore, 1983); Charles L. Stinger, *The Renaissance in Rome* (Bloomington, IN, 1985). For the activities of the Associazione 'Roma nel Rinascimento', see www.romanelrinascimento.it/.

33. For Naples and humanism in the Mezzogiorno: Jerry H. Bentley, *Politics and Culture in Renaissance Naples* (Princeton, 1987); Francesco Tateo, 'Cultura e poesia nel mezzogiorno dal Pontano al Marullo', in *La letteratura italiana: Storia e testi* (Bari, 1972) III.2, pp. 469–542; and David Abulafia's chapter above. For Milan: G. Ianziti, *Humanistic Historiography under the Sforzas: Politics and Propaganda in Fifteenth-Century Milan* (Oxford, 1988); D. Robin, *Filelfo in Milan: Writings, 1451–1477* (Princeton, 1991); on Ferrara: Werner L. Gundersheimer, *Ferrara: The Style of a Renaissance Despotism* (Princeton, 1973); D. Del Nero, *La corte e l'università: Umanisti e teologi nel Quattrocento ferrarese* (Lucca, 1996); T. Tuohy, *Herculean Ferrara: Ercoles d'Este, 1471–1505 and the Invention of a Ducal Capital* (Cambridge, 1996); on Padua and the Veneto: *Storia della cultura veneta* (Vicenza, 1976), II: *Il Trecento*, essays by Guido Billanovich, R. Avesani, L. Gargan, N. Mann and M. Pastore Stocchi (pp. 1–170 and 517–65); III: *Dal Primo Quattrocento al Concilio di Trento*, essays by F. Gaeta, M. Pastore Stocchi, V. Branca and A. Pertusi (pp. 1–264); Benjamin G. Kohl, *Culture and Politics in Early Renaissance Padua* (Aldershot, 2001).

34. Cited above, note 30.

35. In addition to important older works by R. Weiss, *Humanism in England during the Fifteenth Century*, 3rd edn (Oxford, 1967), F. Simone, *The French Renaissance: Medieval Tradition and Italian Influence in Shaping the Renaissance in France* (London, 1969; original French version 1961), and L. Spitz, *The Religious Renaissance of the German Humanists* (Cambridge, MA, 1963), one may consult more recent surveys of the diffusion of humanism in A. Rabil, Jr, ed., *Renaissance Humanism: Foundations, Forms and Legacy*, 3 vols (Philadelphia, 1988); A. Goodman and A. MacKay, eds, *The Impact of Humanism on Western Europe* (London, 1990); R. Porter and M. Teich, eds, *The Renaissance in National Context* (Cambridge, 1992); P. Burke, *The European Renaissance: Centres and Peripheries* (Oxford, 1998); and J. Helmrath, U. Muhlack and G. Walther, eds, *Diffusion des Humanismus: Studien zur nationalen Geschichtsschreibung europäischer Humanisten* (Göttingen, 2002). For the Turks and the humanists see J. Hankins, 'Renaissance Crusaders: Humanist Crusade Literature in the Age of Mehmet II', *Dumbarton Oaks Papers*, XLIX (1995) 111–207, reprinted in my *Humanism and Platonism in the Italian Renaissance*, I (Rome, 2003), pp. 293–424; N. Bisaha, *Creating East and West: Renaissance Humanists and the Ottoman Turks* (Philadelphia, 2004); on humanism and the Huns see A. F.

D'Elia, 'Genealogy and the Limits of Panegyric: Turks and Huns in Fifteenth-Century Epithalamia', *Sixteenth Century Studies*, XXXIV (2003) 973–91.

36. E. Muir, *Civic Ritual in Renaissance Venice* (Princeton, 1981); A. Brown, 'Platonism in Fifteenth-Century Florence', in her *The Medici in Florence: The Exercise and Language of Power* (Florence, 1992), pp. 215–45; A. Brown, ed., *Languages and Images of Renaissance Italy* (Oxford, 1995); A. Brown, 'Demasking Renaissance Republicanism', in J. Hankins, ed., *Renaissance Civic Humanism: Reappraisals and Reflections* (Cambridge, 2000), pp. 179–99; S. J. Milner, 'Citing the *Ringhiera*: The Politics of Place and Public Address in Trecento Florence', *Italian Studies*, LV (2000) 53–82; S. J. Milner, 'Communication, Consensus and Conflict: Rhetorical Principals, the *ars concionandi* and Social Ordering in Late Medieval Italy', in *The Rhetoric of Cicero in its Medieval and Renaissance Commentary Tradition*, ed. V. Cox and J. O. Ward (Leiden, 2004); S. J. Milner, 'Exile, Rhetoric, and the Limits of Civic Republican Discourse', in *At the Margins: Minority Groups in Pre-Modern Italy*, ed. S. J. Milner (forthcoming, Minneapolis and London, 2005), pp. 162–91.

37. J. Hankins, 'Latin and Vernacular Humanism in the Fifteenth Century: The Case of Leonardo Bruni', forthcoming in Festschrift for Ronald G. Witt edited by C. Celenza.

38. J. Hankins, 'Lorenzo de'Medici's *De summo bono* and the Popularization of Ficinian Platonism', in *Humanistica. Per Cesare Vasoli*, ed. F. Meroi and E. Scapparone (Florence, 2004), pp. 61–9 (with further references).

39. From Letizia Panizza's summary of this view in her contribution to *The Cambridge History of Italian Literature*, ed. P. Brand and L. Pertile, revised edn (Cambridge, 1999), p. 131.

40. C. Dionisotti, 'Tradizione classica e volgarizzamenti', in *Geografia e storia della letteratura italiana* (Turin, 1967), pp. 103–44; G. Folena, *Volgarizzare e tradurre* (Turin, 1991); M. Martelli, *Angelo Poliziano: Storia e metastoria* (Lecce, 1995); R. Bessi, *Umanesimo volgare: Studi di letteratura fra Tre e Quattrocento* (Florence, 2004).

41. On this negotiation see J. M. Najemy, 'Civic Humanism and Florentine Politics,' in Hankins, *Renaissance Civic Humanism*, pp. 75–104.

42. A. Grafton and L. Jardine, 'Humanism and the School of Guarino: A Problem of Evaluation', *Past and Present*, XCVI (1982) 51–80, reprinted in their *From Humanism to the Humanities: Education and the Liberal Arts in Fifteenth- and Sixteenth-Century Europe* (London, 1986), pp. 1–28.

43. See the symposium edited by Paul Grendler, 'Education in the Renaissance and Reformation', in *Renaissance Quarterly*, XLIII (1990) 774–824.

44. R. Black, *Humanism and Education in Medieval and Renaissance Italy: Tradition and Innovation in Latin Schools from the Twelfth to the Fifteenth Century* (Cambridge, 2001).

45. R. Schweyen, *Guarino Veronese: Philosophie und humanistische Pädagogik* (Munich, 1973); R. G. G. Mercer, *The Teaching of Gasparino Barzizza, with Special Reference to his Place in Paduan Humanism* (London, 1979); G. Müller, *Mensch und Bildung im italienischen Renaissance-Humanismus: Vittorino da Feltre und die humanistischen Erziehungsdenker* (Baden-Baden, 1984).

46. R. G. Witt, *Hercules at the Crossroads: The Life, Works and Thought of Coluccio Salutati* (Durham, NC, 1983); A. Brown, *Bartolomeo Scala, 1430–1497, Chancellor of Florence: The Humanist as Bureaucrat* (Princeton, 1979); R. Black, *Benedetto*

*Accolti and the Florentine Renaissance* (Cambridge, 1985); on Machiavelli as a humanist secretary see the important article of R. Black, 'Machiavelli, Servant of the Florentine Republic', in *Machiavelli and Republicanism*, ed. G. Bock, Q. Skinner and M. Viroli (Cambridge, 1990), pp. 71–100; on the papal bureaucracy see P. Partner, *The Pope's Men: The Papal Civil Service in the Renaissance* (Oxford, 1990).

47. M. Simonetta, *Rinascimento segreto. Il mondo del Segretario da Petrarca a Machiavelli* (Bologna, 2004); D. Biow, *Doctors, Ambassadors, Secretaries: Humanism and the Professions in Renaissance Italy* (Chicago, 2002).

48. See Chapter 9 below.

49. On humanist philology see L. D. Reynolds and N. G. Wilson, *Scribes and Scholars: A Guide to the Transmission of Greek and Latin Literature*, 3rd edn (Oxford 1991); and on the humanist study of Greek, Wilson's *From Byzantium to Italy: Greek Studies in the Italian Renaissance* (Baltimore, 1992); a useful overview of twentieth-century scholarship on humanist philology may be found in *La Filologia medievale e umanistica greca e latina nel secolo XX: Atti del Congresso internazionale, Roma, Consiglio nazionale delle ricerche, Università La Sapienza, 11–15 dicembre 1989*, 2 vols (Rome, 1993).

50. Anthony Grafton's three major intellectual biographies are *Joseph Scaliger: A Study in the History of Classical Scholarship*, 2 vols (Oxford, 1983–93); *Cardano's Cosmos: The World and Works of a Renaissance Astrologer* (Cambridge, MA, 1999); *Leon Battista Alberti: Master Builder of the Italian Renaissance* (New York, 2000). See also his *Commerce with the Classics: Ancient Books and Renaissance Readers* (Ann Arbor, MI, 1997); *Defenders of the Text: The Traditions of Scholarship in an Age of Science, 1450–1800* (Cambridge, MA, 1991); and *Forgers and Critics: Creativity and Duplicity in Western Scholarship* (Princeton, 1990); on the latter see also my review, 'Forging Links with the Past', in *Journal of the History of Ideas*, LII (1991) 509–18, reprinted in my *Humanism and Platonism*, pp. 511–24.

51. See my *Plato in the Italian Renaissance*; J. H. Gaisser, *Catullus and his Renaissance Readers* (Oxford, 1993); C. Celenza, *Piety and Pythagoras in Renaissance Florence: The Symbolum Nesianum* (Leiden, 2001); D. Lines, *Aristotle's Ethics in the Italian Renaissance (ca. 1300–1650): The Universities and the Problem of Moral Education* (Leiden, 2002).

52. On humanist historiography in general see E. W. Cochrane, *Historians and Historiography in the Italian Renaissance* (Chicago, 1981); *La storiografia umanistica [Convegno internazionale di studi, Messina 22–25 ottobre 1987]*, ed. A. Di Stefano et al., 2 vols (Messina, 1992); R. Fubini, *Storiografia dell'umanesimo in Italia da Leonardo Bruni ad Annio da Viterbo* (Rome, 2003).

53. Some texts are assembled in W. K. Ferguson, *The Renaissance in Historical Thought: Five Centuries of Interpretation* (Boston, 1948), pp. 1–28; see also P. Burke, *The Renaissance Sense of the Past* (London, 1969).

54. Biondo Flavio, *Italy Illustrated*, I, ed. and trans. J. A. White, I Tatti Renaissance Library, XX (Cambridge, MA, forthcoming), 6.26–30.

55. Leonardo Bruni, *Opere letterarie e politiche*, ed. P. Viti (Turin, 1996) and Leonardo Bruni, *History of the Florentine People*, ed. J. Hankins, I Tatti Renaissance Library, III, XVI (Cambridge, MA, 2001–04).

56. Bartolomeo Platina, *Liber de vita Christi ac omnium pontificum*, ed. G. Gaida (Città di Castello, 1917–33), p. 338.

57. An interesting discussion of the survival of medieval elements in humanist Latin well into the fifteenth century may be found in S. Rizzo, *Ricerche sul latino umanistico* (Rome, 2002); for the parallel case of the language of classical architecture, see C. Smith, *Architecture in the Culture of Early Humanism: Ethics, Aesthetics and Eloquence, 1400–1470* (Oxford, 1992).

58. J. A. Owens, 'Music Historiography and the Definition of the Renaissance', *Notes*, 2nd ser., XLVII (1990) 305–30.

59. C. Trinkaus, *In Our Image and Likeness: Humanity and Divinity in Italian Renaissance Thought*, 2 vols (Chicago, 1970); S. I. Camporeale, *Lorenzo Valla: Umanesimo e teologia* (Florence, 1972); C. L. Stinger, *Humanism and the Church Fathers: Ambrogio Traversari (1386–1439) and Christian Antiquity in the Italian Renaissance* (Albany, NY, 1977); O'Malley, *Praise and Blame in Renaissance Rome*.

60. See E. Rummel, *The Confessionalization of Humanism in Reformation Germany* (Oxford, 2000).

61. Bernd Moeller, 'Die deutschen Humanisten und die Anfänge der Reformation', *Zeitschrift für Kirchengeschichte*, LXX (1959) 46–61 at p. 59; discussion with further references in A. A. Strnad and K. Walsh, 'Ohne Humanismus keine Reformation? Zur Stellung von Renaissance-Humanismus und Reformation im neueren Schrifttum', *Innsbrucker Historische Studien*, III (1980) 211–318.

# 5

# the renaissance and humanism: definitions and origins

## robert black

In 1860 Jacob Burckhardt published the most influential work ever written on the Renaissance: *The Civilization of the Renaissance in Italy: An Essay*.[1] Burckhardt's fundamental assumption was that the Renaissance constituted a new and distinct age or period in the history of culture. The job of the historian of civilization was, for Burckhardt, to portray the mentality of a given period, or, in other words, to delineate the spirit of the age. Its distinguishing stamp was, according to Burckhardt, individualism, a quality which he proceeded to relate to the various aspects of Italian culture from the thirteenth to the sixteenth century. Man as an individual – modern, secular man – emerged first, said Burckhardt, in Renaissance Italy; during the Middle Ages, in contrast, man had received his identity not through his own individuality but by association with some corporate body. Burckhardt devoted his book to an analysis of how this new individualism determined the political, cultural, social, moral and religious life of the epoch.

Burckhardt's attempt to portray the Renaissance in Italy as a homogeneous historical period, although powerfully compelling, is inherently flawed; it is impossible to demonstrate that political, social and cultural history moved in marvellous coordination from the thirteenth to the sixteenth century in Italy. The force of logic, for example, compelled Burckhardt to suggest the 'equality of classes'. Radical individualism had to mean that people in the Renaissance were valued not as members of privileged social groups but simply for their own talents, and so he was even led to suggest 'that women stood on a footing of perfect equality with men'.[2] Few sociologists would argue that, even in an era of mass democracy such as the second half of the twentieth century, social class had disappeared, and the perfect equality of men and women is still a distant aspiration.

Burckhardt's thesis not only encouraged him to see an untenable chronological and geographical uniformity in Renaissance Italy, but also to distort the Middle Ages. Individualism was hardly lacking in famous medieval characters such as Peter Damian, Gregory VII, Abelard, Abbot Suger of St Denis, Innocent III or St Francis, some of whom even left autobiographies.[3] It is futile to try to see, in the Burckhardtian manner, the Renaissance as a chronological block informed by a unifying ethos such as individualism. Social, political and cultural developments were far too diffuse and complex to admit of such simplistic harmonization as suggested by Burckhardt. The Renaissance cannot be reduced to a hall-marked period of history.

If the Renaissance was not a period of history in the Burckhardtian sense, then perhaps, as Ernst Gombrich suggested, it was a movement.[4] There is much to recommend this view of the Renaissance. *The Shorter Oxford English Dictionary* defines a movement as 'a series of actions and endeavours by a body of persons, tending more or less continuously towards some special end'. It could be argued that the 'special end' of the Renaissance was the revival of classical learning which was thought to have been eclipsed during the barbarous Middle Ages. Movements work 'continuously' towards their ends; in other words one follower converts his contemporaries and so on. Again, it could be suggested that Petrarch, the first great Renaissance man, communicated to contemporaries such as Boccaccio his enthusiasm for the classical revival and together they handed on the torch to the next generation in the person of Coluccio Salutati, who in turn inspired younger men such as Niccolò Niccoli, Leonardo Bruni and Poggio Bracciolini. Most importantly, movements are the work of a 'body of persons', and the protagonists of the Renaissance soon acquired a special name: humanists, who were, in contemporary parlance, not lovers of humanity or devotees of man rather than God but rather simply teachers or students of the humanities (known from the fourteenth century as the *studia humanitatis*), or in modern parlance, the classics.

There is little question that Renaissance humanism was a movement: Gombrich's insight into the character of humanism is confirmed by many texts in which leading figures such as Bruni and Poggio speak of the *studia humanitatis* as their particular specialism, thus confirming Renaissance humanism as a self-conscious movement, with a genuine *esprit de corps*.[5] It is sometimes said that the Renaissance is the work of the humanists, and yet the equation of the Renaissance with humanism cannot be quite the whole story. If the Renaissance were only or overwhelmingly the work of humanists attempting to substitute the civilization of antiquity for the culture of the barbarous Middle Ages, then it must be wondered why various Renaissance achievements were so deeply indebted to sources other than classical antiquity. The Renaissance was a complex, hybrid phenomenon, with chronologically and geographically diverse and varied roots. Recent research has shown and will continue to show that there can be no simplistic approach to this heterogeneous series of historical developments. It is impossible to turn the clock back to Burckhardt and see the Renaissance as a block of historical time; if the Renaissance was a chronological hybrid, its point of origin and its ultimate end cannot be determined. Distinctive aspects of the Renaissance can be found in the medieval Byzantine tradition of Greek scholarship, in the revival of classical learning characteristic of twelfth-century western Europe, in the practices of medieval rhetoric or *ars dictaminis* (not to mention Jewish and Arabic learned activity); scholars following in the wake of the Renaissance revival of classical antiquity can be found throughout the early modern period of European history and well into the nineteenth or twentieth century. (It could be suggested, without an absurd degree of distortion, that more recent figures such as Francesco Novati, Remigio Sabbadini, Roberto Weiss, Arnaldo Momigliano, Carlo Dionisotti or Paul Oskar Kristeller represented latter-day Renaissance humanists.)

On the other hand, Renaissance humanism, as a coherent and concrete historical movement, was anything but a hybrid. Burckhardt too regarded humanism as a discrete phenomenon; for him, the movement was not fundamentally concerned with the revival of antiquity: 'the essence of the phenomena might still have been the same without the classical revival', which had 'been one-sidedly chosen as the name to sum up the whole period'. Burckhardt painted a portrait of the humanists in which the colours and contours of his subjects were not academic or scholarly but anthropological: superficially the humanists might have been 'mediators between their own age and a venerated antiquity', but their essential definition was human and personal: 'malicious self-conceit', 'abominable profligacy', 'irreligion', 'licentious excess'. What the humanists revived from the mid-thirteenth to the early sixteenth century was, for Burckhardt, not classical antiquity but rather man himself.[6]

Burckhardt's thesis dominated the interpretation of humanism for at least half a century after the publication of the *Civilization*. His definition of humanism and the Renaissance in human, not in scholarly or literary, terms, was adopted by influential figures such as Symonds, Villari, Goetz, Taine and Müntz.[7] Burckhardt had posited a political explanation of the origins of Renaissance individualism, which in his view was the product of the egoistic and amoral political world of the Italian city-states;[8] this particular facet of the Burckhardtian synthesis was soon challenged by a succession of writers, such as Renan, Thode, Gebhart and most eruditely by Burdach, who saw the origins of the Renaissance in the religious world of medieval spirituality.[9] Yet despite their disagreement over the sources of the Renaissance, these early revisionists still carried on with Burckhardt's anthropological approach to the nature of humanism. Similarly Burckhardtian in conception was much of the so-called 'revolt of the medievalists' which gained momentum particularly in the first half of the twentieth century; their continued emphasis on the precocious discovery of the world and of man, on a 'truly Renaissance spirit', individualism, sensuality, rationalism, realism are all obviously Burckhardtian categories of analysis.[10] Even the attempt to deny to the Renaissance the status of a genuine new historical period, devaluing it instead as the decaying afterlife of the Middle Ages – a type of *histoire des mentalités* most famous in the writings of Huizinga[11] – is still painting with a Burckhardtian brush.

Despite all this revisionism, moreover, it is important to remember that Burckhardt continued to have his unabashed champions well into the twentieth century, not least two of the most famous German refugees in modern American academic life – Ernst Cassirer and Hans Baron. Individualism is a central theme of Cassirer's study of the philosophy of humanism; moreover, his emphasis on the interrelation of the elements of a culture and a historical period – 'society, state, religion, church, art, science' – is preeminently Burckhardtian in conception.[12] It might seem paradoxical to connect Baron, who of course highlighted the republican strand of humanism, with Burckhardt, who saw despotism as the determining political influence in Renaissance Italy; nevertheless, Baron's preoccupation with a sharp contrast between the Middle Ages and the Renaissance ('a fundamental transformation of *Weltanschauung*'),[13] with the emergence of modern secular and lay values, with the decline of medieval concepts such as Guelphism and Empire, not to mention his denigration of pure classicism and his attempts to link together the various strands of cultural history (political and historical thought, artistic realism, positive valuation of wealth) – all these features of his interpretation of early Italian humanism are solidly within the Burckhardtian tradition.[14]

However, it is particularly in the Italian scholarly tradition – most notably in the field of the history of philosophy – that Burckhardt has continued to enjoy the most powerful resonance. This is in one sense ironic, since Renaissance philosophy was egregiously ignored in the *Civilization*.[15] Yet Burckhardt had declared,

> Every period of civilization which forms a complete and consistent whole manifests itself not only in political life, in religion, art and science, but also sets its characteristic stamp on social life,[16]

and it has been irrefutably demonstrated by Gombrich that Burckhardt derived this concept of the spirit of the age from the idealist historical philosophy of Hegel.[17] Bertrando Spaventa introduced Hegelian idealism into Italian philosophical circles in the 1860s,[18] and his approach was a determining influence on the two giants of Italian philosophy in the early twentieth century – Croce and Gentile. Croce gave little detailed attention to humanism, although his support for a Hegelian literary historian such as De Sanctis and his implicit criticisms of a pro-Catholic revisionist such as Toffanin added weight to the Burckhardtian tradition in Italy.[19] It was above all Gentile who developed an Hegelian/idealist interpretation of Renaissance humanism in Italy: the Middle Ages had devalued man and life in this world; Italian humanism, by contrast, restored the dignity of man, the potential of the human mind and the value of earthly existence. Gentile thus effectively bolstered the Burckhardtian view of Renaissance Italians as 'the first born among the sons of modern Europe'.[20]

This Burckhardtian/Hegelian approach continues to find powerful support in contemporary Italian philosophical circles. Indeed, the leading Italian post-war Renaissance scholar, Eugenio Garin, was Gentile's protégé; it is not surprising that he has emphasized a coherent outlook in Renaissance humanism, which he sees as a new philosophy of man, in sharp contrast to medieval devaluation of humanity.[21] It also comes as no surprise that Garin has embraced many of Baron's views, including his 'civic humanism';[22] indeed, Garin finds Burckhardt himself particularly sympathetic:

> Humanism consisted in a renewed confidence in man and his possibilities and in an appreciation of man's activity in every possible sense [...] Burckhardt's old and vigorous conception which linked the reaffirmation of man with the reaffirmation of the world, the reaffirmation of the spirit with the reaffirmation of nature, ought to be connected without fear of rhetoric to the old notion that the Renaissance succeeded in bringing about a new harmony. This ideal of the harmony and the measure of a complete man runs [...] through those centuries.[23]

It is also ironic that the most effective and powerful challenge to the Burckhardtian approach to the Renaissance and humanism has come from another of Gentile's protégés from the 1930s, Paul Oskar Kristeller, who offered the most fundamental repudiation of Burckhardt's thesis that Renaissance humanism represented a new philosophy of man. In the single most influential article on Renaissance humanism written last century,[24] Kristeller refuted the interpretation of 'humanism as the new philosophy of the Renaissance, which arose in opposition to scholasticism, the old philosophy of the Middle Ages', declaring 'that the Italian humanists on the whole were neither good nor bad philosophers, but no philosophers at all'. Instead, he saw Renaissance humanism as a literary movement, focusing on grammatical and rhetorical studies; the excursions of humanists into the realm of philosophy were often erratic, amateurish and superficial. Humanism could not have replaced scholasticism as the new philosophy of the Renaissance for the simple reason that scholasticism and Aristotelian philosophy continued to thrive in Italy until the mid-seventeenth century. Because humanism was not a philosophical movement, it could not, for Kristeller, represent a new vision of man:

> If we think or hear of such a topic as 'renaissance concepts of man', we are immediately reminded of a view of the Renaissance period that is widespread and has often been repeated: the Renaissance, according to this view, had a special interest in, and concern with, man and his problems. Very often, and in my view mistakenly, this notion is associated with the phenomenon called Renaissance humanism, and in stressing the difference which distinguishes the Renaissance from the period preceding it, it has been pointedly asserted that the thought of the Renaissance was man-centered, whereas medieval thought was God-centered.[25]

For Kristeller, the essential focus of Renaissance humanism was precisely what Burckhardt had rejected: the revival of antiquity.[26]

The great merit of Kristeller's interpretation of Renaissance humanism – indeed the key to its lasting appeal – is his philological study of primary sources; discarding modern meanings whereby 'almost any kind of concern with human values is called "humanistic"',[27] Kristeller returned to contemporary usage of the late fifteenth century when the term *humanista* was invented to designate a teacher of the humanities, on the analogy of such medieval university labels as *legista, jurista, canonista* or *artista*. Although the term humanism was a nineteenth-century coinage,

Kristeller connected *humanista* with a defined group of subjects, the *studia humanitatis*,[28] a literary programme, focused on grammar and rhetoric and clearly distinguished from philosophical, mathematical, medical, scientific and theological studies.

The definition of humanism is of crucial importance in understanding its origins. In a recent book on the birth of humanism and its early development,[29] Ronald Witt has highlighted Latin poetic style as its key feature:

> My decision to center my discussion of humanism on stylistic change derives [...] from my conviction that a litmus for identifying a humanist was his intention to imitate ancient Latin style. At the least, a dedication to stylistic imitation initiated the destabilization of an author's own linguistic universe through his contact with that of antiquity. As a consequence, I do not regard as humanists those contemporaries who were engaged in historical and philological research on ancient culture but who showed no sign of seeking to emulate ancient style, but rather I consider them antiquarians.[30]

This definition focuses on the implicit, rather than the explicit, meaning of humanism. The nature of every historical phenomenon is not clearly articulated by contemporaries, if only because for them its essential features were so obvious as to require no explanation. In the case of humanism, any moderately informed researcher can detect the presence of a humanist text simply through its Latin: by attempting to show his readers that he is affiliating himself, however imperfectly, with the Latin style of the ancients as opposed to the moderns (or medievals in modern parlance), a writer is making an implicit declaration of his affinity with the humanist movement.

Both Kristeller's and Witt's definitions have their advantages and disadvantages. Witt's helps to identify the novel aims of the humanist movement and to distinguish humanists from their medieval forerunners, while Kristeller's tends to assimilate humanism with the medieval disciplines from which it emerged. Kristeller was aware that his emphasis on humanism as a discipline tended to blur the boundaries between medieval and Renaissance learning. He attempted to overcome this difficulty dialectically. Excluding from his definition precursors of the Italian humanists, such as ultramontane classical scholars and writers of the twelfth century, as well as Italian practitioners of the *ars dictaminis* from the twelfth and earlier thirteenth centuries, he put forward the thesis that humanism was fully born only when ultramontane classicism was merged with Italian rhetorical activities at the end of the thirteenth century.[31] But Kristeller's definition has the advantage not only of contemporary usage, but also of embracing a wide range of activities, writers and scholars under the umbrella of a broad discipline. By applying Kristeller's definition, signs of early humanism in the later thirteenth and early fourteenth centuries could be detected not only in the areas highlighted by Witt, such as Lovato Lovati's attempts to imitate classical verse forms or in Albertino Mussato's revival of Senecan tragedy, but also in Brunetto Latini's study and use of Ciceronian orations and rhetorical texts, in Bartolomeo Benincasa's and Giovanni Buonandrea's lectures on Ciceronian rhetorical handbooks, in Giovanni del Virgilio's teaching of the classical Latin poets, in Geri d'Arezzo's and Giovanni de Matociis' early efforts at critical literary history or in Geremia da Montagnone's and Benvenuto Campesani's reading of rare Latin authors such as Catullus and Martial.

Witt's narrower focus on Latin style as the 'litmus' of humanism can tend to exclude rather than include. While scholars such as Kristeller, Roberto Weiss[32] or Berthold Louis Ullman[33] have recounted the early history of humanism, Witt's definition leads to a preoccupation with distinguishing who and who were not in fact the first humanists: his account can become less a history of humanism than of those figures who meet his criteria as humanists. Thus Witt rejects the humanist credentials of Geremia da Montagnone, despite his 'knowledge of a wide range of ancient authors',[34] as well as of Riccobaldo of Ferrara,[35] Giovanni de Matociis and Benzo d'Alessandria.[36]

Particularly provocative is Witt's treatment of the origins of humanism. For Witt, Latin literacy thrived in north and central Italy for 'the first five centuries following the fall of Rome [...] Broad strata of the general population had frequent contact with documents, and elementary Latin literacy seems to have been relatively widespread.' This Italian Latin literary culture reached its peak in the eleventh century but was shattered by the Investiture Contest at the end of the eleventh century.[37] For Witt, traditional literary culture was replaced by a new practical and professional educational movement:

> The intellectual life of northern and central Italy in the twelfth century was largely driven by legal-rhetorical concerns and directed by *dictatores* and Roman and canon lawyers [...] The extent of grammar training was generally determined by the humble demands of *ars dictaminis*.[38]

According to Witt, classical studies in Italy lay dormant until the end of the twelfth century:

> [the] fortunes of grammar revived after 1180, when a massive invasion of French scholarly and literary influences transformed the intellectual life of Italy north of Rome. At the height of their glory [...] French grammarians and poets made their major contribution to the brilliant future of letters and scholarship in Italy. After almost a century of playing an auxiliary role to rhetoric, grammatical studies required decades to revive; but the burst of Latin poetic composition in northern Italy by the middle of the thirteenth century shows their vigorous development by that time.[39]

Witt's thesis regarding the origins of Italian humanism is that its seeds were sown at the end of the twelfth century but that they took nearly a hundred years (1180 to 1267–68) to germinate in the person of Lovato Lovati and his fellow Latin classicizing poets in the second half of the thirteenth century.

Witt has persuasively identified the key elements in the background to Italian humanism, especially the decline of medieval Italian classical education and the rise of professional and legal studies. But his account of the way and the chronological order in which these elements combined to give birth to humanism, and particularly his emphasis on the role of French classicism in the dawn of Italian humanism have subsequently been challenged.[40]

One can agree with Witt that there was a thriving classical grammar education prevalent in Italian ecclesiastical schools until the twelfth century. However, from that point new evidence does not substantiate Witt's picture of a rapid decline in classical education in Italy nor of a collapse of ecclesiastical grammar schools there during the twelfth century. On the contrary, evidence suggests a coexistence during the twelfth century of a classically based grammar education in ecclesiastical schools together with a rising non-classical education focused on the *ars dictaminis* and professional study. This evidence can be summarized as follows: (1) a survey of Italian manuscript schoolbooks of Latin classical authors now preserved in Florentine libraries shows a strong presence for the twelfth century,[41] a result confirmed by a further continuing survey outside Florence;[42] (2) the anti-classical polemics of the eminent Bolognese professor of rhetoric, Boncompagno da Signa (c.1165–c.1240) at the turn of the thirteenth century, arguing for a liberation of rhetoric from dependence on Roman authors, would make little sense, if these classical authors had not constituted the staple of the Italian educational curriculum before Boncompagno strode forth as a radical modernizer.[43]

There is further difference of emphasis regarding the nature of French influence in Italy at the turn of the thirteenth century. Witt recognizes overwhelmingly the impact of French classicism here. France had been at the heart of the antique revival now generally known as the Twelfth-Century Renaissance, one of whose major centres had been the so-called school of Orléans. There is no doubt that Aurelianism (that is, Orléanism) penetrated the papal chancery, and the Latin elegy (1193) by the period's most important Italian poet, Henry of Settimello, is not only inspired by classical models (Ovid, Vergil, Horace) but also by the French neo-classicizing Latin poets of the twelfth century (Walter of Châtillon, Alain of Lille, Matthew of Vendôme). But there was a more powerful and lasting French influence at the turn of the thirteenth century. This is the new-style logical grammar, developed in twelfth-century Paris by masters such as William of Conches and particularly Petrus Helias. This Parisian grammar was given a decisively anti-classical turn by the arch-enemy of Aurelianism, Alexander of Villedieu, in his verse grammar, *Doctrinale* (1199). This work aimed to displace the traditional basis of grammar, the study of the Roman classics, and replace it with a new grammar based on logic and philosophy. Although *Doctrinale* and the other great French verse grammar, Evrard of Béthune's *Graecismus* (1216), were both northern French works, they reached the Italian schoolroom rapidly in the thirteenth century, when the most important school grammarians not only cited these texts extensively, drawing from them their entire theoretical and practical approach to the subject, but also produced several explicitly named imitations.[44]

At the turn of the thirteenth century, these two conflicting approaches openly clashed, as is clear from the polemics of Boncompagno. On the one hand, there was classicism, traditional to the Italian grammar schoolroom and reinforced by the influx of Aurelianism from France at the end of the twelfth century. On the other, there was anti-classicism, represented by the growing practical and utilitarian tendencies of the native Italian *ars dictaminis*, culminating in Boncompagno's hostility to Aurelianism, and reinforced by the influx of Parisian logical and non-authorial grammar in the wake of Alexander of Villedieu and Evrard of Béthune. There was little doubt about the struggle's outcome as far as Italy was concerned. The thirteenth century not only witnessed the high-water mark of Italian economic and civic growth, requiring a streamlined education system to service the ever-expanding demands of commerce, industry and civic administration; it also saw the definitive establishment of a network of professional universities, whose emphasis on the practical training of lawyers and physicians required rapid fluency in basic Latin, not a profound knowledge of the classical authors.

Anti-classicism is portrayed as triumphant in thirteenth-century Italy according to the famous metaphorical poem by Henri d'Andeli, *La bataille des .VII. ars*, where among the forces ranged against grammar and the authors is rhetoric, marshalling many Lombard knights; the Lombards following rhetoric rode together with dialectic, wounding many honest enemies from the authorial camp.[45] This collapse of classical education in thirteenth-century Italy is confirmed by the recently published survey of schoolbooks now housed in Florentine libraries. In comparison with the forty-one manuscripts of classical Latin authors produced as schoolbooks in twelfth-century Italy, the figure for the next century drops to a total of only ten.[46] This pattern, to some extent, mirrors the drop in overall numbers of classical manuscripts being produced in Europe as a whole in the thirteenth century,[47] but the extremity of the fall suggests that the shift away from the classics was particularly cataclysmic in Italian schools of the thirteenth century.[48] In place of the authors there now burgeoned practical manuals for the study of secondary Latin in thirteenth-century Italy, a genre which had hardly before existed south of the Alps. In none of these works did direct study or citation of the ancients prevail; on the contrary, the methods used were the logical approach to language imported from Paris.

If collapsing, not rising, classicism was the prevailing culture of Italian education in the early thirteenth century, how then can the emergence of humanism beginning with Lovato later in that same century be explained? Here Witt's focus on the rise of Provençal and vernacular poetry in early thirteenth-century Italy is crucial. This period is famous for the rise of the Italian vernacular, and this movement corresponds exactly to the anti-classicism characteristic of Italian grammar and rhetoric teaching in schools and universities at the same time. What Lovato's humanism represented was a reaction against the overwhelming anti-classicism of the preceding generations, as typified by vernacular and Provençal poetry:

Lovato dei Lovati [...] implied that the popularity of vernacular poetry spurred him to write Latin poetry out of a spirit of competition. So he suggested in a letter that he wrote about 1290 to his friend, Bellino Bissolo, a Latin poet who, perhaps only for the purpose of argument, was apparently willing to champion the vernacular against Lovato's criticisms. Lovato told Bellino [...] he had come across a singer [...] 'bellowing the battles of Charlemagne and French exploits' in French, 'gaping in barbarous fashion, rolling them out as he pleased, no part of them in their proper order, songs relying on no effort'. Nevertheless, the listeners had hung on every word.

While recognizing the wisdom of maintaining the middle course between writing verses for the few and for the many, Lovato declared that 'if you must err on one side, it should be on the side of daring' [...] The obvious reference here was to his intention to write his poetry in Latin as opposed to the vernacular.

> Do you despise him [the courageous poet] because he believes that one must follow in the footsteps of the ancient poets (*veterum vestigia vatum*) [...] I won't change my mind. I stand fast, as is my habit, and I won't correct the vice of my long disease.

This letter of ca. 1290 conveys the élitism of Lovato, who looked down on vernacular literature as inferior to Latin [...] Although the immediate antagonist was French poetry – Provençal poetry commonly enjoyed higher status – given Lovato's loyalty to the *veterum vestigia vatum*, there can be no doubt that he considered Provençal poetry also inferior to Latin verse. More generally, the letter indicates the creative tension between vernacular and Latin poetry at the dawn of humanism and injects an element of competition into the mixture of causes leading to the rise of a new Latin poetry around 1250.[49]

Witt is right to see Lovato's humanism as a reaction, one, however, which was not just against the vernacular but also opposed to the anti-classicism of the entire 'secolo senza Roma', to quote Toffanin,[50] or 'l'exil des belles lettres', in the words of Gilson.[51] In line with his definition of humanism in terms of Latin style and classical imitation, Witt resolutely rejects literary developments in prose writing as contributing to or signalling the emergence of humanism.[52] He is certainly correct to maintain that prose literary forms remained tenaciously tied to the medieval patterns of *dictamen* throughout the thirteenth century, and that classicized Latin prose-writing (with a few exceptions such as Geri d'Arezzo and Petrarch's familiar letters) did not emerge until the turn of the fifteenth century.[53] However, other scholars seem not to share Witt's focus on style and imitation as the only indicators of burgeoning classicism. Noteworthy here are several students of Ciceronian rhetorical theory. 'In the second half of the thirteenth century', wrote James Banker, 'Ciceronian rhetoric began to play a more prominent role in certain Italian writers' understanding of persuasion [...] Brunetto Latini in the 1260s revived the precepts of Cicero's teaching.'[54] For Virginia Cox, the

> later thirteenth and early fourteenth centuries in Italy saw a marked new interest in the study of Ciceronian rhetorical theory, in both Latin and vernacular contexts [...] in defiance of recent Italian traditions of rhetorical instruction, both [Brunetto Latini's *Rettorica* and Bono Giamboni's *Fiore di rettorica*] are based more or less directly on classical Roman sources [...] it seems justifiable to speak of a classicizing reorientation of the medieval Italian rhetorical tradition in this period.[55]

John Ward accepts their emphasis on Latini's originality, speaking of a 'revival of classical rhetorical theory': 'Brunetto appreciated the limitations of *dictamen* theory [...] and the need for classical rhetorical theory'.[56] Cox is disinclined

> to interpret this turn towards Ciceronian rhetoric as a protohumanistic phenomenon. There is a certain superficial appeal to this suggestion. The history of the study of Ciceronian rhetoric may be relatively neatly aligned with that of the study of classical literary texts, which, having enjoyed a first phase of intense cultivation in eleventh- and twelfth-century France, [...] was then taken up with enthusiasm in late thirteenth and fourteenth-century Italy [...] It would be mistaken, however, to make too much of these parallels between the literary and rhetorical cases. The French classicizing rhetorical learning of the twelfth century was transplanted in Italy into a powerful existing rhetorical culture, closely bound up with Italian political and civic life and distinguished by its modernizing, utilitarian character. There was little place in this rhetorical-political culture for that impulse to a formal emulation of classical models which is the distinguishing trait of Italian humanism.[57]

Instead, Cox sees as crucial 'the increasing prominence within the civic culture of the Italian communes of practices of oral and adversarial rhetoric which the dominant instrument of rhetorical instruction in this period, the *ars dictaminis*, was ill-equipped to teach'.[58] There is no doubt that the adversarial, oral debate and speech-making characteristic of Italian city life made classical rhetorical theory more attractive in the later thirteenth century, but this can be only part of the story. Indeed,

Cox's thesis has a number of shortcomings, which can be summarized as follows: (1) public debate – whether in general assemblies of the people or in communal councils – had been a feature of Italian civic life since the emergence of the communes at the beginning of the twelfth century. Why then did *ars dictaminis*, a form of rhetoric ostensibly geared more to the letter than to the adversarial speech, take increasing hold during the first 150 years of communal history, and why was it only after 1250 that Ciceronian rhetoric, with its adversarial bias, was revived?[59] (2) Cox exaggerates the weakness of adversarial rhetoric in *dictamen*, citing herself adversarial debates in dictaminal collections by Matteo de' Libri, the *Oculus pastorialis* and Giovanni da Vignano's *Flore del parlare*.[60] (3) There is no surviving evidence of rhetorical practice in communal assemblies from the later thirteenth and early fourteenth centuries to substantiate a connection between classical rhetorical theory and adversarial communal debating: 'we have no reliable documentary evidence of the form that council speaking is likely to have assumed'.[61] (4) Cox places too much emphasis on the objective divergence between classical adversarial rhetoric and *dictamen* and on the objective differences between the non-classical prose of the later thirteenth-century Ciceronian rhetoricians and the later Italian humanists. Strong intrinsic contrasts of course exist in both these cases, but such distinctions can overlook the subjective appeal of the classics. Classical rhetoric (as well as classical prose and poetry in general) may have had a powerful symbolic, emblematic attraction for writers such as Latini or Lovato. The chronological concurrence between the return to Cicero on the part of Latini, Jacques de Dinant, Giovanni di Bonandrea and Bartolomeo Benincasa, and the revival of interest in other classical authors evident in Lovato, Mussato, Geri, Riccobaldo, Geremia, Giovani de Matociis, Benvenuto Campesani and Benzo is too striking to be dismissed as mere superficial coincidence.

The ups and downs of the classical heritage from antiquity itself until the Renaissance and beyond were seldom isolated from wider cultural, social and historical currents. The decline of classical learning and education in the sixth and seventh centuries – associated as it was with efforts by the likes of Gregory the Great or St Benedict to purge early medieval society of the vestiges of paganism[62] – or the reversal of the twelfth-century Renaissance – brought about by the triumphant lay culture of the communes and the rise of the civic professional classes – are two prominent illustrations of how the history of classical learning was part of the broader historical mainstream. But it must be wondered whether an emphasis on literary dimensions alone in considering the birth of humanism can obscure its wider context. Perhaps one should ask what motivated the early humanists to turn their backs on contemporary thirteenth- and fourteenth-century culture. It must be wondered whether there was a social and political context to early humanism, indeed to what extent the birth of humanism had ideological resonances.

In this context, perhaps one should recall the above-mentioned passage that Witt has highlighted, demonstrating Lovato's rejection of the vernacular and call for a return to antique Latinity. Lovato contraposed a singer 'bellowing the battles of Charlemagne and French exploits' in French, 'gaping in barbarous fashion, rolling them out as he pleased, no part of them in their proper order, songs relying on no effort' with '[the courageous poet] [...] [who] believes that one must follow in the footsteps of the ancient poets (*veterum vestigia vatum*)'. Brunetto Latini could proudly identify with Cicero, the new man who rose to confront the conspiratorial Catiline: '[Marcus] Tulius [Cicero] was a new citizen of Rome and not of great stature; but through his wisdom he rose to such eminence that all Rome was commanded by his words'.[63] Latini's formulation recalls Sallust's description of Cicero as 'homo novus' (a new man), previously passed over for the consulate owing to the 'invidia' (envy) and 'superbia' (arrogance) of the 'nobilitas' (nobility);[64] Sallust's anti-aristocratic, pro-popular sentiments complemented Cicero's own *arriviste* biography, giving classical history and literature a powerful social resonance in mid-thirteenth-century Italy. For both Lovato and Latini a return to classical authors or classical language was connected with antipathy to contemporary aristocratic society dominated by courtly mores and hierarchical values; in both cases, it is hard not to detect a reaction against the political dominance of the aristocratic élite in the Italian communes.

Lovato rejected the contemporary vernacular, at least in part, because of its associations with the upper echelons of the social order, and similarly it could be argued that Latini favoured classical rhetorical theory over medieval *dictamen* to some extent for similarly anti-hierarchical motives. The *ars dictaminis* added a new section to the Ciceronian doctrine of the parts of a rhetorical composition: the *salutatio* (greeting). Classical orations began with an *exordium* (introduction) whose purpose was to win the audience's sympathy through various standard arguments (for example, by assuming false modesty [*topos humilis*]), but medieval *dictamen* predisposed the recipient of a letter by deferring to rank, as spelled out in the salutation. The *ars dictaminis* tended to devalue the *exordium* at the expense of the *salutatio*, whereas classical rhetorical theory assumed that neither speaker nor audience commanded authority through standing: it was argument that counted.[65] Latini rejected his predecessors' devaluation of the *exordium*, restoring its full treatment according to the norms of classical rhetorical theory, and it is tempting again to see Latini's wider anti-hierarchical sympathies at work here.

What were the social backgrounds of the first humanists? Latini was Florentine chancellor to the popular regime of the *primo popolo*, exiled after the return of the Florentine aristocrats to power in 1260 but subsequently to enjoy a prominent political role in the popular guild regime established after 1282.[66] Lovato 'was the son of Rolando di Lovato, a notary, and his brother Alberto was also a notary; the fact that the family name established itself only in Lovato's generation suggests that the family background was a modest one'.[67] Geri d'Arezzo was similarly a notary/lawyer from a humble Aretine family, who never even developed a surname. 'Mussato was of poor and humble origins; his acknowledged father was [...] a court messenger who lived in the northern suburbs of Padua.'[68] All the figures associated with humanism from 1260 to 1350 emerged from the notarial/legal class: not one came from a prominent aristocratic family. One could continue in this vein regarding the family origins of Petrarch, Boccaccio et al. This kind of social complexion for early humanists even persisted into the early Florentine period. The leading figure of militant classicism and hostility to vernacular culture was Niccolò Niccoli, whose family became enriched from the wool industry in the fourteenth century but commanded neither wealth nor political prominence in the fifteenth; he was connected with an anti-élitist conspiracy as early as 1400,[69] and he became a prominent Medici partisan. Most practising Florentine humanists were either social arrivistes (Palmieri, Manetti)[70] or emigrants from the Florentine dominions (Salutati, Bruni, Poggio, Marsuppini and Accolti). Leon Battista Alberti's family, though once at the heart of the Florentine élite, had been cast out as exiles in 1393; one has to wonder whether his own antipathy to courtly and aristocratic education and his advocacy of Latinity in its place represented a personal and subjective reversal of social affiliation, caused by his own fate as an exile:

> And who does not know that the first thing useful for children are (Latin) letters [...] And this is so important that someone unlettered, however much a gentleman, will be considered nothing but a country bumpkin. And I should like to see young noblemen with a book in hand more frequently than with a hawk [...] If there is anything which goes beautifully with gentility or which gives the greatest distinction to human life or adds grace, authority and name to a family, it is surely

(Latin) letters, without which no one can be reputed to possess true gentility.[71]

For Alberti, humanism was, at least in a Florentine context, an anti-élitist, anti-aristocratic ideology.

By the fifteenth century, however, Alberti's anti-aristocratic vision of humanism had become, in the rest of Italy and even in Florence itself, an anachronism. After 1400, the humanists would achieve a remarkable reversal. The Italian (and European) idea of a gentleman was redefined in the circle which had originally gathered round Salutati and became even more influential after his death. This group included *gente nuova* such as Niccoli, but it also numbered aristocrats such as Palla Strozzi. In order to vindicate either their own predilections or their own social position, both social elements wished to assimilate classical learning with upper-class status. In such circles, humanist scholarship became an essential ingredient of gentility, a necessary qualification for membership of the social élite – a view which was derived from the study of the ancients themselves. The classical texts which provide the most compelling portrait of the ideal Roman gentleman – Cicero's *Orator* and *De oratore* and Quintilian's *Institutio* – were either studied for the first time or with renewed vigour at the turn of the fifteenth century; from such sources the Florentine *avant-garde* was confirmed in its view that no one should command a high social position, no one could rightfully call himself a gentleman, no one was qualified to rule, without a classical education. Such ideas constituted the core of the first and most influential of all humanist educational treatises, Vergerio's *De ingenuis moribus*, written c.1402 in the wake of the author's stay in Florence and of his association with Salutati's circle as a pupil of the Greek scholar Manuel Chrysoloras. Vergerio's work aimed to guide the education of society's leaders, whether citizens, princes or courtiers; it established classical learning as an essential qualification to merit or retain political power and social leadership. This new humanist ideal of education could be associated with any leader or élite, republican or monarchical, and therefore was adaptable throughout Italy and ultimately throughout Europe. As Anthony Grafton and Lisa Jardine have suggested, the greatest humanist teacher, Guarino, who frequented Chrysoloras' lessons too, later teaching in Florence from 1410 to 1414, was also soon advertising the humanist claims to educate society's rulers, as in this letter to a *podestà* of Bologna in 1419:

I understand that when civil disorder recently aroused the people of Bologna to armed conflict you showed the bravery and eloquence of a soldier as well as you had previously meted out a judge's just sentence [...] You therefore owe no small thanks to the Muses with whom you have been on intimate terms since your boyhood, and by whom you were brought up. They taught you how to carry out your tasks in society. Hence you are living proof that the Muses rule not only musical instruments but also public affairs.[72]

Grafton and Jardine's interpretation of mature humanism as the ideology of the élite, first articulated in 1982,[73] had in fact been suggested, at least in embryo, three years earlier by Lauro Martines.[74] Paradoxically, however, humanism had perhaps not always been the 'program for the ruling classes': in its origins, it may have represented the outcry of the aspiring middling orders, struggling to be heard in a forum dominated since the turn of the thirteenth century by the anti-classical voices of the Italian aristocracy.[75]

## notes

1. The best treatment of Burckhardt's influence in the first century after publication remains W. K. Ferguson, *The Renaissance in Historical Thought: Five Centuries of Interpretation* (Cambridge, MA, 1948).
2. Jacob Burckhardt, *The Civilization of the Renaissance in Italy* (New York, 1958), 5.6, p. 250.
3. See for example C. Morris, *The Discovery of the Individual, 1050–1200* (London, 1972).
4. E. H. Gombrich, 'In Search of Cultural History', in his *Ideals and Idols: Essays on Values in History and in Art* (London, 1979), pp. 50–1 (first published in 1969).
5. See the anthology of citations published by B. G. Kohl, 'The Changing Concept of the *studia humanitatis* in the Early Renaissance', *Renaissance Studies*, VI (1992) 185–209.
6. Burckhardt, *Civilization*, 3.1, p. 175 and 3.11, pp. 272–4.
7. Ferguson, *Renaissance in Historical Thought*, pp. 198–213, 226–7, 245–50.
8. Burckhardt, *Civilization*, 1.1, pp. 21–142.
9. Ferguson, *Renaissance in Historical Thought*, pp. 297–311.
10. Ferguson, *Renaissance in Historical Thought*, pp. 333–41.
11. Ferguson, *Renaissance in Historical Thought*, pp. 373–6; J. Huizinga, *The Waning of the Middle Ages* (London, 1990, first published in 1924).
12. Ferguson, *Renaissance in Historical Thought*, pp. 218–20; E. Cassirer, *The Individual and the Cosmos in Renaissance Philosophy* (Oxford, 1963, first published in 1926).
13. H. Baron, 'Moot Problems of Renaissance Interpretation: An Answer to Wallace K. Ferguson', *Journal of the History of Ideas*, XIX (1958) 26–34, at p. 28.
14. H. Baron, 'Franciscan Poverty and Civic Wealth as Factors in the Rise of Humanistic Thought', *Speculum*, XIII (1938) 1–37; H. Baron, *The Crisis of the*

*Early Italian Renaissance: Civic Humanism and Republican Liberty in an Age of Classicism and Tyranny* (Princeton, 1955, revised edition 1966).

15. P. O. Kristeller, 'Changing Views of the Intellectual History of the Renaissance since Jacob Burckhardt', in T. Helton, ed., *The Renaissance: A Reconsideration of the Theories and Interpretations of the Age* (Madison, WI, 1961), pp. 27–52, at p. 30.
16. Burckhardt, *Civilization*, 5.1, p. 230.
17. Gombrich, 'In Search of Cultural History'.
18. Ferguson, *Renaissance in Historical Thought*, p. 222.
19. Ferguson, *Renaissance in Historical Thought*, pp. 240–1, 350.
20. Ferguson, *Renaissance in Historical Thought*, pp. 222–3, 240–3, 350.
21. E. Garin, *Italian Humanism*, trans. P. Munz (Oxford, 1965, first published in 1947).
22. Garin, *Italian Humanism*.
23. Garin, *Italian Humanism*, p. 221.
24. P. O. Kristeller, 'Humanism and Scholasticism in the Italian Renaissance', in his *Renaissance Thought and its Sources* (New York, 1979), pp. 85–105 (first published in 1944).
25. Kristeller, *Renaissance Thought and its Sources*, p. 167.
26. P. O. Kristeller, *Eight Philosophers of the Italian Renaissance* (Stanford, 1964), pp. 147–65.
27. Kristeller, *Renaissance Thought and its Sources*, p. 21.
28. Kristeller, *Renaissance Thought and its Sources*, pp. 98–9.
29. Ronald Witt, *'In the Footsteps of the Ancients': The Origins of Humanism from Lovato to Bruni* (Leiden, 2000).
30. Witt, *In the Footsteps*, p. 22.
31. Kristeller, *Eight Philosophers*, pp. 160–2.
32. Roberto Weiss, *Il primo secolo dell'umanesimo: studi e testi* (Rome, 1949); Roberto Weiss, *The Dawn of Humanism in Italy* (London, 1947), reprinted with updated bibliography in *Bulletin of the Institute of Historical Research*, XLII (1969) 1–17.
33. B. L. Ullman, 'Some Aspects of the Origin of Italian Humanism', and 'The Sorbonne Library and the Italian Renaissance', in his *Studies in the Italian Renaissance* (Rome, 1955), pp. 27–54.
34. Witt, *In the Footsteps*, p. 113.
35. Witt, *In the Footsteps*, p. 114.
36. Witt, *In the Footsteps*, p. 168.
37. Witt, *In the Footsteps*, pp. 14–16.
38. Witt, *In the Footsteps*, pp. 16–17.
39. Witt, *In the Footsteps*, p. 17. See also R. Witt, 'Medieval Italian Culture and the Origins of Humanism as a Stylistic Ideal', in *Renaissance Humanism: Foundations, Forms, and Legacy*, ed. A. Rabil (Philadelphia, 1988), I, pp. 44–50.
40. R. Black, 'The Origins of Humanism, its Educational Context and its Early Development: A Review of Ronald Witt's *In the Footsteps of the Ancients*', *Vivarium*, XL (2002) 272–97, particularly pp. 275–86.
41. R. Black, *Humanism and Education in Medieval and Renaissance Italy: Tradition and Innovation in Latin Schools from the Twelfth to the Fifteenth Century* (Cambridge 2001), pp. 186–92.

42. So far, I have personally identified the following numbers of twelfth-century Italian manuscript schoolbooks of classical Latin authors now housed outside Florence: Cesena (1); London (10); Milan (18); Montecassino (4); Naples (9); Oxford (3); Padua (2); Pavia (2); Perugia (1); Poppi (2); Ravenna (1); Rome (8); Turin (6); Udine (2); Vatican (30); Venice (7); Verona (1). This handlist will appear in my forthcoming article on the origins of humanism in an anthology entitled *Interpretations of Humanism*, ed. A. Mazzocco, to be published by Brill.

43. Black, 'Origins', 278–9; Black, *Humanism and Education*, pp. 192–3. See also R. Witt, 'Boncompagno and the Defense of Rhetoric', *The Journal of Medieval and Renaissance Studies*, XVI (1986) 1–31.

44. Black, *Humanism and Education*, pp. 70 ff.

45. L. Paetow, ed., *The Battle of the Seven Arts: A French Poem by Henri d'Andeli* (Berkeley, 1914), p. 43, verses 68–9; p. 51, verses 224–5, 228–9.

46. Black, *Humanism and Education*, p. 192.

47. See L. Reynolds, ed., *Texts and Transmission* (Oxford, 1983), p. xxvii, giving a drop of 50 per cent in the overall number of manuscripts cited in the book (from 280 to 140) between the twelfth and thirteenth centuries.

48. Of possible significance is the outcome of the study of parchment fragments of literary texts now housed in the Archivio di Stato di Udine. 241 such fragments have been identified, 16 of which come from classical Latin literary texts. Two of these originate from twelfth-century, but none from thirteenth-century, Italy. See C. Scalon, *Libri, scuole e cultura nel Friuli medioevale* (Padua, 1987), pp. 255–6 and 260. For an analysis of the origins of these manuscripts differing from Scalon's, see Black in Mazzocco, ed., forthcoming.

49. Witt, *In the Footsteps*, pp. 53–4.

50. G. Toffanin, *Il secolo senza Roma* (Bologna, 1942).

51. E. Gilson, *Philosophie au Moyen Âge* (Paris, 1962), pp. 400–12.

52. Witt, 'Medieval Italian Culture', pp. 53–4; Witt, 'Civic Humanism and the Rebirth of the Ciceronian Oration', *Modern Language Quarterly*, LI (1990) 167–84.

53. R. Witt, 'Medieval "Ars dictaminis" and the Beginnings of Humanism: A New Construction of the Problem', *Renaissance Quarterly*, XXXV (1982) 27ff.

54. James Banker, 'Giovanni di Bonandrea's *Ars dictaminis* Treatise and the Doctrine of Invention in the Italian Rhetorical Tradition of the Thirteenth and Early Fourteenth Centuries', Ph.D. thesis (University of Rochester, 1971), pp. 110 and 300, cited by John O. Ward, 'Rhetorical Theory and the Rise and Decline of *dictamen* in the Middle Ages and Early Renaissance', *Rhetorica*, XIX (2001) 196.

55. V. Cox, 'Ciceronian Rhetoric in Italy, 1260–1350', *Rhetorica*, XVII (1999) 239–40.

56. Ward, 'Rhetorical Theory', 201–2.

57. Cox, 'Ciceronian Rhetoric', 247–8.

58. Cox, 'Ciceronian Rhetoric', 239.

59. Cox, 'Ciceronian Rhetoric', 259–60.

60. Cox, 'Ciceronian Rhetoric', 256–7.

61. Cox, 'Ciceronian Rhetoric', 260.

62. See Black, *Humanism and Education*, pp. 175–7.

63. Brunetto Latini, *La Rettorica*, I.16, ed. F. Maggini (Florence, 1915), p. 8: 'Tulio era cittadino di Roma nuovo e di non grande altezza; ma per lo suo senno fue in sì alto stato che tutta Roma si tenea alla sua parola'.
64. Sallust, *Bellum Catilinae*, XXIII.5–6.
65. Banker, 'Giovanni di Bonandrea's *Ars dictaminis*', as cited by Ward, 'Rhetorical Theory', 200–1; Cox, 'Ciceronian Rhetoric', 265–71.
66. On Latini's strong popular affiliations and his powerful anti-aristocratic sentiments, see John Najemy, 'Brunetto Latini's "Politica"', *Dante Studies*, CXII (1994) 33–52.
67. J. K. Hyde, *Padua in the Age of Dante* (Manchester, 1966), p. 134.
68. Hyde, *Padua*, pp. 165–6.
69. G. Brucker, *The Civic World of Renaissance Florence* (Princeton, 1977), p. 172.
70. I am indebted for these insights into the social origins of indigenous Florentine humanists to a reading of preliminary chapters of John Najemy's forthcoming *History of Florence*.
71. L. B. Alberti, *Opere volgari*, ed. C. Grayson (Bari, 1960–73), I, pp. 68, 70.
72. Cited and translated by A. Grafton and L. Jardine, *From Humanism to the Humanities* (Cambridge, MA, 1986), p. 2.
73. 'Humanism and the School of Guarino', *Past and Present*, XCVI (1982) 51–80.
74. L. Martines, *Power and Imagination: City-States in Renaissance Italy* (London, 2002, first published in 1979), pp. 210 ff.
75. On the rise of the middle classes (*popolo*) in the Italian communes during the thirteenth century, see Martines, *Power and Imagination*, pp. 45 ff.

# 6

# renaissance humanism and its development in florentine civic culture

## riccardo fubini

In the light of the task which I have been invited to undertake – to review developments in the historiography of the Renaissance since the work on that subject published long ago, in 1948, by W. K. Ferguson – I cannot but feel a sense of bewilderment, as much for the breadth of the subject itself as for the huge number of historical studies that now exist on it. But let me say straight away that I do not believe – and I don't think I'm the only one – that it is any longer possible to talk in general terms about the Renaissance, whether by that term we mean a coherent epoch in history or rather a philosophical or ideological concept. And in this regard it is instructive to note that the debate on the concept of the Renaissance, which lasted from the end of the nineteenth century to the first half of the twentieth, and about which Ferguson wrote at length, was based on a misinterpretation of Jacob Burckhardt's *Civilization of the Renaissance in Italy* (1860), the work which the discussion took as its starting point. Burckhardt was not, as it has become proverbial to repeat, the principal theoretician of the notion of the Renaissance; on the contrary, he disputed it. In effect he contested the idea, which had been revived in the classicist tradition of the French Enlightenment, that the comprehensive reappropriation of antiquity – what was known as the *Renaissance des sciences et des arts* – was the decisive factor in the departure from the 'eternal sleep' of the Middle Ages.[1] The 'so-called *Renaissance*' was for Burckhardt a 'one-sided' idea ('so einseitige Namen') that he used only reluctantly, 'for want of a better one' ('in Ermanlung eines besser').[2] The traditional *Renaissance des sciences et des arts* gave way in Burckhardt's work to a disenchanted vision of the emancipation of the individual from the prescriptive barriers of tradition, with all the moral risks inherent in such a process. Consequently the section on antiquity's 'rebirth' ('Wiedergeburt', which Burckhardt places in inverted commas) was relegated to third place in the economy of his book, after 'The State as a Work of Art' and, indeed, 'The Development of the Individual'.[3] Beyond any conventional conception of progress, Burckhardt perceived, both in the breakdown of trust in the political principle of legitimacy and in the fading of moral and religious certainties, the arrival of modernity; and on this issue he was engaging with his predecessors in the first half of the nineteenth century, from Sismondi to Guglielmo Libri, from Ranke to Georg Voigt, up to Michelet.[4] And yet Burckhardt was aware of the subjective character of his interpretation. As he writes at the beginning of the book, 'the same studies which have served for this work might easily, in other hands, not only receive a wholly different treatment and application, but lead also to essentially different conclusions'.[5] And thus he came to foresee, as he remarked in private to an early reviewer of the *Civilization*, that

> .each historian, once he has been inebriated by the study of that great era, will believe that he sees the whole where in fact he sees only a part. Each will use his own categories, that then will be found poor and defective; each, once the work is completed, would not want merely to retouch it but to rewrite it completely.[6]

Such mental flexibility, and the pluralistic view of history that it implied, were not in evidence in the later, dogmatic approaches of the various kinds of *Kulturgeschichte* (the 'history of culture') and *Geistesgeschichte* (the 'history of the spirit'), although they claimed to derive from Burckhardt; and they were even less in evidence, of course, amongst the medievalists in revolt against Burckhardt's presumption of the modernity of the Italian Renaissance. The paradigms suggested by Burckhardt became rigidified in the ambit of a philosophically oriented historiography, or, in another context, of a sociology of culture, if they were not actually turned upside down, and presented as ennobling attributes of periods or personalities of the Middle Ages.[7] The prevalent trend was to overemphasize Burckhardt's tendency to generalize and to stress the actual value of historical representations, with the result of a genuine historiographical *impasse*.

To come to a period nearer to our own, the conclusions of W. K. Ferguson, partially followed by Denys Hay, generalized too in their own way.[8] According to them the Burckhardtian claim of modernity is of value only in its cultural and artistic dimensions, and not for those social, economic and political developments of a longer period. Thus the picture is presented of an 'age of transition' that is no longer medieval but not yet modern; the age, that is, that the preference today is to describe as 'early modern'. Generalizing also – but for the opposite reason of its marked ideological character – was the thesis concerning 'civic humanism' which was formulated and reiterated insistently by Hans Baron. Under the influence of Werner Jaeger, the author of *Paideia*, with its theory about the value as a model of the Greek *polis*, Baron combined the paradigm of classical republicanism with the typically German emphasis on the dedication (or 'assent') of the individual citizen to the state.[9]

From these arose a historiography of 'grand theses', from the narrowness of which we are still not entirely liberated. This is a subject to which I shall return. Now it is necessary to address one time again the question posed by Ferguson concerning the crisis in the traditional notion of the 'rebirth of good arts and letters', and with it the complementary notion of the 'dark' Middle Ages. The tendency of the historiography after the Second World War was to blunt the ideological impact of such an idea. If the concept of 'rebirth' was confined by Ferguson to the area of literature and the arts alone, it suffered a further diminution in the methodological and programmatic studies of Paul Oskar Kristeller. In direct contrast to the 'modernity' of Burckhardt, Kristeller's work relies on the core idea of 'tradition'. In fact in his work 'humanism' is identified with the tradition, inseparably both medieval and modern, of ancient grammar and rhetoric. This tradition makes no serious attempt to substitute itself for philosophy and thus for the parallel tradition of scholastic Aristotelianism. (Kristeller dedicated some of his studies to the Renaissance tradition of Thomism.)[10] The essential philosophical truths, which were explicated across 'that golden chain' of the metaphysical tradition 'that leads from the Presocratics and Plato to Kant, Hegel and beyond', are protected from the relativization of history, constituting the prototype, the *raison d'être*, of the very idea of tradition: 'This concept of tradition, which finds its expression in the idea of a *philosophia perennis*, may still serve us as a model and guide.'[11] As Kristeller and other scholars such as Campana and Billanovich have stressed, the very word *humanista* owes its formulation to the terminology in use in the world of institutionalized education in the late fifteenth century, just as it was in connection with the programmes of the schools that the abstract term *humanismus* was coined in Germany in the nineteenth century.[12] But the historiographical perspective of Kristeller was clearly of a scholastic – or, if one prefers, neo-scholastic – character. In fact, how can we not recognize in him the imprint of what has been described as that 'scholastic tradition of talking about the sciences as methodologically distinct entities'?[13] It is Kristeller himself who tells us how, in his formalistic conception of the traditions of culture, he was influenced by the theory of literary *genres* of the classical philologists, and particularly by Werner Jaeger, whose Berlin seminar he frequented.[14] Put another way, in the vision of Kristeller, culture is ultimately to be located in the educational context, and disciplinary boundaries are valuable in ordering learning, whilst the paradigms of ancient philology remain implicitly unaltered. Thus his work converges with Giuseppe Billanovich's programme of 'medieval and humanistic philology', conceived as the endeavour to locate humanism in the field of the material transmission of ancient texts, without paying attention to their actual teachings.[15] Yet, in contrast to the essentially philological and literary character of Billanovich and his school, Kristeller's impact was directed towards promoting a well-disciplined history of culture, understood as a tradition of thought and teaching. I refer to studies specifically on the topic of education, such as those of Paul Grendler[16] and Robert Black,[17] or to the researches of John Monfasani on the Greek humanist George of Trebizond, the author of treatises on rhetoric and dialectic that acquired institutional status;[18] or to the vast study of James Hankins on fifteenth-century interpretations of Plato;[19] or again to Ronald Witt, who has recently completed a comprehensive volume on the transition from medieval *dictamen* to humanist rhetoric.[20]

Kristeller thus offered, above all in the Anglo-American world, a strong impulse towards cultural history. And yet I would hesitate before agreeing with James Hankins – perhaps the closest and most productive of his students – that his intellectual orientation represents 'a radically historicized interpretation of Renaissance humanism'.[21] On the contrary, as Hankins himself puts it, one is dealing with an 'overwhelmingly descriptive' treatment of history, where little or no space is conceded to single individuals, and less again to the inevitably subjective aspects of historical interpretation. In short, the postulate of objectivity overrides that of interpretation. It was from here, for example, that the myth was born of 'rhetoric' as a field of activity belonging by definition to the 'humanist', an idea which has found its most provocative version in the work of Jerrold Seigel;[22] as if every culture – medieval or humanistic as it might be – as if any author who demonstrates some originality, is not in possession of his own rhetoric and his own logic, that is, of a will to persuade and to argue, besides a nucleus of ideas with which he identifies himself. From here in turn one arrives at the paradox according to which Lorenzo Valla, the author of a treatise which overturns the fundamental principles of scholastic dialectic (and thus scholastic philosophy as well), has been classified as the advocate of a concept of rhetoric so wide that it invades also the field of philosophy, precisely because of an absence of suitable categories to describe his thought.[23] The fact is that in the post-war historiography of the Renaissance, the desire to re-establish a sense of tradition has largely prevailed over the nineteenth-century emphasis on progress. (Kristeller represents only the most eminent example.) As a result, the disquieting propositions of Burckhardt about the sudden, revolutionary coming of 'modernity' have been placed in the shade, if not actually confuted. The category of 'humanism', understood in the scholastic terms described above, has also contributed to enlarging the chronological ends of the corresponding 'Renaissance'. So suggests the introduction of the English historian E. F. Jacob to an important collection of Renaissance studies of 1960.[24] The 'Renaissance', in the sense of the general aspects of the epoch, has been considered above all from the point of view of descriptive historical sociology, which by definition is a field of *longue durée*. Characteristic in this regard is the successful book of Peter Burke on 'culture and society' in the Italian Renaissance, which refers especially to the French *Annales* school, and in which, unlike some earlier works by the same author, aspects of the economy, of literature and of art are privileged over those of thought, and even more, of politics.[25] For such reasons the old Burckhardtian notion of 'Renaissance' (and let us reiterate it was a term used by him with reservations) seems hardly to survive except in its external framework, where at any rate the production and market of art does not cease to exert its fascination.[26] Admittedly, contestations of an historiographical vision so frozen by convention have not been lacking. Anthony Grafton and Lisa Jardine have denounced the rhetorical character of the traditional celebrations of humanistic education, which they provocatively consider on the level of a status symbol 'of the Establishment'.[27] Nor are there lacking more recent manifestations of a certain tiredness with the vogue, above all American, for studies of the Renaissance, perceived now as artificial. Anthony Molho, one of the most industrious and original historians of Florentine society of the Renaissance, has, for example, written ironically about what appears to him to be a 'Renaissance made in the USA'.[28]

In reality, I would like to add, one is not dealing so much with the particular results of a Renaissance 'made in the USA' as, more generally, with the consequences of an historiography which is always more exacting in terms of archival documentation and philological competence and, certainly from a quantitative point of view, without comparison to that before the Second World War; but in the specific area which concerns us here, this historiography has been confusing its prime motivations. We no longer discuss the 'Renaissance' because the notion represents an era in all its totality (how could it?) but because some of its most eminent representatives assumed the combative emblem of the reborn *humanae literae*, in order to indicate a new, more direct rapport with the cultural heritage of antiquity, quite separate from the institutional transmission of the Middle Ages. In brief, we normally speak of an age of Renaissance because by that term we affirm the presence of a new culture which, with lasting consequences, set itself against the old, yet still surviving, scholastic background. It is evident that an historiography that approaches such an imposing break with tradition with a traditional spirit cannot but confound its own *raison d'être*.

The best demonstration of this is furnished by studies on Petrarch. Once recognized as 'the first modern man', now he appears only as the most eloquent representative of a culture which had already been oriented towards the study of ancient authors since the time of so-called 'Paduan pre-humanism'. And yet Petrarch, quite differently from people like Lovato Lovati, Guglielmo da Pastrengo or Benzo d'Alessandria, cannot be understood without consideration of his direct conflict with the institutional culture of the time, above all the ecclesiastical one. These were the traditions of scholasticism, understood not so much as a specific doctrine as much as a 'unity of method', and thus cutting across individual disciplines.[29] The whole work of Petrarch moves in an inverse direction to the old principles of tradition and authority. Institutional scholasticism identified the 'author' with a text, and thus with a doctrine, which the Schools had the task to explain and transmit. For Petrarch, instead, the author reverts to being a person; and thus his cultural outlook recovers a space for subjectivity, beyond public regulation and hierarchy. The tradition of exegesis seems to Petrarch not directed towards clarifying doctrine but to obscuring the immediacy of the text. From this very theme Petrarch and his followers drew the metaphor, destined to perpetuate itself down the centuries, of the 'dark ages'; a metaphor certainly of a rhetorical and ideological character but which implicitly carries a serious argument about method. And finally, with regard to Christian scholasticism, which was intended to clarify and uphold the texts of the faith, Petrarch opposed the separation not only of sacred and profane literature but also of religious conviction and moral disposition. Their combination presents for him an 'inappropriate mixture' of things in themselves altogether different.[30] In this way profane literature was permitted to rediscover its own autonomous space, beyond its previous subordination, as in the patristic tradition, to the truths of the faith.

As we can see, Petrarch presents a coherent and homogeneous nucleus of transgressive concepts, though as such they were not openly accepted until about thirty years after his death. In fact Petrarch had jealously guarded his entire Latin *opera*, vetoing their publication. The reasons for this delay, and the historical circumstances in which the postulates of Petrarch's ideology became the watchwords of the movement of *humanae literae*, transforming in a few years a culture which was still marked by scholasticism or at least (as was the case with Coluccio Salutati) by notarial and chancery attitudes, is a vital question which still requires adequate analysis.[31]

There is no doubt that one of the essential factors in such a sudden cultural change must be sought in the context of the rapid emergence of new political entities, such as the Visconti dukedom of Milan, the territorial dominion of Florence, and the acquisition of the *Terraferma* by Venice.[32] To this political dimension I will return later. It was in early 1408, Salutati having recently died, that Leonardo Bruni, papal secretary during the Great Schism, felt that the moment had arrived to publicize Petrarch's old polemic against scholasticism. Such is the explicit sense of the tirade delivered in Bruni's *Dialogi ad Petrum Paulum Histrum* by the character Niccolò Niccoli, who bewails the ruin of the good liberal arts and affirms the consequent necessity of giving up the usual means of argumentation or 'disputation' associated with the Schools. Among various other points, 'Niccoli' adumbrates the programme of new Latin translations which will attend to the *sense* ('ad sensum') of the texts of Aristotle, instead of the *literal* translations of the scholastics. This was a programme that was then inaugurated by Bruni himself with his version of Aristotle's *Nichomachean Ethics* of 1417.[33] One of the areas where one senses the break with scholasticism as much in terms of tradition as of teachings, and not only in the formal aspects of argumentation and style, was without doubt the moral arena, following the new version of the *Nichomachean Ethics* which I have just mentioned.[34] I omit here Bruni's own important *Isagogicon moralis disciplinae*,[35] and the dialogue *De avaritia* of Poggio Bracciolini, about which I say more below. These two writings, typical products of the symbiosis of the humanism of Florence and that of the papal *curia*,[36] acted as potent stimuli as well as models for the young Lorenzo Valla, in his dialogue *De voluptate* (*De vero bono* in later redactions), completed in Lombardy in 1431.[37] In making 'pleasure' (*voluptas*, meaning the sensual, emotional and volitive aspects of the soul) the only motive of human action, and in distinguishing that faculty from 'intellect', Valla achieved a radical break with the entire tradition of classical philosophy, Platonic, Aristotelian and Ciceronian (the latter summarized by the stereotype 'Stoicism'). The effect was to repudiate any clearcut division between vice and virtue or, according to Augustinian theology (but Valla did not accept the distinction between the two levels), of sin and grace. From here derives the radically utilitarian approach to moral questions (the religious dimension constitutes for him but one of its aspects) that coincides with the tendency to consider human actions in the multiplicity of their motives, and not to prejudge them according to defined concepts and classifications. From here Valla was inspired to undertake a further, more general philosophical and epistemological enquiry, which was originally entitled *Repastinatio* or 'digging over' (*Retractatio*, or 'total reworking', was the title of later versions) of dialectic and philosophy.[38] In this work, Valla argued for a radical severance of knowing and acting, in so far as the realm of knowing was delimited to a perception of truth and falsity within the data of experience. This has the effect of taking 'knowing' away from the realm of metaphysics, and, even more, from the realm of theology. Such is the sense of admitting as 'transcendent' only *res* (the 'thing'), thus implying the undermining of *ens* (the 'being') and consequently of ontology. *Res*, in as much as it is a transcendent concept, was understood as a pure 'noun', comprehending in itself all other things, like an ideal lexicon embracing all other words and thus the entire range of the knowable. From this resulted a kind of empirical levelling, from the point of view of the data of experience, of the ancient metaphysical hierarchies, and, with even greater reason, a negation of the legitimacy of theology. Religion was treated as a 'faith' and thus, as Valla points out in the *Elegantiae latinae linguae*, as a profound 'persuasion', 'that does not require the comfort of proof'.[39] Valla's treatise on the Donation of Constantine shows that he did not deal only with theory; on the contrary, this dialectical approach fed into militant polemic. In this treatise, commissioned by King Alfonso of Aragon, Valla applies to the field of history the logical dichotomy of the true and false, scornful of the authoritative canonist tradition which had sanctioned the validity of the contested document. These radical positions made Valla an isolated figure; and although his trial before the Neapolitan Inquisition was interrupted by the intervention of the king, Valla was not permitted to publicize his philosophical works, which for this reason he subjected to revision and rewriting.[40]

In its fundamental challenge to the bases of scholasticism, Valla's work clearly anticipates situations and conflicts that would be perpetuated across the centuries. To give but one example, we immediately think of Valla when we read the following, in a work of our own time, about the relationship of the doctrine of neoscholasticism to English utilitarian hedonism:

> The difference between Hedonism and Scholasticism lies in this: Hedonism inculcates that pleasure is the ultimate criterion of morality, and that an action is good only in so far as it is pleasurable; whereas for Scholasticism goodness is in the nature of the act itself, and pleasure is simply an effect which may follow from a moral act.[41]

The proposition could have been written by Valla himself, although in reverse: in his *De vero bono* he turns against any finalistic conception of ethics (represented in emblematic mode in the Stoic and thus ontological principle of the 'honestum', the upright), and thus refuses the pretense of determining *a priori* the 'nature' of every single act.

For reasons mentioned above, the work of Valla, with the exclusion of the *Elegantiae latinae linguae* (and, for other reasons, the treatise on the Donation of Constantine), had a limited and semi-clandestine diffusion in its own time. Yet its presence was stronger than we can document precisely. We can locate it principally in the reactions it provoked and in the stimulus which it gave to writings inspired by older Christian traditions, above all patristic ones, which were nonetheless characterized by the style, by then in vogue, of humanism. In other words, the ecclesiastical culture, in order to maintain its capacity to persuade and to respond to provocation, had to divest itself of its scholastic appearance and adapt to an already established humanistic culture, and also to solicit the intervention of distinguished humanists for apologetic purposes.[42] The celebrated treatises *De excellentia et praestantia hominis* and *De dignitate et excellentia hominis*, respectively by Bartolomeo Facio (1448) and Giannozzo Manetti (1452), both dedicated to Alfonso of Aragon, were of this nature. They were written at the urgings of, and on the basis of a conceptual scheme made available by, an Olivetan monk, Antonio da Barga, with the aim of celebrating the 'dignity' of the spiritual aspect of man, in contrast to the 'misery' of the physical body. This was a dichotomy, with roots in the works of St Augustine, which had been the main target of Valla's attack in his scandalous *De vero bono*.[43] Aimed more directly at the confutation of Valla are a number of other dialogues, such as *De humanae vitae felicitate*, again by Facio, written in Naples in the wake of Valla's Inquisition trial and inspired by the same environment that had favoured the accusation against him; and the later *De falso et vero bono* of Bartolomeo Platina, written also with the aim of gaining the favour of Pope Sixtus IV, who would shortly thereafter appoint the author as prefect of the Vatican Library.[44] Dedicated to Nicholas V, the *Vitae gestaque sanctorum* of Antonio degli Agli, a Florentine priest then resident in the papal *curia* (he would later become bishop of Fiesole and then Volterra), also responds implicitly to Valla and to the scandal created by Valla's treatise on the Donation of Constantine. Beyond the Donation itself, Valla's work had raised serious doubts about various other devout traditions. Agli tells us that his book resulted from a project originating with Ambrogio Traversari to rewrite the entire collection of saints' lives, not according to the liturgical calendar, but according to a verifiable historical chronology, and in a style that would render it acceptable to the taste of the times.[45] It was from preoccupations such as these that a patronage of culture by the Holy See developed, with increasingly clear manifestations. This in turn gave rise to a strong tradition of curial humanism that stretched from the time of Nicholas V and Pius II to the Medici popes.[46]

Naturally Aeneas Silvius Piccolomini, who became Pope Pius II, deserves separate treatment. In his various metamorphoses he incarnated the double spirit of humanism – the institutional and the rebellious. In the *Commentaries* of his own pontificate he deploys the weapons of a utilitarian voluntarism derived from Valla against all the enemies of the Holy See. This he defends to the last, no less in its spiritual prerogatives (opposing the pretensions of the conciliarist movement) as in its temporal ones, against every kind of adversary, whether the great European princes or the minor feudatories and cities of Italy. In the collection *De viris illustribus*, about the humanists of his youth on whose works he was educated, his judgements are no less unforgiving.[47]

But now it is time to turn to Florence, and in particular to the question of the connections one can establish, thanks to the exceptional richness of the documentary evidence, between the development of humanism and the simultaneous evolution of the political, institutional and social environment.[48] It is precisely in the areas of political, institutional, economic and social history that research in the last few decades has produced the richest results, as is indicated elsewhere in this volume.[49] But the historian of culture should not remain indifferent to these results, and this for two principal reasons: first, a true history of culture cannot exist that is not also, at least implicitly, social history (just as, reciprocally, no good social history can ignore the testimony of culture); and secondly, a real understanding of the historical background serves to guard against the tendency, which has been so characteristic of studies on the Renaissance, to idealize and to generalize.

In the face of such an increase in knowledge, the historian now moves on an altogether different level to that available when Hans Baron formulated his idealizing thesis on Florentine 'civic humanism', according to which, thanks to a fortunate historical coincidence, the eternal values of republican liberty deriving from ancient Greece and Rome were reproduced in fifteenth-century Florence.[50] Yet a real connection between cultural and political developments does lie in the prominent state-building and expansionist tendencies assumed by the government of Florence, at least from the time of the anti-Viscontean wars at the end of the fourteenth century. This is exactly what constitutes the object of emphatic celebration in the precocious *Laudatio Florentinae urbis* of Leonardo Bruni (1404).[51] One can detect in the work a dual polemic. The most outspoken argument was aimed against the arbitrariness of tyranny that from his own times extended back to Caesar and the Roman emperors; the other, more indirect but no less substantial argument was directed against a series of medieval traditions, from the universalistic conception of the Holy Roman Empire to that semi-private organism represented by the civic commune. Bruni's *History*, undertaken a decade later, was not simply entitled a history of the city of Florence but a history of the *people* of Florence (*Historiarum florentini populi libri*). This was the expression which at the time, even in the chancery's legal documents, designated the sovereign state, on the model of the 'populus Romanus' of jurisprudential tradition. The aim of the *Historiae* is indeed to render the citizens aware of a new reality, proposing a novel distinction between private ethics, geared towards constraint and parsimony as in the old commune, and a public ethics, inspired not by individual modesty but by the greatness and dignity of the state.[52]

Yet there is another, more hidden connection between humanistic culture and the social and institutional situation of the time, this one not in the realm of the writing of history but in the moral sphere. Near the conclusion of his dialogue *De avaritia* (1429), which discusses the contemporary preaching of San Bernardino against usury, Poggio Bracciolini delivers a eulogy on the wisdom of Cicero. Rather than urge, like Bernardino, that misers should be expelled, Cicero, pragmatically accepting the realities of this world, proposed the imposition of a fine.[53] Poggio's dialogue ironically brings out a contrast between the solemn canonical rules that Bernardino was preaching should be applied in society, and those common human inclinations which no wise government should leave out of consideration.[54] Such in effect was the position taken by the government of Florence for the whole course of the fifteenth century, in the sense that it withdrew an increasing number of jurisdictions from the ordinary courts of foreign rectors (and also if possible from the ecclesiastical court), substituting them with government offices, which were deliberately given both judicial and administrative powers, aimed at social control. Financial reparation agreed with the convicted person was increasingly preferred to corporal punishments intended to have a deterrent effect. Such a tendency is suggested, for example, in the study of Michael Rocke on homosexuality in Florence, which is based on the acts of the *Ufficiali di notte*, the office that dealt with sodomy and other sexual crimes. This office was established in 1432, that is, near to the time when Poggio wrote his ironic dialogue.[55]

Unlike Bernardino, Poggio deliberately avoids subtle casuistry on the 'licit' and the 'illicit', preferring general categories of a psychological rather than doctrinal character, such as 'luxury' and 'avarice'. As has been remarked, the issue of 'avaritia', greed, was also a question in reality. As in the case of sexual crimes, the government had brought under its own competence all matters concerning lending at interest, both by the direct management of the public debt (the *Monte comune*), and in the complementary way of stipulating with Jewish loan companies the setting up of banks for lending at interest by pawnbroking. These companies, that did not fail to attract local capital, functioned to guarantee the solubility of indirect taxation and thus to feed the public debt itself.[56] To be precise, the Jewish loan bank was established in Florence only in 1437, although it originated in an older plan of 1393 which had been impeded by the intervention of the preacher Giovanni Dominici. However, in the meantime, the new institution had been implanted in several minor centres of the Florentine dominion under the supervision of the *Ufficiali del Monte*. Successive renewals of the 'condotta' (the government's agreement with the Jewish community) were entrusted to this office and to the *Otto di Guardia* as a normal administrative procedure, thus avoiding the need for a papal dispensation that would have been required in similar cases. Meanwhile, as has been seen with sexual crimes, the loan company had been removed from the ordinary jurisdiction of the foreign rector's court.

In an even wider sense we find the distinction between the civil and religious spheres clearly formulated in the documents of the Florentine chancery. This distinction is indicated, for example, in a letter of 11 May 1469, probably dictated by the first chancellor, Bartolomeo Scala. In this letter, inviting the Franciscan Jacopo da Cagli to preach in the following Lent, Scala distinguished between the separate areas of preaching and 'civil discipline':

Our concern ought to be not only to guard the commonwealth with arms and to order it with laws, but, even more, to hold our people together by instruction in the belief and observance of true religion. For even if the republic and civil discipline are excellent things, instituted for the good and happy living of everyone, religion, nevertheless, representing true and holy wisdom, leads to another, much more noble and excellent city than human society and present governments.[57]

To the organization of a state whose internal government had established a large sphere of jurisdictional autonomy and, at least in principle, sovereignty, there thus corresponded a rapid secularization of the cultural environment, from frankly utilitarian assumptions on the one hand to the justification of religious toleration on the other. In his letter, widely diffused at the time, on the punishment as a heretic of Jerome of Prague (1416), Poggio Bracciolini distinguished between points of doctrine (on which he did not pass judgement) and the moral dignity of the condemned man, for which he felt complete admiration.[58] Many years later Cristoforo Landino, speaking from his chair at the university of Florence, illustrated the scepticism of Cicero in terms of the enrichment to truth which derives from a plurality of opinions, and he even justified this claim with a biblical citation:

For we do not arrive at wisdom by one path but by many. There is not one path for all and there are many things which lead us to wisdom. For each person's path to happiness is the best one, if it is combined with honest and right living. Hence the Gospel says 'In my Father's house are many mansions'. (John, 14.2)[59]

The attitudes which we have surveyed thus belonged to a sort of official ideology, embodied by the representatives of those parallel and communicating institutions that were the chancery and the university. 'We do not arrive at wisdom by one path but by many': it would be difficult to imagine something similar, in particular emanating from an institutional organ like the university, in the following century. In Italy, at least from the imperial coronation of Charles V in 1530, the political system of the Quattrocento was progressively undermined, while the highest jurisdictional authorities reassumed the traditional control of their legitimate spheres. An emblematic case in Florence, now under the rule of Duke Cosimo I, is the tacit extinction of the *Monte comune*, together with the investment and insurance body of the *Monte delle doti*; the financing of charitable assistance, meanwhile, passed with the approval of the duke to the competence of the *Monte di pietà*, instituted at the time of Savonarola.[60] Typically, the duke now assumed to himself the ultimate jurisdiction – the *iurisdictio* of medieval memory – over sexual crimes, which in republican times had been transferred to the competence of a special government office. The law of 8 July 1542, observes Rocke, 'appears to signify the end of a certain social, political and cultural environment in which sodomy had long flourished'; from henceforth it would be interpreted 'as a personal affront to the monarch'.[61]

A century after the successes achieved by the daring challenges of humanism, transgressive as they were in relation to the consecrated traditions of scholastic doctrine, the dominant tendency inclined rather (to quote the formula of the last book of William Bouwsma) 'towards a culture of order'.[62] Moreover, as concerns Italy in particular, the writings of the most audacious humanists – of Bruni, Poggio, Valla, the Latin Petrarch and so on – were no longer reprinted, at the beginnings of a real migration of knowledge. And yet, however evident this phenomenon appears to be, one can propose such a sharp contrast of epochs only with reservations. In reality the need of the institutional sector to reestablish an order which had been lost after the great crisis at the end of the Middle Ages was as old as the very ideological propositions that had challenged that order. We have already seen how the anti-scholastic (and anti-theological) provocations of Bruni and Valla had stimulated a learned restatement of the patristic and Christian traditions.[63] Even more important (because perhaps less evident), under the general definition of 'civic humanism', a figure like Leonardo Bruni, the critic of the old traditions of the commune and of the Schools, has been confused with a tendency that was on the rise in civic and educational circles, to revive the intellectual and cultural traditions of the fourteenth century, of Dante and Boccaccio especially. In the essentially individualistic and eudemonistic ethics of Bruni, there is no reference to the *De officiis* of Cicero – the Stoic ethics of duties, against which Valla argues – which is nonetheless the theoretical line pursued in the *Vita civile* of Matteo Palmieri (1437–38), an exhortation to good government and to civil concord aimed at the governing class.[64] Giannozzo Manetti personifies such an endeavour to reinsert the cultural propositions of Bruni into a traditional context, and to bring them into line with both sacred and profane literature.[65] An implicit but nonetheless direct attack on Bruni is to be found in the *Dialogus* written by Benedetto Accolti – the Aretine jurist chancellor of Florence – around 1460, which reverses the drastic propositions of his predecessor in the chancery concerning the superiority of the ancients to the moderns, and thus of the superiority of ancient culture over medieval scholasticism. Accolti on the contrary reevaluates the traditions of the Schools in both the theological and legal fields.[66] In the institutional arena of the university and chancery, an authoritative representative of such civic traditionalism, characteristic of the age of Lorenzo de'Medici in particular, was Cristoforo Landino. In the 'Proemio' to his commentary on the *Divine Comedy* he celebrates in particular, among the civic glories of his age, Giannozzo Manetti and Leon Battista Alberti, not just for their 'eloquence' (for which Bruni and Poggio are praised) but for their 'teaching' ('doctrina'). Thus he locates them in the context of traditional scholastic disciplines, as if they represented a prelude to the efflorescence of Aristotelian and Platonic studies: 'We have lots of peripatetics, but we can also glory in having those who have recalled to light the Platonic discipline.'[67] And, as the personality of Landino well illustrates, the return to the old traditions coincides, in Florence and elsewhere, with a renewed control and reorganization of educational institutions.

The disciplining of institutionalized education and the major control that the university came to be subjected to in the political sphere led to the abandonment of the ideological diversions and ambitious philosophical projects of Bruni and Poggio, Valla and Alberti, in favour of a return to curricular order and a highly structured pedagogical system. Such a development is indicated by the ancient name *enkyclios paideia*; the fulfilment of such educational programmes would eventually be affirmed by the appearance of the new name, 'humanista'.[68]

And with this we can return to the point of departure concerning the problem of periodization that had been addressed long ago by W. K. Ferguson. Contrary to Ferguson, I believe that we can affirm that there certainly existed a moment in which a new current of ideas was declared publicly. These were characterized, as had already been the case with Petrarch, by opposition to scholasticism, understood as a methodology and educational programme, and thus in its historical role set against good old classical literature. The most important referent of this process is not the world of institutionalized education but – as in his own way Burckhardt had indicated – the state, according to its particular evolution in Italy. The territorial state, whether signorial or republican, that emerged in the short space of a few decades, broke in substantial ways with the tradition of the commune or the lordship. This was no different to developments in the following centuries in the rest of Europe, where a culture pursuing Renaissance traditions would develop alongside the evolution of monarchical absolutism, particularly in France and England. Put in this way, to discuss the Renaissance as chronologically definable or as the advent of modernity loses its relevance. It will suffice, rather, to identify and investigate the protagonists of humanistic culture in their histories and motivations, as well as in the reactions they stimulated in others; and this is what the present chapter has aimed to suggest.

## notes

This chapter was translated by Jonathan Woolfson in collaboration with the author.

1. This statement derives from Burckhardt's lectures at Zurich of 1856; see R. Fubini, 'Rinascimento scoperto? Studi recenti on Jacob Burckhardt', in R. Fubini, *L'umanesimo italiano e i suoi storici: Origini rinascimentali – critica moderna* (Milan, 2001), p. 258. The French word *Renaissance*, adopted in the title of Burckhardt's work, indicates his points of reference.
2. See R. Fubini, 'Origini e significato del "Die Kultur der Renaissance in Italien" di Jacob Burckhardt', in Fubini, *L'umanesimo italiano*, p. 213. Again these comments derive from his lectures of 1856.
3. Fubini, 'Origini e significato', p. 213.
4. Fubini, 'Origini e significato', pp. 223 ff.
5. Jacob Burckhardt, *The Civilization of the Renaissance in Italy: An Essay* (London, 1958), 1.1, p. 21.
6. 'Una volta inebbriato di quegli studi sul gran secolo, ognuno crederà di vedere l'insieme laddove non vede che una parte; ognuno farà le sue categorie, che poi si troveranno povere e difettose; ognuno, l'opera compita, vorrebbe non ritoccarla solamente, ma rifarla.' Fubini, 'Origini e significato', p. 227. The letter was written in Italian by Burckhardt. The recipient, whose name is not indicated, was perhaps the geographer G. Dalla Vedova, the author of a review of *Civilization* in *Archivio storico italiano* in 1865.
7. See now P. Ladwig, *Das Renaissancebild deutscher Historiker, 1898–1933* (Frankfurt am Main and New York, 2004).
8. See D. Hay, *The Italian Renaisance in its Historical Background* (Cambridge, 1961); D. Cantimori, 'La periodizzazione dell'età del Rinascimento', in his *Storici e storia. Metodo, caratteristiche e significato del lavoro storiografico* (Turin, 1971), pp. 553–77.
9. See R. Fubini, 'Una carriera di storico del Rinascimento: Hans Baron', in Fubini, *L'umanesimo italiano*, pp. 277–316 (English translation published as 'Renaissance Historian: The Career of Hans Baron', *Journal of Modern History*, LXIV (1992) 541–74).
10. Cf. P. O. Kristeller, *Le Thomisme et la penseé italienne de la Renaissance* (Montréal and Paris, 1967).
11. P. O. Kristeller, *Marsilio Ficino and his Work after Five Hundred Years* (Florence, 1987), p. 16; P. O. Kristeller, *Renaissance Philosophy and the Medieval Tradition* (Latrobe, PA, 1966), p. 80; cf. R. Fubini, 'Interpretazioni dell'umanesimo', in Fubini, *L'umanesimo italiano*, p. 328 ff.
12. See now V. R. Giustiniani, '*Homo, humanus* and the Meaning of "Humanism"', in *Renaissance Essays II*, ed. W. J. Connell (Rochester, 1993), pp. 29–57.
13. R. N. D. Martins, *Pierre Duhem: Philosophy and History in the Work of a Believing Physicist* (La Salle, IL, 1991), p. 91.

14. 'Jaeger's concept of "Formgeschichte" ... which much influenced his later work on the Renaissance': 'Paul Oskar Kristeller and his Contribution to Scholarship', in *Philosophy and Humanism: Renaissance Essays in Honor of Paul Oskar Kristeller*, ed. E. P. Mahoney (Leiden, 1976), p. 3. The text is anonymous but of a clearly autobiographical character, or written by another scholar on the basis of autobiographical materials or memories.
15. Cf. G. Billanovich, 'Premessa', in L. D. Reynolds and N. G. Wilson, *Copisti e filologi*. *La tradizione dei classici dall'Antichità al Rinascimento* (Padua, 1969), pp. vii–xiii. See also G. Billanovich, *La tradizione del testo di Livio e le origini dell'Umanesimo* (Padua, 1981). Billanovich was the founder of the journal *Italia medioevale e umanistica* which began in 1958.
16. P. L. Grendler, *Schooling in Renaissance Italy* (Baltimore and London, 1987).
17. R. Black, *Humanism and Education in Medieval and Renaissance Italy: Tradition and Innovation in Latin Schools from the Twelfth to the Fifteenth Century* (Cambridge, 2001).
18. J. Monfasani, *George of Trebizond: A Biography and a Study of his Rhetoric and Logic* (Leiden, 1976); see also *Collectanea Trapezuntiana: Texts, Documents and Bibliographies of George of Trebizond*, ed. J. Monfasani (Binghampton, 1984). The latest researches of this author are in part gathered in J. Monfasani, *Language and Learning in Renaissance Italy* (Aldershot, 1994) and in his *Greeks and Latins in Renaissance Italy: Studies on Humanism and Philosophy* (Burlington, VT, 2004).
19. J. Hankins, *Plato in the Italian Renaissance*, 2 vols (Leiden, 1991).
20. R. G. Witt, *'In the Footsteps of the Ancients': The Origins of Humanism from Lovato to Bruni* (Leiden, 2000).
21. J. Hankins, 'Two Twentieth-Century Interpreters of Renaissance Humanism: Eugenio Garin and Paul Oskar Kristeller', now in J. Hankins, *Humanism and Platonism in the Italian Renaissance*, I: *Humanism* (Rome, 2003), p. 584. On this subject see also C. S. Celenza, *The Lost Italian Renaissance: Humanists, Historians and Latin's Legacy* (Baltimore and London, 2004), pp. 16–57.
22. J. E. Seigel, *Rhetoric and Philosophy in Renaissance Humanism: The Unity of Eloquence and Wisdom, Petrarch to Valla* (Princeton, 1968). In the numerous writings on Italian humanism of Eugenio Garin there is a completely different but nevertheless essential notion of rhetoric. 'Rhetoric', as the practical arm of ideological and civic persuasion, subtly took the place in his work of the influential formula found in the interpretation of the neo-idealist G. Gentile, of humanism as a 'philosophy of non-philosophers'. See, for example, 'Introduzione', *Prosatori latini del Quattrocento*, ed. E. Garin (Milan and Naples, 1952), p. xiv: 'In fact everything in the fifteenth century is "rhetoric", as long as one bears in mind that, on the other hand, "rhetoric" means humanity, that is spirituality, awareness, reason, human discourse ...' ('Tutto è, veramente, nel Quattrocento "retorica", sol che si ricordi che, d'altra parte, "retorica" è umanità, ossia spiritualità, consapevolezza, ragione, discorso di uomini ...')
23. I am referring to the *Repastinatio dialecticae et philosophiae*, as it was entitled in the first version. See R. Fubini, 'La "Dialectica" di Lorenzo Valla. Saggio di interpretazione', in Fubini, *L'umanesimo italiano*, pp. 184–207. See also for a contrasting interpretation, S. I. Camporeale, *Lorenzo Valla. Umanesimo e teologia* (Florence, 1972).

24. *Italian Renaissance Studies: A Tribute to the Late C. A. Ady*, ed. E. F. Jacob (London, 1960), pp. 15–47, esp. p. 21.
25. P. Burke, *The Italian Renaissance: Culture and Society in Italy*, 4th edn (Cambridge, 1999). The first edition is of 1972. See also the same author's *The Renaissance Sense of the Past* (London, 1969).
26. See, for example, L. Jardine, *Worldly Goods: A New History of the Renaissance* (London, 1996).
27. A. T. Grafton and L. Jardine, *From Humanism to the Humanities: Education and the Liberal Arts in Fifteenth- and Sixteenth-Century Europe* (London, 1986), p. xvi.
28. A. Molho, 'The Italian Renaissance, Made in the USA', in *Imagined Histories: American Historians Interpret the Past*, ed. A. Molho and G. S. Wood (Princeton, 1998), pp. 263–94.
29. See R. Schönberger, *La Scolastica medievale. Cenni per una definizione* (Milan, 1997), p. 22.
30. '... ne res distantissimas importuna permixtione confunderem ...' See R. Fubini, 'Luoghi della memoria e antiscolasticismo in Petrarca. I "Rerum memorandum libri"', in U. Pfisterer and M. Seidel, eds, *Visuelle Topoi. Erfindung und tradiertes Wissen in den Künsten der italienischen Renaissance* (Munich and Berlin, 2003), pp. 171–81.
31. See R. Fubini, 'Pubblicità e controllo del libro nella cultura del Rinascimento. Censura palese e condizionamenti coperti dell'opera letteraria dal tempo del Petrarca a quello del Valla', in *L'Humanisme et l'Eglise du XVe siècle au milieu du XVIe siècle (l'Italie et la France méridionale)*, ed. P. Gilli (Rome, 2004), pp. 201–37; and more generally R. Witt, *Hercules at the Crossroads: The Life, Work and Thought of Coluccio Salutati* (Durham, 1983).
32. See D. Hay and J. Law, *Italy in the Age of the Renaissance, 1380–1530* (London, 1989); G. Chittolini, *La formazione dello Stato regionale e le istituzioni del contado. Secoli XIV–XV* (Turin, 1979); P. J. Jones, *The Italian City-State: From Comune to Signoria* (Oxford, 1997); I. Lazzarini, *L'Italia degli Stati territoriali. Secoli XIII–XV* (Rome and Bari, 2003). For the Renaissance state see the discussions in *The Origins of the State in Italy, 1300–1600*, ed. J. Kirshner (Chicago and London, 1995); the fuller, Italian version of the same collection, *Origini dello Stato. Processi di formazione statale in Italia fra Medioevo ed Età moderna*, ed. G. Chittolini, A. Molho and P. Schiera (Bologna, 1994); *Florentine Tuscany: Structures and Practices of Power*, ed. W. J. Connell and A. Zorzi (Cambridge, 2000); and also the fuller, Italian version of the same collection, *Lo Stato territoriale fiorentino (secoli XIV–XV)*, ed. A. Zorzi and W. J. Connell (Pisa, 2001).
33. See R. Fubini, 'All'uscita dalla Scolastica medievale. Salutati, Bruni e i "Dialogi ad Petrum Histrum"', in Fubini, *L'umanesimo italiano*, pp. 75–103; on the translations see now J. Hankins, 'Translation Practice in the Renaissance: The Case of Leonardo Bruni', and J. Hankins, 'The "Ethics" Controversy', both in Hankins, *Humanism and Platonism*, pp. 177–239. Extensive bibliography on Bruni can be found in J. Hankins, *Repertorium Bruniarum: A Critical Guide to the Writings of Leonardo Bruni*, I, *Handlist of Manuscripts* (Rome, 1997).
34. See R. Fubini, *Humanism and Secularization, from Petrarch to Valla* (Durham, 2003).

35. The work can now be read in L. Bruni, *Opere letterarie e politiche*, ed. P. Viti (Turin, 1996), pp. 195–241.
36. See G. Holmes, *The Florentine Enlightenment, 1400–1450* (London and New York, 1969).
37. See R. Fubini, 'An Analysis of Lorenzo Valla's "De voluptate". His Sojourn in Pavia and the Composition of the Dialogue', in *Humanism and Secularization*, pp. 140–73.
38. See Fubini, 'Dialectica', pp. 184–207.
39. Fubini, 'Dialectica', p. 202.
40. See R. Fubini, 'Lorenzo Valla tra il concilio di Basilea e quello di Firenze, e il processo dell'Inquisizione', in Fubini, *L'umanesimo italiano*, pp. 136–52.
41. J. L. Perrier, *The Revival of Scholasticism* (New York, 1967), p. 138. The first edition was published in 1908.
42. See Charles Trinkaus, *In Our Image and Likeness: Humanity and Divinity in Italian Humanist Thought*, 2 vols (Chicago and London, 1970); and Charles Stinger, *Humanism and the Church Fathers: Ambrogio Traversari (1368–1439) and Christian Antiquity in the Italian Renaissance* (Albany, 1977).
43. See J. H. Bentley, *Politics and Culture in Renaissance Naples* (Princeton, 1987), p. 102; Trinkaus, *In Our Image and Likeness*, I, pp. 200–9, 230–70; and O. Glaap, *Untersuchungen zu Giannozzo Manetti, De dignitate et excellentia hominis'. Ein Renaissance-Humanist und sein Menschenbild* (Stuttgart and Leipzig, 1994).
44. B. Platina, *De falso et vero bono*, ed. M. G. Blasio (Rome, 1999); and R. Fubini, 'Pubblicità e controllo del libro', pp. 231–5.
45. See D. M. Webb, 'Sanctity and History: Antonio Agli and Humanist Hagiography', in *Florence and Italy: Renaissance Studies in Honour of Nicolai Rubinstein*, ed. P. Denley and C. Elam (London, 1988), pp. 297–308; and also R. Fubini, 'Papato e storiografia nel Quattrocento', in R. Fubini, *Storiografia dell'umanesimo in Italia da Leonardo Bruni ad Annio da Viterbo* (Rome, 2003), pp. 230–5.
46. See J. F. D'Amico, *Renaissance Humanists in Papal Rome: Humanists and Churchmen on the Eve of the Reformation* (Baltimore and London, 1983); Charles Stinger, *The Renaissance in Rome*, 2nd edn (Bloomington, 1998); J. O'Malley, *Praise and Blame in Renaissance Rome: Rhetoric, Doctrine and Reform in the Sacred Orators of the Papal Court, c. 1440–1527* (Durham, 1979); J. O'Malley, *Rome and the Renaissance: Studies in Culture and Religion* (London, 1981); J. M. McManamon, *Funeral Oratory and the Cultural Ideals of Italian Humanism* (Chapel Hill and London, 1989). See also the researches of J. Monfasani in his *A Theologian at the Roman Curia in the Mid-Quattrocento: A Bio-Bibliographical Study of Niccolò Palmieri* (Rome, 1992) and in *Fernando of Cordova: A Biographical and Intellectual Profile* (Philadelphia, 1992).
47. The most recent and most relevant bibliography is mentioned and discussed in B. Baldi, 'Enea Silvio Piccolomini e il "De Europa". Umanesimo, religione e politica', in *Archivio storico italiano*, CXI (2003) 619–83.
48. A pioneering work in this sense was that of Lauro Martines, *The Social World of the Florentine Humanists* (Princeton, 1963), but see also the same author's *Lawyers and Statecraft in Renaissance Florence* (Princeton, 1968).
49. See in particular the chapters of Alessandro Arcangeli and John Najemy below.

50. H. Baron, *The Crisis of the Early Italian Renaissance: Civic Humanism and Republican Liberty in an Age of Classicism and Tyranny*, 2 vols (Princeton, 1955). A second, abridged edition was published in 1966. See also H. Baron, *In Search of Florentine Civic Humanism: Essays in the Transition from Medieval to Modern Thought*, 2 vols (Princeton, 1988). On this subject see now *Renaissance Civic Humanism: Reappraisals and Reflections*, ed. J. Hankins (Cambridge, 2000), and above, note 9.

51. See R. Fubini, 'La "Laudatio Florentinae urbis" di Leonardo Bruni: immagine ideale o programma politico?', in *Imago urbis*. *L'immagine della città nella storia d'Italia*, ed. F. Bocchi and R. Smurra (Rome, 2003), pp. 93–164.

52. See Fubini, *Storiografia dell'umanesimo*, pp. 93–164.

53. 'Sed vir prudentissimus, obsecutus forsan termporibus, multa plectendam avaritiam censuit, non addens graviorem poenam.' See Fubini, *Humanism and Secularization*, p. 82. This is an ironic reference to Cicero's treatise *De legibus*.

54. On the problem of lending with interest, see J. Kirshner, *Pursuing Honor while Avoiding Sin: The Monte delle doti in Florence* (Milan, 1977); J. Kirshner, 'Reading Bernardino's Sermon on the Public Debt', in *Atti del Simposio internazionale Cateriniano-Bernardiniano*, ed. D. Maffei and P. Nardi (Siena, 1982), pp. 547–621. On Bernardino's preaching more generally see N. Ben-Aryeh Debby, *Renaissance Florence in the Rhetoric of Two Popular Preachers: Giovanni Dominici (1354–1419) and Bernardino da Siena (1380–1444)* (Turnhout, 2001).

55. See M. Rocke, *Forbidden Friendships: Homosexuality and Male Culture in Renaissance Florence* (New York and Oxford, 1996); and also A. Zorzi, *L'amministrazione della giustizia penale nella Repubblica fiorentina* (Florence, 1988).

56. See R. Fubini, 'Prestito ebraico e Monte di Pietà a Firenze (1471–1473)', in R. Fubini, *Quattrocento fiorentino. Politica, diplomazia, cultura* (Ospedaletto, Pisa, 1996), pp. 159–216.

57. 'Cure nobis esse debet non solum quomodo armis rem nostram publicam tutemur atque instruamus legibus, sed vel multo magis quibus erudimentis populum nostrum in vere religionis cultu atque observantia contineamus. Nam, etsi respublica ac civilis ista disciplina preclara quidem res est, utputa que omnis ad bene beateque vivendum instituta sit, religio tamen, que est vera et casta sapienta, ad alteram civitatem, multo quam sint hi hominum cetus et hec ad tempus societates, nobiliorem prestantioremque perducit.' See R. Fubini, *Quattrocento fiorentino*, p. 191. On Scala and his culture see A. Brown, *Bartolomeo Scala, 1430–1497, Chancellor of Florence: The Humanist as Bureaucrat* (Princeton, 1979) and also B. Scala, *Humanistic and Political Writings*, ed. A. Brown (Tempe, 1997).

58. See Fubini, *Humanism and Secularization*, p. 103; and R. Neu Watkins, 'The Death of Jerome of Prague: Divergent Views', *Speculum*, XLII (1967) 104–29.

59. 'Non enim una via ad sapientiam accedimus, sed pluribus. Non omnibus enim una est via. Plures enim sunt res quae nos ad illam ducunt. Omnis enim via optima est ad ipsam felicitatem, dummodo honeste recteque vivamus. Unde est illud in Evangelio, "In domo Patris mei multe mansiones sunt".' See A. Field, *The Origins of the Platonic Academy of Florence* (Princeton, 1988), p. 265. The text derives from an auditor's note (the 'reportatio') written in the hand of another eminent member of the chancery, Giovanni Guidi, son of the notary of the *Riformagioni*, Bartolomeo, whom he would soon succeed

(Field, *Origins*, p. 237). On Landino see also Fubini, *Quattrocento fiorentino*, pp. 303–32.

60. See C. B. Menning, *The Monte di Pietà of Florence: Charity and State in Late Renaissance Italy* (Ithaca and London, 1993), and, more generally, M. G. Muzzarelli, *Il denaro e la salvezza. L'invenzione dei Monti di pietà* (Bologna, 2001). See also A. Molho, *Marriage Alliances in the Late Medieval Florence* (Cambridge, MA, 1994).

61. Rocke, *Forbidden Friendships*, p. 232.

62. W. J. Bouwsma, *The Waning of the Renaissance, 1550–1600* (New Haven and London, 2000).

63. See the conference proceedings *Ambrogio Traversari nel V centenario della nascita* (Florence, 1988); and above, note 42.

64. See C. Finzi, *Matteo Palmieri dalla 'Vita civile' alla 'Città di vita'* (Milan, 1984). For an updating of the bibliography see M. Palmieri, *La presa di Pisa*, ed. A. Mita Ferraro (Bologna, 1995).

65. The bibliography is noted in G. Manetti, *Biographical Writings*, ed. and trans. S. U. Baldassarri and R. Bagemihl (Cambridge, MA, 2003).

66. See R. Black, *Benedetto Accolti and the Florentine Renaissance* (Cambridge, 1985); and R. Fubini, 'Leonardo Bruni e la discussa recezione dell'opera: Giannozzo Manetti e il "Dialogus" di Benedetto Accolti', in Fubini, *L'umanesimo italiano*, pp. 104–29.

67. 'Abbiamo copia di peripatetici, ma ancora possiamo gloriarci avere chi ha revocato in luce la platonica disciplina.' C. Landino, *Scritti critici e teorici*, ed. R. Cardini, I (Rome, 1974), pp. 100–64, esp. pp. 117, 121.

68. P. Godman, *From Poliziano to Machiavelli: Florentine Humanism in the High Renaissance* (Princeton, 1998). For the connection between encyclopaedic programmes of learning and the term 'humanista', see the important document published by G. Pozzi in 'Da Padova a Firenze nel 1493', *Italia medioevale e umanistica*, IX (1966) 191–227. For the evolution of humanistic culture across the fifteenth century see F. Rico, *Il sogno dell'Umanesimo da Petrarca a Erasmo* (Turin, 1998) and the comments on this work in R. Fubini, 'Sogno e realtà dell'umanesimo. Contributi recenti all'umanesimo italiano', *Archivio storico italiano*, CLX (2002) 87–111.

# part three

# 7
## art

catherine m. soussloff

At the beginning of the twenty-first century any consideration of the significance of the Renaissance for the history of art must contend with two interconnected issues, one of which may properly be called conceptual, the other of which is historiographical. This chapter attempts to establish the centrality of these to the current approaches used by art historians to give meaning to works of art produced in the period, in order that the adequacy of representing and explaining may be ascertained. Together with their relationship to the 'real' events of a given time, works of art have most commonly been seen as *representations* of that time and its events. These assumptions about the historical function of works of art emerged most prominently in regard to art made in the period designated by the term 'Renaissance'. The significance of the Renaissance period for the discipline of art history and its procedures, therefore, attains a magnitude in direct proportion to the importance of a historiography of art. Inasmuch as a historiographical analysis seeks to uncover 'the limit between the imaginary and the real' undertaken in western culture by the concept of art itself, this chapter seeks to understand the transformation wrought by history upon art.[1] The manifestation of these limits will be found in an exploration of the relationship between art history and the cognate disciplines of history and literature, and in the distinctions made between the historiographical terms 'Renaissance' and 'Early Modern'. Given the dominance of the Italian vernacular in the early literature on art in this period and of Italy in the traditional interpretations of the idea of the Renaissance, my argument in this chapter will be specific to that context rather than comprehensive, although significant recent work has addressed issues concerning the Renaissance outside of Italy.

In general, when they appear in Latinate or Italianized usage, the terms most closely related to our 'Renaissance', for example, *rinascita, renovatio, renatum*, appeared in humanist literary texts of the period c.1347 onwards, as M. L. McLaughlin has so admirably demonstrated.[2] These texts used the term as an indication of a regard for the literature and political theory of ancient Rome, and for a newly found appreciation of Ciceronian as opposed to medieval Latin. But where did the visual arts belong in regard to this etymology? In 1971 Michael Baxandall explored the ways in which painting operated in precisely these kinds of humanist texts, arguing that 'the more important modes of humanist comment on painting developed between 1350 and 1450 in Italy'.[3] Moreover, Baxandall revealed that the understanding of pictorial composition of the period, which begins with Leon Battista Alberti's *On Painting* of 1435, the first treatise on art since antiquity, derived from purely linguistic, that is, rhetorical, interests.[4] Humanist texts, rhetorical concerns, the medium of painting, and the theoretical writing of a preeminent humanist and artist of the period converge in Baxandall's brilliant assessment of early Renaissance painting.

Baxandall's seminal book has spawned numerous and important studies of the humanist lineage of, and the theoretical implications for, the literature on art in the field known in art history as 'the Renaissance' (the period c.1400–c.1580). These followed, several generations later, the pioneering studies undertaken by Vienna School art historians at the beginning of the twentieth century.[5] Noteworthy among them are David Summers' book on Michelangelo's art theory, Patricia Rubin's book on Giorgio Vasari's biographies of the artists, and Philip Sohm's recent study of the concept of style in art theory, the last of which expands Baxandall's original apperceptions regarding the construction of art through language not only to Vasari's writing, but also to seventeenth-century writers who fall outside the purview of this chapter.[6] In addition, a good number – too numerous to list here – of scholarly editions and, in some cases, translations of the Latin and early Italian literature on art, have aided these endeavours. Foremost among these is the comparative annotation of the 1550 and 1568 editions of Vasari's *Lives of the artists*, without which most of the recent study of the literature on art would not have been possible.[7] In their concern to examine the variety of ways in which texts exhibit the lineage of theoretical and linguistic models, art historians of the last thirty years who study the literature on art have had much in common with their colleagues in literature and history, just as they have benefited from the more traditional archival, philological, and interpretative approaches that these disciplines have offered.

While this last statement might seem to indicate close congruencies amongst the traditional disciplines of 'Renaissance Studies', in the case of art history such an assumption should not be held in regard to the *idea* of the Renaissance. The idea of the Renaissance in art history continues to capture both the scholarly and the popular imaginations. In popular culture, *The Da Vinci Code* remained on the best-seller list for much of 2004. In art history, the Renaissance assumes a unity in the visual culture of the period, one that is often said to transcend specific geographical, historical, and linguistic boundaries in favour of stylistic coherencies, usually called formalist.[8] While, as David Summers recently argues, the overt practice of formalism as an interpretative method (if it ever could be called that) may have declined overall in the discipline, the continuities found through stylistic analysis, connoisseurship, and iconography in the artefacts from this period confirm the idea of the Renaissance.[9] In historical terms, then, the treatment of the Renaissance by art history may be called anti-relativistic. Written texts, documents, and works of art and craft are brought together so that they can be seen to be the result of simultaneous and 'complementary forces', to use Walter Benjamin's language.[10] Of the Renaissance in art history it may be said that it 'does not contain that generality on which the respective conceptual levels in the system of classification depend: the average'.[11]

What, for example, is the 'average' or usual Renaissance painting? If we were to answer that it is Leonardo da Vinci's fresco of the *Last Supper* in Milan or the portrait of the *Mona Lisa*, today in the Louvre museum in Paris, would we not be forced to admit that neither of these could possibly be characterized as an average Renaissance work of visual culture, much as we might be unwilling to admit that Leonardo himself exemplifies 'the Renaissance man'?[12] Indeed we might want to retort that the art historical term 'High Renaissance' was invented to indicate exactly the sort of *exceptional* achievement evidenced by these works and created by this singular man. In neither case can we argue that these works are the same in their visual form as other history or portrait paintings of their period. Yet, confusingly, the term 'High Renaissance' also encompasses the achievements of numerous other artists of the period c.1500–27.

The work of the artist Leonardo may be said to be complementary to the work of his predecessors and contemporaries from c.1400 to c.1580 in regard both to its aesthetic and to its market value. The art market and many museums commonly use the term 'Old Master' to separate all works of art of this period from those of other periods, although now the seventeenth century, too, is said to be populated with these masters. With this nomination, Renaissance works of art – from Masaccio to Michelangelo – are denoted as venerable and ancient. However, as the term 'Old Master' indicates, it possesses authority within the market and the discipline that has nothing to do with a particular historical situation, other than that the idea of a distant past named the Renaissance is called upon nostalgically, and that each work can be identified as being by the hand of a named artist, or a 'master', to use the rather antiquated locution of the nineteenth century, taken up from the use of the term *maestro* in fifteenth- and sixteenth-century documents. These terms indicate that a certain excellence is expected of works of art from this period, executed as they were by 'masters'. In an important study of the economic and social foundations of fifteenth-century art Baxandall attempted to demonstrate how the concept of the Renaissance painter's *style* did, indeed, develop out of the particular social context of early fifteenth-century Florence, where skill or virtuosity was valued above all other characteristics of the visual culture.[13] The intimate connection between the individual style of a named artist and the technological conditions of a work of art, that became so prominent in the history of western art, began in Florence at the initiation of the Renaissance period. According to Baxandall, then, the original authority of skilful painting would seem to belong quite distinctly to a particular historical situation, the very one that also generated a concept of style based on skill. We might say that Old Masters from the Renaissance represent for us today the extreme examples of skilful excellence against which other, later, works of art may be judged and upon which other comparisons may be based. Yet, Baxandall himself understood the historical ambiguity of his argument and, perhaps, its dangers for the new social history of art to which he hoped to contribute. He states in his conclusion to *Painting and Experience in Fifteenth-Century Italy*:

> This book began by emphasizing that the forms and styles of painting respond to social circumstances; much of the book has been given up to noting bits of social practice or convention that may sharpen our perception of the pictures. It is symmetrical and proper to end the book by reversing the equation – to suggest that the forms and styles of painting may sharpen our perception of the society.[14]

The historically specific moment gives way equally to the idea of a style that can, in some unspecified way, stand in for the society of the Renaissance. The circularity of this concluding statement remains problematic for the establishment of a social history of art that seeks procedures of analysis outside those of the traditional formalism of the discipline of art history.

Paintings may be grouped around the idea of the Renaissance, just as their individual styles may be determined, or 'read' in Baxandall's language, in order to do so. Together with Benjamin, therefore, we might call the Renaissance in its usage in art history an aesthetic, non-historical classification, one that is ultimately determined by a pre-conceived idea capable of affecting perception, taste, and judgement – indeed, determining the very idea of style in the history of art. Benjamin said that to let go of the aesthetic extreme in art criticism, which provides for major differences both between the individual works made in the period as well as between the works of the Renaissance and other periods, means to obscure 'the less obvious original qualities' so as to bring into light 'the chaos of more immediately appealing modern ones'.[15] Many interpreters of Italian Renaissance art from Walter Pater to Kenneth Clark have tended to prefer the comparativity of the aesthetic approach.[16] Following Benjamin, however, a focus on the idea of the Renaissance and formal qualities in works of art may well prevent art historians from addressing historiographical concerns which have arisen in the modern era, just as it encourages discussions of the unique achievements of the individual creator and his work. In addition, the more recent historiographical concerns may well be rather messy, as Benjamin implies. For these reasons and for others discussed below, to choose between these two approaches presents a methodological conundrum of some magnitude for the art historian of the period c.1350–c.1580. How can the work of art of the period be discussed without an idea of the Renaissance and without losing both the early historiography and the idea of the singular artist, his style, and issues of connoisseurship that adhere to the material artefacts themselves?

Unlike other disciplines formerly invoked by the term 'Renaissance studies', art history has not found a letting go of an extreme idea of the Renaissance to be particularly advantageous. For this reason the genre of art history writing known in the discipline as 'the artist monograph', a treatment of the single artist and his work from birth to death, often including a complete catalogue of the works, remains central to the field of the Renaissance. Originality, the singular artist in relation with patrons and peers, virtuosity and technologies in the control of the medium – these remain the central topics of much of the best recent writing on the Renaissance in the discipline of art history, and it would seem unfair to name some of these monographs without naming them all, for they all make significant contributions to the study of individual masters.

In the sense in which it is treated in the history of art the Renaissance remains an essential idea associated with the stylistic characteristics found in works of art or, as David Freedberg calls them, 'figured artefacts', from the period c.1350–c.1580 in Europe, particularly Italy.[17] In the history of art the term Renaissance relies on a series of interrelated historiographic and aesthetic concepts: (1) a mimetic standard against which all visual representations are judged according to their fidelity to nature or reality; (2) material artefacts that function as bearers of meaning intrinsic to themselves, to their makers, and to the wider culture that produced them; (3) a progressive chronology as a significant structuring method in the narration of a history of art; (4) geography as a determining factor in style; (5) style as the preeminent category for the evaluation of visual form.[18] Today, this treatment differs significantly from the one found in other disciplines, such as history and literature, where the Renaissance will be understood according to other concerns and constraints.

In these other fields the usage of the term 'Early Modern' rather than Renaissance indicates 'an important set of conceptual reconfigurations', as Leah S. Marcus has recently put it.[19] She argues that at the institutional level reconfiguration has meant a breakdown in disciplinary boundaries, particularly those between literary studies and history and art history, and between all of these and religious studies.[20] Additionally, according to Marcus, 'Early Modern' indicates historical interpretations that orient towards the modern period and the concepts associated with modernity, rather than retrospectively to the distant beginnings of the Renaissance. Fields that use 'Early Modern' interpret prospectively, while those that use 'Renaissance' orient retrospectively. As we have seen, Benjamin understood that a modern orientation produces a messiness brought on, according to him, by the variety of subjective responses elicited by or from the work of art without the compensatory expression of 'the essence of a field of artistic endeavour' allowed by the aesthetic approaches. Benjamin's concept of modernity requires the confusion that results from a breakdown of Enlightenment beliefs and canons.[21] If, on the other hand, such essences are considered desirable, as they most certainly are when the discernment of individual and period style motivate the discussion of art, then we should expect in Renaissance art history that the view in favour of the modern and/or modernity implied, according to Marcus, by the term 'Early Modern', will not be held in higher regard than other views, whether they be towards the past or the present.

Neither the current widespread endorsement of interdisciplinarity in the humanities, nor the pressure towards a modern orientation, much affects the concepts upon which the idea of the Renaissance rests in the history of art. From its inception as an academic discipline in mid-nineteenth-century Germany to the present day, art history has considered itself interdisciplinary in both its methods and practices. In today's interdisciplinary climate art historians point with pride to the founding fathers of these ecumenical procedures, that were first used to interpret the art of the period 1400–1580 by scholars such as Heinrich Wölfflin, Aby Warburg, and Erwin Panofsky. All of these men looked for inspiration to the German-trained Swiss historian Jacob Burckhardt, whose *Civilization of the Renaissance in Italy* (1860) became the foundation for the idea of the Renaissance that was elaborated in relation to concepts both of individual and period style by his intellectual followers in art history. So too, in regard to an interest in a later modernity rather than to the beginnings of a Renaissance period, art historians have consistently shown a lack of preference. A prominent example of this seeming impartiality may be found in the formulation of the High Renaissance by Heinrich Wölfflin in his important book of 1899, *Classic Art: An Introduction to the Italian Renaissance*, which sought to find stylistic categories for developments in later, rather than earlier, Italian art. Indeed, Wölfflin explicitly resisted a historicizing method, one that perforce would focus either on the beginnings or the endings of a chronological period, by theorizing a 'classic' style for forms that could be applied at various times and places. Thus, he concluded his book with the following remark:

> The classic character of Cinquecento art is founded on these formal elements. Here we are dealing with developments which are repeated everywhere; we are dealing with permanent and pervasive art forms, and that which distinguishes Raphael above all the earlier generations is the same as that which, under entirely different circumstances, makes a Ruysdael a classic among the Dutch landscape painters.[22]

Wölfflin's 'permanent and pervasive art forms' relied on a concept of beauty displaced from the Renaissance literature on art, according to Elizabeth Cropper.[23]

Gombrich and others have demonstrated that the basis of Burckhardt's idea of the artistic Renaissance was the written sources on art of the period, pre-eminently Giorgio Vasari's *Lives of the Most Excellent Painters, Sculptors, and Architects* (1550 and 1568).[24] Given this foundation, Baxandall's focus in his two books on the humanist texts and the fourteenth-century origins of pictorial style, formulated now almost thirty years ago, augment the discussions of Burckhardt's influence in significant ways. Vasari stated in the preface to his book that he concerned himself with 'the summit as perfection' as much as the 'humble beginnings' of art and that he saw the art of his own time as the result of a progress from decay to

rebirth to perfection, a progress that would be repeated.[25] The structure
of the biographies that make up the preponderance of Vasari's texts
replicate in narrative or historical time the life cycle of the human being.
Biographies tell the story of the lives of the artists from birth to death.[26]
These biographies produced a history based on the progress and decline of
the physical body. Given the Christian context in which this writing took
place, the idea of re-birth or resurrection of the body after death is also
entailed in this history writing. In this culture, resurrection and rebirth
were implicitly understood as progress, or the attainment of perfection
in work, and at times in life, by the subject of the biography, the artist.

These structural factors, as found in the early artists' biographies of
the period c.1480–1580, left their mark on the representation of art
in Burckhardt's historical interpretation. As Michael Oakeshott put it
some years ago: 'But what [Burckhardt] was in search of was not a mere
generality, but the propensities of a situation, and the *facta* were used
as the evidences of these propensities ... not a course of events, but the
dispositions revealed in events.'[27] To pursue this point historiographically,
we might add that for Burckhardt, his art historian followers, and even
for Baxandall, works of art contained within themselves the materiality
of the disposition of events. In Burckhardt's account the humanist artist
Leon Battista Alberti figures as the paradigmatic new individual of the
Renaissance, one whose architecture, art theory, and life emerge as
exceptional and exemplary. His biography may be found in Vasari's book.
In *Civilization* Burckhardt used what he believed to be an autobiography
as well. Not surprisingly, Alberti's theoretical writings on art had been the
subject of the first so-called illustrated 'art book' in the Italian vernacular
devoted to the theory and practice of art.[28] Alberti's treatises on art were
published in 1550 and 1565 with woodcuts by Cosimo Bartoli. In 1651
Alberti's treatises on painting and sculpture were published again, together
with his biography. These were included with the lavishly illustrated first
edition of Leonardo da Vinci's *Treatise on Painting*, published in Paris in
French and Italian versions. By virtue of the early historiography of art
devoted to these two artists, as well as to their own prolific writing (in the
case of Leonardo in notebook form only), their art, lives, and theory served
first Burckhardt, and then later historians and art historians, as models
for the idea of the Renaissance in art history. The extensive scholarship
on Leonardo that has appeared over the last ten years supports the view
of him as both exceptional and exemplary that may be found in the
literature of the sixteenth and seventeenth centuries.[29] In recent years,
the fascination with Leonardo persists in exacting studies of his often
obscure legacy in Lombardy and Rome in the two centuries following

his death.[30] Returning to an earlier point in this chapter, Leonardo may be seen in art history as both singular in his achievements and typical of the idea of the Renaissance. So too, such claims have been made for Michelangelo's contribution to the 'dramatic, even volatile, artistic change' that typifies the later Renaissance.[31] To these must be added the name of Raphael, the third major figure in Wölfflin's 'classic' style, discussed above.

How is it, then, that the differences between 'Renaissance' and 'Early Modern', which have been so significant over the last twenty years in other fields in the humanities, do not pertain in art history? If we accept the basic precept that the object of study determines disciplinary methods, then we must look to figured artefacts of all media as the cause of the differences in methodologies between art history and her sister disciplines of literature and history in the field of early modern or Renaissance studies. Marcus points to 'the demotion of authorship and intention as the controlling centre of meaning' in literary studies because it opened up 'a vast panorama of "nonauthorial" writings as part of our study of literature'.[32] The result has not only been a new interest in writings by women and non-canonical literature, including moves away from high to low genres and from individual to communal notions of creativity, but also an acknowledgement of the instability of texts themselves, which in turn has led to new approaches to scholarly editing, printing history, and the establishment of a sociology of texts. Some of these developments in the scholarship of the period impinge on the territory of art and visual culture, despite the overarching reach of singularity and exceptionalism that both the public and scholarship expect. For example, renewed interest in the female 'voice' prompts Fredrika Jacobs to explore the early literature on art for the rhetorical evidence of the *virtuosa*.[33] Studies of the 'art book' have already been mentioned, but to these should be added Brian Richardson's work on the economic and cultural outcomes of the arrival of print in Renaissance Italy, because in it he draws on texts, patrons and printers of importance to the history of art.[34]

A major intervention into the dominant understanding of the Renaissance in art history may be found in recent studies that address the art of the period from within the context of a wider understanding of visual culture, including artefacts of everyday life, collections of natural and crafted artefacts, and every form of luxury acquisition. These interpretations rely on the extensive research on humanist culture that has taken place in the disciplines of history and literature over the last thirty years in order to place material artefacts within a wider context, noting that learning, patronage, and commerce were always overlapping areas of interest in this period.[35] Lisa Jardine's radical 'project of redefining the achievements of the European Renaissance' through an examination of visual culture-as-commodity has as its goal the explication of the historical precedents for the modern forces of consumerism and global capital.[36] Paula Findlen moves outwards from the precious artefact and natural object to consider the intersecting histories of collections and natural history. She demonstrates how the very humanists that Baxandall and others mined for the rhetorical construction of the language on art were equally engaged in the socially élite pastime of organizing the world around them through the collection of natural and artistic rarities. In the process the museum was born, thereby orienting the humanist and artistic culture of the Renaissance to the institution said by some historians to be most emblematic of European modernity itself.[37]

The conclusions drawn by all of these recent studies of the wider context of visual culture in the period turn upon the intersection of art and science in scholarly discourse, mercantile endeavours, and behaviours of the élite. Here, the focus on modernity in early modern studies and the idea of the Renaissance in art history meet in ways that are perhaps unexpected, but possibly productive for future research on this era long considered central to the concept of Europe and of European identity.[38] In recent years, while historians of science have looked backwards to the fifteenth and sixteenth century for the foundations of both the Scientific Revolution of the seventeenth century and the scientific disciplines of the Enlightenment (see Brian Ogilvie's chapter below), there has been a corresponding emphasis on issues of 'visuality' in early modern art history. These studies have emerged out of the felt inadequacy with the narrative that art history had constructed for the meaning of perspective. This most central and original aspect of Alberti's theory on painting had long been recognized as more than simply a means to the pictorial end of a regime of mimetic representation. In 1927 Erwin Panofsky had argued that *in itself* perspective was a 'symbolic form' that allowed the forms seen on a two dimensional surface to possess *their* form and *their* secondary level of symbolic meaning as representations.[39] Panofsky's interpretation supported an idea of the Renaissance in which the depiction of forms could be understood as the glue that held the visible world together. It also supported the Burckhardtian idea of the exceptionality of the work of art. It may also be related to the formalism discussed above as a method of visual analysis used by art historians. In any case, Panofsky's essay served as the seminal discussion of perspective until recent scholarship undertook a re-examination of the topic, its history, and the related fields of mathematics and the earliest descriptive sciences of anatomy and astronomy.

These researches began in the 1970s in two essays by Roberto Klein and in a book by Samuel Edgerton.[40] In a major study of 1987 Hubert Damisch argued that the invention of perspective led to the beginning of the history of art, thereby explaining how 'the form' had become enfolded within the discourse.[41] Following Damisch's work, Martin Kemp placed perspective first in his long history of 'the science of art'.[42] In the work that has appeared on perspective over the last thirty years, art has been understood to be engaged at both its most practical and most highly skilled levels with science, as it was understood at the time. Art historians who have researched perspective and early modern optics have not sought to separate out images and artefacts from a social and an intellectual ambiance. In this regard, the history and dissemination of both manuscript and printed materials dealing with perspective has been an important aspect of these researches. Visual culture, including high art, has been theorized as productive of knowledge in ways as significant as those found in science, history, or philosophy. Does this reflect a desire to maintain a place for art in a world increasingly mediated by science and technology? Do the scientists as well as the public need an account that places art at the beginning of the most advanced thinking on the vision, optics, and visualities which predominate in our present digital era?

These questions cannot be answered satisfactorily without the scholarship on Renaissance perspective that has been produced by the history of art. If history speaks of the present as it invokes the past, then we must agree that the ideas about perspective constructed by art history have given much to our current ways of imaging the world. Whereas, as I have suggested in this chapter, the idea of the Renaissance work of art as exceptional and exemplary may fall down upon the realities of the commodity and the abstraction of the form, a history of Renaissance art still has much to offer in regard to the spectatorial gaze of the future. This does not necessarily mean that the focus of the art historian lies only on what is to come, or that 'presentism' should be the guide for art historical writing, although the persistence in our reality of the tangible and valued artefact from the past may well pressure us in these directions. The long view of the historiography of the Renaissance in art history, which I have presented here, leads to the conclusion that the scholarship, together with the works of art and visual culture, could provide all fields of early modern studies with both an interpretative paradigm and a cautionary example. Holding in tension both the aesthetic approach determined by the artefact and its history and the contributions that have been made in

modernity towards the viewing subject and his/her subjectivities, we may
be able to achieve more than an understanding of what a fixed idea of
the Renaissance prevents for our understanding of visual culture. Indeed,
art history may be asked to show the way to a *combinatory method*, based
not solely upon the apparent clarity that the comparativities of its so-
called objects of research allows, but also upon the complex forms of the
narratives that have been constructed over time about those objects. To
proceed in this manner will be to respond not only to the creations of
the past, but also to our own and future creativity as historians of that
complex field known today as art history *and* visual culture.

## notes

1. My views of the function of historiography have been much influenced
   by Hayden White, 'The Question of Narrative in Contemporary Historical
   Theory', in *The Content of the Form: Narrative Discourse and Historical
   Representation* (Baltimore and London, 1987), p. 45. The imputation of an
   extreme historiographical significance to the Renaissance work of art is my
   own contribution. I appreciate the discussions that I had with my students
   on these topics in my course on the High Renaissance, taught in Fall 2003 at
   University of California Santa Cruz.
2. Whenever possible, English editions of texts cited will be given here. M. L.
   McLaughlin, 'Humanist Concepts of Renaissance and Middle Ages in the
   Tre- and Quattrocento', *Renaissance Studies*, II (1988) 131–42. This important
   essay remains relatively ignored in the historiographical discussions of the
   Renaissance in art history, although it is an important corrective to the views
   expressed by Wallace K. Ferguson, *The Renaissance* (New York, 1940).
3. Michael Baxandall, *Giotto and the Orators: Humanist Observers of Painting in
   Italy and the Discovery of Pictorial Composition* (Oxford, 1971), p. vii.
4. Cecil Grayson's excellent annotated facing translations of Alberti's treatises
   *On Painting* and *On Sculpture* appeared at the same moment as Baxandall's
   book. See Leon Battista Alberti, On Painting *and* On Sculpture: *The Latin
   Texts of* De pictura *and* De statua *by Leona Battista Alberti*, ed. and trans. Cecil
   Grayson (London, 1972). A newer edition of Grayson's *On Painting*, without
   the Latin facing, has been annotated by Martin Kemp. See Leon Battista
   Alberti, *On Painting*, trans. Cecil Grayson (London, 1991). On rhetorics in
   Alberti, particularly his architectural theory, see Mark Jarzombek, *On Leon
   Battista Alberti* (Cambridge, MA, 1989).
5. Foremost among these early researches of the literature on art was Julius von
   Schlosser, *La Letteratura Artistica: Manuale delle Fonti della Storia dell'Arte*, trans.
   Filippo Rossi (Florence, 1964), originally published in German in 1924 as *Die
   Kunstliteratur*.
6. David Summers, *Michelangelo and the Language of Art* (Princeton, 1981); Patricia
   Rubin, *Giorgio Vasari: Art and History* (New Haven, 1995); Philip Sohm, *Style
   in the Art Theory of Early Modern Italy* (Cambridge, 2001).

7.  Giorgio Vasari, *Le vite de' più eccellenti pittori, scultori e archittetori nelle redazioni del 1550 e 1568*, ed. Rosanna Bettarini and Paola Barocchi (Florence, 1966–87), 8 vols.

8.  A recent argument of this sort may be found in Marina Belozerskaya, *Rethinking the Renaissance: Burgundian Arts Across Europe* (Cambridge, 2002), especially pp. 1–46.

9.  David Summers, *Real Spaces: World Art History and the Rise of Western Modernism* (London and New York, 2003), esp. pp. 15–36.

10. Walter Benjamin, *The Origin of German Tragic Drama*, trans. John Osborne (London, 1998), pp. 38–9. I have found Benjamin's articulation of the historiography of the *Trauerspiel* extremely useful to my understanding of the idea of the Renaissance in the history of art. Benjamin's extensive reading in art history would certainly have led him to a consideration of the formulation of *Kultur* found in Jacob Burckhardt and in the idea of style found in some of the early twentieth-century German art historians mentioned in my account. It is tempting to conclude that the originality of his theory of Baroque tragic drama owes much to the assessments of Burckhardt's contribution in *The Civilization of the Renaissance in Italy*. Here, I would point particularly to Wilhelm Dilthey, 'Die Kultur der Renaissance in Italien, ein Versuch von Jacob Burckhardt', in *Gesammelte Schriften* (Stuttgart, 1960), II, pp. 70–6. Further discussion of Burckhardt and Dilthey may be found in Catherine M. Soussloff, *The Absolute Artist: The Historiography of a Concept* (Minneapolis, 1997), pp. 88–93.

11. Benjamin, *Origin*, p. 38.

12. For an exhaustive and excellent discussion of the significance of the *Last Supper* for an understanding of the historiography of Renaissance painting, see Leo Steinberg, *Leonardo's Incessant Last Supper* (New York, 2001). For an analysis of Leonardo's position as the archetypical artist of his time, the Renaissance, see Richard Turner, *Inventing Leonardo* (Berkeley and Los Angeles, 1992).

13. Michael Baxandall, *Painting and Experience in Fifteenth-Century Italy: A Primer in the Social History of Pictorial Style* (Oxford and New York, 1972).

14. Baxandall, *Painting and Experience*, p. 151.

15. Benjamin, *Origin*, p. 39.

16. Walter Pater, *The Renaissance* (1873); Kenneth Clark, *Leonardo da Vinci* (London, 1988).

17. David Freedberg, *The Power of Images: Studies in the History and Theory of Response* (Chicago, 1989). This terminology may be particularly useful in the context of an essay that seeks to distinguish the idea of the Renaissance in the discipline of art history, given that figuration may be considered the basis of the mimetic regime of visual representation in Europe at this time, but that a concept of 'art' emerges at a later time.

18. In the discipline of art history there is no consensus on these methodological issues, but see the following recent scholarship dealing with the history of art history for recent views on the topics named here: Thomas DaCosta Kaufmann, *Toward a Geography of Art* (Chicago, 2004); Hans Belting, *Art History After Modernism*, trans. Caroline Salzwedel, Mitch Cohen, Kenneth Northcott (Chicago and London, 2003); Larry Shiner, *The Invention of Art* (Chicago and London, 2001); Catherine M. Soussloff, 'Historicism in Art History', in *The Encyclopedia of Aesthetics*, ed. Michael Kelly (London and New York, 1998),

I, pp. 130–5; II, pp. 407–12; *The Art of Art History: A Critical Anthology*, ed. Donald Preziosi (Oxford and New York, 1998); *Art and its Histories: A Reader*, ed. Steve Edwards (New Haven and London, 1998); *Art History and its Methods: A Critical Anthology* (London, 1995); Vernon Hyde Minor, *Art History's History* (Englewood Cliffs, NJ, 1994).

19. Leah S. Marcus, 'Renaissance/Early Modern Studies', in *Redrawing the Boundaries: The Transformation of English and American Literary Studies*, ed. Stephen Greenblatt and Giles Gunn (New York, 1992), pp. 41–63. I am grateful to my colleague Deanna Shemek for this reference and for discussing some aspects of my essay in its early stages.

20. On literature see Marcus, 'Renaissance/Early Modern Studies'. On religion see the chapter by John Jeffries Martin in this volume.

21. For an excellent discussion of Benjamin on modernity and the work of art see Timothy J. Clark, 'Reservations of the Marvellous', *London Review of Books*, XXII.12 (22 June 2000) 3, 5–9.

22. Heinrich Wölfflin, *Classic Art: An Introduction to the Italian Renaissance*, trans. Peter and Linda Murray (London, 1952), p. 288.

23. Elizabeth Cropper, 'The Place of Beauty in the High Renaissance and its Displacement in the History of Art', in *Place and Displacement in the Renaissance*, ed. A. Vos (Binghamton, NY, 1995), pp. 159–205.

24. Ernst Gombrich, 'In Search of Cultural History', in *Ideals and Idols: Essays on Values in History and in Art* (Oxford, 1979), p. 37 states that Burckhardt collected 700 excerpts from Vasari's *Lives*.

25. Olga Hazan, *Le Mythe du Progrès Artistique: Etude Critique d'un Concept Fondateur du Discours sur l'Art depuis la Renaissance* (Montréal, 1999).

26. Soussloff, *Absolute Artist*.

27. Michael Oakeshott, 'The Detached Vision', *Encounter*, II (May 1954) 74.

28. Francis Haskell, *The Painful Birth of the Art Book* (London, 1987). See also the recent essays in *The Rise of the Image: Essays on the History of the Illustrated Art Book*, ed. Rodney Palmer and Thomas Frangenberg (Aldershot, 2003). The study of illustrated books in Italy in the Renaissance period owes a great deal to the pioneering work of Armando Petrucci; see his *Public Lettering: Script, Power, and Culture* (Chicago and London, 1993) and his *Libri, Scrittura e Pubblico nel Rinascimento* (Rome and Bari, 1979). For the English context, but also for extremely interesting theoretical considerations that pertain in the Renaissance period, see Adrian Johns, *The Nature of the Book: Print and Knowledge in the Making* (Chicago and London, 1998). A useful survey of early illustrated books may be found in *A Continental Shelf: Books across Europe from Ptolemy to Don Quixote* (Oxford, 1994).

29. The most recent bibliography on Leonardo together with this view of him may be found in the massive exhibition catalogue edited by Carmen C. Bambach, *Leonardo da Vinci Master Draftsman* (New York, New Haven and London, 2003). See also the introduction by Martin Kemp and Margaret Walker in *Leonardo On Painting: An Anthology of Writings by Leonardo da Vinci with a Selection of Documents Relating to his Career as an Artist*, ed. Martin Kemp (New Haven and London, 1989).

30. See especially *The Legacy of Leonardo: Painters in Lombardy 1490–1530* (Milan, 1998).

31. Alexander Nagel, *Michelangelo and the Reform of Art* (Cambridge, 2000).

32. Marcus, 'Renaissance/Early Modern', p. 46.
33. Fredrika H. Jacobs, *Defining the Renaissance Virtuosa: Women Artists and the Language of Art History and Criticism* (Cambridge, 1997).
34. Brian Richardson, *Printing, Writers and Readers in Renaissance Italy* (Cambridge, 1999).
35. Ingrid Rowland, *The Culture of the High Renaissance: Ancients and Moderns in Sixteenth-Century Rome* (Cambridge, 1998).
36. Lisa Jardine, *Worldly Goods: A New History of the Renaissance* (New York, 1996). For an extremely interesting exploration that falls in the main outside the chronological period covered in this chapter but which has much to offer in regard to art and commodification, see Marc Shell, *Art and Money* (Chicago and London, 1995).
37. Paula Findlen, *Possessing Nature: Museums, Collecting, and Scientific Culture in Early Modern Italy* (Berkeley, 1994). For views of the museum as modernity, see *Museum Culture: Histories, Discourses, Spectacles*, ed. Daniel J. Sherman and Irit Rogoff (Minneapolis, 1994) and Donald Preziosi, *Brain of the Earth's Body: Art, Museums, and the Phantasms of Modernity* (Minneapolis, 2003).
38. *The Idea of Europe: From Antiquity to the European Union*, ed. Anthony Pagden (Washington, DC and Cambridge, 2002).
39. Erwin Panofsky, *Perspective as Symbolic Form*, trans. Christopher Wood (New York, 1991). Christopher Wood's introduction in this edition is extremely helpful in situating the contribution of Panofsky's essay to the history of Renaissance art. Significant thinking on a variety of aspects of Renaissance perspective has been assembled in *The Treatise on Perspective: Published and Unpublished*, ed. Lyle Massey (Washington, DC, 2003).
40. Roberto Klein, *Form and Meaning* (New York, 1979); Samuel Edgerton, *The Renaissance Rediscovery of Linear Perspective* (New York, 1975). See also S. Edgerton, *The Heritage of Giotto's Geometry: Art and Science on the Eve of the Scientific Revolution* (Ithaca, 1991).
41. Hubert Damisch, *The Origin of Perspective*, trans. John Goodman (Cambridge, MA, 1994).
42. Martin Kemp, *The Science of Art: Optical Themes in Western Art from Brunelleschi to Seurat* (New Haven, 1990).

# 8
## society
### alessandro arcangeli

A survey of the historiography of Renaissance society faces an embarrassment of riches. At the time of Wallace Ferguson's *The Renaissance in Historical Thought* (1948), social history had emerged as a discipline and been identified as one of the most productive and innovative fields of research; subsequent decades have surely kept that promise. On the other hand, the topic is fairly elusive, even posing some fundamental doubts about its actual legitimacy. I will leave some of these doubts to the end, but an initial one arises from the very definition of the object of enquiry: if the Renaissance is taken in its narrower sense to mean a cultural movement, rather than a whole period in general history, its social dimension covers a fairly limited ground, which could be defined as the social history of art and humanism.

In fact Ferguson, commenting on the first examples of a socio-economic interpretation of the Renaissance, identified exactly this issue. He pointed out that

> for more than half a century after Burckhardt, the interpretation of the Renaissance remained [...] almost entirely untouched by the results of the rapidly growing research in economic and social history. One potent reason for this was that the Renaissance had commonly been regarded as a concept applicable primarily to the history of intellectual and aesthetic culture. [...] As a result, economic and social historians as a rule did not consider the Renaissance their concern, while the historians who did concern themselves with it were equally indifferent to the prosaic discoveries of their materialistic colleagues.[1]

Alfred von Martin's pioneering *Sociology of the Renaissance* was published in 1932. Although Ferguson criticized his thesis – the persistence of the belief in a 'spirit of the age', this time identified with the character of the capitalistic bourgeoisie of Florence, seen as the ideal type of the Renaissance – he welcomed Martin's work as the inauguration of a new approach that, although in a reductively economistic form, offered a new solution to the problem of the origins of the Renaissance. This path was to be followed, over the subsequent few years, by other scholars – noticeably by Martin Wackernagel, whose portrait of the world of Florentine artists considers their social, economic and cultural context, from public and private clients to viewers, collectors and institutions.[2] Throughout variations in subsequent trends of art history, the interest in the social milieu has continued to inspire some of the most recent textbooks assessing Renaissance art.[3]

If we broaden the spectrum and, besides art, consider humanism, we find that the social approach to its interpretation has generated studies in the field of 'culture and society'. Along these lines, Lauro Martines explored *The Social World of the Florentine Humanists* in 1963; and Peter Burke adopted the same approach in 1972 by systematically selecting a corpus of Italian intellectuals ('the creative elite'), and analysing the geographical, social and other factors that may have influenced their careers.[4] Twenty years later, in a review essay on Florentine studies, Ronald Weissman suggested that intellectuals may be considered as a social group in their own right, rather than as the expression of the ideology of the dominant élite. It was once more Peter Burke who most explicitly worked in that direction, introducing the notion of early modern European specialists of knowledge as a 'clerisy'.[5]

As for humanism from the perspective of the fifteenth-century renewal of classical models of education, Anthony Grafton and Lisa Jardine have suggested that, rather than being read in terms of the advancement of humane learning and freedom, it should be set in the context of the needs of the early modern bourgeoisie, and be understood predominantly as a reorientation towards discipline: 'it offered everyone a model of true culture as something given, absolute, to be mastered, not questioned – and thus fostered in all its initiates a properly docile attitude towards authority'.[6] Not entirely opposed to this is the conclusion of a wide-ranging study by William Bouwsma who, although differing in his chronology and subject matter, offered a portrait of the 'waning of the Renaissance' in which the initial drive towards freedom is followed by a retreat and the establishment of the rigid modes of thought and social rules characteristic of absolutism.[7]

If we now take the step of considering the Renaissance as a whole period rather than only as a cultural movement, we find that social aspects – as opposed to purely political, economic or intellectual developments – have been attracting an increasing share of attention over the past forty years, and have consequently influenced the ways in which the latter, more traditional fields, are approached. This reorientation has concerned both research and teaching – with textbooks from the late 1960s onwards offering selections of documents on Renaissance society[8] – thus influencing successive waves of students. Even outside the specific fields of humanism and the arts, 'culture and society' still feature together as a frequent pair in the title of books and articles. In fact, an entire generation of historical research has been built on the connection between these two sides of the coin, to the extent that 'socio-cultural history' is a current denomination for a whole methodological approach, with scholars as a rule specializing on either side, but never completely forgetting to consider the other. As Natalie Davis put it fifteen years ago: 'What is social history at the end of the 1980s? It is at the very least social and cultural history. Classic social history has its closest ties with sociology and economics; the newer social history has them more likely with anthropology and literature.'[9] Of course, it would be untrue to suggest that Burckhardt had excluded society from his consideration. His 'Kultur' – as any reliable translation will tell you – was a whole 'civilization'. In fact, he devoted a specific section of his book to 'Society and Festivals' (in the original German, rather, 'sociability': 'Die Geselligkeit und die Feste'). However, Burckhardt's sources and perspective conditioned his view on these matters, and he assessed 'the equalization of classes' and 'the position of women' in terms entirely unacceptable to our own judgements and sensibilities.

The question of the economic roots of Renaissance culture (which received a first answer in Alfred von Martin's historical sociology) gives us the opportunity to glance at the economic background. An old historiographical cliché would have the Italian Renaissance as an age of inventions and paramount economic dynamism, with particular reference to commerce and banking; the wealth consequently generated laid the grounds for artistic developments (and fuelled a Marxist social history of art).[10] During the 1950s and early 1960s, this paradigm was turned upside down by a revisionist approach, which concentrated on the devastating consequences of the plague of 1348 and a series of other contemporary disasters. Ironically, the depression thesis, whose chief representative was Robert Lopez, could also claim to offer a materialistic explanation for the origins of the cultural Renaissance. The idea was that when, from 1350 to 1500, population and economic activity declined,

Italian cities ruthlessly exploited the countryside [...]. As investment opportunities shrank and a small urban aristocracy controlled a larger share of wealth, the capitalist spirit of earlier generations was eroded. The élite now spent time and money in the leisure of country estates and art. As a cultural phenomenon the Renaissance was inextricably tied to economic depression.[11]

In the wording of historians of Marxist orientation, this counted as a 'treason of the bourgeoisie' when compared with the dynamism of earlier generations, or with the trends in the economies of contemporary northern Europe. Italy became a backward looking, 'refeudalized' society.

Few economic historians still subscribe to this thesis today. The study of the rural world has suggested either that agriculture was never abandoned, or that return to the land was a story of successful exploitation of investment opportunities, rather than of failure and retreat. In its turn, this development opens new directions in the exploration of the connections between culture and the economy. For example, 'new forms of landscape painting emerged when the agrarian landscape itself was being transformed by different crops and settlement patterns'[12] such as Italian sharecropping (*mezzadria*). There is less agreement on the actual conditions of the farmers themselves, and one may indeed ask: did *contadini* have a Renaissance? The case of an illiterate Tuscan farmer who left written memoirs has offered an opportunity for unusual insights into his daily life and diverse forms of economic activity, although it is inevitably bound to remain an exception.[13]

Regional variation also needs to be taken into account, and losses in one sector or area could be compensated by gains in others. Thus, more than one study suggests a sharp improvement in the standard of living of Florentine workers after the Black Death, in clear contradiction to the assumption that all its consequences were disastrous. Even one of the late medieval 'horsemen of the Apocalypse' (Revelation, 6.1–8), namely war, was responsible for an economic boom in Milanese arms and metallurgical production.[14]

On the whole, not many economic historians find the Renaissance a useful concept in the periodization of historical trends in their field. A significant exception is Richard Goldthwaite, who identifies the demand for art and other luxury goods, and a parallel increase in consumption, as one of the most distinctive features of the age. The same scholar has written an authoritative socio-economic history of Renaissance Florentine architecture, drawn against a background of economic growth – though such a portrait has not achieved consensus among peers.[15]

The economic life of the Renaissance was dominated by urban systems which have been described in terms of 'urban archipelagos' (such as the north Italian and Flemish), as well as of decentrings and recentrings. Fernand Braudel (1902–1985), the French historian who first introduced some of these categories, sketched a world economy centred on single dominant cities, a place respectively occupied by Venice, Antwerp, Genoa and, from about 1600, Amsterdam.[16] Even outside the economic field, most of Renaissance historiography has been, in one way or another, an urban history. Florence and Venice take up a large portion of such studies, for a wide and obvious range of reasons, not least the richness of their archives.[17] Indeed mirroring the state of research – or at least the frequency by which research directly addresses 'the Renaissance' as the historical setting of a range of different narratives – most of the work surveyed in the present chapter is centred on Florence (and, subordinately, Tuscany and a wider Italy).[18] Among many individual and collective research itineraries in the area of urban studies, the forty years of work of the Italian historian Marino Berengo (1928–2000) might be mentioned in particular. At its two chronological extremes his scholarly activity produced a case-study of sixteenth-century Lucca and an international fresco of urban civilization from the twelfth to the seventeenth centuries, a period he depicted as the heyday in the history of the European city.[19] Berengo's focus was on citizens, urban social history and the forms in which collective life was organized. His work did not merely conceive of the period under study as an initial phase in a story of urban development, whose later forms are to be found in the history of modern Europe. Following a well-established paradigm, it implied instead that, after an age of characteristically city-centred social life, there arose in the modern period an era of regional and national states, whose central identities and animating dynamics lay beyond the city as such.

Broadly speaking, courts provided this alternative centre; they have been the subject of many significant publications.[20] The most influential of all was the oeuvre of German sociologist Norbert Elias (1897–1990). Although not strictly speaking a historian of the Renaissance (the court society at the centre of Elias' attention was seventeenth- and eighteenth-century Versailles), his historical sketch starts from the Middle Ages, and the Renaissance plays a decisive role in that shift towards the regulation of manners and self-control – what he called 'the civilizing process' – which forms the centre of his narrative.[21]

Elias' model has encouraged reflection on the ways in which political, religious and cultural change – with particular emphasis on the evolution of the practice of reading – redefined the nature and limits of the private and public spheres.[22] This in turn takes us back to that interpretation of the Renaissance most often associated with Jacob Burckhardt: individualism. Not insignificantly, this is an area in which recent scholarship has moved far away from his narrative, with attacks coming from medievalists, cultural and social historians, theorists and comparatists.[23] Literary critic Stephen Greenblatt has been one of the most influential Renaissance scholars of the past two decades. The implications of his analysis of 'Renaissance self-fashioning' – a term that has acquired noticeable popularity among the subsequent generation of researchers – are instructive. As the author reveals in the epilogue to his seminal volume,

> When I first conceived this book several years ago, I intended to explore the ways in which major English writers of the sixteenth century created their own performances, to analyze the choices they made in representing themselves and in fashioning characters, to understand the role of human autonomy in the construction of identity. [...] But as my work progressed, I perceived that fashioning oneself and being fashioned by cultural institutions – family, religion, state – were inseparably intertwined. In all my texts and documents, there were, so far as I could tell, no moments of pure, unfettered subjectivity; indeed, the human subject itself began to seem remarkably unfree, the ideological product of the relations of power in a particular society.[24]

Therefore the 'self' in his key word is not merely reflexive – rather, it connotes a social construction of individual identities.

Since the mid-1970s, the historiography has made popular a few revealing examples of Renaissance 'selves', which have helped us to reflect on the relationship between individual and society. Carlo Ginzburg has retold the story of Menocchio, a sixteenth-century miller from Friuli, whose idiosyncratic interpretation of contemporary oral and written culture led him to clash with the Inquisition. Natalie Davis – and one, or rather two, films – have made us familiar with a fascinating case of doubtful and mistaken identity: Martin Guerre, his impersonator, and the final exposure of the latter.[25] Other Renaissance individuals made popular by well-known case studies include Giovanni and Lusanna – the protagonists of a controversial marriage promise, who bear witness to a shift in the academic style of their modern student.[26] Indeed, concern has been expressed over the fact that 'the name of Martin Guerre becomes as well or better known than that of Martin Luther' (John Elliott):[27] the value of such microhistories, and their relation with the wider, macro-picture, has been the subject of extensive discussion, and ultimately depends on personal preferences in the choice of historical methods.[28]

Frequently in recent work, the autonomy of Renaissance 'selves' has been problematized in the context of enduring social structures such as the family. Over the past few decades, indeed, the family has proved one of the most fruitful units to consider in the history of past societies; historians, sociologists and anthropologists have all produced substantial contributions to its reconstruction, from their different perspectives.[29] Thanks to the work of such specialized research institutions as the Cambridge Group for the History of Population and Social Structure, we are now more aware of different types of family structure (simple, extended, multiple), of family relationships (patriarchal versus conjugal), as well as of the relationships of the family unit with the wider kin. An old paradigm, which regarded the nuclear family as a recent product of social change, has been corrected by the discovery that, among some social groups at least, it was already standard in Europe in the later Middle Ages. Indeed, Alan Macfarlane suggested that it should be considered as a precondition, rather than as a consequence, of the establishment of an industrial society in Britain.[30] Cumulative work has not, however, merely reinforced consensus: there are major disagreements among specialists over the nature and direction of such changes, let alone their geography and chronology. Moreover, 'there is no uniform model of family or clan in the Renaissance world. The size, structure, behaviour, and financial and social status of these kinship groups varied from region to region and changed in response to demographic, political, and economic pressures.'[31] In the long term, there tended to be a contrast between kin and family and, under the pressure of religious and political reforms, family acquired importance at the expenses of kin. 'In principle, the clan prevailed in agrarian economies, where the state was weak and the Church did not regulate marriage, while the family flourished in urban societies, with hereditary or wealth-based social stratification.'[32]

The Renaissance scenario is dominated by the wealth of demographic data collected in the Florentine *catasto* of 1427. In that year the Florentine government organized a census of the population of its dominion and their wealth, which was unprecedented for its detail, down to the names of the individual members of even the poor households. Eventually the census was not exploited for its original fiscal purpose, which was to reform state finances through a better knowledge of everyone's assets. It may, however, have produced its own economic effects, since household goods in a family's main residence were exempt from taxation – a circumstance which stimulated investment in the building and decorating of palaces, and thus diverted resources from commerce and industry. In the late 1970s David Herlihy and Christiane Klapisch-Zuber provided the standard study of this material, which is now available in the form of an on-line database and continues to invite fascinating paths of research.[33]

Louis Haas has recently proposed a revisionist approach to the history of the family, in a book devoted to the topics of childbirth and early childhood in Florence from 1300 to 1600. The target of Haas' criticism is the historiographical paradigm chiefly associated with the work of the French historian Philippe Ariès (1914–1984): the idea that

> premodern childhood was a time of neglect and abuse since high infant mortality rates prevented people from forging close affective bonds with their children. Consequently, according to this theory, premodern Europeans failed to recognize childhood as a distinct stage in the development of the individual. If anything, adults saw children as just miniature versions of themselves; premodern paintings reflect this when they depict children garbed as adults and babies possessing adult features.

Accordingly, childhood became modern because, somewhere between 1600 and 1900, parental 'attitudes and practices changed for the better'. Ariès' thesis has undoubtedly represented historiographical orthodoxy for the past thirty years, among professional historians and lay readers alike. In spite of having been the target of several attempts of criticism, Haas finds it still dominant in studies of the Renaissance family. The core sources for his re-examination of the issue are *ricordi* and *ricordanze* from the Florentine archives. According to Haas, this material reveals affectionate parents who had a variety of motives for wanting children (including a desire for emotional growth, and a sense of civic and Christian duty; not only, that is, for reasons of lineage and inheritance). These parents kept detailed records of their lives and expressed deep feelings concerning them. In this light, rather than being equated with abandonment or even infanticide, the ubiquitous practice of wet nursing appears comparable with modern daycare. The risk for his counter-model – whose reception has been far from warm – is to propose a timeless image of loving family relationships, which denies any historical variation. Nonetheless, its common sense criticism of historians' stereotypes should probably be welcomed and helps to paint a more balanced and shaded picture of the Renaissance family.[34]

As well as birth, research has explored the cultural and social history of death. In the aftermath of the Black Death, there emerged a taste for the macabre and a new love for life, one of the subjects of the iconographical research of Alberto Tenenti, the closest Italian associate of the French *Annales* school.[35] In a comparative analysis of six Italian city-states, Samuel Cohn has studied the contents of wills, in order to measure how important were sentiments such as fame and glory (which were central to Burckhardt's Renaissance), in choices over the distribution of property not only among the élite, but also by representatives of the working classes.[36]

The pandemics that swept through the European population at the end of the 1340s have thus proved one of the most durable watersheds, offering a natural turning point between different stages of European history. This continuous role does not mean that the interpretation of the nature, causes and consequences of what happened in those years have remained invariable. Two above-mentioned scholars, David Herlihy and his former student Samuel Cohn, have recently challenged the dominant epidemiological identification of the Black Death. Herlihy (1930–1991) – one of the most authoritative specialists of the demographic, social and economic history of the later Middle Ages – initially agreed with the Malthusian argument that the Black Death was a man-made calamity, which developed as a consequence of a human population expanding beyond the capacity of the food supply. But he subsequently rejected this model, and argued in favour of a demographic stalemate which had been arrived at a few decades before the late 1340s. In this view, the epidemic should thus be interpreted as a natural variable, one without which European history might have been remarkably different. Herlihy and Cohn have also attacked the etiology of the disease that has been common since the discovery of the plague bacillus in 1894. From that date, the rat and flea have been accused of being the agents of transmission, and the lack of reference to them in contemporary sources was blamed on contemporaries' scientific incompetence. In our own days historians of science are aware of the transformation of diseases through time and are wary of imposing modern epidemiological explanations upon the past. The consequences of the epidemics were wide-ranging and should always be borne in mind when setting the social and cultural achievements of the Renaissance in their historical context. One of Herlihy's suggestions (although not an unproblematic one) points to the plague's role in promoting technological labour-saving innovations, including the printing press, which he interpreted as a response to population depletion.[37]

Along with plague went hunger and other diseases.[38] It is surely not the only topic of medical history which has been revisited by recent scholarship. Among the others, research has explored the range of different medical solutions available in the Renaissance medical marketplace, the patient–doctor relationship, and the interface between charity and medical care.[39] A subject related to health and demographic trends is the history of food, which has been the object of renewed scholarly attention.[40] An even more recent development is the history of the body, a field of cultural history on which significant work has been done by German scholars and which provided the topic for the thirtieth international colloquium of humanist studies, held at Tours.[41]

Marriage, birth and death each represent aspects of the ritual life of past societies, and ritual in its own right has recently formed the subject of research from a variety of disciplinary perspectives. Edward Muir – the author of a case-study of civic ritual in Venice – has offered a general discussion of the topic for the early modern period, suggesting a ritual revolution which occurred in the sixteenth century, and 'shifted attention from the emotive power of rituals to questions about their meaning'. A year before Muir's study of Venice, Richard Trexler had imaginatively applied the same concept to an original reinterpretation of Florentine history, a milestone in urban studies in which a theatrical model of political life is shown to have forged collective identities.[42] Conferences and publications inspired by the latter scholar at Binghamton have transmitted a similar cultural orientation to a subsequent generation of students.[43] Confraternities and guilds were among the protagonists of the ritual life which formed a fundamental element of Renaissance urban society: thus, the guild hierarchy was reflected in the order of precedence in processions. Festivals – as we have seen, an aspect of social life which had attracted Burckhardt's attention – also played an important role in shaping communal identities.[44] There are topics in this area which have been the subject of significant research, but have remained to date the reserve of niche expertise, without fully merging into general assessments of the period. A good example is dance, a field in which there have been scholarly editions of Renaissance dance treatises, and reconstructions of the social and cultural worlds of contemporary practice.[45]

Rituals of violence – as exemplified by vendetta, youth-abbeys and charivari[46] – also need to be mentioned. As one scholar recently put it, 'Renaissance tempers were hot'[47] and violence ubiquitous – even in the 'Most Serene' Republic.[48] A comparison between two collections of essays on violence and crime in Renaissance Italy, published twenty years apart from each other, shows some interesting points of contrast, such as the widening scope of coverage, from an initial stress on group crime and political disorder, to an attention to issues of gender.[49]

As the ultimate manifestation of organized violence, warfare is one field in which a Burckhardtian paradigm of the Renaissance as a significant turning point has on the whole survived. The military revolution of the sixteenth century implied that the myth of aristocratic violence and chivalric codes lost ground, in favour of permanent armies that required huge financial efforts on the part of states, and ultimately of the population. Contemporary societies and communities were directly involved also from the perspective of the prolonged length of military campaigns, and of their effects on civilians.[50] Knightly culture did not disappear altogether, though, as proved by the survival of the duel and of a whole range of 'martial arts'.[51]

In its own way, a special form of collective violence is social unrest, a historical phenomenon that offers the opportunity to interpret the structure and development of social hierarchies. It is well known that interpretations inspired by social theories may overestimate consensus, or at least limit the extent of autonomy allowed to social actors. In this area, the armed Revolt of the Ciompi (1378), the Florentine wool day-labourers, provides by far the most famous episode of popular revolt that occurred during the period in Italy.[52] Samuel Cohn is the scholar who has explored in greatest detail the wider dimensions of the lives of Florentine workers. Cohn positions his view away from both (1) a dominant historiographical paradigm that saw the masses as unchanging and totally manipulated by the oligarchy and (2) a reductively economistic version of Marxism, which had concentrated on the development of capitalist relations of production during the Trecento, and defined class simply in terms of the relationship of groups to the means of production. His aim, on the contrary, was to pinpoint 'crucial changes in the community structures, organization, and consciousness of the Florentine *popolo minuto* within a time span in which there seem not to have been any fundamental transformations in the mode of production'. His findings suggest patterns of behaviour both surprisingly 'modern' and subject to change:

> In fourteenth-century Florence, there were fraternities of workers, industrial strikes, and insurrections that followed falling instead of rising bread prices. By the latter half of the fifteenth century, this picture of the *popolo minuto* had changed radically. The labouring classes turned inward, retreating into communities of parochial protection, and their forms of protest reflected these changes in social structure and the ecology of the Renaissance city. Isolated, individualistic outbursts

of violence against their social betters and the strong arm of the state had taken the place of organized mass insurrection and practical plans for capturing the state apparatus.[53]

As a crisis in the hierarchical order, the subject of revolt naturally leads us to social stratification, another key aspect of past and present societies upon which historians and social theorists have applied different categories. While 'class' is a notion still common (particularly in America) among those historians who, like Cohn, have been influenced by Marxism and tend to express sympathy for the living conditions of the workers, over the past few decades it has virtually been abandoned by British and European historians. That is not necessarily a matter of political orientation, though, since scholars of declared leftist affiliation have also expressed dissatisfaction with the term. What *is* at stake is the range of criteria according to which individuals from past societies adhered to a collective identity, together with the spectrum of implications of that adherence. Regardless of doubts about whether we (or some of us) live in a post-industrial society in which collective identities are formed differently, the heuristic value of the term 'class' for describing pre-industrial social groups and their historical dynamics – most famously stated in Marx and Engels' *Manifesto* of 1848 – has undergone a clear crisis of confidence, and has been at least partially replaced by concepts derived from the sociology of Max Weber. People of pre-modern Europe were assigned to an 'order' (in French, 'état'; in German, 'Stand'; in Italian 'ceto'), often defined in legal terms. It could enrol them in one of the three 'estates' of medieval society still officially in place at the time of the French Revolution: the clergy, nobility, and the common people (with such advantages, for the privileged two, as tax exemptions and judgement by peers). Wealth was a significant element, though not the defining one: there are countless stories of pauper aristocrats, but they testify nonetheless to the continued importance of noble identity, even if some individual noblemen were broke.[54]

So long as the system works properly, conflict should not arise, for orders, as the limbs or organs of the body politic, do different things, and should not compete, as classes do, for shares in the profits of economic enterprise. [...] Structural change may be precluded, but social mobility is not. [...] All such things may be seen by critics as mere expressions of a conservative ideology [...]. Class struggles might not at the time have been recognized for what they were, but that is not to deny that classes existed, representing a grimmer and more deep-rooted version of reality. In defence of orders, however, it should be said that they were not merely figments of the imagination of powerful people, not just the cardboard creations of propagandists, for they were embodied in fiscal systems, in regional and national parliaments, in patents of nobility, in registers of honourable citizens, and officially recognized in many other ways.[55]

This is an opinion that has found much support, but scholars have never been unanimous in this matter: participants at a millennium conference at Villa I Tatti, Florence, had the opportunity to listen to a passionate speech by John Najemy (a contributor to the present volume), in favour of the use of the concepts of class and conflict and against the idealization of the Renaissance élite endlessly proposed by what he called the 'consensus school'.[56]

On the whole, it seems that people tended to belong simultaneously to different collectivities, if one also considers gender and age (with the legal conditions that defined women and children), citizenship (and the privileges of belonging to a particular city), profession or trade (and the rules that regulated their exercise). Such criteria should be considered in their interconnections, rather than in their mere coexistence: throughout the period, membership of a guild, for example, was a decisive element of citizenship. Local variations obviously mattered. The Venetian patriciate was different from landed nobility elsewhere: its special relation with the *popolo* has been cited as an explanation of the republic's social stability, and its myth has itself attracted historiographical attention.[57] Contemporary accounts of Venetian social categories could not mention the clergy, and they thus list nobles, citizens and artisans as the three ranks of society.[58] Incidentally, this is precisely the tripartite division proposed by Najemy on the basis of the roles different social groups played in the political arena of northern and central Italy, with the middling *popolo* siding sometimes with the artisans, sometimes with the ruling élite. Najemy also criticizes the idea that patronage – rather than class – works as a better model for the explanation of social dynamics, and he suggests that frequent promiscuity and personal links that cut across the social divide would make people more, rather than less, aware of their differences.[59]

Below all other strata were beggars and the poor, a category which underwent a substantial change of perception and treatment from the sixteenth-century.

Between the fourteenth and seventeenth centuries, both institutions and attitudes regarding the relief of poverty developed and diversified in western Europe [...]. In most settings a culture of poverty and poor relief evolved which distinguished, perhaps more sharply than in the past, among different causes for poverty and the degrees with which they deserved alleviation: the Elizabethan distinction between the 'deserving poor' and the 'sturdy beggar' is merely the best-known example.[60]

While for the medieval Christian the poor represented the image of Christ and an opportunity for soul-laundering charitable deeds, work ethics and political and religious reforms converged to depict them in a new, negative light, locking them inside institutions (such as the large hospitals which were built from around the mid-fifteenth century), and obliging them to work. The rough doubling of the population of western Europe over the period is one of the most obvious roots of this evolution.

The cultural counterpart of social stratification is the contrast between popular and élite culture. Although it dealt with a wider period, Peter Burke's *Popular Culture in Early Modern Europe* (1978) continues to offer the standard assessment of the matter. It offers an overview of the traditional forms of popular culture and of the world of Carnival. This culture was shared by different social groups, but in the sixteenth century, reformations on both sides of the religious divide intervened, Lent triumphed and the upper classes withdrew.[61] The same scholar has subsequently discussed the methodological issues emerging from further research; this has made both 'popular' and 'culture' more problematic notions than previously envisaged. Following the example of the anthropologists, historians have used the concept of culture very widely. As for the dichotomy of élite and popular classes, it tends to oversimplify social hierarchy; and, by identifying the popular with the radical (under the influence of a leftist scholarly tradition), it tends to ignore evidence for popular conservatism. On the contrary, Russian critic Mikhail Bakhtin's seminal 'definition of Carnival and the carnivalesque, by its opposition not to élites but to official culture, marks an important shift in emphasis which comes close to redefining the popular as the rebel in all of us (as Freud once wrote) rather than as the property of any social group'. Some scholars have gone as far as abandoning the popular/élite dichotomy altogether, substituting it with alternative (though no less problematic) dialectics, such as that between centre and periphery.[62] More recently, a culture/subculture model has been proposed, which represents the complex cultural identity of overlapping segments of society (the rural world, 'national' and religious subcultures, the subcultures of work, the subculture of women).[63]

At the margins of its social and cultural sub-groupings, the Renaissance world inevitably had its outsiders. The poor are a borderline case, the Jews and other minorities a more specific example. Characteristic of the age is the witch, since the period starting from the late fifteenth century witnessed the well-known European witch-hunt. The study of witchcraft is perhaps Carlo Ginzburg's best-known expertise, a field to which he has contributed both with a detailed account of a northern Italian tradition (the *benandanti*) and its prosecution by the Inquisition, and with an ambitious (and coldly received) attempt to root the whole related family of witch beliefs in an elementary perception of the human species.[64] Belief in witchcraft is set in a different context by Stuart Clark, who describes how contemporary language – a language of dual classification, contrariety and inversion – together with science, history, religion and politics convinced intellectuals of the reality of the phenomenon.[65] Among many other studies of the subject, it may be worth singling out the suggestion that the preaching of Bernardino da Siena might have played a significant role in pioneering the cultural shift that, during the course of the fifteenth century, turned most western Christians from medieval incredulity to early modern fear and prosecution of the damned art.[66]

To turn back to an initial question, a troubling issue of anachronism has been raised on the very subject of the present chapter: was there ever such a thing as a 'Renaissance society'? John Bossy has expressly made his case against the use of such a term. The Renaissance was not directly at stake in his analysis, which is concerned with traditional Christianity and the transformation it incurred during the sixteenth century. However, his chronology is totally consistent with the one under consideration here. While he notes the absence of the use of the word 'society' in the Renaissance period (at least in any meaning comparable to our own use of the term), his real point is that the thing itself was not there either.[67] Nineteenth-century social theory repeatedly proposed a distinction between society (in German, *Gesellschaft*), the sphere where atomic individuals meet and relate, and community (in German, *Gemeinschaft*), the group to which people intrinsically belong and in which they are shaped fundamentally. Although the story of this distinction owes much to the Romantic imagination and to the nostalgia for 'the world we have lost', its possible use as a historical tool allows and requires the interpreter to set the transition between the two modes of socialization somewhere in time and space: a past world without 'society' is perfectly thinkable; a complex process of redefinition of human relationships would be responsible for its subsequent establishment. In other words, a remarkable distance separates the conditions and life experiences of individuals and groups who lived between four and seven centuries ago from those that characterize modern western societies. In the previous pages, we have referred to historical research on a variety of topics – from family and kin to the other networks that were webbed around and across individuals, such as confraternities (touched upon in the present volume by John Jeffries Martin) – all of which should help us in assessing the depth of social change.

This conclusion leaves open the question of when, where and how the most significant changes in social structures – which differentiate us from them – occurred. If the Renaissance appears to most of us today less 'modern' than it did to Burckhardt and other scholars of past generations, this does not mean that it was not a period of developments of strategic importance in reshaping Europe and the world beyond.

## notes

I owe valuable bibliographical references to the kindness of Simon Ditchfield, Leo Tedoldi and Jonathan Woolfson.

1. W. K. Ferguson, *The Renaissance in Historical Thought: Five Centuries of Interpretation* (Boston, 1948), p. 235.
2. Ferguson, *Renaissance in Historical Thought*, esp. pp. 229–38. A. von Martin, *Sociology of the Renaissance*, trans. W. L. Luetkens (London, 1952, reprinted 1998). M. Wackernagel, *Der Lebensraum des Künstlers in der florentinischen Renaissance: Aufgaben und Auftraggeber, Werkstatt und Kunstmarkt* (Leipzig, 1938), translated into Italian as *Il mondo degli artisti nel Rinascimento fiorentino* (Rome, 1994).
3. See, for instance, E. Welch, *Art and Society in Italy, 1350–1500* (Oxford, 1997); reprinted as *Art in Renaissance Italy* (Oxford, 2000).
4. L. Martines, *The Social World of the Florentine Humanists* (Princeton, 1963). P. Burke, *Culture and Society in Renaissance Italy, 1420–1540* (London, 1972); revised edn entitled *The Italian Renaissance: Culture and Society in Italy* (Princeton, 1986).
5. R. F. E. Weissman, 'Dal dialogo al monologo: la storia tra i fiorentini', *Cheiron*, XVI (1991) 95–111 (p. 106) – a monographic issue on 'Storici americani e Rinascimento italiano', ed. G. Chittolini; P. Burke, *A Social History of Knowledge* (Cambridge, 2000), esp. pp. 18–31.
6. A. Grafton and L. Jardine, *From Humanism to the Humanities: Education and the Liberal Arts in Fifteenth- and Sixteenth-Century Europe* (London, 1986), quotation from p. xiv.
7. W. J. Bouwsma, *The Waning of the Renaissance. 1550–1640* (New Haven, 2000).

8. A. Molho, ed., *Social and Economic Foundations of the Italian Renaissance* (New York, 1969); G. A. Brucker, ed., *The Society of Renaissance Florence: A Documentary Study* (1971; reprinted Toronto, 1998).

9. N. Zemon Davis, 'The Shapes of Social History', *Storia della storiografia*, XVII (1990) 28–39 (quotation from p. 28). The same scholar has authored one of the best-known occurrences of this pair of terms: *Society and Culture in Early Modern France* (Stanford, 1975).

10. For an example of Marxist interpretation: J. Macek, *Italská Renesance* (Prague, 1965); Italian translation by H. K. Casadei (Rome, 1981).

11. J. C. Brown, 'Prosperity or Hard Times in Renaissance Italy?', *Renaissance Quarterly*, XLII (1989) 761–80 (quotation from p. 761) – here the reader will find all the bibliographical information that can substantiate my brief summary of the matter. For another historiographical survey, see F. Franceschi, 'La storiografia economica sul Rinascimento', in A. J. Grieco, M. Rocke and F. Gioffredi Superbi, eds, *The Italian Renaissance in the Twentieth Century* (Florence, 2002), pp. 153–72.

12. Brown, 'Prosperity or Hard Times', 764.

13. D. Balestracci, *The Renaissance in the Fields: Family Memoirs of a Fifteenth-Century Tuscan Peasant*, trans. P. Squatriti and B. Merideth (University Park, PA, 1999).

14. Brown, 'Prosperity or Hard Times', 771–2.

15. R. Goldthwaite, *Wealth and the Demand for Art in Italy: 1300–1600* (Baltimore, 1993); *The Building of Renaissance Florence: An Economic and Social History* (Baltimore, 1980). Cf. also R. Goldthwaite, *Private Wealth in Renaissance Florence: A Study of Four Families* (Princeton, 1968) – one of many remarkable studies of one or few households of the Tuscan patriciate.

16. J. de Vries, 'Renaissance Cities', *Renaissance Quarterly*, XLII (1989) 781–93.

17. For a wide-ranging study of Venice: E. Crouzet-Pavan, *'Sopra le acque salse': Espaces, pouvoir et société à Venise à la fin du Moyen Âge* (Rome, 1992).

18. Although implications of these and other works for the wider historical context will be expressly drawn, this is not the place for redressing such an imbalance, while the reader will find geographical issues addressed in the first part of this volume.

19. M. Berengo, *Nobili e mercanti nella Lucca del Cinquecento* (Turin, 1965); *L'Europa delle città. Il volto della società urbana europea tra Medioevo ed età moderna* (Turin, 1999). For an even wider chronological survey see P. M. Hohenberg and L. H. Leese, *The Making of Urban Europe, 1000–1950* (Cambridge, MA, 1985).

20. For general overviews, see S. Bertelli et al., *Italian Renaissance Courts* (London, 1986); J. Adamson, ed., *The Princely Courts of Europe* (London, 1999). See also the section on 'La corte' in G. Chittolini, A. Molho and P. Schiera, eds, *Origini dello Stato. Processi di formazione statale in Italia fra Medioevo ed Età moderna* (Bologna, 1994), pp. 425–89, with contributions by T. Dean, M. Fantoni, J. S. Grubb and E. W. Muir; abridged English edition ed. J. Kirshner, *Origins of the State in Italy, 1300–1600* (Chicago, 1995). Over the past twenty-five years the Centro Studi Europa delle Corti – which in 1983 promoted the establishment of the Istituto di Studi Rinascimentali in Ferrara – has published a series of books ('Biblioteca del Cinquecento', Rome, Bulzoni), which covers both historical and literary topics and has already passed the hundredth volume.

21. N. Elias, *The Civilizing Process*, I: *The History of Manners*, trans. E. Jephcott (Oxford, 1978); *The Court Society*, trans. E. Jephcott (Oxford, 1985). Naturally Elias' thesis did not go unchallenged. For two examples of different replies (one a radical confutation, the other a critical reassessment of the model), see H. P. Duerr, *Der Mythos vom Zivilisationsprozess* (Frankfurt am Main, 1988–); and J. Duindam, *Vienna and Versailles: The Courts of Europe's Dynastic Rivals, 1550–1780* (Cambridge, 2003).
22. G. Chittolini, 'Il "privato", il "pubblico", lo Stato', in Chittolini, Molho, Schiera, *Origini dello Stato*, pp. 553–89; P. Ariès and G. Duby, eds, *A History of Private Life*, II–III, trans. A. Goldhammer (Cambridge, MA, 1988–89).
23. J. J. Martin, 'The Myth of Renaissance Individualism', in G. Ruggiero, ed., *A Companion to the Worlds of the Renaissance* (Oxford, 2002), pp. 208–24 – which offers a typology distinguishing between a 'communal', a 'performative', and a 'porous' self.
24. S. Greenblatt, *Renaissance Self-Fashioning, from More to Shakespeare* (Chicago, 1980), p. 256.
25. C. Ginzburg, *The Cheese and the Worms: The Cosmos of a Sixteenth-Century Miller* (Baltimore, 1980); N. Zemon Davis, *The Return of Martin Guerre: Imposture and Identity in a Sixteenth-Century Village* (Cambridge, MA, 1983).
26. G. A. Brucker, *Giovanni and Lusanna: Love and Marriage in Renaissance Florence* (London, 1992).
27. See the interviews collected in M. L. G. Pallares-Burke, *The New History: Confessions and Conversations* (Cambridge, 2002), passim.
28. For methodological discussion on social and cultural history see *Storia della storiografia*, XVII and XVIII (1990).
29. Only a small selection representative of chronologically and geographically wide-ranging surveys can be cited here: J. Goody, *The Development of the Family and Marriage in Europe* (Cambridge, 1983); M. Barbagli, *Sotto lo stesso tetto: mutamenti della famiglia in Italia dal XV al XX secolo* (Bologna, 1984).
30. A. Macfarlane, 'Socio-Economic Revolution in England and the Origin of the Modern World', in *Revolution in History*, ed. R. Porter and M. Teich (Cambridge, 1986), pp. 145–66.
31. J. M. Ferraro, 'Family and Clan in the Renaissance World', in Ruggiero, *A Companion*, pp. 172–87 (quotation from p. 176).
32. Ferraro, 'Family and Clan'.
33. D. Herlihy and C. Klapisch-Zuber, *Les Toscans et leurs familles: une étude du catasto florentin de 1427* (Paris, 1978); English abridged version: *Tuscans and their Families: A Study of the Florentine Catasto of 1427* (New Haven, 1985). The Florentine example has shown the importance of considering the family as something more than a group of co-residents: family units of the same kin lived next door to one another in the same quarter, regularly met and co-operated in their political and economical affairs. See also A. Molho, *Marriage Alliance in Late Medieval Florence* (Cambridge, MA, 1994); and, for an example from a different area, J. S. Grubb, *Provincial Families of the Renaissance: Private and Public Life in the Veneto* (Baltimore, 1996).
34. L. Haas, *The Renaissance Man and His Children* (Basingstoke, 1998); quotations from p. 2. Cf. P. Ariès, *Centuries of Childhood*, trans. R. Baldick (New York, 1962).

35. A. Tenenti. *Il senso della morte e l'amore della vita nel Rinascimento: Francia e Italia* (Turin, 1957). On the macabre, see J. Huizinga, *The Waning of the Middle Ages*, trans. F. Hopman (London, 1965). Here too Philippe Ariès has produced seminal work for a wider chronological period: P. Ariès, *Western Attitudes toward Death: From the Middle Ages to the Present*, trans. P. Ranum (Baltimore, 1974); P. Ariès, *The Hour of Our Death*, trans. H. Weaver (New York, 1981). See also S. T. Strocchia, *Death and Ritual in Renaissance Florence* (Baltimore, 1992).

36. S. Cohn, *The Cult of Remembrance and the Black Death: Six Renaissance Cities in Central Italy* (Baltimore, 1992); S. Cohn, 'Burckhardt Revisited from Social History', in A. Brown, ed., *Language and Images of Renaissance Italy* (Oxford, 1995), pp. 217–34; reprinted in *The Renaissance: Italy and Abroad*, ed. J. J. Martin (London, 2003), pp. 107–23.

37. D. Herlihy, *The Black Death and the Transformation of the West*, ed. S. K. Cohn, Jr (Cambridge, MA, 1998); S. K. Cohn, Jr, *The Black Death Transformed: Disease and Culture in Early Renaissance Europe* (London, 2002).

38. An updated overview in M. Lindemann, 'Plague, Disease, and Hunger', in Ruggiero, *A Companion*, pp. 427–43.

39. K. Park, *Doctors and Medicine in Early Renaissance Florence* (Princeton, 1985); J. Henderson, *Piety and Charity in Late Medieval Florence* (Oxford, 1994); G. Pomata, *Contracting a Cure: Patients, Healers and the Law in Early Modern Bologna* (Baltimore, 1998).

40. Among the most recent contributions see K. Albala, *Eating Right in the Renaissance* (Berkeley, 2002).

41. R. Zur Lippe, *Naturbeherrschung am Menschen* (Frankfurt am Main, 1974); A. Nitschke, *Bewegungen in Mittelalter und Renaissance: Kämpfe, Spiele, Tänze, Zeremoniell und Umgangsformen* (Düsseldorf, 1987); J. Céard et al., eds, *Le corps à la Renaissance* (Paris, 1990); K. Park, 'Was there a Renaissance Body?', in Grieco, Rocke, Gioffredi Superbi, *Italian Renaissance in the Twentieth Century*, pp. 321–35.

42. E. Muir, *Civic Ritual in Renaissance Venice* (Princeton, 1981) and his *Ritual in Early Modern Europe* (Cambridge, 1997), quotation from p. 274; R. Trexler, *Public Life in Renaissance Florence* (New York, 1980). For a discussion of their two models, see M. Casini, *I gesti del principe: la festa politica a Firenze e Venezia in età rinascimentale* (Venezia, 1996).

43. See, for instance: R. C. Trexler, ed., *Persons in Groups: Social Behavior as Identity Formation in Medieval and Renaissance Europe* (Binghamton, 1985).

44. F. Yates, *The Valois Tapestries* (London, 1959); R. Strong, *Art and Power: Renaissance Festivals, 1450–1650* (Berkeley and Los Angeles, 1984); P. Béhar and H. Watanabe O'Kelly, eds, *Spectaculum Europaeum: Theatre and Spectacle in Europe/Histoire du spectacle en Europe, 1580–1750* (Wiesbaden, 1999).

45. For an edition of one of the most important sources see Guglielmo Ebreo of Pesaro, *De Pratica seu Arte Tripudii. On the Practice or Art of Dancing*, ed. B. Sparti (Oxford, 1993); for a detailed study: A. Pontremoli and P. La Rocca, *Il ballare lombardo: teoria e prassi coreutica nella festa di corte del XV secolo* (Milan, 1987); as an example of a recent publication from which dance is remarkable for its absence: L. Panizza, ed., *Women in Renaissance Culture and Society* (Oxford, 2000).

46. E. Muir, *Mad Blood Stirring: Vendetta and Factions in Friuli during the Renaissance* (Baltimore, 1993); N. Zemon Davis, 'The Reasons of Misrule', in her *Society and Culture*, pp. 97–123; C. Klapisch-Zuber, 'The *mattinata* in Medieval Italy', in her *Women, Family, and Ritual in Renaissance Italy*, trans. L. G. Cochrane (Chicago, 1985), pp. 261–82.

47. T. F. Arnold, 'Violence and Warfare in the Renaissance world', in Ruggiero, *A Companion*, pp. 460–74 (quotation from p. 461).

48. G. Ruggiero, *Violence in Early Renaissance Venice* (New Brunswick, 1980). See also G. Ruggiero, *The Boundaries of Eros: Sex, Crime, and Sexuality in Renaissance Venice* (New York, 1985).

49. L. Martines, ed., *Violence and Civil Disorder in Italian Cities, 1200–1500* (Berkeley, 1972); T. Dean and K. J. P. Lowe, eds, *Crime and Disorder in Renaissance Italy* (Cambridge, 1994).

50. J. R. Hale, *War and Society in Renaissance Europe, 1450–1620* (London, 1985); G. Parker, *The Military Revolution: Military Innovation and the Rise of the West* (Cambridge, 1988).

51. S. Anglo, *The Martial Arts of Renaissance Europe* (New Haven, 2000).

52. See *Il tumulto dei Ciompi: un momento di storia fiorentina ed europea* (Florence, 1981).

53. S. Cohn, *The Labouring Classes in Renaissance Florence* (New York, 1980) – a revised version of Cohn's doctoral dissertation supervised by David Herlihy (quotations from pp. 11 and 4). Cohn acknowledges Charles de la Roncière as one of the few scholars of Renaissance Florence who is interested in the Florentine poor.

54. To be accurate, wealth was not Marx's criterion either. His definition of class as determined by one's relation with the means of production is nonetheless clearly rooted in the industrial world. On the stereotype of the 'declassed' aristocrat: G. Ricci, *Povertà, vergogna, superbia: i declassati fra medioevo e età moderna* (Bologna, 1996).

55. B. Pullan, '"Three Orders of Inhabitants": Social Hierarchies in the Republic of Venice', in *Orders and Hierarchies in Late Medieval and Renaissance Europe*, ed. J. Denton (Basingstoke, 1999), pp. 147–68 (quotation from pp. 148–9).

56. J. M. Najemy, 'Politics: Class and Patronage', in Grieco, Rocke, Gioffredi Superbi, *Italian Renaissance in the Twentieth Century*, pp. 119–36.

57. D. Romano, *Patricians and Popolani: The Social Foundations of the Venetian Renaissance State* (Baltimore, 1987); D. E. Queller, *The Venetian Patriciate: Reality versus Myth* (Urbana, 1986).

58. Pullan, 'Three Orders'.

59. Najemy, 'Politics'.

60. L. R. Poos, 'The Historical Demography of Renaissance Europe: Recent Research and Current issues', *Renaissance Quarterly*, XLII (1989) 794–811 (quotation from pp. 809–10); cf. B. Pullan, *Rich and Poor in Renaissance Venice: The Social Institutions of a Catholic State, to 1620* (Oxford, 1971).

61. P. Burke, *Popular Culture in Early Modern Europe* (London, 1978; revised edition Aldershot, 1994).

62. P. Burke, 'Popular Culture Reconsidered', *Storia della storiografia*, XVII (1990) 40–9 (quotation from p. 42); reprinted with slight variations as Introduction to the 1994 edition of his *Popular Culture*, pp. xvi–xxvii (p. xvi).

63. D. C. Gentilcore, 'The Subcultures of the Renaissance World', in Ruggiero, *A Companion*, pp. 299–315.
64. C. Ginzburg, *Night Battles: Witchcraft and Agrarian Cults in the Sixteenth and Seventeenth Centuries*, trans. J. and A. Tedeschi (London, 1983); *Ecstasies: Deciphering the Witches' Sabbath*, trans. R. Rosenthal (New York, 1991).
65. S. Clark, *Thinking with Demons* (Oxford, 1997).
66. F. Mormando, *The Preacher's Demons: Bernardino of Siena and the Social Underworld of Early Renaissance Italy* (Chicago, 1999). On the other hand, the author reduces the role which current historiography often gives to Bernardino in another campaign, that against the Jews: his actual target was money-lenders, most of whom were Christian.
67. J. Bossy, 'Some Elementary Forms of Durkheim', *Past and Present*, XCV (1982) 3–18.

# 9
# gender
## judith c. brown

As other chapters in this book have noted, modern conceptions of the Renaissance begin with the 1860 publication of Jacob Burckhardt's *The Civilization of the Renaissance in Italy*. The emergence of self-conscious individuals in that time and place made them, according to Burckhardt, the 'first-born among the sons of modern Europe'.[1] In their journey of self-discovery, these men were joined by their women, who 'stood on a footing of perfect equality' with them.[2] The discovery of 'man' also meant the discovery of 'woman'.

Although in the decades after its publication, Burckhardt's conception of the Italian Renaissance was challenged by medievalists, as well as by Renaissance historians of religion, science, and the economy, among others, his conception of gender relations remained unchallenged for over a century.[3] Even in the early years of the feminist revolution of the 1970s, when some scholars began to look at the history of Renaissance women from a new perspective, they painted a favourable picture of their power and influence.[4] It was not until later in the decade that this conception of gender relations was challenged, mostly by women historians who were deeply affected by the changes in gender relations in their own societies.[5] The first round of critiques from this direction came in an article by Joan Kelly, aptly titled 'Did Women Have a Renaissance?'[6] 'One of the tasks of women's history', she argued, 'is to call into question accepted schemes of periodization … The Renaissance is a good case in point.' The economic and political developments 'that reorganized Italian society along modern lines and opened the possibilities for the social and cultural expression for which the age is known … affected women adversely, so much so that there was no renaissance for women – at least not during the Renaissance'.[7] The development of the modern state and the emergence of capitalism, which were essential for the expansion of opportunities for men, had, in her view, an inherently negative effect on women. The creation of a public political sphere and the shift of economic activities to locations outside the home, she argued, removed women's ability to hold political and economic power.

Kelly's challenge to reconceptualize the way we organize history and evaluate historical periods, was accompanied or followed by a series of essays whose trenchant arguments and evidence seemed to confirm her thesis. Margaret King wrote of the thwarted ambitions of the élite women of the Renaissance, who in the interests of family ambitions now received a better education than before, but who, by virtue of that education, were also more isolated from their peers, occupying gilded cages that made their education a questionable gain.[8] Diane Owen Hughes' essay, 'From Brideprice to Dowry in Mediterranean Europe', published a year later, argued that the widespread shift to a dowry system by the end of the Middle Ages brought about the marginalization of women in the inheritance system as well as their subjugation to their husbands.[9] And in a powerful series of essays whose titles, 'The Griselda Complex' and 'The Cruel Mother', reveal the bleak picture they paint of women's standing in Renaissance families, Christiane Klapisch-Zuber also argued that family strategies for success in Renaissance politics and society imposed harsher restrictions on patrician women than had been the case before. The patriarchal family system that emerged in Florence, the 'cradle' of the Renaissance, became so intent on the preservation of male lineage that women became passing and barely tolerated guests in their own homes.[10] Only widowhood may have brought some measure of relief, as Renaissance women married older husbands than their medieval predecessors. The prolonged widowhood that often ensued allowed many to regain control of their dowries and a degree of independence that they lacked as wives and daughters.[11] Yet even this possible improvement by middle- and upper-class women was contested by male relatives and was, moreover, balanced in society as a whole by the increasing exclusion of their poorer sisters from the labour force, both as a result of diminished demographic pressures after the Black Death and by increasing guild restrictions against women.[12]

Kelly's thesis and the contention that Renaissance women were worse off than their medieval predecessors did not go unchallenged. On theoretical grounds, some historians argued that the emergence of a public sphere had the potential to increase the roles of women and that capitalism did not appreciably shift the organization of economic activities and production outside of the domestic sphere until the industrial revolution.[13] On empirical grounds, historians such as Isabelle

Chabot and Samuel Kline Cohn showed that women participated in the economy in larger numbers and in more diverse ways than had been previously thought.[14] Others, such as Monica Chojnacka, discovered that women, and working women especially, had a degree of geographical mobility that calls for qualification of the thesis that with the creation of a public sphere, women were consigned to private spaces.[15] Yet others, such as Stanley Chojnacki, observed that some of the same phenomena that appear to have had a negative impact on the lives of Florentine women, such as the increasing importance of ever-larger dowries, gave Venetian women a power that they had not enjoyed before the Renaissance.[16] Even some scholars who agreed with Kelly on the deterioration of women's conditions in the Renaissance argued that this very fact contributed to the emergence of a new self-consciousness among women. Aware of their plight, women began to rail against it in treatises that in some respects could be considered the first modern feminist tracts, thus giving support to Burckhardt's contention that Renaissance women shared with men a new and modern sensibility about the self.[17]

Initially, the dialogue with Kelly's work proceeded along the lines of women's history. The goal was to restore women to historical accounts – to unearth from the rubble of history the lives of women who had been hidden by historical accounts of earlier generations. At first, this meant gaining a deeper understanding of the lives of a small number of famous women – Caterina Sforza, Isabella d'Este, St Catherine of Siena, Vittoria Colonna, and others who, by virtue of their role in political circles, as patrons of the arts, or as well-known religious figures, were able to influence society.[18] Extending outward from this small circle, the project required finding worthy women writers or artists who might be brought into the illustrious company of great men. Finally, it required combing the historical documents – tax records, notarial contracts, family diaries, and so on – for the telltale signs of the activities of everyday women – the bakers, seamstresses, innkeepers and others whose work and social contributions enabled ordinary people to survive.

As these efforts to discover the range of women's activities and influence unfolded, historians also began to turn their attention to the more complicated issue of how legal, political, economic, and social structures may have circumscribed the lives of the vast majority of women, impinging on their actual social conditions and behaviour. What legal restrictions on inheritance or property ownership contributed to the unequal distribution of wealth between men and women? What barriers kept women from receiving the professional training and status to become professional writers and artists? What educational opportunities were denied to women and were available to men and on what grounds? What kinds of guild regulations limited the range of occupational choices available to them? And if restrictions existed, as they undoubtedly did, how did they vary from one Renaissance city to another, from one century to the next, and why?[19]

These questions led to an analysis of the legal and prescriptive sources that was much more self-conscious and nuanced about the relationship between the theoretical and the actual lived experience of women than had been the case before. Whereas some of the earlier scholarly work tended to look at the prescriptive sources – preachers' sermons, treatises on the family, educational tracts, legal codes affecting marriage and dowries, or sumptuary laws – as a full reflection of how the patriarchal society of the Renaissance treated women, the new approach took both a deeper and a wider view.[20] The deeper view led to the concept of agency; the wider view to the concept of gender.

The former resulted in many studies showing how women negotiated and at times subverted the social norms that stood in their way. In these works women are depicted less as passive victims than as individuals who, despite formidable constraints, helped shape their own destinies, those of their families, and those of their social groups. They are also seen as having greater ability to control economic and other resources than was thought. Finally, they are shown in a more complicated social world than was imagined before – a world in which they were often aided by brothers, fathers, and other male kin whose interests at particular moments intersected with their own.[21] Indeed, some of the men who might have denied their sister's claims to their family's patrimony could be found at a different time in the family's history helping that very sister fight legal battles to control her own inheritance upon her husband's death. Perforce then, these studies have resulted in a less pessimistic view of the plight of Renaissance women. They also rehistoricized women's past. 'Woman' was no longer the timeless and classless victim of patriarchy, but an active agent in moulding the world she inhabited.

The wider view, which led to the concept of gender, had even more profound repercussions because it altered the theoretical categories with which to approach the relation between the sexes and the new conceptions of the self. Women's history helped us discover aspects of women's lives that were hidden from history. But it also had the potential to create a timeless, placeless, and essentializing notion of woman, as well as to isolate the history of women in an anachronistic separate sphere.[22]

By means of gender as an analytical category, historians can now examine the ways in which women and men interpreted the meaning of being male and female; what characteristics men and women in the past attached to what they considered 'feminine' and 'masculine'; how those attributes varied by time and place, or age and social class; and how both women and men could appropriate these categories for different purposes. Gender enables scholars to examine the social construction of male and female identities and the meaning attached to different social roles assumed by women and men depending on age, social class, and other social rather than biological characteristics. Using gender, scholars can ask different questions than are possible in women's history: if in some places in Italy men allowed women to be guardians of their children, why did they not allow them to represent themselves in a court of law? What was 'male' and what was 'female' about these two powerful functions that women could and could not practise in one and the same place? Indeed, why could they do so in some Italian cities but not others? Why, in the absence of obvious barriers in the law, did women in some cities located in the same region exercise greater independence in disposing of their property than women in neighbouring towns? Given the theoretical equality of the spirit between men and women in Christian thought, why was it that some of the central practices of the Church divided the spiritual roles of women and men in ways that resembled secular society? In short, what cultural constructs allowed women and men in the past to attach different meaning to similar circumstances and hence to structure social practices along gendered fault lines?

Gender can also direct us to the examination of social organizations – among which the political state is perhaps the most obvious – that excluded women from official roles, but which were based on strong notions of gender which, in turn, affected the most fundamental aspects of the lives of women as well as men. In a city like Venice, for example, that formally barred women from political life, gendered metaphors that depicted the city as Virgin and as Venus were central to the powerful myth of Venice which shaped the Venetian aristocracy's sense of self in the sixteenth century. By analysing this aspect of political discourse and its connection to the cultural and social life of the city, historians can observe the importance of women and reinsert them in spheres from which they at first glance appear to be missing.[23]

Last but not least, gender leads us in the direction of analysing the construction of male identity rather than taking men as the undifferentiated norm and women as the other. The rise of women's history and of gender theory was followed by the emergence of men's history. One might say that the discovery of 'woman' has led to the discovery of 'man'. Pioneering work in this area has been done by Stanley

Chojnacki, showing the consequences for men of the increasing emphasis on patrilineage by which the Venetian ruling class defined itself after 1300.[24] A more rigid patriarchy was not only problematic for women, but also for large groups of men – young adults, permanent bachelors, and others – who were excluded from decision-making powers and from access to political and economic resources.

With the extension of gender theory to include the history of men as men, historians have weakened the link between biological sex and gender. Gender is now seen as a construct in which women and men situate themselves and are situated by others along a shifting range of possibilities. The position that is occupied by any one person or group is influenced by many characteristics, among them age, class, region, and sometimes, but by no means exclusively, biological sex. Perhaps nowhere is this more obvious than in the history of sexuality, another field that has developed in the last two decades. As Michael Rocke's pioneering work on the history of homosexuality shows, homosexual behaviour and perceptions about it in Renaissance Italy 'had little to do with current notions of sexual orientation or identity', but were 'organized instead around notions of gender and life stages'. For most males it was a temporary stage on the way to adulthood.[25]

Having seen the usefulness and elasticity of the concept of gender, it would be remiss not to acknowledge that as a category of historical analysis it is by no means beyond criticism. Judith Bennett has warned that by intellectualizing the inequality of the sexes, the concept of gender can gloss over the injustices faced by medieval and Renaissance women. By emphasizing the agency of both women and men, it can gloss over the powerlessness of women in the face of patriarchy. And by its concern with meaning and metaphor, it can steer historians away from the hard realities of social history.[26] At the other end of the continuum, historians such as Thomas Kuehn believe that as neutral as gender may seem to historians like Bennett, it remains overly divisive because it cannot escape the limitations of 'natural' sexual imagery. For that reason, Kuehn favours the notion of 'social personhood', which he argues 'points to relations between individuals, or even between parts of an individual' in a complex social reality that cannot be simplified along binary lines.[27]

With the development of the conceptual tools discussed above and after roughly three decades of empirical research, what is the state of many of the questions that historians have posed? Consensus has been slow to emerge, in part because much of the initial scholarly work focused on specific places, most notably Florence and Venice, where different political, legal, and social conditions contributed to different results. However, after nearly thirty years of research, it is now possible to examine local experiences in a more comparative framework. Doing so allows us to discern broad patterns and themes across geography and time. Although these have not entirely erased ideological and methodological differences among scholars, and some still emphasize the constraints that Renaissance notions of gender imposed on women, most now focus on the imaginative and resourceful ways in which these notions were subverted by women as well as men. One might argue that they were Renaissance people precisely because of the ingenuity and self-consciousness with which they did so.

Renaissance notions of what was masculine and what was feminine were to a large extent rooted in Renaissance notions about human biology. These were explored by Ian Maclean in his pioneering *The Renaissance Notion of Woman*, which summarizes the Aristotelian and Galenic views of male and female differences in the human body that held sway until the end of the sixteenth century, when the work of Gabriele Falloppio irreversibly changed medical views of the female anatomy.[28] According to the Aristotelian view, women were defective and incomplete males, whose colder, moister humours affected everything from menstruation to intelligence and sexual behaviour. Galen differed on one major point, that is, that women had semen, albeit a colder and less active variant, but semen nonetheless, which contributed to the formation of the human embryo. While the Galenic view gave women a more active role in reproductive biology, this hardly brought them to a position of equality. Scientific theories, whether Aristotelian or Galenic, posited a world of binary oppositions in which men were decidedly on top.[29] Yet Katharine Park has noted that in contrast to the theoretical literature, most medical practitioners and their patients held a variety of opinions that were more gender-neutral. The emphasis of medical practice was on evacuating the substances that impacted on and corrupted the humours. This could be accomplished through urination, menstruation, bleeding, sweating, and so on, with analogous processes among men and women. Indeed, so close were these systems that some physicians discussed them with reference to 'menstruating men'. Because practising physicians did not have a clearly dichotomous view of men's and women's bodies, they tended to interpret female inferiority to behaviour patterns rather than to corporeal imperatives. The importance of this for Renaissance attitudes about gender should not be underestimated. Behaviour could be changed, while human anatomy could not.[30]

Because gender history grew out of the history of women and the latter's initial focus was the private sphere, scholars of gender turned first to social history. Yet the development of the state, as Joan Kelly pointed out from the beginning, was essential to establishing the framework for social relations between men and women and of new notions of the public and private spheres. In the last decade historians have become more aware of the intricate connections between these spheres, of the centrality of gender in the formation of the Renaissance state, and of the essential role of the state in the regulation of gender relations in family life. As a consequence, they have turned to the intersection of gender history and the development of the state.[31]

The symbiosis between public and private in political life is evident in the relationship between state formation and the consolidation of oligarchic hegemonies that were the body politic yet which also needed to be regulated by it. In the process of representing and disciplining the élites in the late fourteenth and fifteenth centuries, the state extended its regulatory reach into areas of social life that had previously been the province of the family. New laws and new public offices to deal with everything from the size of dowries to the regulation of marriage and the protection of children asserted the prerogatives of patriarchy to represent the state and control the behaviour of individuals within the family.[32] Patriarchy, the right of certain males to hold authority, was not a new social construct, but it was newly articulated in these centuries through the revival of Roman law, the systematization of common law (*ius commune*), the development of local laws, and the rediscovery, reinterpretation, and application of Aristotelian and Platonic political texts to political thought and civic institutions. In the process the divide between men and women widened. And for the same reasons, so did the divide between males who were deemed fit to rule and those who were not because of their class, age, or circumstance within the family. The result, according to a number of scholars, was that the conflicts revealed by state efforts to mediate between these different interests created the room that enabled women and sometimes disenfranchised men to manoeuvre more extensively as effective agents in the social landscape. The Renaissance state marks a decisive turning point in the creation of notions about what is public and what is private, and gender lines were the contested boundaries around which these new notions developed.

The role of law in these developments is obviously very important. Whereas earlier work suggested that the revival of Roman law imposed a harsher regime on women than medieval law, and that the systematization of law in and of itself constrained their agency, more recent work has substantially altered these ideas. It seems that new local statutes, rather than *ius commune* or the revival of Roman law, put the most constraints on Renaissance women. Local governments, for example, sometimes tried to limit the ability of women to inherit property by recognizing inheritance only through the male line. Some also tried to limit the power of women to represent themselves legally by requiring them to have a male guardian (*mundualdus*) to represent in court. Yet even these efforts were inconsistent. There were, for example, geographic differences. In Venice wives could bequeath their dowries to their children or their husbands and could represent themselves in court – rights denied to their Florentine sisters. There were also legal inconsistencies within particular places. While Florentine women could not represent themselves in court, they could have principal guardianship over their children, a powerful right, as long as they also appointed a male co-guardian, whom they had the right to choose. Last, there were inconsistencies in the enforcement of laws, of which the most glaring were to be found in sumptuary laws, which for the most part were practised in the breach.[33] The one common denominator was that women could not have *patria potestas* (paternal legal control), but neither could certain categories of males. The study of gender in Renaissance law reveals that clearcut dichotomies between male and female did not exist either in legal theory or in everyday practice.

The lack of a single, uniform body of law, the discrepancies between common law and local statutes, and the increasingly complex reality of family life, contributed to a large number of legal disputes and court cases in which women and men asserted their agency in ways that were contrary to what superficial readings of the law might suggest. These cases have been mined by scholars for many different purposes, ranging from scholarship showing the systematic and deliberate undermining of sumptuary laws designed to curb female and sometimes male displays of clothing and jewellery, to work on disputes over property, inheritance, honour, illegitimate marriages, guardianship of females, forced marriages, and marriage wars that sometimes ended in the dissolution of marriage.[34] They have produced a rich body of work showing that women and subaltern men had many legal rights they could assert both in theory and practice, and that often they were aided by male relatives – husbands, fathers, or children – whose interests coincided with theirs and whose ties of affection bound them beyond self-interest. Thus women and men were able to mitigate the consequences of patriarchy and to contrive ways to circumvent some of the legal barriers that were placed in front of them.[35] The manner in which the laws were interpreted and applied in practice and the plurality of law, both according to time and place, resulted in considerable flexibility.

The absence of rigid boundaries also extended to the world of work. The distribution of men and women in the labour force depended on notions of gender-appropriate work, not on biology. The historical documents that bear on the question, however, conceal as much as they reveal. Among the best sources for learning about occupations in the past are tax records and guild matriculation lists. But pre-modern tax records tend to show only the occupations of heads of households, and guild records tend to show official matriculation lists from which women were often excluded. For that reason, the range of women's occupations and the degree of their participation in them tended to be underestimated by scholars. Yet based on such fraught sources, David Herlihy concluded that because of the allegedly growing power of labour guilds in economic and political life, urban women of the Italian Renaissance were less likely to find employment than their medieval ancestors.[36] Guilds, however, declined in power in the Renaissance and, if one looks at sources other than guild matriculation lists or tax records, one finds women in a surprisingly large range of occupations. Exact quantitative assessment of their numbers are beyond our reach, but guild records, tax records, notarial records, criminal and civil law records, as well as literary and artistic sources, show women in many occupations. While many clustered in traditional sectors, working as servants, spinners and weavers in the wool and silk cloth industries or as sailmakers in maritime cities, and in food-related occupations, where they were bakers, itinerant food vendors, and inn-keepers, some did heavy physical labour as carpenters, blacksmiths, or skinners, carders, and stretchers in the wool industry; and yet others were sheep-herders over long distances, which put them far from home and in potentially dangerous situations. Because few scholars in recent decades have turned their attention to the economic history of the Renaissance, we do not yet know whether such activities were common among women or how the sexual division of labour varied by region or time. Even with partial sources, however, it is possible to know that the experience of different parts of Italy does not support a single model to explain the variety of patterns. It would be unwise, therefore, to subscribe to theories that posit a decline in the overall participation of women in the labour force and in the range of their occupations. It is likely that some women, such as medical practitioners, were edged out of certain fields that were becoming professionalized, and which therefore increasingly required a university education from which women were barred. But there is insufficient evidence to support theories that posit an overall decline due to a culture of honour and shame that allegedly kept women in the domestic sphere, as some have claimed, or due to the rise of capitalism, as Joan Kelly suggested, or due to the stranglehold of guilds in urban economies. Much more detailed research will need to be done before we understand the degree and the range and reasons for gendered patterns in the labour force. The work of recent historians suggests much more variety, a much greater presence, and a far more complex set of reasons for the patterns of women's work than scholars had imagined.[37]

One area to which work extended was behind the walls of monasteries and convents that enclosed a large proportion of the population, particularly the female population, of Italian cities. It is not just that monastic men and women performed the spiritual work of prayer for their own salvation and that of those around them, but that a significant amount of economic activity occurred in those places. Book production, manuscript illumination, miniature painting, lace making, and embroidery of luxury cloths were just a few of the economic activities that took place in women's convents, while men's monastic institutions continued to produce the books, paintings, and, in rural settings, the agricultural products for which they have always been known.

As our view of what took place in monastic institutions and the meaning attached to those activities has become more complex, so has our view of the gendered dimension of the religious landscape of the Renaissance. We are more aware than in previous decades of the large range of religious institutions – from places where deeply secluded anchorites spent their lives in solitary prayer to houses of *pinzochere*, where women lived communal religious lives out in the secular world. We are also more aware of the gender-bending complexity of religious roles that men and women assumed or that were assigned to them. Religious women who were ostensibly secluded from the world sometimes became powerful public figures. Religious men who ostensibly knew little about domestic matters wrote advice books about it and sometimes used female imagery to describe their relationship to Christ. Life in monastic institutions enabled some women to devote their lives to writing, a career that was denied to them outside of convent walls, while it enabled others in the secular world to be architectural and artistic patrons, a role that could more easily be justified for women if the object of patronage was a religious institution.[38]

The gender continuum and role reversal observed in the spiritual landscape of the Renaissance became more difficult to maintain after mid-sixteenth century, when the Protestant Reformation and internal reforms within the Catholic Church resulted in new norms that widened the distance between men and women. After the Council of Trent in the mid-sixteenth century, women's independence was curbed by stricter rules of decorum and of enclosure in convents. The domestic ideal of marriage came to dominate the imagery and the ritual life of women inside and outside the convent while the ideal of the heroic missionary and military conquerors as soldiers of Christ became more pervasive among men. These developments unfortunately took place against a backdrop of increasing monachization for women, particularly women of the urban élites who by the end of the Renaissance found themselves behind the walls of convents in ever greater numbers.[39]

In conclusion, looking at more than a quarter century of scholarship on Renaissance women and men as gendered subjects, it is safe to say that it is no longer tenable to hold dichotomous views of the developments that took place in the Renaissance. While there are still many unanswered questions and topics to explore, it is clear that there was no universal downward slide in the opportunities available to women and that there were enormous regional variations. Moreover, because gender is a culturally produced category, it was constantly tested in practice by the men and women of the time. In the course of their daily lives, they reinvented, reinforced, and subverted the gender classifications that confronted them in scientific, political, legal, and religious doctrines. To be sure, the state, religious institutions, and educational and professional organizations may have tried to impose more restrictive gender categories, yet the men and women of the Renaissance found ways to undermine these restrictions. Their ability to do so often required them to marshal all their intellectual and emotional resources and sometimes to incur considerable risks. In the process, they not only stretched gender categories, but developed new conceptions of what it means to be human and a new awareness of the self in relation to family and social communities. This new sense of self may not have been the autonomous individualism that Burckhardt posited, but it was an important stage in the trajectory towards modernity.

## notes

1. Jacob Burckhardt, *The Civilization of the Renaissance in Italy* (New York, 1958), 2.1, p. 143.
2. Burckhardt, *Civilization*, 5.6, p. 389.
3. For a useful summary of these critiques, see Gene A. Brucker, *Renaissance Italy: Was it the Birthplace of the Modern World?* (New York, 1965).
4. See Stanley Chojnacki, 'Dowries and Kinsmen in Early Renaissance Venice', *Journal of Interdisciplinary History*, V (1975) 571–600; Lauro Martines, 'A Way of Looking at Women in Renaissance Florence', *Journal of Medieval and Renaissance Studies*, IV (1974) 15–28.

5.  This is not to argue that all women scholars or even that all feminist women scholars viewed the status and condition of women in the Renaissance the same way. It is simply to observe that the pessimistic view of the 'progress' made by women in the Renaissance came from scholars who were women.

6.  Joan Kelly, 'Did Women Have a Renaissance?' in *Becoming Visible: Women in European History*, ed. Renate Bridenthal and Claudia Koonz (Boston, 1977), pp. 137–64; reprinted in *Women, History, and Theory: The Essays of Joan Kelly* (Chicago, 1984; hereafter the edition cited), pp. 19–50.

7.  Kelly, 'Did Women Have a Renaissance?', p. 19.

8.  Margaret King, 'Thwarted Ambitions: Six Learned Women of the Renaissance', *Soundings*, LIX (1976) 280–304; see also her 'Book-Lined Cells: Women and Humanism in the Early Italian Renaissance', in *Beyond their Sex: Learned Women of the European Past*, ed. Patricia Labalme (New York, 1980), pp. 66–90.

9.  Diane Owen Hughes, 'From Brideprice to Dowry in Mediterranean Europe', *Journal of Family History*, III (1978) 262–96.

10. Christiane Klapisch-Zuber, 'Le complexe de Griselda', *Mélanges de l'Ecole Française de Rome*, XCIV (1982) 7–43; also 'Maternité, veuvage et dot à Florence', *Annales*, XXXVIII (1983) 1097–109. These and other essays by Klapisch-Zuber have been translated and published in English in *Women, Family, and Ritual in Renaissance Italy* (Chicago, 1985).

11. David Herlihy, 'Growing Old in the Quattrocento', in *Old Age in Preindustrial Society*, ed. Peter N. Stearns (New York, 1982), pp. 104–18.

12. David Herlihy and Christiane Klapisch-Zuber, *Les toscans et leurs familles: Une étude du catasto florentin de 1427* (Paris, 1978), pp. 582–3, translated as *Tuscans and their Families: A Study of the Florentine Catasto of 1427* (New Haven, 1985).

13. For an early critique of Kelly's thesis, see Judith C. Brown's review, 'Women, History and Theory', in *American Historical Review*, XCII (1987) 938–40. On the other hand, for a recent reassertion that terms like 'Renaissance' and conventional periodization schemes do not fit women's history, see Merry Wiesner's essay, 'Women's History and Social History: Are Structures Necessary?' in Anne Jacobson Schutte, Thomas Kuehn, and Silvana Seidel Menchi, eds, *Time, Space, and Women's Lives in Early Modern Europe* (Kirksville, MO, 2001), pp. 3–16.

14. Judith C. Brown, 'A Woman's Place Was in the Home: Women's Work in Renaissance Tuscany', in *Rewriting the Renaissance: The Discourses of Sexual Difference in Early Modern Europe*, ed. Margaret W. Ferguson, Maureen Quilligan and Nancy J. Vickers (Chicago, 1986), pp. 206–24; Isabelle Chabot, 'La reconnaissance du travail des femmes dans la Florence du bas Moyen Age: contexte idéologique et réalité', in *La donna nell'economia secc. XIII–XVIII*, ed. S. Cavaciocchi (Florence, 1990), pp. 563–76. For a brief review of the literature on women's roles in economic activities and an analysis of their participation in Florentine economic life, see Samuel Kline Cohn, 'Women and Work in Renaissance Italy', in Judith C. Brown and Robert C. Davis, eds, *Gender and Society in Renaissance Italy* (London and New York, 1998), pp. 107–26.

15. Monica Chojnacka, *Working Women of Early Modern Venice* (Baltimore, 2001).

16. Stanley Chojnacki, 'The Power of Love: Wives and Husbands in Late Medieval Venice', in *Women and Power in the Middle Ages*, ed. Mary Erler and Maryanne

Kowaleski (Athens, GA, 1988); '"The Most Serious Duty": Motherhood, Gender, and Patrician Culture in Renaissance Venice', in *Refiguring Woman: Perspectives on Gender in the Italian Renaissance*, ed. Marilyn Migiel and Juliana Schiesari (Ithaca, 1991), pp. 133–54.

17. This is not to ignore the enormous intellectual differences that separate these writings from modern works for women's rights, but they share with modern works a desire to improve the condition of women and to critique the cultural assumptions that were the foundations for women's inequality. Some of these writings are examined by Virginia Cox, in 'The Single Self: Feminist Thought and the Marriage Market in Early Modern Venice', *Renaissance Quarterly*, XLVIII (1995) 513–81. In language that coincidentally foreshadowed Burckhardt, one such treatise by Lucrezia Marinella, called on women to 'wake themselves from the long slumber that has oppressed them'. Cox, 'The Single Self', 521. The treatise is now available in translation: Lucrezia Marinella, *The Nobility and Excellence of Women and the Defects and Vices of Men*, ed. and trans. Anne Dunhill (Chicago, 1999). See also Moderata Fonte, *The Worth of Women*, ed. and trans. Virginia Cox (Chicago, 1997).

18. The change in approach is evident in some of the titles themselves; cf. Ernst Breisach, *Caterina Sforza: A Renaissance Virago* (Chicago, 1967), and two later treatments, Natale Graziani, *Caterina Sforza* (Milan, 2001), and Julia Hairston, 'Skirting the Issue: Machiavelli's Caterina Sforza', *Renaissance Quarterly*, XLVIII (2000) 687–712. On Isabella d'Este, see Massimo Felisatti, *Isabella d'Este, la primadonna del Rinascimento* (Milan, 1982). Also see David Wilkins, 'Art, Education, and Medicine: Woman as Artists and Patrons in the Middle Ages and the Renaissance', in *The Roles and Images of Women in the Middle Ages and Renaissance*, ed. Douglas Radcliff-Umstead (Pittsburgh, 1975), pp. 107–31.

19. The most famous and perhaps most influential of these essays, akin to the impact of Joan Kelly's essays, is Linda Nochlin's 'Why Have There Been No Great Women Artists?' originally published in *Art News*, special issue entitled *Women's Liberation, Women Artists, and Art History* (1971), reprinted in the collected writings of Linda Nochlin, *Women, Art, and Power and Other Essays* (New York, 1988), pp. 145–78.

20. A helpful overview of the prescriptive sources that limits itself to laying out the intellectual framework is Ian Maclean, *The Renaissance Notion of Woman: A Study in the Fortunes of Scholasticism and Medical Science in European Intellectual Life* (Cambridge, 1980). Maclean acknowledged that his focus was limited and that a more comprehensive history of women in Renaissance Europe had yet to be written.

21. For examples of the new approaches, see Sharon Strocchia, *Death and Ritual in Renaissance Florence* (Baltimore, 1992); Giulia Calvi, 'Diritti e legami: Madri, figli, stato in Toscana (XVI–XVIII secolo)', *Quaderni Storici*, LXXXVI (1994) 487–510; Stanley Chojnacki, 'Nobility, Women, and the State: Marriage Regulation in Venice, 1420–1535', in *Marriage in Italy, 1300–1650*, ed. Trevor Dean and K. J. P. Lowe (Cambridge, 1998), pp. 128–51; Thomas Kuehn, *Law, Family, and Women: Toward a Legal Anthropology of Renaissance Italy* (Chicago, 1991); and Catherine Kovesi Killerby, *Sumptuary Law in Italy 1200–1500* (Oxford, 2002).

22. Joan W. Scott, 'Gender: A Useful Category of Historical Analysis', *American Historical Review*, XCI (1986) 1053–75. Also see Judith Butler, *Gender Trouble:*

*Feminism and the Subversion of Identity* (New York, 1990), whose theories about gender are always thought-provoking, but whose emphasis on the primacy of language and discourse is greater than most historians would accept.

23. See, for example, Jutta Gisela Sperling, *Convents and the Body Politic in Late Renaissance Venice* (Chicago, 1999).

24. Stanley Chojnacki, 'Kinship Ties and Young Patricians in Fifteenth-Century Venice', *Renaissance Quarterly*, XXXVIII (1985) 240–70; Chojnacki, 'Political Adulthood in Fifteenth-Century Venice', *American Historical Review*, XCI (1986) 791–810; and Chojnacki, 'Subaltern Patriarchs: Patrician Bachelors in Renaissance Venice', in *Medieval Masculinities: Regarding Men in the Middle Ages*, ed. Clare A. Lees (Minneapolis, 1994), pp. 73–90. Although written with a conceptual focus on developmental stages in identity formation, rather than the later developing notion of masculinity as a historical category, the work of Richard Trexler in the 1970s also deals with masculinity; see his 'Ritual in Florence: Adolescence and Salvation in the Renaissance', and '"The Youth are Coming!" Nonsense in Florence during the Republic and Grand Duchy', both now in *Dependence in Context in Renaissance Florence* (Binghamton, NY, 1994), pp. 259–342.

25. Michael Rocke, *Forbidden Friendships: Homosexuality and Male Culture in Renaissance Florence* (New York, 1996).

26. Judith M. Bennett, 'Feminism and History', *Gender and History*, I (1989) 258–9.

27. Thomas Kuehn, 'Person and Gender in the Laws', in Brown and Davis, *Gender and Society*, pp. 89–90.

28. Maclean, *Renaissance Notion*, pp. 28–46.

29. Nancy G. Siraisi, *Medieval and Early Renaissance Medicine: An Introduction to Knowledge and Practice* (Chicago, 1990).

30. Katharine Park, 'Medicine and Society in Medieval Europe, 500–1500', in *Medicine in Society*, ed. Andrew Wear (Cambridge, 1991); and Katharine Park, 'Medicine and Magic: The Healing Arts', in Brown and Davis, *Gender and Society*, pp. 129–49.

31. For a recent example, see Giovanna Benadusi, 'Rethinking the State: Family Strategies and State Formation in Early Modern Tuscany', *Social History*, XX (1995) 157–78.

32. See for example Anthony Molho, *Marriage Alliance in Late Medieval Florence* (Cambridge, MA, 1994), on the creation of the public dowry fund in Florence. See also Stanley Chojnacki, 'Daughters and Oligarchs: Gender and the Early Renaissance State', in Brown and Davis, *Gender and Society*, pp. 63–86; Chojnacki, 'Marriage Regulation in Venice' and 'Getting Back the Dowry', both in Chojnacki, *Women and Men in Renaissance Venice: Twelve Essays on Patrician Society* (Baltimore, 2000), pp. 53–75 and 95–111.

33. Killerby, *Sumptuary Law in Italy*.

34. Kuehn, *Law, Family, and Women*; Killerby, *Sumptuary Law in Italy*; Daniela Hacke, '"Non lo volevo per marito in modo alcuno": Forced Marriages, Generational Conflicts, and the Limits of Patriarchal Power in Early Modern Venice, c. 1580–1680', in Jacobson Schutte, Kuehn, and Seidel Menchi, *Time, Space, and Women's Lives*, pp. 203–21; Joanne M. Ferraro, *Marriage Wars in Late Renaissance Venice* (Oxford, 2001).

35. See Julius Kirshner, 'Materials for a Gilded Cage: Non-Dotal Assets in Florence, 1300–1500', in *The Family in Italy from Antiquity to the Present*, ed. David I. Kertzer and Richard P. Saller (New Haven, 1991), pp. 184–207; Giulia Calvi, 'Diritti e legami: Madri, figli, stato in Toscana', *Quaderni Storici*, LXXXVIII (1994) 487–510.
36. David Herlihy, *Opera Muliebria: Women and Work in Medieval Europe* (New York, 1990)
37. In addition to the works cited in note 14, see Judith C. Brown and Jordan Goodman, 'Women and Industry in Florence', *Journal of Economic History*, XL (1980) 73–80; Christiane Klapisch-Zuber, 'Women Servants in Florence during the Fourteenth and Fifteenth Centuries', in *Women and Work in Preindustrial Europe*, ed. B. Hanawalt (Bloomington, 1986), pp. 56–80; Chojnacka, *Working Women*; Robert C. Davis, *Shipbuilders of the Venetian Arsenal: Workers and Workplace in the Preindustrial City* (Baltimore, 1991); Katharine Park, 'Medicine and Magic: The Healing Arts', in Brown and Davis, *Gender and Society*, pp. 129–49; A. Groppi, *Il lavoro delle donne* (Bari, 1996).
38. Among the many studies on gender, religious institutions, and spiritual life, see Craig A. Monson, ed., *The Crannied Wall: Women, Religion, and the Arts in Early Modern Europe* (Ann Arbor, 1992); Daniel Bornstein and Roberto Rusconi, eds, *Women and Religion in Medieval and Renaissance Italy* (Chicago, 1996); several of the essays in Lucetta Scaraffia and Gabriella Zarri, eds, *Women and Faith: Catholic Religious Life in Italy from Late Antiquity to the Present* (Cambridge, MA, 1999); and Sperling, *Convents and the Body Politic*.
39. Gabriella Zarri, 'From Prophecy to Discipline, 1450–1650', in Scaraffia and Zarri, *Women and Faith*, pp. 83–112; and Zarri, 'Gender, Religious Institutions and Social Discipline: The Reform of the Regulars', in Brown and Davis, *Gender and Society*, pp. 193–212.

# 10
## religion

john jeffries martin

At the height of the Renaissance a young Saxon monk travelled to Rome. Accompanying a superior on official business, the young man – excluded from the more important meetings – found himself with time on his hands. At this very moment (autumn 1510) Michelangelo was recasting the Book of Genesis as a spectacular vision in bold colours on the ceiling of the Sistine Chapel, and Raphael was hard at work on his learned frescos in the papal library. But the Rome this young German monk saw was not a Renaissance city but rather a medieval one, the epicentre of Latin Christendom, a gathering place for pilgrims. The young man visited the city's major churches, saw the relics of saints, climbed the Santa Scala on his knees, and took communion in St Peter's. Immersion in such works was the gate to Heaven. The young man was impressed by the pious opportunities Rome provided, even if he found the intimacy of the sacred in this Mediterranean city disconcerting. He deplored the ecclesiastical extravagance of the Roman prelates. And he overheard other priests making fun of the Eucharist. In later life he would recall that, while in Rome, 'with my own ears I heard the most loathsome blasphemies against Christ and His Apostles'.[1]

On 31 October 1517, only seven years after this visit, the young man, now a doctor of theology, posted his *Ninety-Five Theses* on the door of the cathedral at Wittenberg, the small but bustling Saxon town where he taught. Arguably, this was the act – with its celebrated denunciation of the sale of indulgences – that triggered the Protestant Reformation. Indeed, until the mid or late twentieth century, scholars generally conceived of the Reformation as a protest against abuses in the Catholic Church. Yet, as Martin Luther's earlier experience in Rome suggests, Renaissance Catholicism was rich in spiritual possibilities – penitential acts, devotional exercises, expressions of charity – for setting oneself right with God.

Indeed, evidence from throughout late medieval Europe points to a lush landscape of pilgrimages, processions, eucharistic devotions, and the veneration of saints.[2] The Reformation, accordingly, did not break out in a period in which Christianity was losing its importance, nor was this a time in which abuses were *unusually* widespread. Rather it broke out in a period – the Renaissance – in which a new, intense, lay spirituality was transforming the relations of Christians to one another, and to God. Moreover, even before Luther emerged as a figure of European-wide significance, religious reforms had already begun to make their mark from England to Bohemia, and from the Low Countries to Italy.

Over the last thirty years historians have revolutionized our understanding of the religious history of the Renaissance. To Jacob Burckhardt, writing about this epoch in his famous *Civilization of the Renaissance in Italy* (1860), what mattered in the Renaissance were those forces – the widespread corruption of the Church which drove the people, as he put it, 'into the arms of unbelief and despair', a revival of interest in pagan antiquity, and a growing tendency to explore the world and human nature itself outside the earlier medieval framework of the Christian faith – that laid the foundations for an increasingly secular and modern society.[3] This secularization thesis held sway for a long time. Of course, scholars did not lose all interest in the history of Christianity in this period, but, when they turned their attention to this subject, they tended to focus on the colourful and often scandalous history of the Renaissance popes and the uses and abuses of ecclesiastical power.[4] And Christianity itself was often viewed as an oppressive, guilt-inducing system from which, first, the fresh air of the Renaissance revival of antiquity and, then, the Protestant Reformation would bring deliverance. In an influential series of essays on changing attitudes of individuals to the world and to wealth, Hans Baron – perhaps, after Burckhardt, the single most influential interpreter of the Renaissance – traced what he viewed as a gradual abandonment of a medieval world-denying view to a civic-minded humanism that embraced an active life on the secular stage of politics.[5] St Francis gave way to Leonardo Bruni and other humanists who celebrated an active *vivere civile*. In Baron's narrative, as in Burckhardt's, religion appeared to be a hold-over from the Middle Ages, hardly a central concern of the Renaissance. It was as though these historians and those who followed their views had constructed a great dam to hold religion away from the rest of life in the era. They viewed religion as a reservoir from which Renaissance men and women might occasionally drink, but it was walled off from the everyday life of work, family, politics, and ideas.

In the early 1970s this dam gave way, with a rush of books and essays that swept the traditional paradigm aside. Suddenly religion was no longer viewed as something apart but was recognized as a central aspect of the intellectual, social, and political life of the period. Charles Trinkaus' *In His Image and Likeness: Humanity and Divinity in Italian Humanist Thought*, first published in 1970, made religious concerns and, in particular, a renewed interest in the writings of St Augustine, a central component of the work of the humanists, while Donald Weinstein's *Savonarola and Florence*, which appeared in the same year, linked a late medieval tradition of prophecy to the political idiom of one of the greatest of the Renaissance republics at the end of the fifteenth century. The following year, Brian Pullan's *Rich and Poor in Renaissance Venice* made it clear that the *scuole grandi* – the great city-wide confraternities of Venice – were institutions that simultaneously served social, political, and religious purposes, while Keith Thomas' *Religion and the Decline of Magic* offered an anthropologically-informed analysis of belief systems in the towns and villages of early modern England.[6] In this same period, seminal essays – that are still frequently assigned in courses on religion in the Renaissance – appeared; these included works by John Bossy, Natalie Zemon Davis, and Richard Trexler.[7] That such a historiographical revolution was underway was well known to scholars at the time. In his preface to *The Pursuit of Holiness in Late Medieval and Renaissance Religion* – a collection of magisterial essays by leading scholars on various aspects of the religious life of the period – the editor Charles Trinkaus underscored the revisionist impulses of his fellow scholars. The volume demonstrated, Trinkaus noted, that the study of religion in the late medieval and Renaissance worlds 'has seemed to present to this current generation of scholars a strikingly different, almost unrecognizable image of the religious condition, attitudes, beliefs and practices of this period of the fourteenth, fifteenth, and early sixteenth centuries'.[8] A paradigm shift had taken place. Religion had moved, as David Peterson has put recently put it, from the margins to the centre of Renaissance studies.[9]

The origins of this paradigm shift lay primarily in the growing influence both of social history and of cultural anthropology on the field. As an approach to the history of religion, social history proved enormously successful in demonstrating the limits of a historiography that had been dominated by the institutional history of the churches (Protestant and Catholic), the intellectual history of the élites (again both Protestant and Catholic), and the often artificial lines drawn among confessions. To be sure, Marxist scholars had long searched for the social origins of religious ideologies, but within modern Renaissance and Reformation studies, the decisive work was Bernd Moeller's *Imperial Cities and the Reformation* (1962), which made a compelling case for interpreting the Reformation in relation to the social history of the German cities.[10] In the wake of this essay, the emphasis of scholars began to fall increasingly on ordinary people and their *experience* of religion, with the result that the meaning of religious life could be explained neither purely by confessional doctrines nor by ecclesiastical institutions. In fact, social forces – the experience of family and work – were seen as equally decisive. The growing interest by historians in the discipline of cultural anthropology was similarly important. Clifford Geertz's essay 'Religion as a Cultural System', which offered a new way of conceptualizing the interplay of religion with society, was especially influential.[11] But an additional factor also enabled the emergence of this new paradigm. The scholars who overturned the traditional approach to Renaissance religion had all undertaken research in European archives and libraries in the 1950s and 1960s. There they forged contacts with European scholars who had already begun to secularize the study of religion and to approach its history with new methods, many inspired by the groundbreaking works of Emile Durkheim, Max Weber, and Ernst Troeltsch, whose theories enabled a sociological approach to the history of Christianity. Moreover, and perhaps most decisively, continental scholars were less invested in the Burckhardtian paradigm than either their American or British counterparts for whom Burckhardt's model had served as a myth of modernization. Finally, by the 1960s, it was clear as well that the secularization model itself was riddled with difficulties. The modern world may have had pockets of secularization but religious forces had proven tenacious in the construction of modern culture, perhaps especially in the United States and eastern Europe – and in other places far from Rome and Paris.

To a large degree the agenda established by this remarkable group of historians has continued to shape the historiography of Renaissance religion down to the present, as scholars explore the religious life throughout Europe under a number of new rubrics. Perhaps the most compelling evidence of these new approaches is in the exploitation of sources that earlier generations of scholars would not have dreamed of as important to the study of religion. Where theological treatises and ecclesiastical decrees once predominated, historians now turned with great interest to urban chronicles, broadsides, pamphlets, chapbooks, wills, letters, autobiographies, sermons, votive offerings, episcopal visitation records, manuals of confessors, inquisitorial records, court transcripts, and the iconography of tombs. But equally important have been the new questions that scholars have brought to bear upon the study of religion in this period. They have focused on beliefs and practices: on rituals, processions, pilgrimages, acts of self-mortification and flagellation, fasting, and acts of charity. Tellingly, they have focused on these subjects from an increasingly academic perspective as the study of the history of Christianity has moved beyond seminaries into departments of history and religion in our universities. There is a tendency, that is, to view Christianity not so much as a tradition as a variegated set of beliefs and behaviours that scholars can approach much as they might approach the beliefs and practices within other religious traditions, with an eye to the diverse ways in which religion functions, for better or worse, in the lives of individuals and societies.

One of the most characteristic forms of religious expression in the Renaissance was the confraternity. These organizations, which brought groups of men (and, at times, women) into voluntary devotional societies, were central to the spiritual life of the towns and cities of the late medieval world. They could be found throughout Europe, but they have been studied most intensively in Italy. To a large degree they were institutional expressions of the need Renaissance townsmen had to forge solidarities with one another and to find corporate ways to protect their interest in this world and the next. Their proliferation in the thirteenth through the fifteenth century was in part a response to crises in both church and society; and, in this period, they were largely lay in initiative. One scholar estimates that between ten and twenty per cent of Italian adults were members; and in his *Italian Confraternities in the Sixteenth Century*, Christopher Black observes that 'by the later sixteenth century nearly every sizable village and parish throughout Italy had at least one confraternity'.[12] Black's study, which draws not only on his own research, but also on the vast scholarship on this topic, makes it clear that generalizations are difficult. Some confraternities had an exclusively lay membership; others included clergy. In the early Renaissance, many of these societies were closely associated with guilds, but by the sixteenth century, they were often either city-wide, drawing members from different occupations, or based in particular parishes. In this period as well confraternities came increasingly under clerical control – both in the wake of the Catholic Reform generally and especially in its recognition of the need to respond to the challenges of the Protestant Reformation. The size of a confraternity could also vary enormously, with some including only a handful of members and at least one – the *Compagnia dello Spirito Santo* in Naples – numbering some six thousand.[13] Yet, despite their diversity, it is increasingly clear that the confraternities of Renaissance Europe represented the growing influence of the laity over their own spiritual lives. Issues of salvation had become pressing matters, and laymen and women sought outlets – often beyond the parish and the clergy – in which they could participate in a wide variety of devotional activities – from eucharistic devotions to self-flagellation – that provided them with reassurance about matters of salvation as well as networks of mutual support.[14] Largely on the basis of this evidence alone, historians have come to think of the Renaissance as the first period in western history in which we find widespread manifestations of an intense lay spirituality.

Another important area in which the laity participated in the religious life of the age was the cult of saints. To be sure, ever since the twelfth century, the papacy had gained – at least in a formal sense – the privilege of canonization, or the right to determine who was (and who was not) to be counted among the company of the saints. But late medieval Christians also made the saints their own. Ordinary Christians set up altars, displayed statues of the Virgin Mary and of other saints in porticoes on street corners, and hung religious images of saints in their homes. The saint, while still an intermediary between the faithful and God, nonetheless allowed for an elaboration of religious hopes well outside the control of the Church and therefore, much like the confraternities, served as a powerful expression of lay spirituality. But the significance of the urban experience of the sacred varied significantly from place to place, as Edward Muir has pointed out in an important article. In Venice, the Virgin played a central role in forging political solidarities, while in Naples San Gennaro (St Janarius) was at the heart of many of the political struggles of the city. An icon, therefore, could be the source of either sociability or hostility, its meaning largely determined by the larger context.[15] And devotions to saints and the Virgin were European-wide, though scholars have noted significant differences between the Mediterranean and the northern European image of sanctity, a contrast that has been central to the scholarship of André Vauchez. Vauchez has identified a telling distinction between the Mediterranean saint who was generally a kind of medieval Mother Teresa, identifying with and offering comfort to the poor, and the northern saint, who was often a king or a bishop – a heroic aristocrat – devoted to the protection of his subjects or his flock.[16] Several other studies have also pointed to important distinctions between northern Europe and the Mediterranean in this period – Lionel Rothkrug, for example, has even argued that such distinctions in the relation of Christians to the holy, go a long way in accounting for the tendencies of certain regions to accept the

Reformation.[17] Rothkrug's thesis has not garnered universal acceptance, but his approach is an important yardstick of the growing influence of anthropology on the field.

But the religious landscape of Renaissance Europe was also animated by the lives of charismatic leaders who broke from the traditional approaches to Christianity through mysticism and prophecy. Among the mystics, Meister Eckhard (c.1260–c.1327) and Catherine of Siena (1347–1380), both figures who sought their own direct relation or union with God, point to yet another way in which the relation of the Christian to God was not always mediated by the clergy. Among the prophets, most of whom picked up on medieval millenarian currents that had been formally elaborated by Joachim of Fiore in the twelfth century, the best-known figure was undoubtedly fra Girolamo Savonarola, the charismatic Dominican who effectively ruled Florence from 1494 until his spectacular execution on the Piazza della Signoria in 1498. But recent scholarship has made it evident that prophecies circulated well beyond the better-known figures. The Italian historian Ottavia Niccoli has shown how friars and street singers tried to make sense of the political instability and violence of the early sixteenth century and, more recently, Marion Leathers Kuntz, in a compelling study of an itinerant and eccentric prophet from France who visited many of the most influential Italian courts in the sixteenth century, has made it clear that the prophetic tradition lasted well into the late sixteenth century.[18]

Yet perhaps the most striking recent development within the study of Renaissance religion has been the growing recognition of the important role that women played in the religious culture of late medieval Europe. At times, the spiritual lives of women developed in tandem with those of their husbands or brothers, as, for example, when they joined confraternities. But there is also remarkable evidence that women sought out both traditional and new forms of the religious life as a sphere in which they could achieve a certain independence or dignity. In the Low Countries, many women – who came to be known as Beguines – chose to live in a community, not as nuns but as lay women sharing a common life, while in Italy, a significant number of urban women carved out independent lives for themselves as *pinzochere* or *bizoche* in small groups of fellow penitents on the margins of society. But women did not always set themselves apart from power. In early sixteenth-century Italy, as Gabriella Zarri's work has shown, women such as Colomba da Rieti, who protected her fellow Perugians from the plague, and Stefana Quinzana, who interpreted her own life's mission as the establishment of peace in an age clouded by almost continuous warfare, were viewed as prophets or *sante vive* (living saints); some were even invited to serve as counsellors to princes in the most élite courts of the day.[19] And in the sixteenth century Catholicism in particular continued to provide important options for women who sought a life outside of marriage. New female religious orders such as the Ursulines are evidence of this, as is the active involvement of women in the patronage of religious art and architecture in late Renaissance Rome.[20]

In general, then – even before the Reformation and its doctrine of 'the priesthood of all believers' – the tendency in Renaissance spirituality was one of laicization, meaning specifically the increasingly active and direct participation of lay men and women (often alongside priests, monks, and nuns) in the Christian life. Equally, Renaissance spirituality was not so much one of secularization (as scholars used to believe) as one of the sacralization of the everyday: of family life, of the neighbourhood, and of the workplace. If reform tendencies in the Middle Ages, beginning with the Investiture Contest in the late eleventh century, had led to an intense effort to set the sacred apart from society, as we see, for example, in the proliferation of new religious orders and the construction of hundreds of monasteries, reform tendencies in the Renaissance tended to move in the opposite direction, with society itself becoming sacralized and, in Protestant lands at least, the monasteries dissolved. The history of the word 'religiosus' captures this change. In the Middle Ages, the term most often was used as a noun that referred to 'a religious', that is a monk or the member of a religious order (or, in the case of 'religiosa' a nun). By the fourteenth century, by contrast, many writers had begun to use the term as an adjective. In this new context a painting, a family, an individual too could be 'religious'.[21] The sacred had moved outside the walls of monasteries and flowed quite freely into the everyday world of late medieval and Renaissance Christians.

In this sense, neither the Protestant nor the Catholic Reformations represented so much departures from Renaissance spirituality as deepenings of tendencies already underway. Luther's protest against the traditional Catholic emphasis on works as well as his protests against the great emphasis that late medieval Catholicism placed on the sacraments stemmed in part from the growing perception that the religious life could no longer be contained within specific acts or monopolized by a specific ecclesiastical hierarchy. At the same time the Catholic Church itself underwent far-reaching changes, perhaps especially in the growth of new religious initiatives that offered increasingly large numbers of lay men and women an opportunity to participate in the religious life through such movements as the Company of Divine Love, founded in Genoa in 1497, which developed a more outward-looking spirituality in which philanthropy and the care of the poor were emphasized.[22] Indeed, these shifts also help explain some of the more radical developments in this period such as the Savonarolan episode in late fifteenth-century Florence and the brief political reign of radical Anabaptists in early sixteenth-century Münster, both cases in which spiritual leaders put themselves up as representatives of cities which viewed themselves as sacred.[23] It also helps explain the larger political developments of the sixteenth century as political rulers – princes and town councils – set themselves up as leaders of nations and cities in which religious and political authority were frequently intertwined. Henry VIII of England made himself head of the English Church; his contemporary Francis I brought the French episcopate increasingly under his control; the Venetians, always sceptical of Rome's meddling in the republic's affairs, kept a tight rein on ecclesiastical appointments, and the town councils of such cities as Augsburg and Basel regulated not only secular but also religious life, even appointing the ministers of Protestant congregations.

While the study of popular and lay religious practice has thrived in the past forty years, scholars have also re-interpreted the institutional history of the Church, again often from within the framework of social history. What is plain is that earlier models that emphasized the corruption of the Church have been eclipsed by efforts to understand in greater detail the way in which religious power actually developed in the Renaissance world and intersected with the interests of particular families and groups. Ronnie Po-Chia Hsia has mustered impressive evidence to demonstrate the way in which Italian families came to dominate the ecclesiastical hierarchy (its popes, its cardinals, even its saints) in the Renaissance, with the result that 'increasingly, religious dissent and criticisms of ecclesiastical corruption assumed an anti-Italian, anti-Roman, and anti-papal stridency'.[24] And this was clearly a trend that alienated many of the reformers outside Italy. But even within Italy, ecclesiastical institutions seemed largely impervious to reform. Giovanni Miccoli has put forth the fascinating thesis that alliances not only between merchants and friars but also between such influential families as the Medici and the papacy led to the privatization of religious ethics, passive Christianity, failure to reform, and tended to divorce the Church from society.[25] Nonetheless there were efforts throughout Europe to reform religious orders, as we see among the Franciscans as well as certain Benedictine houses such as those at Camaldoli and Vallambrosa. Other scholars have also begun

202 palgrave advances in renaissance historiography

to cast new light on the institutional history of the Church, from Paolo Prodi's emphasis on the absolutist tendencies of the late Renaissance papacy to Angelo Torre's nuanced analysis of the early modern parish in the Piedmont. In Torre's study the more traditional institutional histories of parochial life have been replaced by an examination of the parish as a site of social tensions and the ritual construction of community among the lords and villagers of rural Italy.[26]

But the gulf between the religious needs of the people and the Church was not only the result of subtle shifts in lay piety. Equally important were the disruptions in the social order of the later Middle Ages. Social and economic historians have long seen the fourteenth century as an age of crisis. The century opened with a series of famines – most notably the Great Famine of 1315–18 which brought hunger and death to much of northern Europe, but it was the Black Death, which struck Europe in 1347–51, that caused the greatest trauma. This epidemic, which carried away between one third and one quarter of the population, inevitably changed the religious sentiments of Europeans. Accordingly, late medieval Christianity focused with a new intensity on the themes of death and punishment. Members of confraternities flagellated themselves in elaborate public processions to deliver their world from the epidemics, while artists explored the intimacy of death in popular representations of the *danse macabre*. Historians of Christianity, therefore, must keep in mind that the transformations in the religious life in the Renaissance took place not merely within the serene cityscapes of fifteenth-century Italian cities but also within the context of major crises in the social and economic order of Europe.

The fourteenth century was also marked by a series of protracted institutional crises within the Church, prompted in part by the growing power of monarchs over the papacy. From 1309 to 1377, as a result of the machinations of the French king, the seat of the papacy was moved from Rome to the southern French city of Avignon; and then from 1378 to 1417 Latin Christendom had not one but two popes, one in Rome, the other in France, each supported by a different constellation of political rulers. In fact, for a brief period (1409–17), three men claimed the papal title. The papal hierarchy, moreover, struggled to control the growing influence of the conciliarists who wished to move the source of religious authority away from the papacy and to councils of representatives of the Church so as to locate supreme ecclesiastical authority not at the summit of its hierarchy but rather at its base in the *congregatio fidelium* (the gathering of the faithful).

In this late medieval world of such protracted social, economic, and demographic crises – crises exacerbated by contemporaneous institutional failings in the Church – it is hardly surprising that men and women questioned traditional beliefs and practices. To a large degree it was disruptions such as these that accounted for the development of Lollardy in England under the leadership of John Wycliffe, who made Scripture central to salvation, the *Devotio Moderna* and the Beguines in the Low Countries, and the Hussite movement in Bohemia, each one of which gave expression to the desire of the laity to be more directly involved in the religious life.[27] Indeed, from the beginnings of the Franciscan Order in the early thirteenth century down to the early seventeenth century, Renaissance Christianity was characterized above all by intense experimentation, innovation, and reform, as older models of devotion and piety continually gave way to new ideals and practices.

Yet, in the end, these late medieval movements failed. While many factors no doubt conspired to make both Protestant and Catholic reforms in the sixteenth century far more successful, two in particular stand out. One was the increasing importance of humanist practices. As an approach to ancient texts humanism, for example, breathed new life into the teachings of St Augustine, whose influence on late medieval and early modern culture was enormous. Humanists also inevitably invited a critical stance towards many received interpretations of Scripture, as we see, first, with Lorenzo Valla's annotations on, and then with Erasmus' edition of, the *New Testament*, both of which significantly altered the way in which theologians and, eventually, ordinary people understood the Bible.[28] Indeed, humanism is without question one of the key threads that ties the Renaissance and the Reformation together, especially as the approaches of the Italian humanists influenced those of their counterparts in England, Germany, and France. But the study of humanism has also been transformed, as older models of the Christian humanists – which stressed the moderating values of this learned élite – give way to newer approaches that examine the work of the humanists from new angles, stressing both the patterns of patronage and the ambitions that shaped their work.[29]

The second and related major development involved the growing capacity of Renaissance humanists to reach a larger and larger readership as a result of the invention of the printing press and the rapid spread of this technology to many of the major commercial centres of late fifteenth- and early sixteenth-century Europe. The influence of this new technology on all fields of knowledge was enormous. While religious texts constituted the overwhelming majority of early printed books, some printers – most notably the Venetian printers Nicolas Jenson and Aldus Manutius – devoted themselves to the production of classical Latin and (in the case of Aldus) Greek texts. But most critically the printing press enabled those scholars who were drawing on humanist methods and new religious ideas to transform the nature of the religious texts that circulated and reached the people. The most conspicuous result of this transformation was the proliferation of translations of the Bible into all the major European languages in the sixteenth century, a process that undoubtedly reinforced the development of 'national' churches in the period. But printing brought about other shifts as well. Miriam Usher Chrisman's comprehensive study of printing in Strasbourg from the late fifteenth to the end of the sixteenth century shows a clear pattern of the eclipse of the influence of Catholic writers and a growing literature of Protestant and lay writings.[30] And historians have only recently begun to explore the impact of printing from the vantage point of an increasingly literate urban population and the development of new reading practices (both collective and individual) in this age.[31]

'A society, like a mind, is woven of perpetual interaction', so the great French historian Marc Bloch wrote in the early twentieth century.[32] The history of religion in the Renaissance exemplifies this perfectly. Social, political, and intellectual developments had transformed the nature of Christianity in profound ways in the Renaissance. The Reformation and the Counter-Reformation may, in certain respects, be seen as outgrowths of these transformations, but they, in turn, did much to remake European culture, society, and politics in the late Renaissance. The current generation of scholars – the intellectual children and grandchildren of those responsible for the paradigm shift of the early 1970s – has tended to take a less optimistic view of these transformations. In particular, they have focused on the repressive dimensions of Christianity which, now often tied to political regionalism, became increasingly combative and repressive. The history of anti-Semitism in late medieval and Renaissance Europe illustrates this. From the First Crusade on, many Christians in Europe frequently turned with hostility and violence towards the Jews. They killed them in pogroms, forced them to convert, and depicted them as hostile to Christianity, often accusing them of the ritual murder of Christian children and the profanation of the Host. The Jews were expelled from France (or at least the lands ruled directly by the king) in 1182 and from England in 1291. The outbreak of famine and plague in the following century led to a renewed hostility towards the Jews, with the result that many of the Jewish communities in Germany were entirely eliminated and in 1391 the most massive killing of Jews in the history of Spain took place.[33] Throughout the Renaissance the Franciscans, including Bernardino da Siena, often fanned the flames of Christian hostility towards the Jews. Indeed, by 1492, with the expulsion of Jews from Spain, western Europe was essentially emptied of Jews, apart from a few cities such as Antwerp and Venice where the Jewish communities lived in relative peace, though behind ghetto walls. Yet, despite the hostility of Christians to Jews in the late Middle Ages and the Renaissance, a remarkable number of Jewish communities thrived in this period. Robert Bonfil even believes it possible to argue that in Italy at least the Jews themselves experienced a Renaissance. Though confined to the ghettoes of the Italian cities, the Jews were able to elaborate their own rich intellectual traditions – especially the study of the Kaballah.[34] But aspects of their social and cultural history present deep parallels with the Christian society around them. In Venice, they established what David J. Malkiel has called the 'Ghetto Republic'; they founded their own confraternities; and at least one of the Venetian Jews – Leon Modena – has left a record of his life in an autobiography, an emerging genre in this period.[35]

But Jews were not the only target of Christian authorities in this period. The Reformation – and to a lesser extent – the Counter-Reformation constituted a major impetus behind the attacks by European political and intellectual élites on witchcraft and superstitious beliefs and practices. At the height of the Renaissance, with the late fifteenth-century publication of the *Malleus maleficarum*, an inquisitorial manual aimed at the repression of witchcraft, down to the end of the seventeenth century, both religious and secular élites tended to demonize and persecute these beliefs and practices. Perhaps as many as sixty thousand individuals accused of witchcraft were executed between 1485 and 1700.[36] Indeed, in general, intellectual and political élites in the Renaissance and Reformation placed enormous stress on conformity. As often happens, such acts of repression have left not a positive image of a triumphant orthodoxy but insights into the beliefs and practices of ordinary Christians as scholars are able to reconstruct them through the careful study of inquisitorial documents and other court records. Here witchcraft is the most prominent example. It has become increasingly clear that men and women in late medieval and early modern Europe approached supernatural forces not only through officially-sanctioned channels but also through a wide variety of traditional practices that involved village cunning women as well as urban healers who offered solace. The notion of witchcraft as an organized conspiracy of men and women who had entered into a pact with the Devil was not a popular but rather an élite belief. Nonetheless the interplay between learned and popular culture was enormously complex, as Carlo Ginzburg has shown in his suggestive study of the cult of the *benandanti*, men and women in the Friuli who saw themselves as able to enter into supernatural battle against witches but who gradually, under the pressure of the inquisitorial courts, came to internalize the language of witchcraft that the authorities used against them.[37] Ultimately, it is difficult not to see the Renaissance, with its triumphant orthodoxies turned both against the Jews and witches – both groups represented as anti-Christians – as a prelude to the destruction of indigenous beliefs in the New World that, first the Spanish and Portuguese, and then the English and Dutch conquered.[38]

But Christians also turned on one another. The acceptance of the principle that the religion of a particular state would reflect the religion of its ruler – the principle of *cuius regio, eius religio* worked out at the Peace of Augsburg in 1555 – laid the groundwork for decades of horrific religious warfare both within and between States, beginning with the Wars of Religion in France and continuing down through the Thirty Years War (1618–48) and the Puritan Revolution in England (1640–60). If the early Renaissance had been a period in which the laity came to participate more fully in the religious life, the later Renaissance itself became a period of growing religious intolerance. The result of such a shift has led to a fundamental rethinking of the Renaissance. Historians no longer view this watershed period as rational and secular as they once did; instead they see and stress the symbolic dimensions of religious behaviours which shaped both individual and collective identities, forged urban solidarities as well as conflict, and led to an era of repression in those places (of which there were many) in which a need was felt for religious conformity. The implications for Renaissance studies as a whole have therefore been significant.

This is not to say that there were not voices in this divisive age that called for greater religious concord or toleration, among them those of Desiderius Erasmus, Sebastiano Castellio, and Michel de Montaigne. The late Renaissance even witnessed a new set of understandings of religion itself. Writers such as Machiavelli who looked back to the early history of the Roman republic were able to see religion in abstract and not purely Christian terms as a fundamental element of human society – a notion that was deepened by the growing awareness in the sixteenth century of the diverse religious practices and beliefs of the New World. Religion, which had once been a triad of Abrahamic religions – Judaism, Christianity, and Islam – gradually came to be seen as a far more inclusive category of the relation of the human to the divine. The explorations of religion from this perspective were, of course, for a long time confined to a minority within the intellectual élites. Nonetheless, in the final analysis, these explorations developed not only in response to new circumstances, they also drew upon the intellectual practices and assumptions of both humanists and scholastics – scholars attuned to questions of context and theories of natural law. The historical anthropology of Renaissance religion, in this sense, owes much to the intellectual life of the very period it seeks to understand.[39]

## notes

1. Cited in Heiko A. Oberman, *Luther: Man Between God and the Devil* (New York, 1992), p. 149; see also Ingrid D. Rowland, *The Culture of the High Renaissance: Ancients and Moderns in Sixteenth-Century Rome* (Cambridge, 1998). Erik Erikson's account of Luther's Roman sojourn, *Young Man Luther* (New York, 1962), is poetic.

2. Two classic works on late medieval and early modern piety are Jacques Toussaert, *Le sentiment religieux en Flandre à la fin du moyen-âge* (Paris, 1963) and William Christian, *Local Religion in Sixteenth-Century Spain* (Princeton, 1981).

3. Jacob Burckhardt, *The Civilization of the Renaissance in Italy* (New York, 1958), esp. p. 290. See also Jonathan Woolfson's chapter above.

4. Here the works of Leopold von Ranke and Ludwig Pastor were most influential: see von Ranke, *Deutsche Geschichte im Zeitalter der Reformation*, 6 vols (Munich, 1925) and Pastor, *History of the Popes* (Wilmington, NC, 1978).

5. Hans Baron, *In Search of Florentine Civic Humanism: Essays on the Transition from Medieval to Modern Thought*, 2 vols (Princeton, 1988), I, pp. 158–257.

6. Charles Trinkaus, *In Our Image and Likeness: Humanity and Divinity in Italian Religious Thought*, 2 vols (Chicago, 1970); Donald Weinstein, *Savonarola and Florence: Prophecy and Patriotism in the Renaissance* (Princeton, 1970); Brian Pullan, *Rich and Poor in Renaissance Venice: The Social Institutions of a Catholic State, to 1620* (Cambridge, MA, 1971); and Keith Thomas, *Religion and the Decline of Magic: Studies in Popular Beliefs in Sixteenth and Seventeenth-Century England* (New York, 1971).

7. John Bossy, 'The Counter-Reformation and the People of Catholic Europe', *Past and Present*, XLVII (1970) 51–70; Natalie Zemon Davis, 'The Rites of Violence: Religious Riot in Sixteenth-Century France', *Past and Present*, LIX (1973) 51–91; and Richard Trexler, 'Florentine Religious Experience: The Sacred Image', *Studies in the Renaissance*, XIX (1972) 7–41 are merely a few of the more significant works of these authors.

8. Charles Trinkaus, 'Forward', in *The Pursuit of Holiness in Late Medieval and Renaissance Religion*, ed. Trinkaus and Heiko A. Oberman (Leiden, 1974), p. x.

9. David Peterson, 'Out of the Margins: Religion and the Church in Renaissance Italy', *Renaissance Quarterly*, LIII (2000) 835–79 – includes an invaluable bibliography.

208       palgrave advances in renaissance historiography

10. Bernd Moeller, *Imperial Cities and the Reformation*, ed. and trans. H. C. Erik
    Midelfort and Mark U. Edwards, Jr (Philadephia, 1972).
11. Clifford Geertz, 'Religion as a Cultural System', in his *The Interpretation of
    Cultures* (New York, 1973), pp. 87–125; this essay originally appeared in
    1966.
12. Nicholas Terpstra, *Lay Confraternities and Civic Religion in Renaissance Bologna*
    (Cambridge, 1995); Christopher Black, *Italian Confraternities in the Sixteenth
    Century* (Cambridge, 1989); Ronald F. E. Weissman, *Ritual Brotherhood in
    Renaissance Florence* (New York, 1982).
13. Black, *Italian Confraternities*, p. 51.
14. The social functions of confraternities are emphasized in Weissman, *Ritual
    Brotherhood in Renaissance Florence*.
15. Edward Muir, 'The Virgin on the Street Corner: The Place of the Sacred in
    Italian Cities', in *Religion and Culture in the Renaissance and Reformation*, ed.
    Steven Ozment (Kirksville, 1989), pp. 25–40.
16. André Vauchez, *Sainthood in the Later Middle Ages* (Cambridge, 1997).
17. Lionel Rothkrug, *Religious Practices and Collective Perceptions: Hidden Homologies
    in the Renaissance and Reformation* (Waterloo, 1980).
18. Ottavià Niccoli, *Prophecy and the People in Renaissance Italy*, trans. Lydia
    G. Cochrane (Princeton, 1990), but see now Marion Leathers Kuntz, *The
    Anointment of Dionisio: Prophecy and Politics in Renaissance Italy* (University
    Park, PA, 2001).
19. Gabriella Zarri, 'Living Saints: A Typology of Female Sanctity in the Early
    Sixteenth Century', in *Women and Religion in Medieval and Renaissance Italy*,
    ed. Daniel Bornstein and Roberto Rusconi (Chicago, 1996), pp. 219–303.
20. Carolyn Valone, 'Piety and Patronage: Women and the Early Jesuits', in
    *Creative Women in Medieval and Early Modern Italy*, ed. E. Ann Matter and
    John Coakley (Philadelphia, 1994), pp. 157–84.
21. Réginald Grégoire, '"Religiosus": Etude sure le vocabulaire de la vie religieuse,'
    *Studi medievali*, ser. 3, X (1969) 415–30.
22. Black, *Italian Confraternities*, p. 8
23. Weinstein, *Savonarola and Florence*; Ronnie Po-Chia Hsia, *Society and Religion
    in Münster, 1535–1628* (New Haven, 1984).
24. Hsia, 'Religious Cultures', in Guido Ruggiero, ed., *A Companion to the Worlds
    of the Renaissance* (Oxford, 2002), p. 335.
25. Giovanni Miccoli, 'La storia religiosa', *Storia d'Italia*, II, pt. 1: *Dalla caduta
    dell'impero romano al secolo XVIII*, ed. Ruggiero Romano and Corrado Vivanti
    (Turin, 1974).
26. Paolo Prodi, *The Papal Prince: One Body and Two Souls: The Papal Monarchy
    in Early Modern Europe*, trans. Susan Hankins (Cambridge, 1987) and Angelo
    Torre, *Il consumo di devozioni: religione e comunità nelle compagne dell'Ancien
    Régime* (Venice, 1995).
27. R. R. Post, *The Modern Devotion* (Leiden, 1968).
28. Deborah Shuger, *The Renaissance Bible: Scholarship, Sacrifice, Subjectivity*
    (Berkeley, 1994).
29. Lisa Jardine, *Erasmus, Man of Letters: The Construction of Charisma in Print*
    (Princeton, 1993).
30. Miriam Usher Chrisman, *Lay Culture, Learned Culture: Books and Social Change
    in Strasbourg, 1480–1599* (New Haven, 1982).

31. Guglielmo Cavallo and Roger Chartier, eds, *A History of Reading in the West*, trans. Lydia G. Cochrane (Amherst, 1999), especially the chapters on the Renaissance and Reformation.

32. Marc Bloch, *Feudal Society*, trans. L. A. Manyon, 2 vols (Chicago, 1961), I, p. 59.

33. František Graus, *Pest-Geissler-Judenmorde: das 14. Jahrhundert als Krisenzeit* (Göttingen, 1987); Philippe Wolff, 'The 1391 Pogrom in Spain: Social Crisis or Not?' *Past and Present*, L (1971) 4–18.

34. Robert Bonfil, *Jewish Life in Renaissance Italy*, trans. Anthony Oldcorn (Berkeley, 1994).

35. David J. Malkiel, 'The Ghetto Republic' and Elliott Horowitz, 'Processions, Piety, and Jewish Confraternities', both in *The Jews of Early Modern Venice*, ed. Robert C. Davis and Benjamin Ravid (Baltimore, 2001); on autobiography and Renaissance Jewish culture, see *The Autobiography of a Seventeenth-Century Venetian Rabbi: Leon Modena's* Life of Judah, ed. and trans. Mark R. Cohen (Princeton, 1990), with special attention to the introductory essay by Natalie Zemon Davis in which she draws comparisons and contrasts between Jewish and Christian autobiography ('Fame and Secrecy: Leon Modena's *Life* as an Early Modern Autobiography', pp. 50–70).

36. Brian Levack, *The Witch-Hunt in Early Modern Europe* (New York, 1987), p. 21.

37. Carlo Ginzburg, *Witchcraft and Agrarian Cults in the Sixteenth and Seventeenth Centuries*, trans. John and Anne Tedeschi (Baltimore, 1983).

38. Adriano Prosperi, *Tribunali della coscienza: inquisitori, confessori, missionari* (Turin, 1996).

39. James Samuel Preus, *Explaining Religion: Criticism and Theory from Bodin to Freud* (Atlanta, 1996).

# 11
## literature

warren boutcher

In 1603, the English poet and humanist Samuel Daniel picked a fight in print with Thomas Campion. He came to the defence of rhyme. Both men backed up their arguments with histories of the revival of literature. Their narratives allow us to sample in detail the story of pre-1600 European literature as it was told and contested in the period itself. There are three things worth emphasizing in advance. Firstly, there is no mention of the general cultural 'Renaissance' or of the story of art as told by a contemporary such as Vasari. Secondly, they are not histories of 'literature' in the primary modern sense of original fictional works of poetry, prose and drama in the vernaculars. Literature meant any text in any area of humane or divine learning, and particularly editions and imitations of ancient works. It followed, thirdly, that to be highly valued in the Renaissance period, new vernacular works had to present themselves as antique and learned in some sense. They had to be rhetorically effective local forms of an ancient and global tradition of knowledge, and to be worthy of learned comment. So Campion and Daniel link local histories of learning connected with particular households and texts in England to a universal revival also connected with particular figures and texts. They agree that the context for new poetry in English is the global survival and revival of antique learning, but they specify that context in different ways.

## campion versus daniel

Campion dedicates his work to Thomas Sackville, Lord Buckhurst, as both a judge of poetry and a protector of learning. He thereby associates it with the Erasmian new learning of Edwardian and early Elizabethan Cambridge, and with Roger Ascham in particular. Ascham's *The Scholemaster* (1568) had been written as advice on the education of Sackville's son. It advised against following the 'Goths' in rhyming rather than the Greeks in true versifying. From the start of his own treatise, Campion assumes that poetry is a form of humane learning closely related to the other arts and sciences, and particularly to knowledge of music and of Latin. In the first chapter he cites the Latin playwright Terence speaking of art and music as though they were the same thing. He then offers a potted history of global learning as a way of justifying his stance on the composition of poetry in English.[1]

Learning first flourished in Greece but was then 'derived unto' the Romans, who observed the number and quantity of syllables in Latin verse and prose. But after the decline of the Roman Empire, and the conquests of the barbarians, learning (and Latin with it) lay deformed until the age of Erasmus, More and Reuchlin in the early sixteenth century. These scholars took the Latin tongue out of the hands of the illiterate monks and friars with whom it had rested for centuries. In the meantime, however, 'in those lack-learning times', the vulgar custom of rhyme had crept into barbarized Italy and spread thence to the rest of Europe. Campion associates this history, and the grouping of Erasmus, More and Reuchlin as revivers of true learning, with a satirical Latin book issued in a series of expanding editions and known all over Europe in the sixteenth century: the *Epistolae obscurorum virorum* ('Letters of obscure men'), first printed in 1515. These letters were associated with the 'Reuchlin controversy' and with the Louvain school of trilingual (Latin–Greek–Hebrew) scholarship – the institutional base of what is now often known as 'Low Countries humanism'. The *Epistolae* satirized the conservative theologians who condemned Reuchlin for his opposition to the proposed destruction of Hebrew books in the Holy Roman Empire, and by extension for his reformed approach to the interpretation of Scripture.[2]

Campion's potted history of the global revival of learning lasts only a few lines before he moves swiftly on to the detail of his metrical proposals. But when Daniel replies, he takes issue with this history at great length. He starts by invoking an alternative 'school' to Campion's in his dedication of the treatise to William Herbert, Earl of Pembroke. Wilton, the household of the Earl's mother, the Countess of Pembroke, famously associated with Philip Sidney's vernacular compositions, is the place where Daniel first learnt to rhyme.[3] But he proceeds from this local context to *remind* Campion and his readers of something they and every educated person at the time already knew. This is the key to his rebuttal of Campion's charge that rhyme should be rejected as barbarous and vulgar on the basis that it was not used by Greeks or Romans. For there is but one global source for all knowledge and learning or letters (*litterae* – the forms in which knowledge is acquired, transmitted, and recorded by man) and it is not – *originally* – Graeco-Roman literature, or any literature. Rather, it is God's original gift of wisdom. The gift comes in two forms: natural and divine, corresponding to the book of the world (nature) and the book of God (Scripture). The distribution of this gift is universal, and to be found to some degree in all countries and times.[4] Daniel takes us on a global and historical tour of literary civilizations, from the Druids to the Turks, from Russia to Spain, from Asia to Africa.

So we should not so soon yield our consents captive to the authority of antiquity; all our understandings are not to be built in every area of learning by the square of Greece and Italy. Even the Goths, the Vandals and 'Longobards' (Lombards), who are supposed to have overwhelmed the glory of learning in Europe, left durable monuments of their wisdom in the form of the laws and customs still informing the constitutions of Christian Europe. And how could Campion say that learning lay deformed in Europe between the decline of the Roman Empire and the age of Erasmus, when three hundred years previously, about the time Tamburlaine came down into Europe, Petrarch had shown all the best notions of learning, both in Latin prose and verse and in vernacular Italian? Daniel catalogues Petrarch's various works in moral philosophy, poetry and history, including his vast Latin epic on the subject of the last Punic War (the *Africa*). But he says that Petrarch is most famous for his poems in Italian, poems which use vernacular metres and rhyme, not classical quantitative schemes.[5]

Daniel then plots the succession of learning from Petrarch to Boccaccio and on to a whole line of famous Italian writers including Bruni, Valla, Poggio and Biondo. The next momentous event in this alternative history is the arrival in Venice of the Greek scholar Manuel Chrysoloras, sent by the Byzantine emperor to raise support from Christian princes against the Turk. The result is another succession of scholars from Bessarion to Gaza and beyond who transport philosophy 'beaten by the Turke out of Greece, into christendome': '[H]ereupon came that mighte confluence of Learning in these parts, which returning, as it were *per postliminium* [by right of repatriation], and heere meeting then with the new invented stampe of Printing, spread itselfe indeed in a more universall sorte th[a]n the world ever heeretofoore had it'. So scholars from Poliziano to Pico adorned Italy and woke up the other nations with desire of glory well before the age of Reuchlin, More and Erasmus. The result was a *confluence* of the streams of universal learning, in which the diverse nations of 'this lettered world' had their portions of spirit and worthiness. One of these is of course Britain. Daniel then produces a catalogue of illustrious British authors from before Petrarch's time, authors that would now be thought of as 'medieval': Bede, Bracton, Ockham and so on. In the same way he later adduces other European 'medieval' authors who had no less portion of wisdom than Erasmus and co., with their 'new revived wordes': Thomas Aquinas, Bartolus, Duns Scotus.[6]

The Daniel–Campion debate and its fortunes shall serve in what follows as a touchstone for modern approaches to the story of pre-1600 literature. For modern scholars have found this debate fundamental both to that story and to the humanities more generally: what role has the notion of a classical antiquity had – what role should it have – in the formation of modern literature and society? Daniel appeared to offer an advance in historical perspective on Campion. But the advance has been interpreted in different ways depending on the historicism of the modern scholar doing the interpreting. Some have seen in Daniel one of the Elizabethan pioneers of a British literary history and criticism not dependent upon Greece and Rome, and more respectful of the native medieval heritage. Others have taken him to be showing that there is a larger history of classical European humanism beyond More and Erasmus, a history going back to Petrarch. More recently, he has been seen as one of the pioneers of a new non-Eurocentric attitude; in the 'Defence' the traditional emphasis on the Greek and Roman legacy is rejected in favour of a broad comparative approach that anticipates social history and the *histoire des mentalités*.[7]

The end of the present chapter will suggest what an advance on all of these interpretations might currently be held to look like. But the point for now is that the 'Defence' has been used to address a modern question about the place of a classical tradition in the study of the literature of the pre-1600 period. To call that period the 'Renaissance' was for much of the twentieth century a way of placing the classical literary revival in early Renaissance Florence at the centre of things. To refer instead to the 'early modern period' became in the later twentieth century a way of de-centralizing the classical Renaissance. There is now as a result a 'Renaissance versus early modern' historiographical debate.[8] In what follows, I approach the developments behind this debate as a matter of changing scholarly formations, and of changing relations to the documentary record in the modern period.

## from italian renaissance man to early modern woman

The typical scholar in the field as it first emerged in the 1830s was a continental European man educated first in Latin and Greek and in classical civilization. He was attracted into the study of Italian Renaissance civilization via an experience of research and cultural tourism in Italy or the Renaissance galleries of European museums such as the Louvre.[9] One such man, Jules Michelet, compares passing from scholasticism to the splendid antiquity he had encountered with Vergil in his youth to the experience of passing from the sharp cobblestones of a Swiss street to the smooth paving stones of Florence and Milan.[10] Michelet visited the Italian Renaissance as a crucial stop in a tour of the whole global background to the history of France in the sixteenth century. Jacob Burckhardt was a classically trained Swiss historian who took his germanophone readers from the streets of Basel and elsewhere on a more confined and detailed tour of Renaissance Italy alone. As institutionalized in the twentieth century by the central European émigrés forced out of continental Europe by the Nazis, this kind of scholarly formation is most associated with the Renaissance Society of America and the Warburg Institute in London.

Scholars with a different kind of formation entered the field in the post-war period, typically North American men or women of European ancestry. They trained first in Anglo-American vernacular study of the western canon, then branched via a broader and less familiar range of texts into medieval and early modern studies, either in search of contexts for the canon, or in search of a history beyond the canon. One such scholar, Stephen Greenblatt, describes the crucial experience not as the voyage to Italy and classical antiquity but as the 'touch of the real' to be found in historical documents and archives. He refers to 'verbal traces less self-consciously detached [than poetry or fiction] from the lives real men and women actually live'.[11] Natalie Zemon Davis started out in Renaissance studies, publishing sociological analyses of northern humanists, but is now known principally for her discovery of 'fiction in the archives' of early modern France.[12] Where Davis has pursued a social and intellectual history beyond the canon, Greenblatt has remained a critic of the major literary monuments and figures of the English Renaissance. The institution most associated with the formation shared by these two scholars is the Folger Shakespeare Library in Washington DC.

Two moments transformed the field and shaped the practice of the scholars profiled above: the 1830s and 1840s, and the 1960s and 1970s. These were moments at which distinctively modern modes of historical enquiry – 'historicisms' – combined with changes in the relationship of scholars to the documentary record of the pre-1600 past. In the earlier of the two moments, the change amounted to the emergence of a new, medieval and Renaissance antiquity (c.1100 to c.1600). Between the late eighteenth century and the mid-nineteenth century, the heritage of the middle age between the fall of the Roman Empire and the modern period became visible – in the growth of cultural tourism, in newly reorganized and inventoried museums and archives, in new publications of unedited documents, in new editions of the literature – at a faster rate than ever before.[13] The new antiquity was part of a broader historical revolution, centred in Germany, France and Britain, that took in both classical and biblical scholarship and oriental studies (described as 'orientialism' by Edward Said).[14] This global change in the sense of past and present culture is much more evidently the context for Michelet's volume on the Renaissance – conceived during the 1830s and 1840s – than for Burckhardt's famous work, even though Burckhardt's formation at the new humanistic Pädagogium (classical school) in Basel and the University of Berlin made him every bit as much of a universal historian.[15] To re-read Michelet's global history now is to wonder how Renaissance studies ever came to be so closely identified with early Italian humanism in the twentieth century. The answer is that Burckhardt's work was used to license a fierce *concentration* on the revival of Greek and Latin antiquity in the Trecento and Quattrocento.

The 1960s and 1970s paved the way for the extension of the new antiquity to c.1800 and its redescription as the '[late] medieval and early modern period'. But it was not just a matter of changing periodization. The crucial challenge was to the concept of culture underpinning the old historicisms. For the new historicisms questioned the premise that the relationship of the scholarly community to the documents and monuments of c.1100 to c.1600 (and later to c.1800) should take the form of a relationship to a 'classical' civilization in the traditional, nineteenth-century sense. Study of a classical civilization was of course defined by the study of Graeco-Roman antiquities. It essentially meant selection of a canon of artistic and literary monuments from the Elgin marbles to Vergil's *Aeneid*, held to stand not just for the civilizations of Athens and Rome but for cultivated *humanity*. 'Culture' was essentially identified with reflective literature and the fine arts and with a way of life expressed most intensely in their making and consumption.[16] We shall see that the same kind of general approach was taken to the new medieval and Renaissance antiquity by historicists from Michelet to Erich Auerbach, though the stories they told and the definitions of 'humanity' they used varied enormously. The new historicists' challenge to these old historicisms and their concept of culture – to which we shall return below – did not exclude adoption of their tactics and concerns. This was especially the case when the essential task remained historical criticism centred on a canon of monuments.

By identifying the Renaissance as the workshop in which modern Europe was forged, Michelet and Burckhardt in different ways showed modernity fashioning itself with classical literary and artistic tools. Michelet may have turned the Renaissance into a precedent for the French Revolution, but he also turned the French Revolution into a Renaissance of antiquities in the present. Burckhardt believed, however melancholically, that modernity should take the form of a revival of antiquities in the humanistic formation – *Bildung* – of each individual.[17] This was precisely the belief that in the late nineteenth century drove conservative educationalists to reclaim 'the tradition of classical humanism' for modern institutionalized education. From the later nineteenth-century, classical languages and erudition lost primacy in many countries, but textual interpretation of a canon of classics – centrally including Renaissance classics – was retained as the vital core of liberal education.[18] This is ultimately why Renaissance studies was re-founded in the twentieth century on the study of humanism and its texts. The field's core subject matter became the *origins* of the revival of classical humanism for modern society.

## artistic or textual renaissance?

In the general culture of nineteenth-century Europe the Renaissance was almost exclusively associated with art museums and exhibitions. Michelet built his history on this fact. He tells the story of the first time the transalpine peoples, led by the French, discovered Italy and were changed for ever – the second was the contemporary moment that had begun in the Napoleonic era. His point is that the despoiling of Italy by the transalpine European powers in the early sixteenth century *should have been* a revolution like that of 1789.[19] So he and the historians who followed him re-enact the *aesthetic* experience of 'going' – actually and virtually – to Renaissance Italy and to classical Roman antiquity from Switzerland, Germany, France and England as a form of revolutionary *historical* sensibility, as a quasi-religious substitute for Christianity whose sacred artefacts are to be found in museums of culture.

The strong association between the Renaissance and the guided tour of art continues to this day even if, since the 1950s, modern art museums have not themselves been defined to quite the same extent by the Renaissance. At the same time, in the twentieth-century universities, the Renaissance increasingly came to mean texts and thought – even for academic art historians, who made literary knowledge and philosophical insight the basis of their approach.[20] The founding figure for *university* study of the Renaissance, Burckhardt, hardly mentioned art in his great work; he concentrated on humanistic literary sources. But there are nevertheless significant continuities that justify treating the whole period from the 1830s to the 1960s as a single era in the history of Renaissance studies.

The gothic revival, especially as championed by the Catholic Church in France, put much stress on gothic painting and cathedrals. From Michelet's point of view, it was the taste for gothic art that had made his generation initially sympathetic to the medieval Catholic worldview. He even describes how the French government, keen for a rapprochement with the clergy, deliberately handed the Church a programme of investment in gothic architecture as a way of avoiding handing them a bigger cultural prize – such as control of education. This was the contemporary political reason why Michelet retorted with the radical *thinking* behind Brunelleschi's and Michelangelo's buildings and paintings. If the gothic cathedral was the medieval Church's poetry, then the great sceptical doubter of the medieval worldview had to be the builder of Florence's cathedral dome. The Church did not understand that an enfranchized art could open the way for an enfranchized literature and philosophy.[21] This was the *purpose* of art. It was itself *already* a radical form of thought and poetry. In this sense, then, Michelet shared an idealist mindset with twentieth-century art historians such as Panofsky.

But in the nineteenth century, the texts were not there. The literature and philosophy of the Renaissance – especially translations, editions and imitations of ancient works – could not, as the art in the museums could, stand on its own to tell a story. There was simply no general taste either for its humanistic Neo-Latin or for its vernacular texts. Michelet himself had little taste for anything between Dante and Rabelais.[22] Historians of the national vernacular literatures – as we shall see below – were building a taste for medieval and modern forms of romantic and gothic literature, not for classical or rhetorical literature. So Michelet turned the Renaissance art vividly present in his readers' mindseyes into the key literary and philosophical artefacts that – in the same readers' eyes – the period lacked. In so doing he pursued an embarrassingly radical and nationalistic purpose – another reason why his tradition was erased in favour of Burckhardt's in the twentieth century.

## literary pictures of the renaissance

In his volume on the Renaissance, Michelet takes us on a dizzying tour of the classical sites and literary monuments of the new medieval and

Renaissance antiquity, from the tomb of Abelard and Heloise to the Rue St Jacques in Paris where crowds gathered in 1500 to purchase the 'popular prudence of antiquity' – Erasmus' *Adagia*.[23] He does so because he needs rapidly to reverse the more positive image of the Middle Ages he had offered in previous volumes of his history. It now emerges as a long counter-revolution, a deliberate effort by the Church to smother the secular rebirth of man, an effort that continues in Michelet's present. For at the heart of the 'Renaissance' Michelet places the *politics* of documentary culture in the past and present. So on the one hand he points us towards the Reuchlin controversy and the failure of Francis I of France to support his and Ulrich von Hutten's humane stance against the Church's burning of Hebrew books. On the other hand, he points us to Didron's 1843 *Iconographie chrétienne*, part of a vast new series of unedited documents on the history of France. Had the author, says Michelet, removed some sheets that offended the ecclesiastical censor before going to press, we would have been plunged back into ignorance – by which he means 'medieval' ignorance.[24]

So literature *is* crucial. Indeed, the politics of the printing-press is at the heart of Michelet's revolutionary Renaissance. He describes how his own father, a master-printer, set up his printing-house *in* a church in 1793, and how he himself, persecuted as a revolutionary in 1843, ran straight to another publisher to print his free thoughts. Revolutionary publishing features in other ways. The sixteenth-century 'Discourse of voluntary servitude' by Montaigne's great friend La Boétie was published or quoted in print several times during the French Revolution, including by Marat himself. It was then printed again in revolutionary contexts in the mid-1830s. This is the context for its appearance in Michelet's history as practically the only literary text he cites from the period that gives heroic expression to the revolutionary dream of a revived antiquity.[25]

But we are never invited to *read* Italian Renaissance literary or philosophical antiquities in any detail. We are, instead, ushered into the grand gallery of the Louvre, where on one side – with Fra Angelico – we can see the Middle Ages, while on the other – with Leonardo da Vinci – we can see the genius of the Renaissance.[26] We are asked to slip alone into the Sistine Chapel, or – barring that – to equip ourselves with good reproductions of Michelangelo's famous frescos. The reader is then guided to see them as part of French revolutionary history, which means above all *turning them into* a literary monument. The frescos become the politically prophetic Vergilian epic that the 'original' literature of the time disappointingly could not offer. They become, also, a popular epic, the avatar of a whole social revolution. The poetic voice of the frescos is on first hearing that of Savonarola, the popular preacher and leader of Florence. But the deeper voice is that of Joachim of Fiore, the twelfth-century prophet of the 'eternal gospel' whose teachings were – according to Michelet – the *alpha* of the Renaissance. And Michelet asks us to pay particular attention to the figures listening to the various prophets depicted, to the families of pilgrims sat in the dark corners. For the prophetic voice behind the whole work expresses above all the contemporary popular thirst for *Droit*, for law and justice.[27]

Where Michelet made prophetic poetry out of frescos, Burckhardt made urbane portraits out of humanistic sources.[28] It is the traditional task of Renaissance studies rhetorically to shape the effect of the monuments on a contemporary audience, to turn them into speaking pictures of individuals – posed against national or civic backgrounds – with a resonantly 'humane' or 'liberal' message for modern ears. Different permutations of visual and literary arts are used, as well as different – lighter and darker – versions of what is 'classical' and what is 'humane'. Post-war examples range from Hans Baron's lifelong portrait of the adopted Florentine Leonardo Bruni to Kenneth Clark's televisual image of Montaigne in his Périgord tower. The tradition survives in a transmuted form, more attentive to the artifice of representation, in Greenblatt's use of Holbein's *The Ambassadors* as a way of grasping both the *Utopia* and the estrangement of Thomas More's interior self.[29] But notice in these examples how texts – as in Burckhardt – have come to the forefront.

## finding a canon of texts

Between the 1920s and the 1970s the Renaissance acquired the philosophical underpinnings and the canon of texts it had lacked in Michelet's work and in nineteenth-century historiography more generally. The Renaissance was purposefully reinvented as an *intellectuals'* tradition – a continuous intellectual history – of a self-conscious, historically aware revival of 'antiquity'. This tradition was built on the model of its close relation, the history-of-ideas version of the Enlightenment, which was likewise seen as a continuous intellectual tradition.[30] It was reinvented to forge a link between practitioners of the humanities in the mid-twentieth century and the historical and moral self-consciousness of pre-Enlightenment humanists and philosophers from Petrarch and Ficino to Montaigne and Bruno. In the process, Michelet's search in the monuments for the voice of early modern people was left behind.

The pivotal, the crucial, figure in this reinvented tradition was Erasmus, who linked southern and northern Europe, Renaissance and Reformation. He emerged as the author of a new theology and a new rhetoric. But above all it was his dynamic activity as a scholar, intellectual and editor, the vast amount of textbooks and editions he produced, that made him so important for inter-war and post-war scholars. For with Erasmus 'humanism' became a verifiable phenomenon in European history.[31] At the same time the history of humanism spread beyond the Renaissance. It linked medieval thought to Enlightenment philosophy and science. Its more strictly literary-historical corollary, a narrative about the transmutation of the Petrarchan Latin revival and subsidiary currents of thought into the various vernacular humanisms and literatures, was itself transmuted into various forms in the scholarship on the separate national literatures in the fifteenth and sixteenth centuries.[32] This is the great period of discovery of Renaissance humanistic literature (including philosophical literature) in both Latin and the vernaculars and of the intellectual background to that literature.[33] Every writer could now potentially be viewed as a 'humanist' in some sense, while their texts could be viewed as rhetorically constructed pieces of affective persuasion. Every writer and national revival could be assessed for reflections of medieval and of Renaissance thought.[34]

The new *textual* and *intellectual* foundations included a tradition of historiographical texts showing a continuity of historical consciousness of the Renaissance.[35] This was the way out of the problem of the Renaissance as it had developed in the inter-war years. The Renaissance had been declared by Burckhardt and Michelet the first modern era in every respect from social life to natural science. But the declaration and the concept of the Renaissance as a datable period in general history could not hold in the face of revolts by medievalists, who disputed it on many fronts.[36] Now the claim was to be staked on the sole basis of the Renaissance's historical self-awareness – its role, that is, in the founding of the modern, historicist humanities. In the 1940s, Herbert Weisenger wrote a series of articles gathering passages from all sorts of Renaissance texts that showed awareness of the revival of learning. The most important English texts he cited were Daniel's and Campion's. Weisinger uses Daniel's text to establish that the Italian tradition attributing the origin of the revival of learning to Petrarch had been accepted in England. He goes on to argue that 'the intense self-awareness of the Renaissance is a real historical phenomenon' and a 'satisfactory criterion for the identification of the Renaissance'.[37] The importance of this for post-war Renaissance studies is clear when, for example, the famous art historian Michael Baxandall quotes Daniel from Weisenger's article at the beginning of his 1971 study *Giotto and the Orators*. Baxandall uses Daniel to justify his treatment of the 'early humanists' between 1350 and 1450 as more than just a transitional interlude between the scholastics and the international humanists of the sixteenth century.[38]

Michelet had used a dilettantish, multimedia, interdisciplinary combination of archival scholarship, art criticism and cultural tourism. He had made overtly political, nationalistic interventions and had attempted to address the Renaissance as a European social revolution on the scale of the French Revolution. But now nationalistic competition for possession of medieval and Renaissance antiquities was to be transcended. The Renaissance was to be moved into the ether of the international history of ideas, of intellectuals and education. It was to be provided with a canon of works for university study, and a set of canonical intellectual movements for research. Sources were accordingly divided up amongst the various disciplines of the new humanistic pluridiscipline – the history of political and historical thought, the history of Neo-Latin and vernacular literatures, the history of philosophy – and separated from those judged suitable for general political, ecclesiastical and social historians.[39] These movements stretched before and after the Renaissance to form a larger *éta umanistica* (humanistic age), as Delio Cantimori called it, out of the new, medieval and Renaissance antiquity, the seventeenth century and the Enlightenment. They included the twelfth-century Renaissance, medieval humanism and Dante, Petrarchan humanism, Florentine civic humanism, neo-Platonism from Ficino to Pico, the sixteenth-century revolution in historical thought, and so on.[40]

It was not only the revolt of the medievalists which forced this shift into the history of ideas and texts. Renaissance historiography in the conservative Burckhardtian tradition was less capable than Michelet's tradition might have been to account for the emergence of modernity in the *new*, post-war sense. It was difficult enough to claim that the beginnings of the modern period in the old idealist sense of the spiritual awakening of modern man (traditionally dated to c.1500) should be thrust back into the fourteenth and fifteenth centuries and equated solely with the Italians' discovery of nature and antiquity. But there was now a new sense of a modernity that had begun with the French and industrial revolutions c.1800.

So the post-war Anglo-American institutionalization of the 'Renaissance' as a pluridisciplinary history of ideas coincided with the moment when the old concept of the 'modern' upon which its force *in general historiography* had depended, was declared obsolete. When Auerbach and

Ernst Robert Curtius published their great works of literary history and
criticism in 1946 and 1948, this concept was just losing its hold. Curtius
was saying that a new 'modern' period must be begun with the origins of
'industry' and 'technique' in the eighteenth century. It was the menace
and barbarism of this new modern period and its warring nation-states
that compelled Curtius to reinvent the tradition of humanism, to root it
more profoundly in the common European Latin tradition.[41]

Auerbach was more of a modernist and reacted differently. He
reoriented the whole of literary history around the dual emergence of
a 'modern contemporaneous realism' and of *historismus* ('historicism')
in France between 1789 and 1815. The cause was the first great mass
movement of modern times and its broad social effects (such as the
spread of elementary education) in the next decades.[42] To anchor this
modernity in a common global past he reinvented not Graeco-Roman
but biblical antiquity and the tradition of medieval realism derived from
it. Curtius and Auerbach, Burckhardt and Michelet, all *now* look equally
like Campions, like men of letters shoring up an old world – even though
Auerbach vernacularized the classical tradition in a highly influential
way and Michelet went looking for a revolutionary people in the art
of the Renaissance. The new concept of the 'modern' in the post-war
academic humanities, with its broad social and cultural scope and its
long revolutionary consequences, altered the sense of possible agents
and agencies of general historical change in European history; hence the
need for a commensurate 'early modern' period (1500–1800) in social
and cultural history.

So at the moment when it was challenged, the 'traditional' Renaissance
was only residually the Renaissance in general history sketched for the
nineteenth century by Michelet. It had been diverted via a selective
reading of Burckhardt into the various branches of the history of ideas
– everything from Baron's history of humanistic political thought to
Panofsky's iconological art history. This is clearest in the magisterial
interventions of Elizabeth Eisenstein in the late 1960s and 1970s. In
her classic article and subsequent debate with Theodore Rabb in 1969,
Eisenstein squarely took on the fundamental premise of post-war work
in Renaissance studies. German émigré scholars such as Panofsky and
Kristeller had come together with American colleagues within a reinvented
Burckhardtian tradition to claim that the foundations of their Renaissance
lay in the historical self-awareness of the period's own humanists and
philosophers. Eisenstein pointed out that these very humanists – including
Daniel himself – had pointed to an agent of change that was not one of
Burckhardt's Renaissance individuals (though it was one of the sacred

artefacts of Michelet's new secular religion): the printing press. She made the printing press the focus of a new kind of account of Renaissance intellectual history, one which emphasized the conditions, circumstances and collaborations that enhanced opportunities to combine learning by doing with learning by reading.[43]

A whole series of new intellectual histories followed on, revisiting the classic topics of post-war Renaissance studies and reassessing them root-and-branch. The new object of study, as in Eisenstein, was the social and intellectual matrix from which the classic text had been abstracted by idealist historians.[44] Artefacts from printed books to altar-pieces were re-read as deposits of social relations and exchanges, not as expressions of an individual's culture rooted in a particular western European nation or city. This would eventually change and expand the cultural geography of the Renaissance, the sense of the 'centres and peripheries' that nineteenth-century French, German and English scholars put in place.[45]

For during the later eighteenth and nineteenth centuries it was – as described earlier – the intellectual communities of France, Germany and Britain who defined the past and future directions of 'Europe' and its other, the 'Orient'. This was true in both literary and cultural historiography. The most important early books on the Italian Renaissance were written from the perspective of revolutionary France, Basel (a Swiss city-state perched precariously between France and the emergent German state), Prussia, and England (by Michelet, Burckhardt, Voigt and Symonds). Twentieth-century American historians of the Renaissance co-opted – with the help of the émigrés – this transalpine discovery of Italian cultural and historical capital as a useable past for their own country.[46] The western European nation that is interestingly excluded from this international discovery of the Renaissance is the one that controlled much of Renaissance Europe in the sixteenth century: Spain. Its Arabic cultural heritage made it not quite European enough in the Franco-German-British sense.

A sense of changing cultural geographies affects both literary-critical and cultural-historical approaches to artefacts. The geocultural setting of Shakespeare's *The Tempest* would first be identified with New World colonialism, then with trade and conflict between the Eurasian powers in the Mediterranean.[47] In broader cultural history, instead of seeing only what static national and civic traditions render visible and significant, the idea would be to follow people, objects and knowledge commodities as they circulate across boundaries from context to context, to explore the process by which cultural activities associated with a particular location or network come to remain private or to be publicized as of regional, national or international significance. Now we study transactions and relations, new patterns of collecting and consuming, rather than artistic expressions of metaphysical and historical consciousness.

## challenging the traditional renaissance in the 1960s and 1970s

The historicisms – new intellectual and social histories – that began to transform Renaissance studies in the 1960s and 1970s were new because they went back to the original questions and looked for new sources and new approaches to existing sources. They went back to do what Michelet and Burckhardt had done in their own context – to discover the patterns of ideas and mentalities that had shaped and changed early modern Europe. There was a political aspect to this return which made it – if unwittingly – a revival of Michelet's place in the tradition. In the 1840s and 1850s, Michelet saw an urgent need to wrest the medieval and Renaissance past from the hands of the clerical élite who were determining its contemporary significance. The new historicists of the 1960s and 1970s saw an urgent need to challenge not élite clerics' but élite humanists' view of the medieval and Renaissance past. Just as Michelet had done, they used new conjunctions of materials, new archival documents, new approaches to iconography and new readings of literary texts to *question* the 'civilization' bequeathed them by previous generations.

Michelet had used new archival documents to reveal the operations of the medieval Church as a police state, as the agent of an organized counter-revolution. The sources revealing the historical revolution in *popular* worldview which the Church could no longer repress by the early sixteenth century remained *artistic*, however. Mid-twentieth-century scholars, headed by Paul Oskar Kristeller, had taken things in a post-Burckhardtian direction. They had documented and canonized the literary sources – the corpus of manuscript and printed works of humanistic and philosophical literature centred on the ancients – that gave access to continuities and changes in the intellectuals' worldview between medieval and Renaissance eras. Kristeller segregated these sources from archival documents, the fodder of the general historian.

But Natalie Zemon Davis and Carlo Ginzburg took their skills of literary interpretation back to the archival documents of early modern France and Italy in search of popular voices and mentalities.[48] The archetypal experience was no longer the aesthetic encounter with medieval and Renaissance antiquities – Michelet slipping us into the Sistine Chapel, or Burckhardt showing us a literary portrait of Alberti. It was noticing the startling or strange vernacular narrative in archival or non-fictional documents. Davis and Ginzburg found popular narratives that had been fictively shaped, that uncannily resembled – in some respects – the novels, poems and treatises of the published vernacular literature. In other respects, they revealed mentalities and cultural possibilities that the version of cultural history gleaned exclusively from the polished humanistic sources had not hinted at. This archival experience could then be taken back to the high literary sources – such as, for example, the humanist Coras' account of the Martin Guerre case – as a new way of reading those sources against their own grain.[49] The new histories of late medieval and early modern French and Italian communities were another direct challenge to the Renaissance France of Michelet and the Renaissance Italy of Burckhardt. Early modern vernacular literature and vernacular literary agency had been discovered in a new sense.

A whole variety of new reading and research strategies developed. Advances were made partly by a harder, more empirical look at the history of humanistic scholarship and education; partly by valuing alternative or popular forms of thought and experience; partly by revealing the operations and structures of old regime power. This could mean reconstructing the worldview of a Friulian miller, or the thought behind a popular riot in early modern France. It could mean embedding the canonical works back in their patronage and transactional contexts. It could mean reviewing Castiglione's *The Courtier* and asking whether women really had a 'Renaissance'.[50] It could mean asking what the barbarism evident in travel accounts of the European invasion of the New World had to do with great works of the English Renaissance such as Marlowe's *Tamburlaine* and Shakespeare's *Othello*, and with the glorious image of the Renaissance as a civilized age of discovery.[51]

## the rise of the english literary renaissance

By the 1980s, an Anglo-American literary training (including literary theory) and familiarity with the new, north Atlantic social history and anthropology had firmly displaced a training in the Greek and Latin classics and in Italian Renaissance art and civilization as the main route into study of late medieval and early modern culture. In the contemporary humanities, the Italian Renaissance and early Italian humanism no longer enjoy an assured role as major *agents of change* in general political or literary histories of the individual western European nations.[52] Many practitioners in those fields nevertheless retain a Burckhardtian confidence in the *general* significance of their work (a confidence often shared by funding bodies). Meanwhile, other social and cultural historians have continued to bring the study of fourteenth- to sixteenth-century Italy into the fold of early modern community studies.

The centre of intellectual gravity has shifted from the Renaissance Society of America to the international centre of early modern studies, the Folger Shakespeare Library in Washington DC. The central artwork in Michelet's narrative of the revolution between medieval and Renaissance was Michelangelo's Sistine Chapel. The central artwork in Greenblatt's account of the shift in religious belief and practice between medieval and early modern is Shakespeare's *Hamlet*.[53] One result is that it is perfectly acceptable for someone in an English or English and Comparative Literature department who never reads texts in other languages to think of themselves as in 'Renaissance studies'. What is not acceptable is for them not to subscribe to some form of new historicism, and not to know something of the institutions and politics of early modern Britain. The rise to centrality of early modern Britain and British text studies in international historiography has brought both advances and distortions in historical perspective – just as the rise to centrality of Florence and the study of Florentine humanism did in the earlier period. Let us return to our starting-point to explore this further.

The orthodox approach to Daniel's text is now to be found in one of the canonical books of new historicism and comparative literature, Richard Helgerson's *Forms of Nationhood* (1992). Helgerson collects texts from different fields – including cartographic and legal texts – authored by men of Shakespeare's generation. They all participate in the writing of England. The purpose of the poets amongst them, including Daniel, was to make poetry serve the nation, 'to articulate a national community whose existence and eminence would then justify their desire to become its literary spokesmen'. Helgerson's own critical task, of course, is to deconstruct this writing of England, to show that there is no 'stable and unified national self' to be found in these texts, but a whole variety of representations, complete with dialectics and oppositional voices.[54]

Though from different fields the texts are linked by common themes. Renaissance humanism, for example, made the cultural dialectic between classical antiquity and the Middle Ages available to the discourses of both poetry and law. This is where the debate between Campion and Daniel comes in. Campion would impose a classical form on the nation. Daniel defends rhyme as a more inclusive form of nationhood and associates quantitative prosody with royal absolutism, which he rejects. He opposes the whole plan to 'write the nation' on a plan borrowed from a classical antiquity. Together, Campion's and Daniel's texts reveal a rift in the larger literary and cultural project of 'writing the nation'. Furthermore, neither the 'Greek' line, nor the 'gothic' line, was particularly English – something Daniel obscures.[55] The cultural historian Carlo Ginzburg was later to follow up this aspect of Helgerson's argument. He was likewise concerned with Daniel's role in the constructing of an English identity in the Elizabethan age. But Ginzburg shows that Daniel's declaration of independence from the classical continent is a revival of a cosmopolitan historiographical argument made by the mid-sixteenth-century French historian François Bauduin, and that Daniel elsewhere quotes Montaigne without acknowledgement.[56]

Helgerson and Ginzburg have advanced understanding of Daniel's text. But let us conclude by asking why, in the first place, they take the context of Daniel's text to be the role of literature in the formation of national identity. It is because they are ultimately addressing the role of Daniel's and others' texts in nation-formation in the Victorian and Edwardian, not the Elizabethan and Jacobean, eras. The cultural dialectic between classical antiquity and the Middle Ages was a nineteenth-century not a sixteenth-century phenomenon. By the First World War, the medieval and Renaissance period – Chaucer, Spenser, Shakespeare – had become the classical antiquity of the new discipline of English literature. The Victorians used Elizabethan and Jacobean literature – especially Shake-speare – to spread English civilization across the globe. The rise of English literary studies as the classical culture of American liberal arts programmes would make the revival of literature in the Elizabethan Renaissance the very model of national self-writing for Americans of Helgerson's and Greenblatt's generation.[57] Thanks most recently to the American movie industry, the bard is now left standing as the only truly global icon whose literary works date to the period between c.1300 and c.1650.

In historical terms this is nothing short of a paradox. For what was really interesting in this respect about Tudor and early Stuart England was that it had *no* credible claim before the later seventeenth century to international recognition as a distinct literary nation-state.

## european literary history before the first world war

Over three hundred years after its first publication, the Professor of Poetry at Oxford, W. P. Ker, included a long extract from Daniel's critique of Campion's history of learning in the introduction to his *The Dark Ages* (1923).[58] Though Daniel's poetry remained in print during the eighteenth century, his critical treatise was first revived and re-edited in the nineteenth century as part of the enterprise of collecting a national

tradition of vernacular literary criticism. The definitive collection for the
Elizabethan period proved to be that used here and published by George
Gregory Smith in 1905: *Elizabethan Critical Essays*. Smith was a lecturer
in the University of Edinburgh and had published a volume (1900) on
the fifteenth century in the same series as Ker's. According to critical
tradition, Smith says in the preface to his volume, the fifteenth was the
century when 'the ideals of the medieval world were transformed to the
fashions of modern art'. But Smith's goal was to show that there was no
sudden break between the old and the new, that 'things medieval and
things modern' could not be discriminated so exactly.[59] He might well
have taken the moral of Daniel's treatise to be something similar.

The series in which both volumes appeared was edited by George
Saintsbury, Professor of English Literature at Edinburgh University, and
was entitled 'Periods of European Literature'. Like Daniel's universal
history of learning this history of European literature was conceived
in a particular context at a specific moment for specific purposes. This
moment was the period *before* the First World War when a new wave of
histories of the national vernacular literatures written by professional
scholars all over Europe had been coming to notice. For during the long
nineteenth century between the end of the Napoleonic conquests and the
First World War the literary and cultural past was nationalized and inter-
nationalized in a vigorous way. 'European literature' became a matter of
international relations between national vernacular entities claiming
cultural primacy.

The specific context for Saintsbury's series in Britain was the rise of
English studies, the advent of university teaching and research in English
literature, which now meant 'original' literary prose, poetry and drama.
The motto of the series was a comment by Matthew Arnold calling for
a 'criticism which regards Europe as being, for intellectual and spiritual
purposes, one great confederation, bound to a joint action and working to
a common result'. The goal was therefore to *confederate* the new national
literary histories. It is specifically the relations between the powers that
went to war as the series came out – France, Germany (only unified as
Germany from 1871) and England – that are at the heart of its account
of European literary history.

The introduction to Ker's volume on *The Dark Ages* records and
reinforces a change in the prevailing sense and evaluation of the periods
of European literature. There traditionally used to be a middle age that
meant the time between ancient and modern civilization, everything
between the end of antiquity and the taking of Constantinople by the
Turks and the revival of learning. In this old, eighteenth-century and

Enlightenment reckoning, there was nothing worth reading between the end of antiquity and the revival of antiquity in the vernaculars. But now, says Ker, the Renaissance does not speak with such conviction, the term 'medieval' has lost its meaning of 'dark' and come to denote the period from about 1100 to 1500, the period of a highly valued gothic and romantic culture: '[the] Crusades, cathedrals, tournaments, old coloured glass and other splendid things, [having come] to be popularly known and appreciated'.[60] There is a direct line between the rhymes of twelfth-century Provence and European romantic writers in France, Germany and England such as Hugo, Goethe and Wordsworth. The so-called 'dark age' before Provençal poetry, though not modern, is still – *pace* the eighteenth century – part of the humanities and deserves the study it receives in Ker's volume.[61]

It is not that the classical tradition is simply displaced by the vernacular traditions in this type of history. The classical tradition now *is* the leading national literature during a particular period, the literature most authoritatively in possession of the 'joint-stock' (including Graeco-Roman stock) of all European nations: first French literature in the early medieval period, then Italian literature in the early Renaissance.[62] So Saintsbury's series does have a strong period concept of the Renaissance of literature in Europe, and of the role of 'classic models' in the history of that literature. No less than five of the twelve volumes narrate some phase of the period. The concept is recognizably Michelet's, though with an English pedigree supplied through the historical precedent of Daniel. Saintsbury describes how the Renaissance of literature began when the 'converging influences of the capture of Constantinople, the invention of printing, the discovery of America, and the final uprising against the ecclesiastical tyranny of Rome' were successively brought to bear.[63] The Renaissance consists of a series of differentiated national revivals with different life-spans and with different consequences.

The nations compete in a race in which the fastest starters collapse exhausted with no future, and the slower starters prove vigorous enough to run on into a longer history. This nicely divides the dead-end literary cultures of southern Europe from the two great national literatures of northern Europe: the French and the English. Italy's national (that is vernacular) literature is first to form, directly influenced by humanism and the classical revival, but is stifled by the Counter-Reformation. The synthesis of Italian classical humanism and Italian vernacular literature successively forms other nationalized humanisms and literatures. It kick-starts the Spanish Golden Age, then, slightly later, the French Renaissance, and latest, but strongest of all, the English revival. A German national literature does not emerge at all in this period.[64] The Spanish Golden Age proves to be the most isolated and short-term of the national vernacular revivals. For in Spain, the Renaissance met something 'barbarous, not quite European, and recalcitrant to all classic influences'. This 'something' had to do with the similarity of the Spanish to 'some oriental races'.[65]

This, I am suggesting, is representative of the new and explicitly racist view of European literary history that emerged towards the end of the nineteenth century. The cultural and historical geography informing this view centres on non-oriental, non-Mediterranean Europe and on the modern tradition leading from medieval Provence to romantic Germany via the literary Renaissances of France and especially England.[66] In the process, the literary humanities are given a new medieval-romantic antiquity and a new vernacular and national origin c.1100. This is why the message of Daniel's work of distinctively English and Elizabethan literary criticism seemed so familiar to scholars such as Ker and Saintsbury.

## building national literary cultures in renaissance europe

But was it in fact familiar? In the new literary history a western European tradition *consisting* of the general drift and relations of the primary national literatures was substituted for Campion's and Daniel's links between global and local literary contexts. The divine original source of literary wisdom was now the nation, the race at home in its own language. This nineteenth-century trend was of course modified by developments in the twentieth century. But it was still largely responsible for shaping the way that Renaissance literature and humanism have been studied in national literature departments for much of the period since. Wherever you end up, you are highly likely to be starting in a study environment shaped by the nineteenth-century Idea of a national literature.

Traditionally, if you work in an English or Modern Languages department on sixteenth-century literature you must either be a specialist in the canons of one of the national vernacular Renaissances – French, English, Spanish – and/or in the minor specialism of European, Neo-Latin literature. You can also, of course, become a comparatist. But traditional comparative literary study presupposes the nineteenth-century discovery and institutionalization of distinct and discrete national tongues, spirits and cultures, complete with their own 'antiquities'.[67] And this is the point about Helgerson. His new historicism is shaped by the way the Victorians and Edwardians collected and edited their literary antiquities. The context for Daniel's text is established by its collection in a volume of 'English literary criticism'.[68]

This is important because sixteenth-century English literary studies of the last thirty years has refounded itself on the study of the writing of the early modern English nation. In recent Oxford and Cambridge reference works, the history of early modern English literature *means* the post-Reformation history of the self-conscious construction of a national literary identity, and the converse shaping of literature by national institutions and customs.[69]

There *was* of course a move towards the formation of distinct national literatures in the sixteenth century. Literary nationalism does amplify between about 1500 and 1530 in the context of international cultural rivalry and of confessional and dynastic schism. This is the moment of the Reformation and the epoch-making vernacular translations of the Bible. There are suddenly vigorous rhetorical and antiquarian efforts to gather, or rather *list*, the materials and writings of national traditions. Daniel's treatise is testimony to this. Literary canons are gathered together more regularly and competitively by nation; Dante, Petrarch and Boccaccio are identified as the 'national' canon of Tuscany; Chaucer, Gower and Lydgate pop up to match them. In Skelton's 'Garlande or Chapelet of Laurell', written (possibly in several stages) between the late 1490s and early 1520s, the palace of literary fame is a global court at which writers of all nations and periods congregate. They press for entrance into the global court *via* their national archway, just as Skelton is aided in his suit by Chaucer, Gower and Lydgate; once inside they mingle indiscriminately with writers that subsequent tradition would divide into 'classical', 'medieval' and 'Renaissance': Quintilian and Theocritus, Poggio and Robert Gaguin, Plutarch and Petrarch.[70]

But Skelton's allegory indicates that this is a change in the whole system of literature and literary values. Another way of describing what happens in the early sixteenth century is to say that there is a new sense of the transnational or *global* nature of literary learning that is the precondition for international recognition of the strength of particular national archways. From this perspective, Campion and Daniel are doing the same, not different things. They both draw on internationally reputed, transnational revivals of learning – revivals consisting of networks and groups of texts – to give authority to their arguments about English literature. Campion associates poetry with musical knowledge and with 'Low Countries humanism' (as it would be labelled in the twentieth century) and its English adherents More and Ascham. Daniel associates poetry with judicial and historical knowledge and implicitly with the so-called 'revolution in historical thought' of the 1560s and 1570s, and its English adherents in Philip Sidney's circle.

And we have to consider what it meant at the time in practical terms for a particular political entity or region to stake a claim as a distinct national or civic centre of literary culture in the sixteenth century. The ability to list a catalogue of famous authors of the 'nation' was just one small, rhetorical part of the overall process; likewise to write works full of nationalistic sentiments. To possess a national or civic literary culture meant to be recognized as an independent reviver and collector of the global tradition of humane and divine learning. This meant a large financial investment in literary culture. You had to produce home-grown scholarly editions of the Graeco-Roman, biblical and patristic classics in the ancient languages. Around these both in Latin and your local vernacular you had to develop your own traditions of commentary and translation, as well as works of *new* learning in the various spheres of knowledge associated with the canonical classical authors. And all this in the context of rivalry both with the ancients themselves and with contemporary scholars and translators of other nations. In other words, Seneca had to be French both in the sense that France had an internationally regarded Latin edition and vernacular translation, and in the sense that Montaigne was internationally recognized as the most authentic vernacular imitator of Seneca. England was not even in the race for possession of the classical tradition in this sense.

You then of course had to have internationally significant institutions that produced humane and divine learning in various forms: universities and colleges, courts, academies, publishing houses. You had to have famous dynastic or civic libraries, including, of course, a grand royal collection. You had to have home-grown scholars and humanists with international reputations, and the ability to attract internationally famous scholars to your own institutions, especially your royal court. The evidence of this should be clear in international editions of familiar letters showing the intimate links between scholars and humanists and the wider world of learning.

England, then Great Britain (1603), had fragmentary elements of a national literary culture in this sense: Erasmus' stay in Cambridge and his links with Thomas More and John Colet; Henry VIII's investment in his library; Philip Sidney's international reputation; the King James Bible; the Bodleian Library, and so on. But the list of the elements it lacked, the sheer paucity of investment and independent literary production compared with other European nations and cities, would take another chapter in itself to enumerate. France, the Habsburg Empire, the Papacy, Venice, Tuscany and even a small Italian state like Urbino were all ahead of England and Britain in the international competition for recognition as culturally distinct centres of literary production – not least because their vernaculars were international languages.

From this perspective, the rise of English studies in the modern period blocks our view of the historical culture of literature in Renaissance Europe. In the contemporary world of learning the language of English, of English studies, of Anglo-American historiography is slowly colonizing more and more of the space and pedagogy of classical Latin and of major modern languages such as French, Spanish and Italian.[71] But in sixteenth-century England, imported continental expertise and learning, including not only Latin books but French, Italian and Spanish vernacular translations, filled the space left by the *absence* of a comprehensively nationalized culture of literary learning. Insofar as it existed during the period traditionally described as the European Renaissance (c.1350 to c.1600), Britain's 'national' literary culture (in the sense I have been developing) was an unachieved and marginal enterprise swamped by the importation and consumption of international learned commodities on the one hand, and by the vernacular oral and literary culture connected with popular and devotional texts, and with the contingent occasions of domestic, civic and courtly speech, on the other. It is the permeability of these two cultures that makes the 'original' English writing of the period historically interesting, not the model it provides of national self-writing.

It is this permeability that we can see in Daniel's work, especially if we approach it less as an abstracted text and more as a print-event. As Helgerson did point out, Daniel's 'Defence' was first printed in 1603 in a small volume that began with 'A Panegyric Congratulatory, delivered to the King's Most Excellent Majesty'. He noted in general terms that the concerns of the poem are those of the 'Defence' – worries about political innovations tyrannically imposed by absolute power – and that Daniel was quite consciously taking his stand in the face of the new king, James VI of Scotland.[72] But he does not see that the *real* occasion of Daniel's text as published in 1603 is not what it appears to be, namely, his staged debate with Campion about the nature of history and the best way to write true English verse. The full title of Daniel's poem goes on to specify that the poem was delivered to James 'at Burley-Harington in Rutlandshire'. The real occasion is the literary publicity surrounding James' progress from Edinburgh to London in the late spring of 1603. James' progress consisted of a mixture of private entertainments in élite households such as Lord Harrington's, and civic occasions connected with his entrance into particular towns. The pair of texts to be looking at, then, is not so much Campion's and Daniel's as Daniel's 'Panegyric' and Daniel's 'Defence'. Both are offered as private literary works – a poem delivered as part of a private courtly entertainment, and a private letter to a gentleman at court – whose publication is warranted by the occasion of the king's succession. As a vernacular humanist tutor employed in households such as Harrington's, Daniel had been chosen to compose an elegant and learned vernacular poem appropriate to the occasion. It would show the household to be an environment of courtly vernacular letters. In this context, the outcome is no surprise. The Harringtons were awarded the costly honour of educating James' daughter, the Princess Elizabeth, in their household.[73]

Daniel's text turns a defence of rhyme into a treatise on how to read history and a petition for the preservation of customs against tyrannical intervention. So one context is the importation of new historical and legal – 'judicial' – knowledge from the continent, especially France, and its application in vernacular household tuition. As Weisinger already demonstrated, Daniel's history of the revival of learning is mainly borrowed from authoritative expansions of Italian accounts by international French scholars and historian-jurists such as Estienne Dolet and Louis Le Roy.[74] But the new historical perspective offered by his text more generally depends on the mid-century effort to rethink the reading of the ancients and reshape the history of the world – not, as once thought, the 'origins' of modern historical thought and criticism but a range of scholarly activities linking the producing of historical and jurisprudential knowledge in Paris, Basel, Heidelberg and other continental centres.[75] Many of the important figures – Bauduin, Bodin, Postel – were French, as was the greatest lay follower and critic of their enterprise in new critical learning, Montaigne, making France the main national gateway into this international scene. The centre of *transmission* of this new historical knowledge in England is the international figure of Philip Sidney and the milieu of courtiers and scholars with which he is associated.[76]

What was the status of Daniel, author for the Victorians of a 'classic' text of Elizabethan literary culture, within the post-Sidneian milieu? His appearance in an inset portrait in the left panel of Lady Anne Clifford's famous 'Great Picture' confirms that he was primarily known as a vernacular humanist tutor to young noblewomen. He appears alongside Lady Anne's governess above shelves full of her books. The picture indicates that an élite literary culture consisting entirely of English vernacular works did indeed exist; it was considered suitable in aristocratic households for the education of young noblewomen – as well as for non-university educated gentlemen in the shires. The relevant canon of vernacular works included a majority of translations and a minority of what we would distinguish as 'original' literary works by the likes of Sidney, Spenser, Camden, and Daniel himself.[77] The English sub-canon – not clearly demarcated in the collection – only made sense, if you like, as *part* of this vernacularized international context.

The other context for Daniel's 'Defence' takes us back, once again, to its occasion. By placing it alongside its companion piece (by Campion) and collecting it with other vernacular English treatises to do with poetics, G. G. Smith ensured that future scholars would think of its occasion primarily as the writing of a national literary criticism, of the nation itself. But the context in which another nineteenth-century scholar, the antiquarian John Nichols, collected its true companion piece, the 'Panegyric', is more helpful in furthering historical understanding of the text. In his chronologically arranged but otherwise pell-mell collection of archival and printed documents bearing on James' 1603 progress, Nichols provides us with the type of opportunity cherished by new historicists of the 1960s and 1970s. He juxtaposes the poem with various other archival letters and published speeches asking 'in real life' for James' encouragement, as Daniel puts it, 'to go on with what we do', to expect *not* to be checked by any innovation.[78]

For a progress, especially that of a new king arriving for the first time from another country, was punctuated by variations on a particular kind of social event. It consisted of some tense, some routine occasions upon which the people subjected themselves, their lives and goods, to the will of the king, and the king ceremoniously handed them back, encouraging them to think he would not interfere with their wonted customs and liberties. Nichols offers examples of both sides of this social exchange from Berwick's 'Oathe booke', from the king's and mayors' correspondence, from speeches and orations delivered on the various occasions of the progress. The speech that is closest in its topics and rhetoric both to Daniel's poem and treatise is that delivered outside London by Master Richard Martin in the name of the sheriffs of London and Middlesex.[79] Daniel's 'Panegyric' is in this context a poetic appropriation of a type of civic oration; it is delivered in the name of private courtiers – the Harringtons – during a household entertainment that is later publicized. Daniel's 'Defence' *draws* on a contemporary understanding of the conventions of these occasions. It does so to make its argument against checking of the custom of rhyme and to associate itself – via a particular print-event – with the advent of the new king and the revival of learning he will (hopefully) foster and finance. The most significant historical outcome, however, is the entrusting of the Princess Elizabeth to the Harringtons.

Daniel's text can take us out, then, into the new social and intellectual history of the early modern period. But to do so it must relinquish its dual status as a canonical text of Renaissance historical self-awareness and of Elizabethan national self-writing.

## notes

1. G. G. Smith, ed., *Elizabethan Critical Essays*, 2 vols (London, 1904), II, pp. 325–7; Carlo Ginzburg, *No Island is an Island: Four Glances at English Literature in a World Perspective*, trans. John Tedeschi (New York, 2000), pp. 27–8.
2. Smith, *Elizabethan Critical Essays*, II, p. 327.
3. Smith, *Elizabethan Critical Essays*, II, pp. 357–8.
4. Smith, *Elizabethan Critical Essays*, II, pp. 367, 371 and compare p. 372 ('There is but one learning which *omnes gentes habent in scriptum in cordibus suis* [all peoples have written in their hearts], one and the selfe-same spirit that worketh in all ... one bodie of Wisdome thorowout the whole world').
5. Smith, *Elizabethan Critical Essays*, II, pp. 366–8 (Daniel's chronology is wrong).
6. Smith, *Elizabethan Critical Essays*, II, pp. 369–70, 372. Daniel is wrong again: Chrysoloras' impact was far more important in Florence than in Venice.
7. Ginzburg, *No Island*, pp. 33, 37, 40.
8. See, for example, Leah S. Marcus, 'Renaissance/Early Modern Studies', in *Redrawing the Boundaries: The Transformation of English and American Literary Studies*, ed. Stephen Greenblatt and Giles Gunn (New York, 1992), pp. 41–63.
9. Paula Findlen, 'The Renaissance in the Museum', in A. J. Grieco, M. Rocke and F. Gioffredi Superbi, eds, *The Italian Renaissance in the Twentieth Century* (Florence, 2002), pp. 93–116.
10. Jules Michelet, *Œuvres complètes*, ed. Paul Viallaneix, VII: *Histoire de France au seizième siècle: Renaissance et Reforme*, ed. Robert Casanova (Paris, 1978), pp. 200–1.
11. Stephen Greenblatt, 'Touch of the Real', *Representations*, LIX (1997) 14–29, at 14.
12. Natalie Zemon Davis, *Fiction in the Archives: Pardon Tales and their Tellers in Sixteenth-Century France* (Oxford, 1987).
13. J. B. Bullen, *The Myth of the Renaissance in Nineteenth-Century Writing* (Oxford, 1994), p. 18 and passim.
14. Edward W. Said, *Orientalism*, 3rd edn (London, 2003).
15. For further background to Michelet see the introduction to his *Œuvres*, VII, and Bullen, *Myth of the Renaissance*, pp. 156–82. There is a large literature on Burckhardt but I have found Lionel Gossman, 'Cultural History and Crisis: Burckhardt's *Civilization of the Renaissance in Italy*', in *Rediscovering History: Culture, Politics and the Psyche*, ed. Michael S. Roth (Stanford, 1994), pp. 404–27, most helpful.
16. See David Harris Sacks, 'Searching for "Culture" in the English Renaissance', *Shakespeare Quarterly*, XXXIX (1988) 465–88, at 466, an article that shares some concerns with the present chapter.

17. On Burckhardt's historical melancholy see Michael Ann Holly, 'Cultural History, Connoisseurship, and Melancholy', in Grieco, Rocke and Gioffredi Superbi, *Italian Renaissance in the Twentieth Century*, pp. 195–206.
18. Fritz Ringer, *Fields of Knowledge: French Academic Culture in Comparative Perspective* (Cambridge, 1992), p. 94 and passim.
19. See especially Michelet, *Œuvres*, VII, p. 145.
20. Findlen, 'The Renaissance in the Museum', p. 116; Christopher S. Wood, 'Art History's Normative Renaissance', in Grieco, Rocke and Gioffredi Superbi, *Italian Renaissance in the Twentieth Century*, pp. 65–92, at p. 82; Erwin Panofsky, *Renaissance and Renascences in Western Art* (New York, 1969); and Erwin Panofsky, *Meaning in the Visual Arts* (London, 1991), especially 'Introduction: The History of Art as a Humanistic Discipline'.
21. Michelet, *Œuvres*, VII, pp. 49, 77–8, 108–10.
22. Michelet, *Œuvres*, VII, pp. 437–8.
23. Michelet, *Œuvres*, VII, pp. 99–100, 202.
24. Michelet, *Œuvres*, VII, pp. 102–5, 247–8.
25. Michelet, *Œuvres*, VII, pp. 61–2, 203; Nicola Panichi, *Plutarchus Redivivius? La Boétie e i suoi interpreti* (Naples, 1999), pp. 45–53.
26. Michelet, *Œuvres*, VII, pp. 83–4; Bullen, *Myth of the Renaissance*, p. 180.
27. Michelet, *Œuvres*, VII, pp. 72–3, 149–50, 209, 213–16.
28. See, for example, the portrait of Alberti in Jacob Burckhardt, *The Civilization of the Renaissance in Italy* (New York, 1958), 2.2, pp. 149–50, and the comment in Anthony Grafton, *Leon Battista Alberti: Master Builder of the Italian Renaissance* (London, 2001), pp. 14–18.
29. Hans Baron, *In Search of Florentine Civic Humanism: Essays on the Transition from Medieval to Modern Thought*, 2 vols (Princeton, 1988); George Hoffmann, *Montaigne's Career* (Oxford, 1998), pp. 11, 13; Stephen Greenblatt, *Renaissance Self-Fashioning, from More to Shakespeare* (Chicago and London, 1980), pp. 16–27; and the commentary by Lisa Jardine, 'Strains of Renaissance Reading', *English Literary Renaissance* XXV (1995) 289–306.
30. See *La Reinvenzione dei lumi: percorsi storiografici del novecento*, ed. Giuseppe Ricuperati (Florence, 2000).
31. See Bruce Mansfield, *Erasmus in the Twentieth Century* (Toronto and London, 2003); Cesare Vasoli, *Umanesimo e rinascimento*, 2nd edn (Palermo, 1976), p. 500 (an extract from Delio Cantimori's crucial essay originally dating to 1955, 'La periodizzazione dell'età del Rinascimento', also available in Cantimori, *Storici e storia. Metodo, caratteristiche e significato del lavoro storiografico* (Turin, 1971), pp. 553–77).
32. See William M. Jones, ed., *The Present State of Scholarship in Sixteenth-Century Literature* (Columbia, 1978) for illustrations of this.
33. For a general account of the genres of scholarly and philosophical literature in the medieval and Renaissance periods see P. O. Kristeller, 'The Scholar and his Public in the Late Middle Ages', in *Medieval Aspects of Renaissance Learning: Three Essays by Paul Oskar Kristeller*, ed. and trans. Edward P. Mahoney (Durham, 1974), pp. 4–25.
34. See, for English Renaissance studies, E. M. W. Tillyard, *The Elizabethan World Picture* (Harmondsworth, 1943) and further illustrations for other countries in Jones, *Present State of Scholarship*.

35. The classic textbooks are Wallace K. Ferguson, *The Renaissance in Historical Thought* (Cambridge, MA, 1948) and Vasoli, *Umanesimo e rinascimento*.
36. See Ferguson, *Renaissance in Historical Thought*, pp. 329–85, and Vasoli, *Umanesimo*, pp. 491–9 (from Cantimori's essay).
37. Herbert Weisinger, 'Who Began the Revival of Learning? The Renaissance Point of View', *Papers of the Michigan Academy of Science, Arts and Letters*, XXX (1944) 625–38, at 626–9 and 637; and 'The Renaissance Theory of the Reaction against the Middle Ages as a Cause of the Renaissance', *Speculum*, XX (1945) 461–7, at 466–7.
38. Michael Baxandall, *Giotto and the Orators: Humanist Observers of Painting in Italy and the Discovery of Pictorial Composition* (Oxford, 1971), pp. 4–5. Baxandall's book as a whole made precise and historically grounded connections between the revival of letters and the revival of the arts during this early period.
39. Paul Oskar Kristeller's finding-list of Renaissance humanist manuscripts (*Iter Italicum*) is a classic example. His basic principle was cleanly to distinguish between humanistic manuscript texts and books and archives for general history (which he did not list). See Warren Boutcher, 'Literature, Thought or Fact? Past and Present Directions in the Study of the Early Modern Letter', in *Self-Presentation and Social Identification: The Rhetoric and Pragmatics of Letter Writing in Early Modern Times: Proceedings of the International Colloquium, Leuven-Brussels, 24–28 May 2000*, ed. Jan Papy, Toon van Houdt and Gilbert Tournoy (Leuven, 2002), pp. 137–63.
40. This trend is brilliantly described – and endorsed – by Cantimori in his 1955 essay (Vasoli, *Umanesimo*, p. 501).
41. Ernst Robert Curtius, *European Literature and the Latin Middle Ages*, trans. W. R. Trask (London and Henley, 1953), pp. vii–viii, 23. This work was first published in German in Berne in 1948.
42. Erich Auerbach, *Mimesis: The Representation of Reality in Western Literature* (Princeton, 1953), pp. 458–9, 473. This work was first published in German in Berne in 1946.
43. Elizabeth Eisenstein, 'The Advent of Printing and the Problem of the Renaissance', *Past and Present*, XLV (1969) 19–89, esp. 62; Theodore K. Rabb, 'The Advent of Printing and the Problem of the Renaissance: A Comment', and Elizabeth Eisenstein, 'A Reply', *Past and Present*, XXV (1971) 135–44.
44. Quentin Skinner, *The Foundations of Modern Political Thought*, 2 vols (Cambridge, 1978), I, pp. x–xi.
45. The best general synthesis of this kind of approach is Lisa Jardine, *Worldly Goods* (London, 1996).
46. On Voigt see Vasoli, *Umanesimo e rinascimento*, pp. 123–5; on Symonds see Bullen, *Myth of the Renaissance*, pp. 251–5, 301–7. Edward Said described how the major steps in Oriental scholarship were first taken either in Britain or France, then elaborated upon by Germans, then taken up from the Second World War by Americans (*Orientalism*, pp. 17–18). There are clear and close parallels with the history of Renaissance scholarship. See Edward Muir, 'The Italian Renaissance in America', *American Historical Review*, C (1995) 1095–118.
47. See *'The Tempest' and its Travels*, ed. Peter Hulme and William Sherman (London, 2000).

48. Zemon Davis, *Fiction in the Archives*, and Carlo Ginzburg, *The Cheese and the Worms: The Cosmos of a Sixteenth-Century Miller*, trans. John and Anne Tedeschi (Harmondsworth, 1992) – first published in Italian in 1976.

49. Natalie Zemon Davis, *The Return of Martin Guerre* (Cambridge, MA, 1983).

50. See Joan Kelly's 1977 essay, 'Did Women have a Renaissance?' reprinted in *Women, History, and Theory: The Essays of Joan Kelly* (Chicago, 1984), pp. 19–50, and in the important collection *Feminism and Renaissance Studies*, ed. Lorna Hutson (Oxford, 1999), pp. 21–47.

51. See the classic papers given by Greenblatt at the English Institute in 1976 and 1978: 'Marlowe and Renaissance Self-Fashioning', in *Two Renaissance Mythmakers: Christopher Marlowe and Ben Jonson*, ed. Alvin Kiernan (Baltimore and London, 1977), pp. 41–69; and 'Improvization and Power', *Literature and Society*, ed. E. Said (Baltimore and London, 1980), pp. 57–99. Both were later republished in different forms in Greenblatt's *Renaissance Self-Fashioning*.

52. David Loewenstein and Janel Mueller, eds, *The Cambridge History of Early Modern English Literature* (Cambridge, 2002) is not in any sense a history of something called the 'Renaissance' in England. Arlette Jouanna's history of sixteenth-century France still uses the nomenclature of the 'Renaissance' but drastically plays down the general cultural importance of the French invasions of Italy. See Arlette Jouanna, *La France au XVIe siècle 1483–1598*, 2nd edn (Paris, 1997), pp. 267–8.

53. Stephen Greenblatt, *Hamlet in Purgatory* (Princeton, 2001).

54. Richard Helgerson, *Forms of Nationhood: The Elizabethan Writing of England* (Chicago, 1992), pp. 2, 8.

55. Helgerson, *Forms of Nationhood*, pp. 23, 37–9.

56. Ginzburg, *No Island*, 30–42.

57. Helgerson, *Forms of Nationhood*, pp. 15–18.

58. W. P. Ker, *The Dark Ages*, Periods of European Literature, I (Edinburgh and London, 1923), pp. 19–20.

59. G. G. Smith, *The Transition Period*, Periods of European Literature, IV (Edinburgh and London, 1900), pp. v–vi.

60. Ker, *The Dark Ages*, pp. 1–4, quotation at p. 4.

61. Ker, *The Dark Ages*, pp. 5–9.

62. F. J. Snell, *The Fourteenth Century*, Periods of European Literature, III (Edinburgh and London, 1899), p. 421.

63. George Saintsbury, *The Earlier Renaissance*, Periods of European Literature, V (Edinburgh and London, 1901), p. vi.

64. See Smith, *The Transition Period*, especially pp. 118–26; Saintsbury, *The Earlier Renaissance*, especially p. 405; David Hannay, *The Later Renaissance*, Periods of European Literature, VI (Edinburgh and London, 1911), especially pp. 367–78.

65. Hannay, *The Later Renaissance*, pp. 375, vii.

66. See George Saintsbury, *The Flourishing of Romance and the Rise of Allegory*, Periods of European Literature, II (London, 1897), pp. 422–3.

67. William Moebius, 'Lines in the Sand: Comparative Literature and the National Literature Departments', *Comparative Literature*, XLIX (1997) 243–58, and for a more optimistic view of the capacity of comparative literature to overcome its nationalist foundations see Claudio Guillén, *The Challenge of Comparative Literature*, trans. Cola Franzen (Cambridge, MA, 1993).

68. This is truer still of a much more recent collection than Smith's: *English Renaissance Literary Criticism*, ed. Brian Vickers (Oxford, 1999).
69. See Loewenstein and Mueller, *Cambridge History of Early Modern English Literature* and James Simpson, *The Oxford English Literary History*, II: *1350–1547, Reform and Cultural Revolution* (Oxford, 2002).
70. John Skelton, *The Complete English Poems*, ed. John Scattergood (New Haven, 1983), pp. 319–31.
71. Spanish is once again an interesting exception, at least in the United States, but the resurgence in Hispanic studies has brought Golden Age studies to the forefront of Renaissance or early modern studies.
72. Helgerson, *Forms of Nationhood*, p. 38.
73. John Nichols, *The Progresses, Processions, and Magnificent Festivities of King James the First, His Royal Consort, Family, and Court*, 4 vols (London, 1828), I, pp. 121, 93–4; Smith, *Elizabethan Critical Essays*, II, p. 356.
74. Weisinger, 'Who Began the Revival of Learning?', p. 627.
75. See Anthony Grafton, *Defenders of the Text: The Traditions of Scholarship in an Age of Science, 1450–1800* (Cambridge, MA, 1994), pp. 94–101; Donald R. Kelley, *Foundations of Modern Historical Scholarship: Language, Law and History in the French Renaissance* (New York, 1970); Ginzburg, *No Island*, p. 31.
76. See A. Grafton and L. Jardine, '"Studied for Action": How Gabriel Harvey Read his Livy', *Past and Present*, CXXIX (1990) 30–78 and Blair Worden, *The Sound of Virtue: Philip Sidney's 'Arcadia' and Elizabethan Politics* (New Haven, 1996), pp. 253–66.
77. Richard T. Spence, *Lady Anne Clifford, Countess of Pembroke, Dorset and Montgomery (1590–1676)* (Stroud, 1997), pp. 181–99.
78. Nichols, *Progresses*, I; Smith, *Elizabethan Critical Essays*, II, p. 357.
79. Nichols, *Progresses*, I, pp. 32–3, 128–32.

# 12
## science
### brian w. ogilvie

For historians of science, the Renaissance has long been the neglected stepchild, standing in the shadow of the Middle Ages and the seventeenth-century Scientific Revolution.[1] Historians have written about scientific developments in the period from 1400 to 1600, but by and large they have had little interest in whether the Renaissance forms a coherent period in the history of science distinct, on the one hand, from developments in late medieval natural philosophy and, on the other, from the 'new science' of seventeenth-century figures like Galileo, Descartes, Boyle, and Newton.

When writing about the historiography of science in the Renaissance, there are thus two issues to address. First, what was science like in the Renaissance, and on what have modern historians of Renaissance science focused? What approaches have they taken, how do those approaches differ from earlier historical approaches to Renaissance science, and what are their fruits? Underlying these questions about recent and contemporary historical research is a second, deeper – though not necessarily more important – question: is the Renaissance a coherent period in the history of science?

In the following pages, I chart a path from the first to the second of these questions. I begin by sketching briefly the historiography of Renaissance science from Jacob Burckhardt's *Civilization of the Renaissance in Italy* (1860) through the following century. I then address the substance of historical research on science during the Renaissance, emphasizing the shift from study of scientific theories and institutions, with an eye on the origins and development of modern science, to an interest in science as practice and culture done by historians who are less concerned with explaining how Renaissance science contributed to modern science than with understanding what role science played in Renaissance culture and society.

Historians have only occasionally reflected on the Renaissance as a category in the historiography of science. My own views of the subject have been informed not only by my reading in the literature but also by four of these reflections: Eric Cochrane's 1976 article on 'Science and Humanism in the Italian Renaissance'; Antonio Beltrán's 1985 considerations on 'El Renacimiento en la historiografía de la ciencia' ('The Renaissance in the Historiography of Science'), Pamela O. Long's 1988 essay on 'Humanism and Science', and Brian Copenhaver's 1992 article, 'Did Science have a Renaissance?'[2]

As these historians point out, history of science has rarely addressed the Renaissance as a distinct period. Beltrán notes that historians in the 1960s and 1970s – Frances Yates, D. P. Walker, Allen Debus, P. M. Rattansi, and Margaret C. Jacob – acknowledged the importance of the mystical or hermetic tradition on the development of modern science, but they framed the issue not in terms of Renaissance science but, rather, in terms of contributions to the Scientific Revolution. Paolo Rossi emphasized in his study of Francis Bacon the specifically Renaissance elements in Bacon's thought: his logic was an offshoot of Renaissance logic, while his notion of the natural philosopher as 'interpreter of nature' drew heavily on the Renaissance idea of the magus.[3] But more commonly, historians of science either neglected the Renaissance or treated it as only an indirect influence on the history of science. As Beltrán portrays developments through the 1970s, there were three main approaches to the question of Renaissance science and its relation to the history of science more generally. One strand pointed to the indirect importance of later fifteenth- and sixteenth-century humanism for recovering ancient Greek scientific knowledge, which stimulated seventeenth-century developments. A second strand, dating back to the work of Pierre Duhem in the early twentieth century, stressed the theoretical and methodological continuities between medieval physical science and its seventeenth-century successor, treating the Renaissance as an irrelevant or retarding interlude. A third strand emphasized the continuity between the seventeenth-century scientific revolution and the mystical-magical Hermeticism of the Renaissance.[4] Peter Damerow and Jürgen Renn have recently suggested that the last two approaches are not so much opposed as complementary: the body of scientific knowledge of the Scientific Revolution shows many continuities with medieval science, but the 'image of science' of the Scientific Revolution – with its grand claims to remake man and society – is a Renaissance innovation. Moreover, Renaissance and seventeenth-century 'scientist-engineers' confronted new 'objects of knowledge' that led to significant changes and refinements in the theoretical and methodological inheritance of the Middle Ages.[5]

Damerow and Renn's approach is fruitful for understanding the historiographical state of study on Renaissance science. But the very title of the article in which they state their position is revealing: 'Scientific Revolution, History and sociology of.' Scholars who explicitly address the overall character of science in the Renaissance have been interested almost exclusively in relating the Renaissance to the subsequent Scientific Revolution. A chief exception is the work of Michel Foucault (addressed below), which in turn explains why Copenhaver and others take Foucault to task for positing a rupture at the transition both from the Middle Ages to the Renaissance and from the latter to the 'classical age' of early modern thought (and science).

In what follows, we will consider how historians have treated the body of science, the image of science, and the object of science in the Renaissance, in the context of who was doing science and how that changed. I will emphasize the period from 1450 to 1600; as we will see, the sixteenth century has received much more attention from historians of science than the fifteenth. I have made no attempt to be comprehensive; the reader who wishes for a complete bibliography should consult the *Isis Current Bibliography* and the collections produced on its basis.[6]

## background: renaissance science from 1860 to 1970

Jacob Burckhardt's powerful interpretation of the Renaissance created a historical myth that has both structured and distorted subsequent scholarship.[7] Following Jules Michelet, Burckhardt characterized the Renaissance as a period of the 'discovery of the world and of man'. A lively interest in natural phenomena was one element in Burckhardt's Renaissance picture.[8] But Burckhardt knew little and said little about science itself. The 'revolt of the medievalists' against Burckhardt's characterization of the Renaissance as the birth of modern Europe affected the history of science too.[9] Careful study of the achievements of medieval natural philosophers in the mathematical study of motion led the French physicist and historian Pierre Duhem to conclude that the birthplace of modern science lay in the thirteenth and fourteenth centuries, and that the mechanical work of Leonardo da Vinci, essentially medieval, served to transmit this mechanics to its most important student, Galileo Galilei.[10] This conception was vigorously opposed by other historians of science, who identified the late sixteenth and seventeenth centuries as the period when modern science was born. In particular, for E. A. Burtt and Alexandre Koyré, the development of astronomy and physics from Copernicus to Newton marked not only the birth of modern scientific theories and methods but also a more fundamental shift in metaphysics, producing the infinite, mechanized, mathematically tractable universe in which we live.[11] Thus, in the early twentieth century, the most important debate about the origins of modern science was over whether it was to be found in the Middle Ages or the seventeenth century.

This emerging notion of the Scientific Revolution largely eliminated the Renaissance as a distinct period in the history of science. The Scientific Revolution began with the astronomical innovation of Nicholas Copernicus, whose 1543 *On the Revolutions* posited a heliocentric mathematical model for planetary astronomy. Copernicus began a scientific revolution that challenged the dominant Aristotelian physics and Ptolemaic astronomy of the Middle Ages. Later revolutionaries, like Galileo Galilei, Johannes Kepler, and René Descartes, strove both to justify heliocentrism against its opponents and to devise a mathematical theory of local motion that made sense in a world that no longer admitted Aristotle's fundamental distinction between celestial and terrestrial physics. Their endeavours culminated in Isaac Newton's *Mathematical Principles of Natural Philosophy* (1687), whose theory of universal gravitation tied together a century and a half of developments in terrestrial and celestial physics.

When the Renaissance did receive attention, it was generally either as a period of scientific stagnation or as a preparation for the more important developments of the seventeenth century, as in Marie Boas' 1962 survey of 'the scientific Renaissance'.[12] For Boas, the characteristic aspect of the Renaissance in the history of science was confusion and tension between the heritage of ancient science, recovered by humanist scholars, and the increasing demands of scientific empiricism, which was driven by practical needs. The result was a 'paradoxical blend':

> Striving to master Greek scientific texts, while keenly aware of later technical progress, mathematicians, botanists and physicians, like astronomers, strangely combined reverence for the literal word of the remote past with a desire for novelty. Endeavouring to see in nature what Greek writers had declared to be there, European scientists slowly came to see what really was there.[13]

Torn between the conflicting demands of recovering past texts and discovering the world, Renaissance science possessed no individual character of its own.

By the 1970s, the Renaissance had largely been written out of the history of science. Generations of scholars had emphasized the divide between the medieval scholastic tradition, with its strong scientific bent, and the rhetorical, political concerns of Renaissance humanists, who held most scientific knowledge in contempt. Moreover, by emphasizing the continuities between Galileo's work in the 1590s and that of Paduan Aristotelians two centuries earlier, J. H. Randall had effectively removed from the Renaissance its most prominent scientific light. Galileo, according to Randall, was not a product of the humanist culture of the Renaissance but, rather, of a scholastic counter-culture that had persisted in Padua.[14]

Admittedly, there were other currents. George Sarton initially dismissed the Renaissance as a retrograde period whose scholars substituted ancient texts for independent thought and personal observation of nature. But late in life, in the 1950s, Sarton came to appreciate the importance of Renaissance humanism for reviving aspects of ancient Greek science that had been neglected in the Middle Ages.[15] As will be discussed further below, the art historian Erwin Panofsky characterized the Renaissance as a period of 'decompartmentalization' during which the medieval barriers between artists, engineers, and intellectuals broke down, resulting in such universal geniuses as Leonardo da Vinci and Albrecht Dürer.[16]

Nonetheless, these were exceptions. In the middle of the 1970s, Thomas Kuhn summed up what he saw as two different traditions of early modern science. The mathematical tradition, above all astronomy and physics, achieved a true scientific revolution in the seventeenth century. The experimental tradition – chemistry, natural history – did not; their revolutions would come only in the eighteenth and nineteenth centuries.[17] The Renaissance played no role in either of Kuhn's traditions: for the mathematical tradition it was irrelevant, while for the empirical tradition it, like the Middle Ages, was a period of indiscriminate fact-collecting by artisans that began to develop seriously only in the seventeenth century. Insofar as Kuhn considered the Renaissance, he did so in the guise of neoplatonic Hermeticism, a negative force that had to be overcome by the founders of modern science in the seventeenth century.

## revitalizing the renaissance in the 1970s

By the time Kuhn's article was published, though, historians were revitalizing the study of Renaissance science. The major focus of rehabilitating the Renaissance was in the history of chemistry. Allen G. Debus and Owen Hannaway took a new look at sixteenth-century developments in the alchemical tradition from Paracelsus to the seventeenth-century experimentalists and medical chemists. Unlike Boas and other earlier historians, who distinguished sharply between progressive developments and the blind alleys of alchemy, Debus insisted that alchemy was central to scientific developments in the sixteenth century. His studies had roots in the innovative study of Renaissance neoplatonism, especially in its Hermetic varieties, conducted in the 1950s and 1960s by D. P. Walker and Frances Yates.[18] But where Yates had exaggerated the mystical element in Renaissance thought, and Walker had dismissed Paracelsus as a madman, Debus worked to domesticate Paracelsian thought and bring it into the mainstream of Renaissance science. Drawing on the work of the historian of medicine Walter Pagel, Debus first approached the subject in his 1965 *The English Paracelsians*, which established the presence in sixteenth-century England of a number of experimentally-inclined physician-alchemists who accepted Paracelsian medical chemistry despite their suspicions of his elaborate metaphysics.[19] But it was his 1977 synthesis, *The Chemical Philosophy*, that presented most forcefully the argument that a distinctly Christian, anti-Aristotelian chemical philosophy, developed in the sixteenth century out of Renaissance Hermeticism and medieval alchemy, was a vibrant area of scientific enquiry in the sixteenth and seventeenth centuries. In the early seventeenth century, this philosophy offered an alternative to the atomistic or corpuscular philosophies of Gassendi, Galileo, and Descartes.[20]

Debus' work was well received by scholars like P. M. Rattansi, Charles Webster, and Betty Jo Dobbs, who were reformulating the received view of the seventeenth-century Scientific Revolution. His work intended to show, *inter alia*, that sixteenth-century developments, even those that 'lost', were crucial to the development of modern science. Owen Hannaway took a similar approach but with a different focus in his 1975 *The Chemists and the Word*.[21] For Hannaway, the chemical philosophy – represented by the Paracelsian Oswald Croll – was the foil against which Andreas Libavius defined chemistry in the first chemical textbook.[22] Croll was caught up in a Foucauldian world of similitudes. He emphasized the immanence of the Word in the world and held that the alchemist must have ineffable experience of the world. Libavius, on the other hand, took a didactic, operational approach to chemistry. He contributed to forming the discipline of chemistry by deferring any discussion of its theoretical or metaphysical basis, grounding this exclusion in the sixteenth-century didactic method of Peter Ramus. Ramus and his followers developed a method for presenting any art or science systematically while taking for granted its fundamental axioms. Libavius applied Ramist methods to the tools, operations, and products that were part of chemistry, thus systematizing it as a set of practices and results that could be taught regardless of theoretical commitments.

In a later, influential article, Hannaway continued to contrast Paracelsian alchemy with Libavian chemistry in terms of laboratory design.[23] The astronomer and alchemist Tycho Brahe located his chemical laboratory deep in the most secret parts of his palace on the island of Hven. He pointed backwards to the medieval contemplative ideal of knowledge, while Libavius' humanistically-informed notion of science for the public good pointed the way toward the Scientific Revolution. Here as before, Hannaway integrated standard themes in Renaissance intellectual history – Ramism and the humanist praise of the active life – with the history of science.[24]

Hannaway's emphasis on humanism's positive contribution to science was echoed in studies of other disciplines. Karen Reeds' important 1976 article on Renaissance botany emphasized the role of humanist philology and sociability in reshaping the study of plants.[25] In attempting to reform medical study along the lines of the ancients, humanist physicians studied the text of the ancient pharmaceutical writer Dioscorides and revived the Greek physician Galen's programmatic call for physicians to have knowledge of plants. To understand these ancient works, they turned to direct observation of nature.[26] Humanism was thus part of the route to modern natural history, not a dead end that had to be overcome. Mathematics, too, owed much to humanists who gathered, edited, published, and commented on Greek mathematical manuscripts, as Paul Rose demonstrated in his 1975 study.[27] As in natural history and chemistry, Renaissance mathematicians contrasted the dark state of knowledge in the Middle Ages with the revival of learning in which they were taking part.

These studies demonstrated that despite disciplinary differences, Renaissance scientists shared the general attitude of Renaissance culture toward the ancients and the Middle Ages. They did not merely denigrate the Middle Ages and praise antiquity. By the sixteenth century, particularly in northern Europe, scholars recognized that medieval scientists had made positive advances that were worthy of study. Naturalists, mathematicians, and chemists drew extensively on medieval works. Nonetheless they adopted the humanist rhetoric of rebirth and renewal, the rhetoric that drove Francis Bacon's *Instauratio magna* or 'Great Renewal' of the sciences on the threshold of the seventeenth century.

The new canonical view was stated in Allen Debus' 1978 survey, *Man and Nature in the Renaissance*.[28] Despite the importance of fifteenth-century humanism, Renaissance science really began in the sixteenth century with Paracelsus, Copernicus, the anatomist Andreas Vesalius, and the botanist Leonhart Fuchs. Its *annus mirabilis* was 1543, the year in which both Copernicus' *On the Revolutions* and Vesalius' *The Structure of the Human Body* were published; Fuchs' path-breaking *Notable Commentaries on the History of Plants* had appeared the previous year, and Paracelsus' influence was just beginning to spread. From the middle of the sixteenth century through the first decades of the seventeenth, medieval Aristotelian natural philosophy was under assault from heliocentrism, the new empirical sciences of medicine and natural history, and the chemical philosophy. The Scientific Revolution would ultimately establish the mathematico-mechanical natural philosophy of Galileo, Descartes, and Newton, but their achievement would have been impossible without sixteenth-century developments. In this view, Renaissance science was important not because it comprised a unified approach to nature but because, in a time of intellectual turmoil, it tore down old certainties, leaving room for the Scientific Revolution to establish new ones.

## rehabilitating the 'non-progressive' sciences since the 1980s

The work of Debus, Hannaway and others in the 1970s contributed to a historiographical trend that continues to the present: the rehabilitation of alchemy and other 'non-progressive' or dead-end sciences as legitimate subjects of enquiry for historians of science. For the founders of history of science as an academic discipline, these cul-de-sacs of knowledge were of interest only as part of the history of human folly. They had no place in the history of science itself, which they conceived as a record of intellectual progress. Lynn Thorndike's massive *History of Magic and Experimental Science* was an exception, but Thorndike was not trained as a historian of science and he treated magical procedures as a kind of unsystematic empiricism.[29] True, the journal *Ambix*, devoted to 'alchemy and early chemistry', had been founded as early as 1937, but it remained a venue for specialists. Debus, Hannaway, and their contemporaries made alchemy a key part of the history of Renaissance and seventeenth-century science, a position it has continued to hold until the present: no serious historian of Renaissance science can afford to be contemptuous of alchemy.

Contemporary work in the history of alchemy and chemistry has tended to emphasize two elements: first, its connection with princely courts, and second, its cultivation by canonical figures of the Scientific Revolution. Bruce T. Moran and Pamela Smith have emphasized the former. Moran's work on Landgrave Moritz of Hessen underscores the importance of princely support, interest, and practice for developments in alchemy.[30] Smith's study of Johann Becher emphasizes the place of alchemy, and alchemical collections, at the intersection of princely power, scientific enquiry, and economic development in the period immediately following the Thirty Years War.[31] The second aspect, though beyond the chronological scope of the Renaissance, cannot be wholly separated from it. In a series of important studies, Betty Jo Teeter Dobbs uncovered the central importance of alchemy to Isaac Newton.[32] Her pioneering work encouraged William Newman and Lawrence Principe to direct their attention to the alchemical interests of Robert Boyle, and, through Boyle, to the alchemical thought of George Starkey and other forgotten figures of the late seventeenth century.[33] Their scholarship demonstrates that some of the vital questions debated during the Scientific Revolution had been shaped by Renaissance alchemy.

No one writing on Renaissance science can avoid being struck by the attention natural philosophers gave to 'magic'. Marie Boas, in a chapter entitled 'Ravished by Magic', simultaneously acknowledged and dismissed the place of magic in Renaissance science. Since then, Michel Foucault's pioneering study of what he called the *episteme* of the Renaissance (on which see further below), and the work of historians of alchemy, have combined to make magic respectable – at least as a subject of historical enquiry. In fact, Renaissance magicians distinguished two forms of magic: one that invoked intelligent spirits or demons and another that simply drew on knowledge of the properties of things to produce unusual, but wholly natural, effects. This 'natural magic' is being written into the history of Renaissance science, in particular through studies of the 'books of secrets' in which natural magic and craft tricks were set out and of these books' authors. The work of William Eamon has played a key role in this development.

Books of secrets and their authors are humbler than the contemporary works of Latin-writing alchemists, but Eamon argues that the empiricism preached in these books, if not always practised by their authors, contributed to seventeenth-century philosophers' attacks on scholastic natural philosophy.[34] According to Eamon, 'secrets of nature' provided a powerful metaphor for understanding the relationship between common sense and the true structure of the world. Hellenistic esoteric thinkers and their successors considered nature's secrets (*arcana naturae*) as accessible only through divine revelation; they were the province only of a religiously initiated élite. In the Latin Middle Ages, on the other hand, many of nature's secrets fell outside the realm of scholastic *scientia* because they were accessible only to experience. Eamon argues that the early modern notion of the 'secret' as the inner workings of natural processes, a notion popularized by printed books of secrets, informed the seventeenth-century idea of natural philosophy as an attempt to understand the way nature worked and the concomitant criticism of the scholastic notion of 'occult qualities' as a cover for ignorance. Although the word 'Renaissance' does not figure prominently in Eamon's book, his research illuminates an important aspect of late Renaissance intellectual life.

Artisans and natural philosophers shared an interest in natural magic with princes. The court of the Holy Roman Emperor Rudolf II in Prague was a particular focus of the promiscuous pursuit of natural knowledge by almost any path. As Richard Evans showed in a classic study of Rudolf's court, the occult arts were among those the emperor cultivated. John Dee, his medium Edward Kelly, and Giordano Bruno were only three of the magicians who passed through Rudolfine Prague, in the company of naturalists, artists, humanist scholars, and miscellaneous courtiers.[35] In a series of lapidary studies on Rudolf's court, Thomas DaCosta Kaufmann has illuminated how Rudolf's pursuits were intended to do no less than create a microcosm, a small world, through which Rudolf could exercise control over the large world, the macrocosm, in which he lived.[36] Such notions of a correspondence between microcosm and macrocosm, central to Renaissance Hermeticism and the chemical philosophy, shaped – disastrously for Rudolf himself, it must be admitted – not only the quest for scientific knowledge but also imperial policy.

Astrology, the 'irrational' and backwards-looking pseudo-science *par excellence* for historians of science through the 1960s, depended on the same assumptions about correspondences between the greater and the lesser world. Historians of medicine have long taken astrology seriously, for learned medicine in the Middle Ages and Renaissance had a strong astrological bent.[37] Historians of science have begun to take it equally seriously: an indication is Anthony Grafton's recent study of Girolamo Cardano, astrologer, physician, and shameless self-promoter.[38] Grafton is less concerned with the truthfulness of Cardano's astrology – though he points out where the astrologer went wrong according to his own techniques and theories – than in the history and contemporary meaning of astrological practice. This approach emblematizes the changes that have occurred in the historiography of Renaissance science (and science in general) in the past two decades or so.

## from theory and institutions to practice and culture

The rehabilitation of 'non-progressive' Renaissance science took place as part of a broader change in approaches to the history of science. In broadest terms, historians of science have shifted their emphasis from scientific theories and institutions to scientific practice and culture. These developments draw upon a wide range of intellectual traditions. One important strand was the work of Thomas Kuhn, whose classic *The Structure of Scientific Revolutions* undermined confidence in science as a cumulative, progressive enterprise; Kuhn emphasized instead the 'incommensurability' of competing scientific theories, insisting that choices between them had a subjective, cultural element (though the culture in question might be that of a narrowly defined professional community).[39] Kuhn's and others' work legitimated the interests of the historians of the 1970s in alchemy, astrology, and other historical dead ends.

More recently, the sociology of scientific knowledge has had a great impact on historical approaches to early modern science. This tradition, which developed out of Karl Mannheim's sociology of knowledge and the later work of the philosopher Ludwig Wittgenstein, emphasized that early modern European scientists argued not only about specific theories but, more fundamentally, about the very nature of science and the methods by which to pursue it.[40] The rules of the game could not be taken for granted; they were in the process of being worked out. The key work in the transfer of these sociological approaches to history was Steven Shapin and Simon Schaffer's 1985 book *Leviathan and the Air-Pump*.[41] In this work, the authors – a historically-minded sociologist and a historian – examined the dispute between Robert Boyle and Thomas Hobbes over the nature of air and the existence of the vacuum not as a contest between two ideas, one right and the other wrong, but as a dispute over the proper way to conduct natural philosophy. Boyle's victory helped resolve the question of what kind of science would be done in the seventeenth century and beyond, but it was not a foregone conclusion and it depended as much on Boyle's skills as a scientific politician and communicator, his ability to convince others that the 'matters of fact' he observed were true, as it did on the way things really were.

Shapin and Schaffer's book encouraged historians to take a cultural approach not only to 'bad' sciences like astrology and alchemy but also to 'good' science, like Boyle's and Newton's physics. By emphasizing that science changes through controversy and that the old distinction between 'internal' (scientific) and 'external' (cultural) sources of change was untenable, this and similar works encouraged attention to scientific culture and practice as key aspects of the history of science. It appeared at a time when the 'linguistic turn' was at its height in the human sciences: that is, attention to the ways in which linguistic representations of the world do not merely reflect reality but shape our perceptions of it, and to the specific communities within which representational schemes were developed and contested.[42] Together, these approaches have brought new vigour and methodological richness to the study of Renaissance science.

The most obvious impact of the linguistic turn on the history of science has been in the study of scientific terminology and concepts. Hans Blumenberg's massive study of *The Genesis of the Copernican World* is concerned not with where Copernicus got his ideas but how it became possible for Copernicus to think in heliocentric terms.[43] Coming from the German tradition of *Begriffsgeschichte* (history of concepts), Blumenberg's work has not received the attention it deserves from historians of science, perhaps because it is more abstract and less attached to specific historical circumstances than Anglo-American historians prefer. Paula Findlen and Ann Moss have produced more concrete studies of the language of Renaissance science. Findlen's substantial article on *lusus naturae* (jokes of nature) and scholarly playfulness examines both the conceptual value of ideas of natural variability, of nature 'at play', and the sociological effects of scholarly jokes on the practice of Renaissance science.[44] Moss turns her attention to commonplace-books, works in which Renaissance readers jotted down classified notes from their readings. A study of printed versions of these books reveals both how the commonplaces of Renaissance pedagogy were shaped by reading practices and how they structured the way that Renaissance scholars and scientists thought about the world.[45]

As these examples suggest, Anglophone scholarship that takes a linguistic approach to the history of science tends to have a narrow chronological focus and emphasize specific communities and practices. A signal exception is Lorraine Daston and Katharine Park's 1998 study of *Wonders and the Order of Nature* from the twelfth through to the eighteenth century.[46] Daston and Park approach how Europeans thought of nature over this span of six centuries by looking at its boundary: the concept of wonders. By tracing where scholars, physicians, and scientists drew the border between natural occurrences on the one hand, and preternatural or supernatural (wondrous or miraculous) events on the other, the authors construct a rich history of changing ideas of nature. Despite its breadth, this history is connected with specific communities: medieval university scholars scornfully neglected wonders, while medieval courts were fascinated by them; Renaissance physicians collected them; anti-Aristotelians used them to attack received theories of the world; seventeenth-century natural philosophers thought they were the gateway to knowledge; and at the end, Enlightenment scientists and *philosophes* domesticated them while scorning the emotion of wonder as an obstacle to knowledge.

One particular community whose contributions to science in the Renaissance has been fundamentally reevaluated since the 1970s is that of Renaissance humanists. Paul Rose's work, already mentioned, challenged the myth that humanists were opposed to science. Like most myths, this one had a kernel of historical truth: some humanists, above all the fourteenth-century poet Petrarch, disdained the study of the natural world. But the myth depended more on twentieth-century divisions between the humanities and the sciences than on the historical realities of the Renaissance. In the last two decades the myth has become untenable in the light of historical scholarship that has revealed how Renaissance scientists were stimulated by ancient alternatives to medieval Aristotelian natural philosophy, and how textual methods were intimately connected with the study of nature.

A case in point is the early seventeenth-century philosopher Pierre Gassendi. As Lynn Joy has shown, Gassendi became an early defender of atomism on the basis of his studies of Epicurean texts, texts that became tools to dismantle contemporary physical theories.[47] Gassendi, his contemporary and friend Fabri de Peiresc, and others saw no conflict between their antiquarian investigation of the past and the study of nature. On the contrary, one of their models was Galileo Galilei's empirical investigations of heavenly phenomena.[48] Johannes Kepler, too, was both astronomer and classical scholar, though he distinguished carefully between the methods proper to each.[49] Even Isaac Newton, at the end of the seventeenth century, devoted himself not only to physics and alchemy but also to his true passion, biblical chronology.

For seventeenth-century atomists, the support of prestigious ancient texts was indispensable; as Christoph Meinel has shown, atomism lacked sufficient empirical support, even by seventeenth-century standards, to stand on its own merits.[50] In this regard, humanist methods played a key role in the development of modern science, even at a period when scholars began to distinguish more sharply between the methods of the 'new science' and those of the humanities. The study of sixteenth-century humanism and science thus provides a necessary foundation for understanding the Scientific Revolution.

Earlier accounts of sixteenth-century humanism and science tended to emphasize the conservative aspects of the former: for instance, Lisa Jardine's study of Francis Bacon, where the humanist method of Peter Ramus appears as a hindrance to the development of Bacon's new science.[51] More recently, Ann Blair's exemplary study of Jean Bodin sets out the intimate connections between sixteenth-century humanism and science.[52] Bodin set out to encompass the world within the covers of a book, aptly titled the *Theatre of Nature*. His method was empirical, but in a sixteenth-century sense that did not distinguish sharply between an individual's personal observations and those gathered from books. Hence Bodin's empiricism was stamped more by the study than the laboratory. Blair's study underscores that there were several competing forms of empiricism in the sixteenth century. Humanists like Bodin mined books for facts. Empirics like Paracelsus urged their followers to cast away their books and turn to nature – though in fact, Paracelsians depended heavily on the books of their master and others. Naturalists like Conrad Gesner of Zürich and Ulisse Aldrovandi of Bologna did both: by reading old books and studying natural objects in the field and the cabinet, by employing humanist methods of comparison and distinction, they attempted to catalogue the world more comprehensively than anyone before them.

Books, ancient and modern, were essential to the task of humanist science. The invention of the printing press in the middle of the fifteenth century had an undeniable impact on the development of science, an impact recognized by the traditional emphasis on publication dates as landmarks in the history of science (for example, the 1542–43 publications of Fuchs, Copernicus, and Vesalius). A bolder claim, that printing was responsible for the Renaissance, the Reformation, and the Scientific Revolution, was advanced by Elizabeth Eisenstein in 1979.[53] Printing, Eisenstein argued, allowed scholars to amass libraries far larger than had been possible in the age of manuscript. Moreover, it allowed scholars scattered across a continent to consult identical, error-free copies of the same works, thus permitting more intensive long-distance collaboration than ever before. Whereas medieval scholars had striven merely to get access to books, by the middle of the sixteenth century, scientists could compare works, sift through them for reliable information, and work to transcend them. In short, print gave ideas a fixity that they had lacked before, a fixity that was necessary for scientific progress.

Eisenstein's premises have been scrutinized critically ever since the work was published.[54] But her work was immensely stimulating to research in the connection between print culture and the development of science; directly or indirectly, it led to works like those by Moss and Blair on books and the sciences in the Renaissance.[55] Despite its historical and conceptual limitations, it remains essential for the study of Renaissance science. Eisenstein emphasized the importance of material objects, institutions (above all, printers' shops), and communications in the formation of modern science: in those respects, she was at the crest of the wave sweeping across the history of science in the late 1970s and early 1980s. And in engaging critically with her arguments, historians of science have been forced to take a new look at the role of material culture, institutions, and communications in early modern science.

Historians of medieval and early modern Europe had long studied the history of science in two institutional contexts: the universities, often seen as the bastions of outdated Aristotelian thought, and the new academies and societies of the seventeenth century, from the Accademia dei Lincei, founded in 1603, through the Royal Society of London (1660/62) and the Académie des Sciences of Paris (1666). Recent scholarship on the universities has tended to revise the earlier emphasis on their conservatism.[56] Along with this reappraisal, scholars have increasingly focused on a third institutional setting for Renaissance and seventeenth-century science: royal and princely courts. Again, Richard Evans' study of Rudolfine Prague (mentioned above) pointed the way to examining the court as a place where scientists met, exchanged ideas, and vied for the prince's attention. Beginning in the 1990s, this research has dramatically altered how we view Renaissance science. Of particular note is a collection of essays edited by Bruce Moran on *Patronage and Institutions*.[57] The contributions to that volume emphasize how the transformations in the nature of scientific knowledge and activity were intimately connected with princely politics and, above all, court patronage from the sixteenth through the eighteenth century. A particularly influential (and controversial) study of patronage and science is Mario Biagioli's book *Galileo, Courtier*.[58] Biagioli argues that Galileo sought out patronage from the Medici Grand Duke of Tuscany not only to pay his bills but also to gain the right to call himself a 'philosopher', despite his doing what university faculties considered mathematics, a discipline that in their eyes could not offer causal explanations of natural phenomena. Though many of Biagioli's specific claims have been disputed, his work has encouraged a lively debate over the question of patronage and the legitimation of new claims to knowledge. Peter Dear's study of sixteenth-

and seventeenth-century Jesuit mathematics differs greatly in spirit from Biagioli's book, but it is motivated by many of the same questions.[59]

The recent emphasis on informal institutional settings for science, like courts and academies, has encouraged attention to the intersections of science and other courtly pursuits, especially art. The great German refugee scholar Erwin Panofsky was a pioneer; his 1962 essay 'Artist, Scientist, Genius' explicitly addressed the connections between the new spirit of the Renaissance and contemporary developments in science and art, above all in the figures of Leonardo da Vinci and Albrecht Dürer.[60] Panofsky's idealist scholarship emphasized a unitary spirit of the age; at a time when historians are more likely to exorcize *Zeitgeister* than seek them, his approach is out of fashion. But (as noted above) he stimulated attention to specific links between art and science by arguing that the Renaissance was a period of 'decompartmentalization': traditional medieval distinctions between the 'liberal arts' (including science) and the 'mechanical arts' (including painting, sculpture, and architecture) had been effaced, while the modern separation between the cultures of science and humanities had not yet been constructed. Two important collections of essays from 1985 illuminate specific aspects of the connection.[61] In 1991, the art historian Samuel Edgerton revived an element of Panofsky's thesis, arguing that the key to the origins of modern science lay in the new geometrical conception and depiction of space represented by Renaissance perspective theory.[62] Other scholars, such as James Elkins, have responded that 'perspective' is a modern historian's construct, and that Renaissance artists used several different, incompatible systems to create the illusion that a two-dimensional surface had three dimensions.[63] A recent collection of essays, resulting from a 1997 conference, illuminates the continuing fruitfulness of examining such questions, which now include the cognitive role of illustrations in early modern science.[64]

Contemporary scholarship on the history of Renaissance science is epitomized in recent studies of Renaissance natural history. Natural history, Harold Cook has noted, was the 'big science' of the sixteenth and early seventeenth century.[65] Universities, princes, and private individuals collected natural curiosities, established gardens for rare and exotic plants, and stalked urban markets and dockyards for unusual specimens. Naturalists exchanged specimens and descriptions in their correspondence. They used woodcut, and later copperplate engraving, to depict plants and animals while simultaneously developing a powerful descriptive language for natural history. With a few exceptions,

Renaissance naturalists did not attempt to develop new classifications of the natural world; instead, they sought to catalogue nature's productions as exhaustively as possible. And their results were presented in large, often lavish books from Europe's finest presses.

Until recently, these developments were the province of specialists in the history of botany, zoology, and geology.[66] Some scholars did see natural history as emblematic of broader transformations in European thought: for example, Charles Raven and Michel Foucault.[67] The key development that brought natural history to the centre of the historiography of science and culture in the Renaissance was, however, a turn to the history of collecting. In 1985 and 1986, two signal collections of essays were published, resulting from conferences in France and England. The papers in *La Curiosité à la Renaissance* addressed the broad range of meanings of 'curiosity' and its connection to collecting, while *The Origins of Museums* examined more specifically the cabinets of 'curiosities' or 'wonders' that enjoyed an immense popularity beginning in the middle of the sixteenth century.[68] These studies linked natural history to other late Renaissance currents in collecting. Krzysztof Pomian and Antoine Schnapper soon followed with the first important book-length studies since Julius von Schlosser's work at the beginning of the twentieth century.[69] Sustained interest in the subject was marked by the foundation of the *Journal of the History of Collections* in 1989.

This interest in collecting came at a time when Italian scholars were revitalizing the history of natural history. In a series of articles beginning in the late 1970s, Giuseppe Olmi began a detailed study of Renaissance natural history based on the papers of the Bolognese naturalist and physician Ulisse Aldrovandi.[70] Margherita Azzi Visentini, Fabio Garbari, Lucia Tongiorni Tomasi, and Alessandro Tosi complemented this work with important studies of the botanical gardens at the universities of Padua and Pisa.[71] It is in this context that Paula Findlen produced her masterful 1994 account of natural history collecting in Renaissance and Baroque Italy.[72] Findlen examined not only collections of *naturalia* (plants, animals, and minerals) but also the extensive collections of manuscript notes and drawings gathered by Italian naturalists. Both kinds of collections were used reciprocally to understand the natural world. Renaissance scientific empiricism depended not only on examining and comparing objects but also, crucially, on notes, books, and other aids to memory: by the middle of the sixteenth century, the number and variety of species known to naturalists exceeded their unaided cognitive capacity.[73] Collections also helped define the identity of collectors, who formed networks of correspondence and patronage to enhance their collections and their own social standing; some individuals, not collectors themselves, became important brokers in the early modern economy of scientific exchange.[74]

The historiography of natural history has also been shaped by the history of the book. Large and, by the 1540s, usually copiously illustrated, natural histories were expensive and had to be carefully marketed.[75] Laurent Pinon has traced the evolution of Renaissance zoological publications in a catalogue that is a prelude to his forthcoming study of Renaissance zoology.[76] The printed and manuscript illustrations in natural histories have attracted the attention of art historians and historians of science. William Ashworth pointed out that natural history illustrations were widely copied and plagiarized in the sixteenth century, raising the question of what it meant to have an image 'drawn from life' in a published work.[77] Claudia Swan, in a study of natural history illustrations done in the Low Countries, has underscored the pedagogical function of illustrations as well as the distinctive character of natural history illustrations in the artistic landscape of the sixteenth and early seventeenth centuries.[78] I have traced the connections between illustration, text, and the market for natural history books in the sixteenth and seventeenth centuries; illustrations and texts developed in tandem according to naturalists' cognitive needs and publishers' sense of their market.[79]

In summing up developments in the historiography of Renaissance science, natural history also points the way toward resolving the second question with which this chapter is concerned: was there some distinctive 'Renaissance science', in addition to specific developments during the Renaissance period? Natural history as we know it was invented in the Renaissance, and Renaissance natural history, from about 1490 to 1620, was motivated by a specific concern with description, unlike subsequent natural history, in which the problem of classification took on increasing prominence.[80] Nonetheless, the transition from Renaissance to seventeenth century was a matter of a gradual shift, not an abrupt change. In a detailed, magnificently illustrated study of the early seventeenth-century Accademia dei Lincei, the art historian David Freedberg has argued that these 'lynx-eyed' academicians created modern natural history through careful visual documentation of nature, aided by the newly discovered microscope. Freedberg carefully reconstructs the Linceans' painstaking efforts to study nature, but he exaggerates the novelty of their approach.[81] In the case of natural history, it is very hard to draw a line in the sand and say that the Renaissance lies on one side, the Scientific Revolution on the other. The position of the line shifts depending on whether one considers naturalists' conceptual framework, their working methods, their tools, or the nature of their publications. It is hard to escape the conclusion that Renaissance science, if it is to be defined at all, must be defined prototypically: that is, by identifying a series of characteristics that are shared by many Renaissance sciences but that do not necessarily distinguish them sharply from predecessors and successors.

## did science have a renaissance? does it matter?

Nonetheless, the question has been hotly debated: significantly, in terms that hark back to the earlier historiographical notion that science is a matter chiefly of concepts and theories, not practices and culture. I have already noted that historiography before the 1970s tended to efface the Renaissance as a distinct period in the history of science. As the careful reader will have noted from the above, more recent writers also tend to elide the distinction between the sixteenth and seventeenth centuries. Connections between the period are the focus of the essays on *Renaissance and Revolution* edited by J. V. Field and Frank A. J. L. James.[82] The varied contributions to that volume share an interest in continuity, with a focus on cultural and social context and the interactions of science and practical knowledge (for example, J. V. Field on perspective theory and Frances Willmoth on military mathematics). This kind of scholarship, typical of the field at present, recognizes that science participated in Renaissance developments (humanism, exploration, printing, to name only three) but is reluctant to posit any Platonic ideal of 'Renaissance science' that distinguishes it from medieval and seventeenth-century science.

About a decade ago Brian Copenhaver raised the question explicitly: 'Did science have a Renaissance?' In an elegant article Copenhaver argued that there was no transformation in science in the fifteenth and sixteenth centuries that could be seen as equivalent to the Renaissance in art or letters, and that the period was characterized by incoherence and competition among many scientific views, not by any Renaissance scientific world view that was distinct both from the medieval science that preceded it and the mechanical, corpuscular philosophies of the Scientific Revolution that followed. As his focus on world views implies, Copenhaver had a specific target in mind: the Renaissance *episteme* (way of thinking) whose existence was brilliantly, yet ultimately unconvincingly, presented by Michel Foucault in *The Order of Things*.[83]

Foucault characterized Renaissance thought as 'the prose of the world': a metaphorical understanding of nature, in which sympathies and antipathies, resemblances and 'signatures' dominated people's way of thinking about the world. Such a way of thinking, argued Foucault, was a 'grill' that structured people's perceptions of the world in which they lived: it was not so much a conceptual structure as the foundation that made concepts possible. In this sense, Foucault went far beyond earlier accounts of Renaissance mentalities, like E. M. W. Tillyard's version of *The Elizabethan World Picture*, which had also emphasized neoplatonic thought and metaphorical visions of the world.[84] Take the doctrine of signatures as an example: the view that certain natural things were 'signed' by God to indicate their natural sympathies. The plant liverwort bore, in its liver-shaped leaves, the signature of its efficacy against diseases of the liver. For Foucault, the meaning of this particular signature had to be determined by Renaissance thinkers, but the idea that the world was composed of signatures was an *a priori* of Renaissance thought.

Natural history played a large role in Foucault's account. He marked the transition from Renaissance thought to that of the 'classical age' in the 1660s natural histories of John Johnston, the first, he claimed, to eschew symbolic meaning in favour of naked description. In this new period, the metaphorical *episteme* of the Renaissance was succeeded by a metonymical *episteme* in which classification became the dominant approach to the world. Foucault had little interest in explaining this rupture; he considered his work to be an archaeology of knowledge, not a history. And like some archaeologists, Foucault drew grand conclusions from selective evidence. In the realm of natural history, Foucault ignored botanical and zoological works that had, a century before Johnston, no place for fables, emblems, and other symbolic forms of knowledge. And more broadly, as Ian Maclean pointed out devastatingly, Foucault neglected the Aristotelian natural philosophy that still dominated sixteenth-century thought.[85] In the end, Copenhaver concluded that science had no Renaissance, certainly not in a Foucauldian sense and probably not in any sense, due to the multiplicity of views and approaches that characterized science in the sixteenth century.

Others have not been satisfied with this negative answer. The Spanish historian Antonio Beltrán argued that the Renaissance was a coherent period, situated distinctly between the Middle Ages and the seventeenth century:

> The Renaissance constitutes a theoretical period that can be delimited even if it has not been. And only when we narrate [*historiamos*] the period from the fifteenth to the sixteenth century as the succession of the 'Aristotelian-scholastic' frame or paradigm, the 'magical-naturalist', and the 'mechanistic', will we be able to address in an appropriate

fashion questions such as the topic of 'experimental' or 'scientific method', and reject the fallacious oppositions between 'recourse to experience' and 'speculation.' These conceptual frames or paradigms constitute one of the clearest objectives of the historian of 'science', insofar as he is considering the scientific revolution.[86]

Beltrán's use of the term 'paradigm' indicates his debt to Thomas Kuhn, a 'historian-philosopher' whose work, Beltrán hoped, would help explicate this frame.

Beltrán's sequence of periods and his identification of the Renaissance with a 'magical-naturalist' paradigm bears a strong resemblance to Foucault's archaeological approach. The 'magical-naturalist' frame Beltrán describes is *mutatis mutandis* the 'prose of the world' of Foucault's *Order of Things*, and like Foucault's Renaissance *episteme*, it is subject to serious faults. It takes one strand of Renaissance thought and makes it characteristic of the age as a whole, ignoring the persistent vitality of Aristotelian thought and its contributions to scientific debates well into the seventeenth century. Moreover, it perpetuates an unhealthy priority in history of science to conceptual schemas and worldviews at the expense of lower-level theories and scientific practice. It is striking that Beltrán's 1985 article makes no mention of work done after the middle of the 1970s.[87]

Though rejected by experts in Renaissance science, Foucault's work continues to be influential outside of the history of science. This alone justifies continued study of the general presuppositions of Renaissance systems of thought – with an emphasis on their plurality. James Bono has recently returned to the Foucauldian stomping-grounds, but he has done so with a refined historical sense.[88] Where Foucault posited a single Renaissance *episteme* based on metaphor that gave way to a classical *episteme* based on metonymy, Bono posits not two but three early modern approaches to reading the Book of Nature: two competing Renaissance versions and a third, radically different one that characterizes the seventeenth century. In the Renaissance, the 'exegetical' tradition that attempted to uncover the original Adamic language through study of the world competed with a neoplatonic view of hidden correspondences, sympathies, and antipathies. These competing approaches to understanding the meaning of the world were in turn challenged, from the late sixteenth century, by a radically new hermeneutics of nature. Its representatives – Francis Bacon and Galileo Galilei, among others – argued that the connection between human language and the world of nature was arbitrary; God did not inscribe the world in the same idiom in which He produced Scripture. Empirical research, not hermeneutics, was for these thinkers the only way to understand nature; as Galileo put it, God wrote the Book of Nature not in Adam's language but in the language of geometry.

Bono's work returns to the thesis of a rupture between Renaissance and seventeenth-century modes of apprehending the world, while recognizing that all three views competed for adherents in the seventeenth century. Bono emphasizes the incontestable fact that ways of thought are connected with specific individuals located in identifiable, if intersecting, communities of thinkers, each with its own traditions and reference points – traditions and references that extend well beyond the boundaries of an anachronistic notion of 'science'. Bono epitomizes a signal, welcome development in the history of Renaissance science in the past three decades: even historians of science with an intellectual bent have become cultural and social historians. Other contemporary studies that make broad claims about transformations in thought, such as Daston and Park's study of *Wonders and the Order of Nature*, also connect patterns of thinking with identifiable groups and traditions.

This development occurred late in the history of science. Like all subdisciplines of history, history of science has its own conferences, its own points of reference, and its own traditions. These traditions have, until recently, been opposed to drawing the consequence of living in a historicist age – possibly because historians of science had been seduced by the philosopher Karl Popper's unfortunate confusion of historicism with amoral historical materialism.[89] Today, historians of science, intimately aware of subtle differences between individuals, communities, and traditions in Renaissance science, shy away from *ex cathedra* judgements about 'the Renaissance mind' and its place in the history of thought.

Where does this leave the question of Renaissance science? Ultimately, it is without an answer. In one sense, the sciences in the Renaissance participated in the great intellectual and cultural movements of the Renaissance: they were deeply humanist in their critical engagement with classical texts and, throughout the period, in the importance of Latin as a scientific language (though Latin was by no means the only language of science).[90] Renaissance naturalists and geographers engaged with new information, peoples, and objects from European voyages of discovery and conquest. Scientists were closely associated with the efflorescence of princely and royal courts in the Renaissance, and they offered their services to the emerging absolutist rulers of Europe. These cultural and social processes shaped the methods and goals of the study of nature from 1450 to 1600. In that sense, Renaissance science was part of the Renaissance.

In another sense, though, Copenhaver is right: there was no single 'Renaissance science'. All historical periods seem to be in flux when examined closely, but science, in the period from 1450 to 1600, was more in flux than immediately before or after. From the thirteenth to the early sixteenth century, university natural philosophers dealt with natural phenomena within an agreed-upon intellectual and institutional framework that emphasized deductive reasoning and 'final causes', the purposes or reasons behind natural things. By the end of the seventeenth century, empirical, experimental, and quantitative-mathematical approaches to nature had triumphed, and final causes had been expelled from science proper, taking refuge in natural theology.[91] In between, informal institutions and petty courts supported and lent their sometimes dubious prestige to many competing approaches to the study of nature. Panofsky's notion of 'decompartmentalization' seems as good a label as any to define Renaissance science, but it is a negative label: it characterizes the scientific Renaissance by what it was not, not by what it was.

The absence of a definitive answer to this question does not bother most historians of Renaissance science. They are more interested in local contexts and in scientists' *bricolage* – their 'making do' or adaptation of the intellectual tools available to them to new problems, with consequences that might go far beyond their intentions. Ironically, this notion of *bricolage* is adopted from the French structuralist Claude Lévi-Strauss, who himself posited deep conceptual structures, far below the conscious surface, in the world views of human societies.[92] Such structures undoubtedly do exist; the error of Foucault and his followers was to see them as cultural universals. For the most part, they are more akin to habits of thinking inculcated in specific communities; the way to seek them out is by carefully investigating those communities: that is, to adopt, insofar as the historian may, the techniques of ethnographers. In adopting those methods, historians had to abandon the will-o'-the-wisp of 'Renaissance science'. But in exchange they have gained a more subtle, satisfying, and accurate account of what scientists actually thought and did in the European Renaissance.

## notes

1.  *Note on terminology:* The word 'science' in our modern sense is anachronistic for the Renaissance. *Scientia* and its vernacular cognates referred to any organized body of knowledge; in philosophical circles it meant, specifically, knowledge

that was derived through logical demonstration from universal principles. 'Scientist' is equally anachronistic; the word appeared in French in the late eighteenth century and entered English in the early nineteenth century. These days, careful historians tend to use specific words to designate Renaissance scientists: naturalists, natural philosophers, astronomers, alchemists and so on. The very profusion of terms suggests that no single conception of natural science reigned in the Renaissance. Nevertheless, for want of a better general term, I often use 'science' and 'scientist' to refer to the investigation of nature and its practitioners in the Renaissance when a more specific term is impossible.

Note on sources: I have concentrated on English-language scholarship. But the history of science, like other fields of Renaissance historiography, is polyglot, even though more and more European historians of science are publishing their works in English. When referring to works originally published in a foreign language, I have cited English translations if they are available.

2. Eric Cochrane, 'Science and Humanism in the Italian Renaissance', *American Historical Review*, LXXXI (1976) 1039–57; Antonio Beltrán, 'El Renacimiento en la historiografía de la ciencia', in *Filosofía y ciencia en el Renacimiento: Actas del simposio celebrado en Santiago de Compostela, del 31 de octubre al 2 de noviembre de 1985* (Santiago de Compostela, 1988), pp. 141–9; Pamela O. Long, 'Humanism and Science', in *Renaissance Humanism: Foundations, Forms, and Legacy*, ed. Albert Rabil, Jr (Philadelphia, 1988), III, pp. 486–512; Brian P. Copenhaver, 'Did Science have a Renaissance?', *Isis*, LXXXIII (1992) 387–407.
3. Beltrán, 'Renacimiento', p. 144.
4. Beltrán, 'Renacimiento'.
5. Peter Damerow and Jürgen Renn, 'Scientific Revolution: History and Sociology of', in *International Encyclopaedia of the Social and Behavioral Sciences* (Amsterdam, 2001), adopting the terminology of Yehuda Elkana, 'Experiment as a Second-Order Concept', *Science in Context*, II (1988) 177–96.
6. *Isis Cumulative Bibliography: A Bibliography of the History of Science formed from Isis Critical Bibliographies 1–90, 1913–65*, ed. Magda Whitrow, 6 vols (London, 1971–84); *Isis Cumulative Bibliography 1966–1975: A Bibliography of the History of Science formed from Isis Critical Bibliographies 91–100 Indexing Literature Published from 1965 through 1974*, ed. John Neu, 2 vols (London, 1980–85); *Isis Cumulative Bibliography 1976–1985: A Bibliography of the History of Science formed from Isis Critical Bibliographies 101–110 Indexing Literature Published from 1975 through 1984*, ed. John Neu, 2 vols (Boston, 1989); *Isis Cumulative Bibliography 1986–95: A Bibliography of the History of Science formed from the Annual Isis Current Bibliographies*, ed. John Neu, 4 vols (Canton, MA, 1997); and the *Isis Current Bibliography* published annually as a supplement to *Isis*.
7. Peter Burke, *The Renaissance* (Houndmills and London, 1987), pp. 1–5.
8. Jacob Burckhardt, *The Civilization of the Renaissance in Italy* (New York, 1958), 4, pp. 279–344.
9. Wallace K. Ferguson, *The Renaissance in Historical Thought: Five Centuries of Interpretation* (Boston, 1948), pp. 329–85.
10. Pierre Duhem, *Etudes sur Léonard de Vinci: Ceux qu'il a lus et ceux qui l'ont lu*, 3 vols (Paris, 1906–13); Pierre Duhem, *Medieval Cosmology: Theories of*

*Infinity, Place, Time, Void, and the Plurality of Worlds*, ed. and trans. Roger Ariew (Chicago, 1985).

11. Edwin A. Burtt, *The Metaphysical Foundations of Modern Physical Science*, revised edn (Atlantic Highlands, NJ, 1952); Alexandre Koyré, *Etudes galiléennes*, 3 vols (Paris, 1939); Alexandre Koyré, *From the Closed World to the Infinite Universe* (Baltimore, 1957); H. Floris Cohen, *The Scientific Revolution: A Historiographical Inquiry* (Chicago, 1994).

12. Marie Boas, *The Scientific Renaissance, 1450–1630* (New York, 1962).

13. Boas, *Scientific Renaissance*, 49.

14. Cochrane, 'Science and Humanism in the Italian Renaissance', 1041; J. H. Randall, *The School of Padua and the Emergence of Modern Science* (Padua, 1961).

15. George Sarton, *Six Wings: Men of Science in the Renaissance* (Bloomington, 1957); George Sarton, *Appreciation of Ancient and Medieval Science during the Renaissance, 1450–1600* (New York, 1955).

16. Erwin Panofsky, 'Artist, Scientist, Genius: Notes on the "Renaissance-Dämmerung"', in *The Renaissance: Six Essays* (New York, 1962), pp. 123–84.

17. Thomas S. Kuhn, 'Mathematical vs. Experimental Traditions in the Development of Physical Science', *Journal of Interdisciplinary History*, VII (1976) 1–31.

18. D. P. Walker, *Spiritual and Demonic Magic from Ficino to Campanella* (London, 1958); Frances A. Yates, *Giordano Bruno and the Hermetic Tradition* (Chicago, 1964).

19. Allen G. Debus, *The English Paracelsians* (London, 1965).

20. Allen G. Debus, *The Chemical Philosophy: Paracelsian Science and Medicine in the Sixteenth and Seventeenth Centuries*, 2 vols (New York, 1977).

21. Owen Hannaway, *The Chemists and the Word: The Didactic Origins of Chemistry* (Baltimore, 1975).

22. See the review of Hannaway by Audrey B. Davis, *American Historical Review*, LXXXI (1976) 813–14.

23. Owen Hannaway, 'Laboratory Design and the Aim of Science: Andreas Libavius versus Tycho Brahe', *Isis*, LXXVII (1986) 584–610.

24. This theme was taken up by Peter Dear in his recent survey of the Scientific Revolution, which begins with humanism: *Revolutionizing the Sciences: European Knowledge and its Ambitions, 1500–1700* (Princeton, 2001).

25. Karen M. Reeds, 'Renaissance Humanism and Botany', *Annals of Science*, XXXIII (1976) 519–42; see also Karen M. Reeds, *Botany in Medieval and Renaissance Universities* (New York and London, 1991).

26. The ramifications of this turn have been explored most recently by Peter Godman, *From Poliziano to Machiavelli: Florentine Humanism in the High Renaissance* (Princeton, 1998) and Brian W. Ogilvie, *The Science of Describing: Natural History in Renaissance Europe, 1490–1620* (Chicago, forthcoming, 2005).

27. Paul Lawrence Rose, *The Italian Renaissance of Mathematics: Studies on Humanists and Mathematicians from Petrarch to Galileo* (Geneva, 1975).

28. Allen G. Debus, *Man and Nature in the Renaissance* (Cambridge, 1978).

29. Lynn Thorndike, *A History of Magic and Experimental Science*, 8 vols (New York, 1923–58).

30. Bruce T. Moran, *The Alchemical World of the German Court: Occult Philosophy and Chemical Medicine in the Circle of Moritz of Hessen* (Stuttgart, 1991).
31. Pamela H. Smith, *The Business of Alchemy: Science and Culture in the Holy Roman Empire* (Princeton, 1994).
32. Betty Jo Teeter Dobbs, *The Foundations of Newton's Alchemy* (Cambridge and New York, 1975); Betty Jo Teeter Dobbs, *The Janus Faces of Genius: The Role of Alchemy in Newton's Thought* (Cambridge, 1991).
33. William R. Newman, *Gehennical Fire: The Lives of George Starkey, An American Alchemist in the Scientific Revolution* (Cambridge, MA, 1994); Lawrence M. Principe, *The Aspiring Adept: Robert Boyle and his Alchemical Quest* (Princeton, 1998); William R. Newman and Lawrence M. Principe, *Alchemy Tried in the Fire: Starkey, Boyle, and the Fate of Helmontian Chymistry* (Chicago, 2002).
34. William Eamon, 'Books of Secrets in Medieval and Early Modern Science', *Sudhoffs Archiv*, LXIX (1985) 26–49; William Eamon, *Science and the Secrets of Nature: Books of Secrets in Medieval and Early Modern Culture* (Princeton, 1994).
35. R. J. W. Evans, *Rudolf II and his World: A Study in Intellectual History, 1576–1612* (Oxford, 1973).
36. Thomas DaCosta Kaufmann, *The Mastery of Nature: Aspects of Art, Science and Humanism in the Renaissance* (Princeton, 1993).
37. See Nancy G. Siraisi, *Medieval and Early Renaissance Medicine: An Introduction to Knowledge and Practice* (Chicago, 1990).
38. Anthony Grafton, *Cardano's Cosmos: The Worlds and Works of a Renaissance Astrologer* (Cambridge, MA, 1999).
39. Thomas S. Kuhn, *The Structure of Scientific Revolutions*, 2nd edn (Chicago, 1970).
40. David Bloor, *Knowledge and Social Imagery* (London and Boston, 1976; 2nd edn, Chicago and London, 1991); Malcolm Ashmore, *The Reflexive Thesis: Wrighting Sociology of Scientific Knowledge* (Chicago, 1989); Peter L. Berger and Thomas Luckmann, *The Social Construction of Reality: A Treatise in the Sociology of Knowledge* (Garden City, NY, 1966); Peter Winch, *The Idea of a Social Science and its Relation to Philosophy* (London, 1958).
41. Steven Shapin and Simon Schaffer, *Leviathan and the Air-Pump: Hobbes, Boyle, and the Experimental Life* (Princeton, 1985).
42. The linguistic turn can be found in many disciplines, from literary criticism and philosophy to anthropology. Some key works in English are Clifford Geertz, *The Interpretation of Culture: Selected Essays* (New York, 1973); Hayden V. White, *Tropics of Discourse: Essays in Cultural Criticism* (Baltimore, 1978); Richard Rorty, *Philosophy and the Mirror of Nature* (Princeton, 1979); and Stanley Fish, *Is There a Text in This Class? The Authority of Interpretive Communities* (Cambridge, MA and London, 1980).
43. Hans Blumenberg, *The Genesis of the Copernican World*, trans. Robert M. Wallace (Cambridge, MA, 1987).
44. Paula Findlen, 'Jokes of Nature and Jokes of Knowledge: The Playfulness of Scientific Discourse in Early Modern Europe', *Renaissance Quarterly*, XLIII (1990) 292–331.
45. Ann Moss, *Printed Commonplace-Books and the Structuring of Renaissance Thought* (Oxford, 1996).

46. Lorraine Daston and Katharine Park, *Wonders and the Order of Nature, 1150–1750* (New York, 1998).
47. Lynn Sumida Joy, *Gassendi the Atomist: Advocate of History in an Age of Science* (Cambridge, 1987).
48. Peter N. Miller, *Peiresc's Europe: Learning and Virtue in the Seventeenth Century* (New Haven and London, 2000); Arnaldo Momigliano, *The Classical Foundations of Modern Historiography* (Berkeley, Los Angeles, and Oxford, 1990).
49. See the chapter on Kepler in Anthony Grafton, *Defenders of the Text: The Traditions of Scholarship in an Age of Science, 1450–1800* (Cambridge, MA, 1991).
50. Christoph Meinel, 'Early Seventeenth-Century Atomism: Theory, Epistemology, and the Insufficiency of Experiment', *Isis*, LXXIX (1988) 68–103.
51. Lisa Jardine, *Francis Bacon: Discovery and the Art of Discourse* (Cambridge, 1974).
52. Ann Blair, *The Theater of Nature: Jean Bodin and Renaissance Science* (Princeton, 1997).
53. Elizabeth L. Eisenstein, *The Printing Press as an Agent of Change: Communications and Cultural Transformations in Early Modern Europe* (Cambridge, 1979).
54. Anthony Grafton, 'The Importance of being Printed', review of *The Printing Press as an Agent of Change* by Elizabeth Eisenstein, *Journal of Interdisciplinary History*, XI (1980) 265–86; Anthony Grafton, Elizabeth L. Eisenstein, and Adrian Johns, 'AHR Forum: How Revolutionary was the Print Revolution?' *American Historical Review*, CVII (2002) 84–128.
55. For a recent collection of essays on the subject, see Marina Frasca-Spada and Nick Jardine, eds, *Books and the Sciences in History* (Cambridge and New York, 2000).
56. See, for example, John Gascoigne, 'A Reappraisal of the Role of the Universities in the Scientific Revolution', in *Reappraisals of the Scientific Revolution*, ed. David C. Lindberg and Robert S. Westman (Cambridge, 1990), pp. 207–60.
57. Bruce T. Moran, ed., *Patronage and Institutions: Science, Technology, and Medicine at the European Court, 1500–1750* (Rochester, NY, and Woodbridge, Suffolk, 1991).
58. Mario Biagioli, *Galileo, Courtier: The Practice of Science in the Culture of Absolutism* (Chicago, 1993); see also Mario Biagioli, 'Galileo the Emblem Maker', *Isis*, LXXXI (1990) 230–58, and Mario Biagioli, 'Scientific Revolution, Social Bricolage and Etiquette', in *The Scientific Revolution in National Context*, ed. Roy Porter and Mikulás Teich (Cambridge, 1992), pp. 11–54.
59. Peter Dear, *Discipline and Experience: The Mathematical Way in the Scientific Revolution* (Chicago, 1995).
60. Panofsky, 'Artist, Scientist, Genius'.
61. John W. Shirley and F. David Hoeniger, eds, *Science and the Arts in the Renaissance* (Washington, DC, London and Toronto, 1985); *The Natural Sciences and the Arts: Aspects of Interaction from the Renaissance to the Twentieth Century: An International Symposium* (Uppsala, 1985).
62. Samuel Y. Edgerton, Jr, *The Heritage of Giotto's Geometry: Art and Science on the Eve of the Scientific Revolution* (Ithaca, 1991). Again, Panofsky's work on perspective was a key starting-point: see, for example, Erwin Panofsky, *Renaissance and Renascences in Western Art* (New York, 1969).

63. James Elkins, 'Renaissance Perspectives', *Journal of the History of Ideas*, LIII (1992) 209–30.
64. Wolfgang Lefèvre, Jürgen Renn, and Urs Schöpflin, eds, *The Power of Images in Early Modern Science* (Basel, 2003). On the relationship between Renaissance art and science see also Catherine Soussloff's discussion above, Chapter 7.
65. Harold J. Cook, 'The Cutting Edge of a Revolution? Medicine and Natural History near the Shores of the North Sea', in *Renaissance and Revolution: Humanists, Scholars, Craftsmen and Natural Philosophers in Early Modern Europe*, ed. J. V. Field and Frank A. J. L. James (Cambridge, 1993), pp. 45–61.
66. See, for example, Frederick Simon Bodenheimer, 'Towards the History of Zoology and Botany in the Sixteenth Century', in *La science au seizième siècle: Colloque international de Royaumont, 1–4 juillet 1957, Histoire de la pensée*, II (Paris, 1960), pp. 285–96; Reeds, 'Renaissance Humanism and Botany'; and Martin J. S. Rudwick, *The Meaning of Fossils: Episodes in the History of Palaeontology*, 2nd edn (Chicago, 1985).
67. Charles E. Raven, *English Naturalists from Neckam to Ray: A Study of the Making of the Modern World* (Cambridge, 1947); Michel Foucault, *Les mots et les choses: Une archéologie des sciences humaines* (Paris, 1966).
68. Jean Céard, ed., *La curiosité à la Renaissance* (Paris, 1986); Oliver Impey and Arthur MacGregor, eds, *The Origins of Museums: The Cabinet of Curiosities in Sixteenth- and Seventeenth-Century Europe* (Oxford, 1985).
69. Krzysztof Pomian, *Collectionneurs, amateurs et curieux: Paris, Venise, XVIe– XVIIIe siècle* (Paris, 1987), translated as *Collectors and Curiosities: Paris and Venice, 1500–1800*, trans. Elizabeth Wiles-Portier (Cambridge, 1990); Antoine Schnapper, *Le géant, la licorne et la tulipe: Collections et collectionneurs dans la France du XVIIe siècle* (Paris, 1988); Julius von Schlosser, *Die Kunst- und Wunderkammern der Spätrenaissance: Ein Beitrag zur Geschichte des Sammelwesens* (Leipzig, 1908).
70. Many of these papers are collected in Giuseppe Olmi, *L'inventario del mondo: Catalogazione della natura e luoghi del sapere nella prima età moderna* (Bologna, 1992).
71. Margherita Azzi Visentini, 'Il giardino dei semplici di Padova: Un prodotto della cultura del Rinascimento', *Comunità*, XXXIV (1980) 259–338; Margherita Azzi Visentini, *L'Orto botanico di Padova e il giardino del Rinascimento* (Milano, 1984); Fabio Garbari, Lucia Tongiorni Tomasi, and Alessandro Tosi, *Giardino dei semplici: L'Orto botanico di Pisa dal XVI al XX secolo* (Ospedaletto, Pisa, 1991).
72. Paula Findlen, *Possessing Nature: Museums, Collecting, and Scientific Culture in Early Modern Italy* (Berkeley and Los Angeles, 1994).
73. This particular problem has been addressed most effectively by the ethnobotanist Scott Atran in his *Cognitive Foundations of Natural History: Towards an Anthropology of Science* (Cambridge, 1990).
74. See also Jay Tribby, 'Body/building: Living the Museum Life in Early Modern Europe', *Rhetorica*, X (1992) 139–63.
75. Karen M. Reeds, 'Publishing Scholarly Books in the Sixteenth Century', *Scholarly Publishing*, XIV (1983) 259–74.
76. Laurent Pinon, *Livres de zoologie de la Renaissance: Une anthologie, 1450–1700* (Paris, 1995).

77.  William B. Ashworth, Jr, 'The Persistent Beast: Recurring Images in Early Zoological Illustration', in *The Natural Sciences and the Arts: Aspects of Interaction from the Renaissance to the Twentieth Century: An International Symposium* (Uppsala, 1985), pp. 44–66; William B. Ashworth, Jr, 'The Scientific Revolution: The Problem of Visual Authority' (paper presented at the Conference on Critical Problems and Research Frontiers in History of Science and History of Technology, 30 October – 3 November 1991, Madison, WI, 1991).

78.  Claudia Swan, '*Ad vivum, naer het leven*, from the Life: Defining a Mode of Representation', *Word & Image*, XI (1995) 353–72; Claudia Swan, 'Lectura-imago-ostensio: The Role of the *Libri picturati* A.18-A.30 in Medical Instruction at Leiden University', in *Natura-cultura: L'interpretazione del mondo fisico nei testi e nelle immagini: Atti del Convegno Internazionale di Studi Mantova, 5–8 ottobre 1996*, ed. Giuseppe Olmi, Lucia Tongiorni Tomasi, and Attilio Zanca (Florence, 2000), pp. 189–214; cf. H. Wille, 'The Albums of Karel van Sint Omaars, 1533–1569 (*Libri picturati A.16-A.31*)', *Archives of Natural History*, XXIV (1997) 423–37.

79.  Brian W. Ogilvie, 'Image and Text in Natural History, 1500–1700', in *The Power of Images in Early Modern Science*, ed. Wolfgang Lefèvre, Jürgen Renn, and Urs Schöpflin (Basel, 2003), pp. 141–66.

80.  Brian W. Ogilvie, 'Natural History, Ethics, and Physico-Theology', in *Historia: Explorations in Early Modern Empiricism*, ed. Gianna Pomata and Nancy Siraisi (Cambridge, MA, forthcoming); Ogilvie, *Science of Describing*.

81.  David Freedberg, *The Eye of the Lynx: Galileo, his Friends, and the Beginnings of Modern Natural History* (Chicago and London, 2002); cf. Brian W. Ogilvie, 'In Galileo's Orbit', review of *The Eye of the Lynx* by David Freedberg, *American Scientist*, XCI (2003) 256–9.

82.  J. V. Field and Frank A. J. L. James, eds, *Renaissance and Revolution: Humanists, Scholars, Craftsmen and Natural Philosophers in Early Modern Europe* (Cambridge, 1993).

83.  Copenhaver, 'Did Science have a Renaissance?'; Foucault, *Les mots et les choses*, translated as *The Order of Things: An Archaeology of the Human Sciences* (New York, 1970).

84.  E. M. W. Tillyard, *The Elizabethan World Picture*, first American edn (New York, 1943).

85.  Ian Maclean, 'Foucault's Renaissance *episteme* Reassessed: An Aristotelian Counterblast', *Journal of the History of Ideas*, LIX (1998) 149–66.

86.  Beltrán, 'Renacimiento', p. 148.

87.  Cf. Antonio Beltrán, *Revolucíon científica, renacimiento e historia de la ciencia* (Mexico City and Madrid, 1995), which I have been unable to consult.

88.  James J. Bono, *The Word of God and the Languages of Man: Interpreting Nature in Early Modern Science and Medicine* (Madison, 1995).

89.  Karl Popper, *The Poverty of Historicism* (Boston, 1957).

90.  C. Longeon, 'L'usage du latin et des langues vernaculaires dans les ouvrages de botanique du XVIe siècle', in *Acta Conventus Neo-Latini Turonensis (6–10 Septembre 1976)*, ed. Jean-Claude Margolin (Paris, 1980), pp. 751–66.

91.  Margaret J. Osler, 'From Immanent Natures to Nature as Artifice: The Reinterpretation of Final Causes in Seventeenth-Century Natural Philosophy', *Monist*, LXXIX (1996) 388–407.

92.  Claude Lévi-Strauss, *The Savage Mind* (Chicago, 1966).

# 13

# politics and political thought

## john m. najemy

## politics and the state

To gain perspective on the recent historiography of Renaissance politics and political ideas requires a general (if unavoidably schematic) understanding of what preceded it. In the generation after the Second World War, a fairly stable set of assumptions characterized the study of Renaissance politics in its focus on institutions of statecraft and government and the élites that created them. First was the notion that the Renaissance witnessed the beginnings, even the creation, of the modern state, an idea that emerged from the broader conviction that the Renaissance was the harbinger of modernity and the precursor of the presumed modern rationalization of politics. Second was a generally favourable judgement of Renaissance political élites that emphasized the enlightened quality of their leadership and their command and implementation of principles of good government. The rather uncritical adoption of this view of the élites was reinforced, especially in Anglophone historiography, by prevailing ideologies of consensus that denied the reality, or legitimacy, of class conflict. The aristocratic and oligarchic regimes of fifteenth- and sixteenth-century Italy were seen as benevolently paternalistic and sufficiently dedicated to the common good to blunt class antagonisms and win broad support. A third underlying assumption was that politics in the Renaissance was essentially secular and liberated from theological postulates that had previously structured political life and thought. Facilitating this assumption was the secularism that dominated post-war intellectual and political life in the West, when religion was seen as a declining force with little relevance to politics, and political aims and differences were held to emerge from rational calculations of interests rather than religious belief or behaviour. Rationalization in state-building, consensus in class relations, and secularism were projected back onto the Renaissance from the post-war generation's favourite image of itself. A few examples may help to illustrate this cluster of assumptions.

Garrett Mattingly's 1955 study of Renaissance diplomacy viewed the Italian invention of resident ambassadors as part of a state-building process that spread to the rest of Europe by 1500 and heralded its modernity: 'like other Renaissance innovations, [resident ambassadorships] continued to develop along the lines laid down throughout the period which ended in 1914 .... The new Italian institution of permanent diplomacy was drawn into the service of the rising nation-states.' Although Mattingly did not see nation-states as the apex of political evolution (he even observed that diplomacy and standing armies fostered 'their idolatry'), he did believe in the 'new Renaissance state' and saw diplomatic institutions as having been 'successfully adapted' to its uses.[1] A similar focus on emergent state structures characterizes D. M. Bueno de Mesquita's 1941 study of Milan's Giangaleazzo Visconti, still the best book in English on the Visconti *signoria*. He argued that 'Giangaleazzo's system of government was designed to work smoothly with a minimum of personal intervention – to be a state rather than a despotism' (this despite his characterization as a 'despot' in the book's subtitle). Although Giangaleazzo ultimately failed, the aim was a 'new system' in which 'centralization was the keynote'. Even as Bueno de Mesquita allowed that the 'administrative system' he aspired to create aimed above all at the 'greater glory of the dynasty', he attributed to Giangaleazzo a recognition that the alleged 'waste and extravagance of communal government' and the 'obstructions of class privilege' were 'incompatible with the demands of an efficient and powerful state'.[2]

In studies of the republics, the emphasis on emerging state systems easily meshed with the consensus view of politics in which ruling élites were perceived as guardians of the common good. Frederic Lane, the great economic historian of Venice, saw republicanism, not capitalism, as the 'most distinctive and significant aspect' of the Italian city-states, insisting that it was 'not a class product' and 'depended on the readiness of its leaders to share power with others as equals'.[3] In his magisterial 1973 history of Venice, he interpreted the rise and consolidation of its 'aristocratic polity' as an expression of consensus both within the nobility and between it and other classes – what he called 'a general feeling of solidarity and loyalty among the Venetian nobility, and even in the relations between the ruling class and the rest of the people'. Although Lane rejected many aspects of the 'myth of Venice', he accepted that the ruling nobility was 'the part of the population best able to rule well' and that it generally 'ruled in the interests of the whole community'. The Venetian constitution 'provided better government than was generally found elsewhere, and all signs indicate that it enjoyed popular support ... . The lower classes were never incited to revolt ... by vengeful nobles offering to be their leaders.'[4]

The modern study of Renaissance politics in Anglophone historiography began in the 1960s with Nicolai Rubinstein, Gene Brucker, Lauro Martines, Marvin Becker, and Donald Weinstein. While not openly contesting prevailing assumptions about Renaissance states and élites, they nonetheless sowed the seeds of innovation. To speak of 'Anglophone' historiography is of course only a convenient shorthand, which obscures the profound influences of a variety of European traditions. Rubinstein went from Berlin to study in Florence with the Russian emigré historian Nicola Ottokar, who introduced prosopographical methods (much as Namier did for eighteenth-century England and Syme for ancient Rome) to deconstruct class-based interpretations of politics. Rubinstein inherited Ottokar's scepticism of grand theses and focused on how Florentine institutions worked and officeholders were selected, first for the Great Council instituted in 1494 and then, in *The Government of Florence under the Medici* (1966), for the preceding sixty years. Although he rarely spoke of a 'state' that acted on its own interests or aims, his underlying assumption was that institutions – the constitutional framework – constrained and moulded behaviour. Arguing that the Medici modified republican institutions, no doubt to their advantage, but did not ignore or destroy them, he insisted that such interventions were moderate and characterized by 'an almost pedantic concern with legality and technical efficiency'. For example, concerning the election of officials through whom Lorenzo tightened his control over the office-holding group, he wrote that, 'whatever the ultimate political motives and purposes of these officials, the minutes of their proceedings show them as civil servants who are reluctant to depart too much from precedent, and do not reveal any arbitrary abuse of authority'. This judgement stands side-by-side with the acknowledgment that they had 'vast powers in selecting citizens for qualification for the highest office' and that 'their treatment of the Pazzi' – seven years *before* the famous conspiracy – 'shows how they could use their powers to penalize a great family'.[5] In his many students (and others influenced by him) he inspired the conviction that politics needed to be studied in the details of how things actually worked.[6]

Gene Brucker's studies of Florentine politics cover nearly a century from the crises of the 1340s, stopping just short of the factional conflicts that brought the Medici to power. The influential innovation of Brucker's work is his analytical integration of politics and social structures. This is already present in *Florentine Politics and Society* (1962), which opens with a survey of the 'social and economic background' and consistently highlights tensions among the patriciate, the 'new men', and the working classes as central to understanding fourteenth-century politics. *The Civic World of Early Renaissance Florence* (1977) is structured around a profound shift from a commune shaped by the values of its guild community to the increasingly élitist polity of the fifteenth century. Brucker sought to listen to the voices of Florence's citizen politicians (he was among the first to systematically exploit the records of speeches in advisory sessions, the *Consulte e pratiche*) and to reconstruct their social relations in families, patron–client ties, and neighbourhoods. His understanding of politics never loses sight of the 'changing social order' and the 'transformation of the forms of association that underlay politics'.[7] The influence of Brucker's conviction that Florentine politics was inseparable from its social structure was profound.

The early work of Lauro Martines was equally influential in turning the study of politics toward society and, in his case, also toward culture and the intellectual and professional groups that mediated between ideas and power. His 1963 *Social World of the Florentine Humanists* established a conceptual framework for understanding social place and identified the elements – wealth, public office, antiquity of lineage, and marriage connections – that characterized Florence's political élite. But he also took politics into the sociology of ideas, exploring the symbiosis between the political élite and the humanist contribution to discourses of power. In *Lawyers and Statecraft in Renaissance Florence* (1968), he similarly explored the ways in which the élite collaborated with jurists (mainly from its own ranks) to use law in the project of building and legitimating a strong state. Martines studied this 'statecraft' in both Florence and Milan, emphasizing the rationalization of political authority achieved by jurists trained in Roman law who articulated the sovereignty of these emerging states and focused it on the powers of a strong executive. The two studies have in common the perception of an ever more powerful élite that appropriated the services and ideas of key professional groups in the pursuit of an increasingly aristocratic polity and centralized state.[8]

Marvin Becker also saw the rise of a powerful state in Florence, although in a much earlier period, and promoted bold hypotheses concerning its origins in *Florence in Transition* (1968). This state pushed aside all competing forms of authority (guilds, confraternities, *consorterie*, and even the church) and increased its coercive power over citizens. Becker's greatest contribution was his thesis that expanding state power was driven above all by fiscal necessity. Government deficits created by war led to massive borrowing, a huge public debt, and the need for more revenue to pay both military costs and interest on the debt. In addition to increasing the taxes on citizens, the government turned to the *contado*, and then to territories beyond the *contado*, ultimately constituting a territorial state whose wealth was exploitatively taxed to feed the hungry public debt. Thus did the medieval commune transform itself into the Renaissance territorial state. The many Florentines of both the middle and upper classes who had substantial portions of their wealth in the public debt and relied on it for income and dowries became in effect investors in a state on whose success in foreign policy and stability in domestic politics they were ever more dependent. Becker thus offered a powerful explanation for the emergence of civic humanism and the territorial state as well as stronger government.[9] His perception of fiscal policy as the motor driving the evolution of government has remained influential.

Donald Weinstein's *Savonarola and Florence* (1970) was among the major early influences that would ultimately integrate political and religious history. Because the thesis of Renaissance political secularism was incompatible with the explosive mix of religion and politics in Savonarola's Florence, older studies of the charismatic Dominican had seen him either as a relic of the medieval world or an anticipation of the Reformation. Weinstein turned the problem on its head by showing how profoundly Savonarola himself was transformed by a Florentine civic culture that had always had a strong sacred component. His classic essay 'The Myth of Florence' traced the city's belief in its unique destiny as the new Jerusalem, its special relationship to the Church, and the 'idea of Florence as the centre of rebirth and Christian renewal'.[10] In demonstrating that this was already deeply rooted in Florentine civic and religious culture and that Savonarola was in effect converted to its millenarian vision, Weinstein uncovered a religious dimension of politics and political thought that opened the way to much recent work.

Another development of this period of transition was the increasing attention to the previously neglected principalities, or *signorie*. Although Burckhardt had seen the principalities as the defining centres of Renaissance culture and politics, modern Anglophone historiography after the war focused heavily on the republics. Bueno de Mesquita continued to produce important articles on the Visconti-Sforza *signoria* in Milan, but it was not until the 1960s and 1970s that historians turned to the other principalities. While most of these studies accepted the old thesis of state-building, in the process underscoring continuities with developments elsewhere in western Europe, they also revised the assumed contrast between republics and *signorie*. John Larner's 1965 *Lords of Romagna* saw in cities accepting one-family rule 'the same process which was repeated in all Western society at the same period: the birth of the state. The *signoria* came as the result of the development of administration, of an increasing centralization, of a new professionalism in government.' But he also argued that 'there was no antithesis, moral or otherwise, between communal and signorial government ... . Of course, [the *signoria*] was not democratic. But then neither was the commune from which it had emerged.'[11] Breaking down (at least the assumptions that had surrounded) the old dichotomy between republics and principalities was likewise among the objectives of Philip Jones' famous 1965 essay, 'Communes and Despots'.[12] Werner Gundersheimer's 1973 study of Ferrara under the Este followed Larner and Jones in rejecting the old antithesis between 'tyrannical' *signorie* and 'free' republics. He argued that the 'relationship between the Ferrarese *popolo* and its Estense *signori* rested upon a solid foundation of consent' and that the Ferrarese willingly accepted the loss of political freedom in return for security and stability in an 'implicit social contract' that succeeded because the Este were 'enlightened despots'. Although they ruled 'personally and directly', they also fashioned an 'elaborate, articulated chain of command ... through their bureaucracy' and an 'administration ... characterized by increasing centralization and bureaucratic differentiation'.[13] Alan Ryder's 1976 study of Alfonso the Magnanimous' rule in Naples, subtitled *The Making of a Modern State*, interpreted Alfonso's innovations as putting Naples on a path, shared by 'most states of Europe', 'towards a greater emphasis on sovereignty, the consolidation of monarchical power against the competing authority of magnates, and the associated concentration of military, bureaucratic, and judicial powers in the apparatus of a centralized state'.[14] One more example of increasing interest in Italy's monarchical states is Eric Cochrane's *Florence in the Forgotten Centuries* (1973), which lauds the sixteenth-century state-building of Duke Cosimo as guided by principles of efficiency, continuity, justice, and equality in transforming Florence 'into the capital of a modern, bureaucratic territorial state'. In the ultimate idealization of élites, Cochrane attributed this to the genius of a boy prince (only seventeen when he was plucked from obscurity to replace his murdered cousin) who somehow knew how to 'turn a worn-out republic into a well-run monarchy' pretty much all on his youthful own.[15]

Through the first half of the twentieth century, interest in the state (with perhaps less emphasis on its modernity) was strong in Italy as well, from Antonio Anzilotti's interpretation (certainly in the background of Cochrane's similar treatment) of how Duke Cosimo created an 'impersonal state' to Federico Chabod's study of the sixteenth-century Milanese state. To the famous question posed by his own 1958 essay – 'Was there a Renaissance State?' – Chabod answered in the affirmative, locating its essence in bureaucracy and administrative structures.[16] But, as in Anglophone historiography, by the 1970s the Renaissance state began to seem a more problematic concept. Even those who continued to accept it gave it different meanings. Gaetano Cozzi, for example, saw Venice's stronger state as an expression of the power of its dominant class and the result of conflicts between a small oligarchy at the apex of the ruling class and the rest of the lesser nobility. He showed how the oligarchy made the repressive Council of Ten its instrument for consolidating a kind of 'authority' that undermined republican equality.[17] The study of Florentine politics took a still different turn, as a number of historians began to explore Florence's factions and parties more closely, especially for the Medici period and the subsequent popular government, for which an abundance of private letters, memoirs, and the records of the *pratiche* have survived. In Sergio Bertelli's essays on Piero Soderini and the politics behind his election as lifetime Standardbearer of Justice in 1502, ideology, institutions, law, and even class give way to personal and family ambitions and rivalries and the always shifting alliances of powerful patrons and party bosses for whom the 'state' mattered less than the loyalty of clients. Bertelli applied this view of early sixteenth-century Florentine politics back onto all the city-states of late medieval and Renaissance Italy.[18] Riccardo Fubini, whose early work had focused on humanism and political thought, came to political history as the editor of the first two volumes of the letters of Lorenzo de'Medici. In excursuses to these volumes and many other essays, Fubini made original use of private documentation and letters to illuminate the factional, personal, and family networks of the Medici domination. Of his many contributions, two uncovered the complex backgrounds of crucial crises in Lorenzo's period of leadership: the Volterra massacre and the Pazzi conspiracy.[19]

Italian historians of the principalities similarly sought to ground a new political history in personal bonds and feudal ties that significantly redefined the 'Renaissance state'. Giorgio Chittolini and Elena Fasano Guarini have been particularly influential in this regard. In her 1973 study of ducal Tuscany, Fasano Guarini showed that, while Cosimo may have aimed at centralization, he had to contend with, and even contributed to, a negotiated, fragmented, piecemeal mosaic of separate agreements and jurisdictions. She underscored the 're-feudalization' of Tuscany – the survival of a surprising number of fiefs, some that had escaped the suppression of feudal jurisdictions by the republic and others created by the dukes – five under Cosimo alone.[20] In 1979 Chittolini gathered his early essays into a book that has powerfully affected both Italian and Anglophone scholarship. His discovery of not only the persistence but the increasing use of the fief by the dukes of Milan shifted the perception of their 'state-building'. However much the dukes may have aspired to extend their authority, or that of their law and 'state', uniformly over the entire territory, the regular practice of enfeoffment reflected the irreducible local power of noble families and actually reinforced 'ties of personal dependence that hark back to forms of state organization once thought to have been superseded' and which seemed 'antithetical to the new territorially based political organization'.[21] Finding either early modern absolutism or the origins of the modern state in the Renaissance became much more difficult after Chittolini and Fasano Guarini began illuminating the feudal and personal nature of state-building in these territorial formations.

Thus by 1980 the ground had been prepared for the developments that transformed the field. These can be categorized (no doubt somewhat artificially) under the following rubrics: (1) the rise of anthropologically-grounded social history; (2) a rethinking, similarly inspired by anthropology, of the political role of religion; (3) a deepening interest in the courts of the *signori*; (4) a new focus on the territorial states; and (5) greater attention to the expanding intervention of Renaissance governments in social and moral issues. Much of the political historiography of the last two decades has been influenced by one or more of these frequently intersecting developments.

(1) In the 1970s social historians brought new, anthropologically informed approaches to demography, family, lineage, gender, women, marriage, sexuality, ritual, patronage, the working classes, and many other topics. No list of the leaders of this collective achievement could be complete without mentioning David Herlihy's and Christiane Klapisch-Zuber's pioneering work on Tuscany's demography, family history, and its radically uneven distribution of wealth, as revealed by the 1427 *Catasto*; Klapisch-Zuber's analysis of the precarious status of married women between their natal and marital families; Julius Kirshner's and Anthony Molho's enquiries into the significance of the dowry and the Florentine government's dowry investment fund; Richard Goldthwaite's study of the Florentine élite's family structures, living spaces, and palace-building; F. W. Kent's exploration of the developmental cycle of Florentine households and the persistence of the lineage; Samuel Cohn's investigation of the marriage patterns of Florentine workers; and Stanley

Chojnacki's studies of the Venetian patriciate and his discovery of a surprising degree of economic autonomy enjoyed by Venetian women.[22] The effect on political history was twofold. The new focus on women, children, workers, and a variety of liminal groups who had little or no place in politics as traditionally understood made the élite's political institutions and conflicts seem less relevant in some eyes. But in other hands the new social history held the promise of innovative approaches to the study of politics and indeed of an expansion of the 'political'. For those who saw these innovations as an opportunity to rethink political history in an anthropological framework, the building blocks of politics began to be seen everywhere.

A particularly important and precocious book in this regard was Dale Kent's *Rise of the Medici* of 1978. Her analysis of how Cosimo de'Medici and his allies put together their faction and party through the mechanisms of patronage and personal bonds begins with an analysis of private correspondence, relations within the Medici family, marriage connections, neighbourhood ties, bonds of friendship, and ritual expressions of ascriptive kinship. On the basis of these aspects of what previously would have been considered 'private' life, Kent reconstructed the factions and their conflicts. Building on anthropological and sociological insights, she saw in Florence a 'highly personalized and face-to-face environment [in which] a multitude of concrete loyalties competed with the abstraction of the commune in their claims on every citizen'. For Kent, public and private were inseparable:

> Where individual concerns were so powerfully affected by the possession of political influence and the exercise of political office, and the public sphere so intimately related to the private, the interest groups based on non-political associations whose members turned traditionally to each other for support might swiftly be transformed into political action groups or parties in times of crisis.[23]

More than their powerful banking connections or great wealth, and before they had the chance to modify and manipulate the institutions of government, it was personal bonds and patronage obligations that gave the Medici party its strength and made it a political force.

Others similarly influenced by social history also began to write political history in a new key. Anthony Molho analysed Cosimo de'Medici's power as a function of patronage as revealed in correspondence. Similar approaches inform Melissa Bullard's study of Filippo Strozzi and the Medici; Humfrey Butters' reconstruction of Florentine politics in the early sixteenth century (in his case without the anthropological dimension, but still grounded in the conviction that 'an understanding of the nature of *amicizia* is fundamental if one wishes to make sense of Florentine politics'); Mark Phillips' study of Marco Parenti, the Strozzi, and the political crisis of 1465–66; and Paula Clarke's family history of the Soderini. Although not explicitly a work of political history, Carol Lansing's investigation of the Florentine magnates sheds new light on the politics of the late thirteenth century by focusing on the formation and nature of élite lineages, their inheritance practices, marriage patterns, cultural style, use of violence, and penchant for factionalism.[24]

Italian scholarship similarly registered the turn to the social. Identifying ruling groups through complex networks of family, business, and patronage – in addition to officeholding – was the goal of the collaborative enquiry by Sergio Raveggi, Massimo Tarassi, Daniela Medici and Patrizia Parenti into the 'holders of power' in Florence in the late thirteenth century.[25] The collaborative volumes on the *ceti dirigenti* (or ruling élites) of Tuscany also displayed the expanding concern with the social underpinnings of politics. The volume on the Quattrocento contains essays on patronage, patron saints, ecclesiastical institutions, artistic patronage, architecture, prosopography, family history, neighbourhoods, testamentary practices, and education, as well as diplomacy, government, and public finance. In the introduction Riccardo Fubini recalled Ernesto Sestan's remark (during the conference from which the volume emerged) that the very concept of the 'ceto dirigente', theoretically descended from Mosca, Pareto, and Weber, meant that research naturally focused 'on the social and the political, not the juridical-institutional, which was understood merely as a legitimation of the exercise of power'. But Fubini lamented the declining attention to the 'institutional thread and nervous system' and warned that a history that ignores institutions will inevitably lack moorings.[26] Appropriately, Fubini's own essays on Florentine politics merge the institutional with analyses of social forces,[27] as does Giorgio Cadoni's study of the conflicts between *ottimati* and middle-class *popolo* over the control of electoral and governmental institutions between 1494 and 1502.[28]

(2) The rethinking of Renaissance religion[29] has had equally momentous consequences for political history. Revived by Weinstein around 1970, religion reclaimed the attention of historians who made the religious aspirations, anxieties, and behaviour of the urban laity, as well as professional religious, men and women alike, central to the understanding of a society whose culture and politics had long been seen as secular. The impact of anthropology made religious ritual central to

the understanding of both political power and protest. Three particularly influential books of the early 1980s pointed the way to a new integration of religion and politics: Richard Trexler's *Public Life in Renaissance Florence*, Edward Muir's *Civic Ritual in Renaissance Venice*, and Ronald Weissman's *Ritual Brotherhood in Renaissance Florence*. Rejecting the well-established paradigms of Renaissance individualism and secularism, Trexler argued that identity, both individual and collective, was constituted by ritual and group behaviour in processions, ceremonies, prayer and worship, and that through ritual the republic sought honour and legitimacy. Not all readers have accepted his assumption that the republican commune lacked (or feared it lacked) 'trust, honour, and credit' and thus looked to ritual to compensate for its 'ignoble' character. But the 'ritual revolution' that Trexler saw in processions of boys and working-class festive organizations and in the search for a 'charismatic centre' (embodied by Lorenzo de'Medici, Savonarola, and Lorenzo's son Giovanni, who became Leo X) recast Florence's passage from republic to monarchy in entirely new terms that were less a function of constitutional struggles and political theory than of collective behaviour in streets and squares, and in ceremonies and processions that continually reshaped the polity. After *Public Life*, it became impossible to think of Florentine politics between Lorenzo and the principate apart from its fusion of politics and religion, sacred and profane.[30]

What Trexler did for Florence Edward Muir simultaneously accomplished for Venice, demonstrating the way ritual created political meaning and social order: for example, how the ducal procession 'created in its ranking of officials a constitutional ideal for Venice that existed nowhere else, neither in visual nor even in written form; in effect, the ducal procession was the constitution'. The crowded calendar of Venetian ritual occasions imbued political institutions with a sacral character, and the hierarchical dimension of Venice's republicanism was constantly re-created in ceremonies and processions. The 'myth of Venice' as the stable and long-lasting republic built on social peace and a mixed constitution emerged from rites, ceremonies, and festivals central to the urban civic theatre.[31] Ronald Weissman opened up the political and social dimensions of confraternal life in Florence. Assuming that 'relations between individuals were as intensely political, that is, concerned with power and obligation, as were relations among groups', he argued that confraternities provided their members with a 'symbolic means of repairing and renewing their communal bonds' and a 'ritualized escape' from a social order he depicted as agonistic, competitive, and conflictual, 'teaching members the duties of brotherhood and imparting to them a sense of participation in the honours and obligations of the dominant republican culture'.[32]

The merging of politics and religion through ritual has become a staple of contemporary political historiography. Among the works that politicize ritual and ceremony and/or explore the ritual dimension of politics are Sharon Strocchia's analysis of mourning rituals in Florence; Nicole Carew-Reid's study of festivals in the time of Lorenzo (whose concluding section is entitled '*Festaioli* ou agents politiques'); Giovanni Ciappelli's investigation of the rituals of Carnival and Lent in Florence; and Matteo Casini's comparative analysis of 'festa politica' in Florence and Venice.[33] The last twenty years have seen a steady expansion of confraternal studies, with attention to the social and political roles of these lay organizations that straddled politics and private devotion. Particularly noteworthy are John Henderson's work on Florentine confraternities and Nicholas Terpstra's on those of Bologna.[34] Lorenzo Polizzotto's comprehensive history of the Savonarolan movement simultaneously explores the religious convictions of the friar's followers and the political impact of the movement's survival and ultimate suppression under the principate.[35] Paolo Prodi reintegrated the papacy into the history of state formation.[36] And local church history became part of political history. Two significant examples are Roberto Bizzocchi's work on the Florentine church as a field of lucrative patronage for the Florentine *ottimati* (especially the Medici) and David Peterson's investigations of local ecclesiastical politics and the role of the church as a legitimizing institution in shaping Florentine political development.[37]

(3) The growing interest in the *signorie* led to their courts. The main focus of Gundersheimer's book on Ferrara was the Este court and the ways in which this circumscribed and highly ritualized space of aristocratic manners, cultural patronage, and deference to the prince functioned, not merely as the centre of signorial administration, but as a theatrical and performative legitimation of Este rule and a visible expression of the 'style' of 'enlightened despotism'. A decade later, Jerry Bentley's study of politics and culture at the Neapolitan court of Ferrante showed the influence of Gundersheimer's model.[38] By then, courts were all the rage. In Italy the collaborative interdisciplinary project known as the Centro Studi Europa delle Corti promoted the publication of a wide series of theoretical studies on courts and studies of particular courts. The underlying interest was less political – politics indeed often being slighted – than cultural and sociological, as much of the inspiration came from revived interest in Norbert Elias' 'civilizing process'. Court studies proliferated – on Savoy, Milan, Parma, Piacenza, Mantua, Ferrara, Urbino, Camerino,

the papal court in Rome, the Angevin-Aragonese court in Naples, and the new court of the Medici duchy in Florence. The success of a richly illustrated collection of essays published in Italian as *Le corti italiane del Rinascimento* (Milan, 1985) and then in English as *The Courts of the Italian Renaissance* (New York, 1986) underscored the growing fascination with courtly culture. In 1993 Trevor Dean could note with satisfaction that the 'natural inclusion of the court in a conference on the origins of the modern state is a demonstration of the great distance travelled by court studies'. Whereas two decades earlier the court would not 'automatically have figured among historians' conceptions of the modern state', court and state had finally come to be 'seen as complementary, confused, or identical'. Historians had 'become more seriously interested in the ritual and symbolic aspects of rulership as part of, not extraneous to, the political system', and recognized 'that princely government remained personal government'.[39] By the mid-1990s the conviction that courts were integral to the political systems at whose centre they stood produced a number of books that explicitly linked them to politics: Gregory Lubkin on the Milanese court of Galeazzo Maria Sforza; Marcello Fantoni on the Medicean court in sixteenth- and seventeenth-century Tuscany; Benjamin Kohl on the Carrara court in fourteenth-century Padua; the special issue devoted to culture and politics at the court of Mantua in the journal *Renaissance Studies*; and Samantha Kelly's recent book on Robert's court in Naples.[40]

(4) Studies of the territorial states have become a veritable growth industry. Italian scholars were originally drawn to the topic rather more than their Anglophone colleagues, partly because of their traditional focus on rural and agrarian society and thus on ties between city and *contado*, and also because of their interest in the long-term process that led from Renaissance regional states to the nineteenth-century national state. New directions of research and the conceptual apparatus of this spatial expansion of political history from cities to territorial states were defined largely under the influence of models provided by Chittolini and Fasano Guarini. Recent work on Lombardy influenced by Chittolini's approach includes Letizia Arcangeli's investigation of the 'territorial aristocracy' and its feudal character, Jane Black's enquiry into the legal dimension of the fief and the ways in which feudal ties limited ducal prerogatives, and Marco Gentile's study of Parma and its territory in the Visconti duchy.[41] For the Veneto, James Grubb's study of Vicenza as a test case for the Venetian territorial state abandons arguments for modernity to reaffirm a 'Renaissance state', neither medieval nor modern, encompassing both unity and particularism – an uneasy coexistence

of Venice's power of intervention and the subject city's privileges and autonomies.[42] The persistence of local autonomies and jurisdictions of both subject communes and feudal nobles is emphasized in the recent study by David Chambers and Trevor Dean of the attempts in the 1470s and 1480s by the rulers of Mantua and Ferrara to impose a uniform and stern system of justice throughout their territories through the appointment of a judicial strongman (the same man in each case). The experiment failed as nobles and communes reacted defensively to safeguard their immunities and liberties and accused the prince's hated bureaucrat of 'tyranny'. Here too the regional state is characterized by limitations on central power.[43]

The main approach to the Florentine territorial state is now through the mechanism of patron–client ties forged by Florentine patricians with subject towns and local élites. Extending to the regional state the conceptual tools applied to Florentine domestic politics by Dale Kent and others, a growing number of historians have uncovered a heretofore only dimly glimpsed dimension of Renaissance politics. The *annus mirabilis* of this collective achievement was 2000, which saw the publication of Patrizia Salvadori's illuminating study of Lorenzo de'Medici's dominion patronage, William Connell's analysis of factions and Florentine patronage in Pistoia, and the collaborative volume *Florentine Tuscany*. These studies confirm, with a wealth of detail, Fasano Guarini's picture of the territorial state as a patchwork of separate and for many purposes still largely autonomous legislative entities. They illuminate the patronage ties of influential Florentines, sometimes over long periods of time, in specific localities, and they show the extent to which the Medici, especially Lorenzo, increasingly monopolized dominion patronage. In the light of these findings we are more distant than ever from the centralization, much less the absolutism, of law or administrative structures once imagined by those seeking the origins of the modern state in Renaissance Italy. A different and novel approach has come from Samuel Cohn, who maintains the notion of state-building but with a focus on Florence's changing relations with the highlanders of the mountain areas whose protests against fiscal inequality elicited more equitable treatment and a stronger regional state.[44]

(5) In one respect perhaps – the expanding agenda of governments – recent scholarship has vindicated the modernity of the Renaissance state. Fiscal necessity drove Italian governments to develop complex institutions for measuring wealth and assessing tax obligations. William Bowsky illuminated taxation and public finance in Siena. Elio Conti revealed the increasing sophistication of Florentine fiscal institutions,

from the forced loans and *estimi* of the fourteenth century to the *Catasto* that required self-assessment by every household in the dominion and experiments with graduated tax rates. Anthony Molho demonstrated how the fiscal crisis of the 1420s and 1430s made government dependent on loans from the wealthy, and ultimately on the vast wealth of the Medici. And Lawrin Armstrong has recently inscribed the debates over whether interest-bearing public debts were compatible with the ban on usury into Florence's political development.[45]

A second aspect of the expansion of government concerned the regulation of marriage, dowries, inheritance, sexual morality, conspicuous consumption, health and hospitals, and the protection of children, widows, and the poor. Guido Ruggiero investigated Venice's management of violence and sexual crime. Richard Trexler and Serena Mazzi studied the regulation and licensing of prostitutes in Florence. Michael Rocke explored Florentine homosexuality through the magistracy created to sift through thousands of anonymous denunciations and decide whom to prosecute and punish, mostly with fines.[46] Anthony Molho unravelled the complexities of the Florentine government's dowry fund.[47] Governments took an active role in regulating and administering hospitals. Philip Gavitt studied Florence's Foundling Hospital, created by private bequest but exempted from taxation and protected from ecclesiastical interference by the government. Carol Bresnahan Menning investigated the development of the state lending-bank created at Savonarola's urging into an instrument of statecraft under the dukes. Caroline Fisher has unravelled the changing policies of the Florentine magistracy that managed the estates of orphans. And Catherine Kovesi Killerby has surveyed sumptuary legislation by governments the length and breadth of the peninsula.[48] These and other studies reveal the extraordinary array of responsibilities assumed by Renaissance governments. They also show, as Anthony Molho has recently remarked, that after all the innovations and challenges to political history, inevitably 'we come back to the question of power, its organization, and its use'.[49]

## political thought

The notion of breakthroughs toward modernity also pervaded the historiography of political thought after the war. The great German refugee scholars Hans Baron and Felix Gilbert established the dominant paradigms. Building on essays that went back to the 1930s, Baron brought to fruition in *The Crisis of the Early Italian Renaissance* of 1955 his powerful interpretation of the emergence of civic humanism in early fifteenth-century Florence, chiefly in Leonardo Bruni. Baron argued that in defending Florence's republican tradition against 'despotic' Milan the civic humanists articulated Florence's inheritance from Rome of a mission to protect republican liberty, proclaimed an ethic of active citizenship, and developed secular and proto-modern modes of historical and political analysis. Earlier, in Petrarch and Salutati, Baron saw tentative but ultimately failed attempts to approach the same breakthrough, and later, in Machiavelli, its recovery and mature legacy.[50] In Italy, Eugenio Garin developed a parallel and compatible view of the humanists' positive assessment of worldly activity, politics, wealth, and marriage. Like Baron, he underscored the political commitment of Florentine culture in the age of Salutati and Bruni, emphasizing the crucial role of the chancery in promoting a 'vision of the duties of man as a citizen'. Claudio Varese saw the same cluster of civic values in fifteenth-century Florentine authors of memoirs and histories. And the Swiss historian Rudolf von Albertini produced a comprehensive synthesis of Florentine political and historical thought in the long transition from the resurgent republicanism of 1494 to the 'political ideology' of the Medicean principate.[51]

Felix Gilbert likewise found in the Renaissance a radical reshaping of traditional assumptions and the beginnings of modernity, defined in terms of a realistic, rational, secular approach to politics. He too saw it as a response to a political crisis, in this case the sudden loss of political moorings following the French invasion of 1494, the collapse of the Medici regime, the ascendancy of Savonarola, and the creation of the popular government. Gilbert saw the controversies between supporters and aristocratic opponents of the popular republic as the incubator of transformed political assumptions that ultimately led to the revolutionary theorizing of Machiavelli and Guicciardini. The thesis of a nascent modernity is explicit in the title of Gilbert's 1949 article on Bernardo Rucellai and 'the origin of modern political thought', and is elaborated in his 1965 book on Machiavelli and Guicciardini, where, to cite one example, he states that Machiavelli's works 'signify the beginning of a new stage – one might say, of the modern stage – in the development of political thought'.[52]

William Bouwsma approached Venetian political thought in ways broadly compatible with Baron's and Garin's view of republicanism and Gilbert's emphasis on the Renaissance's modernity. His *Venice and the Defense of Republican Liberty* (1968) presented Renaissance republicanism as a worldview that decisively broke with the 'medieval conception of reality' in which 'every aspect of human existence [was] seen as part of an objective and cosmic system of order'. By contrast, the Renaissance saw only 'the incessant flux of things' and a 'particular, located reality'. In place of 'the unity of all Christians in a single body, the *ecclesia* or *respublica christiana*', in which 'authority ... descended from above' and man 'could not be a citizen', the Renaissance placed at the 'heart of republicanism' a claim to liberty and a 'rejection of subordination'. This entailed, first, 'the independence of the state' (the 'republic was free because it belonged to no eternal system and acknowledged no earthly superior') and, second, 'self-government by citizens' (because 'human interests appeared as discrete and self-determined, not coordinated from above'). Bouwsma accepted as axiomatic that this 'Renaissance vision of reality is more like our own' than what preceded it and argued that Venice 'made available to the rest of Europe' and bequeathed to the Enlightenment the 'central political values of Renaissance republicanism' – secularism, the 'dignity of the lay estate and of political activity', the 'integrity of particular states', constitutionalism, and a 'sophisticated historicism'.[53]

As with political history, so also in the historiography of political thought an important moment of transition combined old questions with new perspectives and mediated between traditional certitudes and the innovations that were to come. Central to this transition were the landmark books of J. G. A. Pocock and Quentin Skinner, in which familiar issues coexisted with a new interest in excavating political 'vocabularies' or 'languages' shared by communities of discourse. The quest for the origins of modern 'secular political self-consciousness' in Pocock's great *Machiavellian Moment* (1975) exhibited important continuities with the work of Baron, Gilbert, and Garin. The 'moment' was 'the moment in conceptualized time in which the republic was seen as confronting its own temporal finitude, as attempting to remain morally and politically stable in a stream of irrational events'. Republicanism as the bearer of a modern mode of self-consciousness clearly evokes Baron and Bouwsma. Indeed, Pocock generously acknowledged that 'the presence of Hans Baron looms numinously if controversially (and entirely without his prior knowledge) over the whole scene'. Like Bouwsma, Pocock set the first Machiavellian moment against the background of medieval ideas about time that saw the particular only 'in its relation to eternity'. And, again like Baron, he saw in the early fifteenth century the first 'decisive break' with earlier Christian modes of conceptualizing time in the full recovery, by Leonardo Bruni, of the Aristotelian notion of the citizen, 'the particularity and historicity of the republic' and thus the 'particularization of history and its secularization'. But for Pocock the 'moment' also 'had a continuing history', in which 'modes' and 'patterns' of thought became detached from their original contexts and transplanted in very different cultural soils. He traced that history from late fifteenth- and sixteenth-century Florence and Venice to the English seventeenth-century republicans and finally to the eighteenth-century Americans as bearers of a republican tradition that went back to the Florentine civic humanists and Machiavelli. 'What started with Florentine humanists as far back as Leonardo Bruni is affirmed to have played an important role in the shaping of the modern sense of history, and of alienation from history.' Although great thinkers are present and accounted for, this is a history in which 'the actors in the narrative ... are seen to be the languages rather than (or on an equal footing with) the human individuals who have used them'.[54]

In announcing that one of his purposes was 'to indicate something of the process by which the modern concept of the state came to be formed', Quentin Skinner linked his 1978 *Foundations of Modern Historical Thought* to the traditional aim of locating in the Renaissance and early modern Europe the roots of the modern state conceived as autonomous, sovereign, and secular. Although he found three of the four prerequisites for this concept already present in Italy by the mid-fourteenth century, he argued that its mature formulation came only in late sixteenth-century France (with Bodin) and seventeenth-century England (chiefly with Hobbes). 'With this analysis', begins the book's last sentence, 'of the state as an omnipotent yet impersonal power, we may be said to enter the modern world.' But *Foundations* was also a foundational work in announcing itself as 'a history centred less on the classical texts and more on the history of ideologies'. Skinner proposed that recovering 'the nature and limits of the normative vocabulary available at any given time will also help to determine the ways in which particular questions come to be singled out and discussed'. Moreover, 'the adoption of this approach might also help us to illuminate some of the connections between political theory and practice', for, 'in recovering the terms of the normative vocabulary available to any given agent for the description of his political behaviour, we are at the same time indicating one of the constraints upon his behaviour itself'. Reconstructing normative vocabularies meant taking seriously a range of less well-known 'minor' texts and tracing long-term continuities. For example, in thirteenth-century advice books on city government and handbooks on the composition by public officials of speeches and letters Skinner found 'the vocabulary of Renaissance republicanism' already fully elaborated on the basis of its key Roman sources, Cicero and Sallust. This led him to conclude that Machiavelli, in inheriting and embracing this vocabulary, was actually offering a quite 'traditional' defence of republicanism in the *Discorsi*.[55]

Skinner's methodological and theoretical writings have exerted considerable influence on the study of political thought in the last twenty-five years. Compatible in approach, for example, is the survey by Maurizio Viroli, which traces the sea-change in political assumptions and vocabulary from civic and republican 'politics' (in the Aristotelian sense) to 'reason of state' in the sixteenth century.[56] Some historians have extended Skinner's method to a broader range of sources – statutes, legislation, court and guild records, private and chancery letters, and debates in advisory sessions – to search for political vocabularies in everyday politics and institutions. The use of these sources is of course not new. Long before the recent theoretical attention to political languages, Rubinstein tested the claims of civic humanists (and their modern interpreters) against what governments actually said to each other and their citizens.[57] Felix Gilbert and Gene Brucker demonstrated the value of the speeches in advisory sessions (the *Consulte e pratiche*) for understanding Florentine political thought.[58] Ronald Witt and Daniela De Rosa utilized the chancery letters as well as the *De tyranno* to explore Salutati's political ideas, as Paolo Viti has similarly done for Bruni.[59] More recently, Alison Brown has advanced the search for political vocabularies in the documents of everyday political life in a series of groundbreaking studies that reveal whole new facets of Renaissance political thinking: the complexities of the 'language of empire' in Florentine discourse, especially concerning the territorial state; the emergence under Lorenzo of 'new men' espousing a 'self-interested morality as a realistic basis for practical politics'; and the appearance during the Savonarola years of a group of '*politiques avant la lettre*', 'empiricists and sceptics' who, two decades before Machiavelli, theorized a political view of religion as 'an instrument of power and flexibility'. In these and other studies Brown fruitfully combines, as perhaps no other student of Florentine political ideas has, her command of both the canonical texts and the archives to uncover new strains of thought. In a study that relies on more traditional sources of intellectual history she has also illuminated a heretofore dimly perceived current of political and philosophical speculation engendered by the recovery of Lucretius' *De rerum natura*.[60]

Recent work has generally eschewed the grand theses that animated the post-war decades, especially the search for modernity and the modern state. The most cogent syntheses have come from medievalists intent upon showing the medieval, rather than humanist, origins of Renaissance political ideas. Brian Tierney, nearly three decades after excavating the origins of the conciliar theory in the thirteenth-century canonists, similarly found in medieval legal thought the intellectual

origins of early modern constitutionalism.[61] James Blythe published a
magisterial enquiry into the evolution of the Aristotelian theory of the
mixed constitution and its influence on political thought from Aquinas
to Machiavelli. In what is perhaps the most cogent synthesis since Pocock
and Skinner, Blythe demonstrates that Italian Renaissance political
thought was but a late chapter of the general European response to the
Aristotelian paradigm first developed by the scholastics.[62] Other general
treatments have come from Antony Black, Joseph Canning, and Kenneth
Pennington, who likewise stress the medieval origins and larger European
context of Italian political thought.[63] Another fruitful development has
been the intensifying connection between political thought and the
history of law. Building on classic studies of legal thought by medievalists,
some historians have turned to jurists, not merely as sources, but indeed
as a crucial component of Renaissance political thinking. In *Lawyers and
Statecraft* Martines identified jurists as major contributors to the concept of
sovereignty. Julius Kirshner has produced a stream of pioneering essays on
the influence of legal doctrines and debates on a wide variety of political
(and social) issues, including citizenship and the public debt.[64] Diego
Quaglioni has reconstructed the political thought of the jurist Bartolo
of Sassoferrato, as Canning has done for Baldo degli Ubaldi. Osvaldo
Cavallar has revealed the importance of Guicciardini's legal training. And
Lawrin Armstrong has brought Lorenzo Ridolfi, jurist and theorist of the
Florentine public debt, into the house of civic humanism.[65] The growing
awareness of the centrality of law has also yielded studies on the juridical
dimension of statecraft, including Jane Black's essay on the fragmented
'legal realities' of the Florentine regional state and Victor Crescenzi's book
on the legal process of defining the Venetian nobility.[66]

Nor have the connections between humanism and political thought lost
their fascination. While few scholars cling to Baron's narrow interpretation
of the 'crisis' of 1402 as the stimulus that politicized humanism, many
have continued to ponder humanism's political character and proposed
new interpretations of its relationship to power and politics. Cesare Vasoli,
whose leadership of the Istituto Nazionale di Studi sul Rinascimento and
whose contributions (as author, reviewer, and member of the editorial
board) to the journal *Il pensiero politico* (founded in 1968) have anchored
two central institutions for the exploration of Renaissance thought, has
devoted many essays to illuminating the broad and variegated applications
of political humanism, even in the principalities.[67] In addition to Skinner's
discovery of the core of civic republicanism in thirteenth-century political
advice books,[68] Mikael Hörnqvist finds in civic humanism an ideology
of expansion and imperialism that Baron never glimpsed. I explore civic

humanism's role in the changing relations between the Florentine élite and guild community. James Hankins has reopened the debate over the commitment of the civic humanists to republican ideology.[69] And Ronald Witt, Daniela De Rosa, Alison Brown, and Robert Black have produced major studies of the political ideas of the Florentine humanist chancellors Salutati, Bartolomeo Scala, and Benedetto Accolti.[70]

The powerhouse of the historiography of Renaissance political ideas continues to be the huge amount of attention devoted to the generation from Savonarola to Machiavelli and Guicciardini. The outpouring of Italian scholarship on Savonarola occasioned by the anniversary of his death, especially the volumes in the series 'Savonarola e la Toscana', amply confirms the friar's importance as an influential political theorist.[71] It would be impossible to give even a sampling of the ongoing scholarship on Machiavelli. The old debates about whether he was chiefly a republican or a prophet of the new princely order no longer animate scholarship as they did in the era of Baron and Gilbert. Earlier attempts to assess the totality of his thought have largely given way to studies of particular works and themes. Gennaro Sasso, for over forty years the undisputed master of Machiavelli studies, whose first major contribution in 1958 was a comprehensive assessment of the evolution of his thought to 1520, has produced a stream of learned and original essays (many on the philosophical underpinning of Machiavelli's ideas) and a monograph on his historical writing.[72] The interpretation of Machiavelli has been heavily influenced by what might be called a literary turn – increasing attention to language, genre, and literary tradition. Among the major contributors have been Carlo Dionisotti, Ezio Raimondi, Mario Martelli, Giulio Ferroni, Wayne Rebhorn, Albert Ascoli, Ronald Martinez, and Peter Godman. My study of Machiavelli's correspondence with Francesco Vettori has much in common with their attempts to see how the literary and the political were inextricably linked in the Renaissance.[73]

Perhaps the most original work of Anglophone scholarship on Machiavelli in the last quarter-century is Hanna Pitkin's *Fortune Is a Woman*, which explores Machiavelli's concepts of manhood and masculinity in their anxious relationship to images and fears of women. Taking seriously and analytically the most famous of his metaphors, Pitkin uncovered a Machiavelli deeply ambivalent about the possibility of a political order built on manly *virtù*.[74] Even when the influence is not always direct, Pitkin's feminist deconstruction has given birth to a new chapter in the study of Renaissance political thought and humanism in bringing gender to the forefront. From Stephanie Jed's analysis of the myth of the rape of Lucretia to Constance Jordan's reading of Alberti, Castiglione and other humanists on women, and Pamela Benson's study of the debates on the equality of women and men, the pursuit of the gendered construction of Renaissance ideas about politics and society has been particularly fruitful.[75] The study of Renaissance political thought, like that of politics, has thus moved away from the narrow focus on constitutional forms and the organization of government to embrace the discourses, ideas, assumptions, fears, and desires with which all components of the body social and political understood their relationship to power of all kinds. If politics is now found in places where it would not have been fashionable to look for it two generations ago, the same is true of political ideas, which are now found in the household and family and between men and women as well as in the state and government.[76] Both disciplines have enriched themselves by rethinking their foundations and expanding their horizons.

## notes

My warmest thanks to Alison Brown, Anthony Molho, and David Peterson for generously reading a first draft of this essay and for their many valuable suggestions and criticisms.

1.  G. Mattingly, *Renaissance Diplomacy* (Boston, 1955; reprint Baltimore, 1964), pp. 10, 87.
2.  D. M. Bueno de Mesquita, *Giangaleazzo Visconti, Duke of Milan (1351–1402): A Study in the Political Career of an Italian Despot* (Cambridge, 1941), pp. 316, 312.
3.  F. C. Lane, 'At the Roots of Republicanism' (his 1965 presidential address to the American Historical Association), *American Historical Review*, LXXI (1966) 403–20, at 404, 417, 407.
4.  F. C. Lane, *Venice: A Maritime Republic* (Baltimore, 1973), pp. 117, 101, 271.
5.  N. Rubinstein, 'I primi anni del Consiglio Maggiore di Firenze (1494–99)', *Archivio storico italiano*, CXII (1954) 151–94, 321–47; *The Government of Florence Under the Medici (1434 to 1494)* (Oxford, 1966; 2nd edn, Oxford, 1997), p. 215.
6.  Among the studies that exhibit the imprint of Rubinstein's model: D. Kent, 'The Florentine *Reggimento* in the Fifteenth Century', *Renaissance Quarterly*, XXVIII (1975) 575–638; R. Pesman Cooper, 'The Florentine Ruling Group under the *"Governo popolare"*, 1494–1512', *Studies in Medieval and Renaissance History*, VII (1985) 71–181; J. Najemy, *Corporatism and Consensus in Florentine Electoral Politics, 1280–1400* (Chapel Hill, 1982); R. Ninci, 'Lo "Squittino del Mangione": il consolidamento legale di un regime (1404)', *Bullettino dell'Istituto Storico Italiano per il Medio Evo*, XCIV (1988) 155–250.
7.  G. A. Brucker, *Florentine Politics and Society, 1343–1378* (Princeton, 1962); 'The Ciompi Revolution', in N. Rubinstein, ed., *Florentine Studies: Politics and Society in Renaissance Florence* (Evanston, IL, 1968), pp. 314–56; 'The Florentine *Popolo Minuto* and its Political Role, 1340–1450', in *Violence and Civil Disorder*

*in Italian Cities, 1200–1500*, ed. L. Martines (Berkeley and Los Angeles, 1971), pp. 155–83 (both articles reprinted in Gene A. Brucker, *Renaissance Florence: Society, Culture, and Religion* [Goldbach, 1994], pp. 37–109); *Renaissance Florence* (New York, 1969); *The Civic World of Early Renaissance Florence* (Princeton, 1977), p. 11.

8. L. Martines, *The Social World of the Florentine Humanists, 1390–1460* (Princeton, 1963); *Lawyers and Statecraft in Renaissance Florence* (Princeton, 1968).

9. M. Becker, *Florence in Transition*, 2 vols (Baltimore, 1967–68); 'The Florentine Territorial State and Civic Humanism in the Early Renaissance', in Rubinstein, *Florentine Studies*, pp. 109–39.

10. D. Weinstein, 'The Myth of Florence', in Rubinstein, *Florentine Studies*, pp. 15–44; *Savonarola and Florence: Prophecy and Patriotism in the Renaissance* (Princeton, 1970), p. 35.

11. J. Larner, *The Lords of Romagna: Romagnol Society and the Origins of the Signorie* (Ithaca, NY, 1965), p. 200.

12. P. J. Jones, 'Communes and Despots: The City-State in Late Medieval Italy', *Transactions of the Royal Historical Society*, 5th ser., XV (1965) 71–96. See also his *The Malatesta of Rimini and the Papal State: A Political History* (Cambridge, 1974).

13. W. L. Gundersheimer, *Ferrara: The Style of a Renaissance Despotism* (Princeton, 1973), pp. 3–4, 275, 285.

14. A. Ryder, *The Kingdom of Naples Under Alfonso the Magnanimous: The Making of a Modern State* (Oxford, 1976), p. 369.

15. E. Cochrane, *Florence in the Forgotten Centuries, 1527–1800* (Chicago and London, 1973), pp. 11, 58–66.

16. A. Anzilotti, *La crisi costituzionale della Repubblica fiorentina* (1912; reprint Florence, 1969); *La costituzione interna dello Stato fiorentino sotto il duca Cosimo I de' Medici* (Lumachi, 1910). F. Chabod, *Lo Stato di Milano nella prima metà del secolo XVI* (Rome, 1955); 'Y a-t-il un état de la Renaissance?' in *Actes du colloque sur la Renaissance* (Paris, 1958), pp. 57–74; English trans. in *The Development of the Modern State*, ed. H. Lubasz (New York, 1964), pp. 26–42.

17. G. Cozzi, 'Authority and the Law in Renaissance Venice', in J. R. Hale, ed., *Renaissance Venice* (London, 1973), pp. 293–345, at pp. 308, 337.

18. Of Bertelli's many essays on Soderini between 1969 and 1980, one is in English: 'Machiavelli and Soderini', *Renaissance Quarterly*, XXVIII (1975) 1–16; for his overview: *Il potere oligarchico nello stato-città medievale* (Florence, 1978).

19. Lorenzo de'Medici, *Lettere*, I and II, ed. R. Fubini (Florence, 1977); R. Fubini, 'Lorenzo de' Medici e Volterra', first published in 1994, reprinted in Fubini, *Quattrocento fiorentino: politica, diplomazia, cultura* (Ospedaletto, Pisa, 1996), pp. 123–39; 'La congiura de' Pazzi: radici politico-sociali e ragioni di un fallimento', in B. Toscani, ed., *Lorenzo de'Medici: New Perspectives* (New York, 1993), pp. 219–47.

20. E. Fasano Guarini, *Lo Stato mediceo di Cosimo I* (Florence, 1973).

21. G. Chittolini, 'Infeudazioni e politica feudale nel ducato visconteo-sforzesco', in *La formazione dello stato regionale e le istituzioni del contado, secoli XIV e XV* (Turin, 1979), pp. 36–100, at pp. 36–7; 'L'onore dell'officiale', in *Florence and Milan: Comparisons and Relations*, ed. S. Bertelli et al., I (Florence, 1989), pp. 101–33; and 'The "Private", the "Public", the State', in J. Kirshner, ed., *The Origins of the State in Italy, 1300–1600* (Chicago, 1995), pp. 34–61.

22. D. Herlihy and C. Klapisch-Zuber, *Les Toscans et leurs familles: Une étude du catasto florentin de 1427* (Paris, 1978); partial English trans. *Tuscans and Their Families: A Study of the Florentine Catasto of 1427* (New Haven, 1985). C. Klapisch-Zuber, *Women, Family, and Ritual in Renaissance Italy*, trans. L. Cochrane (Chicago, 1985). J. Kirshner, *Pursuing Honor While Avoiding Sin: The Monte delle doti of Florence* (Milan, 1977). J. Kirshner and A. Molho, 'The Dowry Fund and the Marriage Market in Early Quattrocento Florence', *Journal of Modern History*, L (1978) 403–38. R. Goldthwaite, *Private Wealth in Renaissance Florence: A Study of Four Families* (Princeton, 1968); 'The Florentine Palace as Domestic Architecture', *American Historical Review*, LXXVII (1972) 977–1012; *The Building of Renaissance Florence: An Economic and Social History* (Baltimore, 1980). F. W. Kent, *Household and Lineage in Renaissance Florence: The Family Life of the Capponi, Ginori, and Rucellai* (Princeton, 1977). F. W. Kent and D. Kent, *Neighbours and Neighbourhood in Renaissance Florence: The District of the Red Lion in the Fifteenth Century* (Locust Valley, NY, 1982). S. K. Cohn, Jr, *The Laboring Classes in Renaissance Florence* (New York, 1980). S. Chojnacki, 'In Search of the Venetian Patriciate: Families and Factions in the Fourteenth Century', in Hale, *Renaissance Venice*, pp. 47–90; *Women and Men in Renaissance Venice: Twelve Essays on Patrician Society* (Baltimore, 2000).
23. D. Kent, *The Rise of the Medici: Faction in Florence, 1426–1434* (Oxford, 1978), pp. 33–135, at pp. 15, 18.
24. A. Molho, 'Cosimo de' Medici: *Pater Patriae* or *Padrino?*' *Stanford Italian Review*, I (1979) 5–33. M. M. Bullard, *Filippo Strozzi and the Medici: Favor and Finance in Sixteenth-Century Florence and Rome* (Cambridge, 1980). H. C. Butters, *Governors and Government in Early Sixteenth-Century Florence, 1502–1519* (Oxford, 1985), p. 11. M. Phillips, *The Memoir of Marco Parenti: A Life in Medici Florence* (Princeton, 1987). P. C. Clarke, *The Soderini and the Medici: Power and Patronage in Fifteenth-Century Florence* (Oxford, 1991). C. Lansing, *The Florentine Magnates: Lineage and Faction in a Medieval Commune* (Princeton, 1991).
25. S. Raveggi et al., *Ghibellini, Guelfi e popolo grasso: I detentori del potere politico a Firenze nella seconda metà del Dugento* (Florence, 1978).
26. *I ceti dirigenti nella Toscana del Quattrocento* (Florence, 1987), pp. ix, xii.
27. For example, Fubini's 'From Social to Political Representation in Renaissance Florence', in *City-States in Classical Antiquity and Medieval Italy*, ed. A. Molho et al. (Stuttgart, 1991), pp. 223–39.
28. G. Cadoni, *Lotte politiche e riforme istituzionali a Firenze tra il 1494 e il 1502* (Rome, 1999).
29. For an excellent overview (with comprehensive bibliography), see D. S. Peterson, 'Out of the Margins: Religion and the Church in Renaissance Italy', *Renaissance Quarterly*, LIII (2000) 835–79. See also John Jeffries Martin's essay in this volume, Chapter 10.
30. R. Trexler, *Public Life in Renaissance Florence* (New York, 1980); also *The Spiritual Power: Republican Florence under Interdict* (Leiden, 1974).
31. E. Muir, *Civic Ritual in Renaissance Venice* (Princeton, 1981), pp. 189–90.
32. R. F. E. Weissman, *Ritual Brotherhood in Renaissance Florence* (New York, 1982), pp. 92, 235.
33. S. Strocchia, *Death and Ritual in Renaissance Florence* (Baltimore, 1992). N. Carew-Reid, *Les fêtes florentines au temps de Lorenzo il Magnifico* (Florence,

1995). G. Ciappelli, *Carnevale e Quaresima: Comportamenti sociali e cultura a Firenze nel Rinascimento* (Rome, 1997). M. Casini, *I gesti del principe: la festa politica a Firenze e Venezia in età rinascimentale* (Venice, 1996).

34. J. Henderson, *Piety and Charity in Late Medieval Florence* (Oxford, 1994). N. Terpstra, *Lay Confraternities and Civic Religion in Renaissance Bologna* (Cambridge, 1995).

35. L. Polizzotto, *The Elect Nation: The Savonarolan Movement in Florence, 1494–1545* (Oxford, 1994).

36. P. Prodi, *Il sovrano pontefice: un corpo e due anime. La monarchia papale nella prima età moderna* (Bologna, 1982).

37. R. Bizzocchi, *Chiesa e potere nella Toscana del Quattrocento* (Bologna, 1987). D. S. Peterson, 'An Episcopal Election in Quattrocento Florence', in *Popes, Teachers, and Canon Law in the Middle Ages*, ed. J. R. Sweeney and S. Chodorow (Ithaca, NY, 1989), pp. 300–25; 'Conciliarism, Republicanism and Corporatism: The 1415–1420 Constitution of the Florentine Clergy', *Renaissance Quarterly*, XLII (1989) 183–226.

38. J. H. Bentley, *Politics and Culture in Renaissance Naples* (Princeton, 1987).

39. T. Dean, 'The Courts', in Kirshner, *Origins of the State*, pp. 136–40.

40. G. Lubkin, *A Renaissance Court: Milan under Galeazzo Maria Sforza* (Berkeley and Los Angeles, 1994). M. Fantoni, *La corte del granduca: forme e simboli del potere mediceo fra Cinque e Seicento* (Rome, 1994), with an important theoretical introduction, pp. 9–20. B. G. Kohl, *Padua under the Carrara, 1318–1405* (Baltimore, 1998). *Renaissance Studies*, XVI, n. 3 (2002). S. Kelly, *The New Solomon: Robert of Naples (1309–1343) and Fourteenth-Century Kingship* (Leiden, 2003).

41. L. Arcangeli, *Gentiluomini di Lombardia: Ricerche sull'aristocrazia padana nel Rinascimento* (Milan, 2003). J. W. Black, 'The Limits of Ducal Authority: A Fifteenth-Century Treatise on the Visconti and their Subject Cities', in *Florence and Italy: Renaissance Studies in Honour of Nicolai Rubinstein*, ed. P. Denley and C. Elam (London, 1988), pp. 149–60; and '*Natura feudi haec est*: Lawyers and Feudatories in the Duchy of Milan', *English Historical Review*, CIX (1994) 1150–73. M. Gentile, *Terra e poteri: Parma e il Parmense nel ducato visconteo all'inizio del Quattrocento* (Milan, 2001).

42. J. S. Grubb, *Firstborn of Venice: Vicenza in the Early Renaissance State* (Baltimore, 1988).

43. D. S. Chambers and T. Dean, *Clean Hands and Rough Justice: An Investigating Magistrate in Renaissance Italy* (Ann Arbor, 1997).

44. P. Salvadori, *Dominio e patronato: Lorenzo dei Medici e la Toscana nel Quattrocento* (Rome, 2000). W. J. Connell, *La città dei crucci: fazioni e clientele in uno stato repubblicano del '400* (Florence, 2000). W. J. Connell and A. Zorzi, eds, *Florentine Tuscany: Structures and Practices of Power* (Cambridge, 2000), especially the contributions of Jane Black, Laura De Angelis, Patrizia Salvadori, Robert Black, and Stephen Milner. S. K. Cohn, Jr, *Creating the Florentine State: Peasants and Rebellion, 1348–1434* (Cambridge, 1999).

45. W. M. Bowsky, *The Finance of the Commune of Siena, 1287–1355* (Oxford, 1970). E. Conti, *L'imposta diretta a Firenze nel Quattrocento (1427–1494)* (Rome, 1984). A. Molho, *Florentine Public Finances in the Early Renaissance, 1400–1433* (Cambridge, MA, 1971). On the fiscal aspects of the Florentine territorial state, see also G. Petralia, in Connell and Zorzi, *Florentine Tuscany*, pp. 65–89.

L. Armstrong, *Usury and Public Debt in Early Renaissance Florence: Lorenzo Ridolfi on the Monte Comune* (Toronto, 2003).

46. G. Ruggiero, *Violence in Early Renaissance Venice* (New Brunswick, NJ, 1980); *The Boundaries of Eros: Sex Crime and Sexuality in Renaissance Venice* (Oxford, 1985). R. Trexler, 'Florentine Prostitution in the Fifteenth Century: Patrons and Clients', first published in French in 1981, now in English in Trexler's *Dependence in Context in Renaissance Florence* (Binghamton, NY, 1994), pp. 373–414. M. S. Mazzi, *Prostitute e lenoni nella Firenze del Quattrocento* (Milan, 1991). M. Rocke, *Forbidden Friendships: Homosexuality and Male Culture in Renaissance Florence* (Oxford, 1996).

47. A. Molho, *Marriage Alliance in Late Medieval Florence* (Cambridge, MA, 1994).

48. P. Gavitt, *Charity and Children in Renaissance Florence: The Ospedale degli Innocenti, 1410–1536* (Ann Arbor, 1990). C. Bresnahan Menning, *Charity and State in Late Renaissance Italy* (Ithaca, NY, 1993). C. Fisher, 'The State as Surrogate Father: State Guardianship in Renaissance Florence, 1368–1532', Ph.D. dissertation (Brandeis University, 2003). C. Kovesi Killerby, *Sumptuary Law in Italy, 1200–1500* (Oxford, 2002).

49. Personal communication, 19 June 2004.

50. H. Baron, *The Crisis of the Early Italian Renaissance: Civic Humanism and Republican Liberty in an Age of Classicism and Tyranny*, 2 vols (Princeton, 1955; revised one-volume edn Princeton, 1966). His early essays are republished in Baron, *In Search of Florentine Civic Humanism: Essays on the Transition from Medieval to Modern Thought*, 2 vols (Princeton, 1988).

51. E. Garin, *Der Italienische Humanismus* (Bern, 1947); English trans. *Italian Humanism: Philosophy and Civic Life in the Renaissance* (New York, 1965), chapter 2; 'The Humanist Chancellors of the Florentine Republic from Coluccio Salutati to Bartolomeo Scala', first published in 1961, English trans. in Garin, *Portraits from the Quattrocento*, trans. V. and E. Velen (New York, 1972), p. 3. C. Varese, *Storia e politica nella prosa del Quattrocento* (Turin, 1961). R. von Albertini, *Das florentinische Staatsbewusstsein im Ubergang von der Republik zum Prinzipat* (Bern, 1955); Italian trans. *Firenze dalla repubblica al principato: Storia e coscienza politica* (Turin, 1970).

52. F. Gilbert, 'Bernardo Rucellai and the Orti Oricellari: A Study on the Origins of Modern Political Thought', *Journal of the Warburg and Courtauld Institutes*, XII (1949) 101–31, reprinted in Gilbert, *History: Choice and Commitment* (Cambridge, MA, 1977), pp. 215–46; *Machiavelli and Guicciardini: Politics and History in Sixteenth-Century Florence* (Princeton, 1965), p. 153.

53. W. J. Bouwsma, *Venice and the Defense of Republican Liberty: Renaissance Values in the Age of the Counter Reformation* (Berkeley and Los Angeles, 1968), pp. 1–18; 'Venice and the Political Education of Europe', in Hale *Renaissance Venice*, pp. 445–66.

54. J. G. A. Pocock, *The Machiavellian Moment: Florentine Political Thought and the Atlantic Republican Tradition* (Princeton, 1975), pp. viii–ix, 8, 52, 54; 'The Machiavellian Moment Revisited: A Study in History and Ideology', *Journal of Modern History*, LIII (1981) 49–72, at 52.

55. Q. Skinner, *The Foundations of Modern Political Thought* (Cambridge, 1978), I, ix–xiii; II, 349–58; 'The Vocabulary of Renaissance Republicanism: A Cultural

*longue-durée?*' in A. Brown, ed., *Language and Images of Renaissance Italy* (Oxford, 1995), pp. 87–110, at p. 110.

56. M. Viroli, *From Politics to Reason of State* (Cambridge, 1992).

57. N. Rubinstein, 'Florence and the Despots: Some Aspects of Florentine Diplomacy in the Fourteenth century', *Transactions of the Royal Historical Society*, 5th series, II (1952) 21–45; 'Florentine Constitutionalism and Medici Ascendancy in the Fifteenth Century', in Rubinstein, *Florentine Studies*, pp. 442–62.

58. F. Gilbert, 'Florentine Political Assumptions in the Period of Savonarola and Soderini', *Journal of the Warburg and Courtauld Institutes*, XX (1957) 187–214; *Machiavelli and Guicciardini*, pp. 7–152. Brucker, *Civic World*, pp. 283–318.

59. R. G. Witt, 'The "De tyranno" and Coluccio Salutati's View of Politics and Roman History', *Nuova rivista storica*, LIII (1969) 434–74; *Hercules at the Crossroads: The Life, Works, and Thought of Coluccio Salutati* (Durham, NC, 1983). D. De Rosa, *Coluccio Salutati: Il cancelliere e il pensatore politico* (Florence, 1980). P. Viti, *Leonardo Bruni e Firenze: Studi sulle lettere pubbliche e private* (Rome, 1992). Viti has also edited a volume on Bruni: *Leonardo Bruni cancelliere della Repubblica di Firenze* (Florence, 1990).

60. A. Brown, 'The Language of Empire', in Connell and Zorzi, *Florentine Tuscany*, pp. 32–47; 'Lorenzo de' Medici's New Men and Their Mores: The Changing Lifestyle of Quattrocento Florence', *Renaissance Studies*, XVI (2002) 113–42, at 141; 'Ideology and Faction in Savonarolan Florence', in *The World of Savonarola: Italian Elites and Perceptions of Crisis*, ed. S. Fletcher and C. Shaw (Aldershot, 2000), pp. 22–41, at pp. 27 and 40; 'Lucretius and the Epicureans in the Social and Political Context of Renaissance Florence', *I Tatti Studies*, IX (2001) 11–62.

61. B. Tierney, *Foundations of the Conciliar Theory* (Cambridge, 1955); *Religion, Law, and the Growth of Constitutional Thought* (Cambridge, 1982).

62. J. M. Blythe, *Ideal Government and the Mixed Constitution in the Middle Ages* (Princeton, 1992); '"Civic Humanism" and Medieval Political Thought', in J. Hankins, ed., *Renaissance Civic Humanism: Reappraisals and Reflections* (Cambridge, 2000), pp. 30–74.

63. A. Black, *Guilds and Civil Society in European Political Thought from the Twelfth Century to the Present* (Ithaca, NY, 1984); *Political Thought in Europe, 1250–1450* (Cambridge, 1992). J. Canning, *A History of Medieval Political Thought, 300–1450* (London, 1996). K. Pennington, *The Prince and the Law, 1200–1600: Sovereignty and Rights in the Western Legal Tradition* (Berkeley and Los Angeles, 1993).

64. Three essays on citizenship: 'Paolo di Castro on *Cives ex privilegio*: A Controversy over the Legal Qualifications for Public Office in Early Fifteenth-Century Florence', in *Renaissance Studies in Honor of Hans Baron*, ed. A. Molho and J. Tedeschi (Florence, 1971), pp. 227–64; '*Civitas sibi faciat civem*: Bartolus of Sassoferrato's Doctrine on the Making of a Citizen', *Speculum*, XLVIII (1973) 694–713; and '*Ars Imitatur Naturam*: A *Consilium* of Baldus on Naturalization in Florence', *Viator*, V (1974) 289–331.

65. D. Quaglioni, *Politica e diritto nel Trecento italiano: Il 'De tyranno' di Bartolo da Sassoferrato (1314–1357)*; 'Tirannide e democrazia: Il "momento savonaroliano" nel pensiero giuridico e politico del Quattrocento', in *Savonarola: Democrazia, tirannide, profezia*, ed. G. C. Garfagnini (Florence, 1998), pp. 3–16. J. Canning,

*The Political Thought of Baldus de Ubaldis* (Cambridge, 1987). O. Cavallar, *Francesco Guicciardini giurista* (Milan, 1991). For Armstrong, see note 45.

66. J. Black, 'Constitutional Ambitions, Legal Realities and the Florentine State', in Connell and Zorzi, *Florentine Tuscany*, pp. 48–64. V. Crescenzi, *Esse de maiori consilio: Legittimità civile e legittimazione politica nella Repubblica di Venezia (secc. XIII–XVI)* (Rome, 1996). See also A. Mazzacane, 'Law and Jurists in the Formation of the Modern State in Italy', in Kirshner, *Origins of the State*, pp. 62–73.

67. For example, C. Vasoli, 'Riflessioni sugli umanisti e il principe: il modello platonico dell'ottimo governante', in *Per Federico Chabod (1901–1960)*, ed. S. Bertelli (Perugia, 1980–81), pp. 147–68; 'La trattativa politica a Firenze e a Milano', in Bertelli, *Florence and Milan*, I, pp. 67–78; and 'Modelli teorici della storiografia umanistica' (first published 1992), in Vasoli, *Civitas mundi: studi sulla cultura del Cinquecento* (Rome, 1996), pp. 211–33.

68. Skinner, *Foundations*, I, pp. 69–112.

69. M. Hörnqvist, 'The Two Myths of Civic Humanism', and J. M. Najemy, 'Civic Humanism and Florentine Politics', both in Hankins, *Renaissance Civic Humanism*, pp. 105–42 and 75–104. J. Hankins, 'The Baron Thesis after Forty Years', *Journal of the History of Ideas*, LVI (1995) 309–38.

70. A. Brown, *Bartolomeo Scala, 1430–1497, Chancellor of Florence: The Humanist as Bureaucrat* (Princeton, 1979). R. Black, *Benedetto Accolti and the Florentine Renaissance* (Cambridge, 1985). For Witt and De Rosa, see above, note 59.

71. For example, *Savonarola e la politica*, ed. G. C. Garfagnini (Florence, 1997), with essays by Garfagnini, Paolo Prodi, Claudio Leonardi and others; and Garfagnini, *Savonarola: Democrazia, tirannide, profezia*, with essays by Diego Quaglioni, Mario Turchetti, Paolo Viti, Mario Martelli, Garfagnini, Armando Verde and Innocenzo Cervelli.

72. G. Sasso, *Niccolò Machiavelli: Storia del suo pensiero politico* (Naples, 1958; revised edn Bologna, 1980); *Machiavelli e gli antichi e altri saggi*, 4 vols (Milan and Naples, 1987–97); *Niccolò Machiavelli*, II: *La storiografia* (Bologna, 1993).

73. The work of Dionisotti, Raimondi, Ferroni, Ascoli and Martinez can be sampled in *Machiavelli and the Discourse of Literature*, ed. A. R. Ascoli and V. Kahn (Ithaca, NY, 1993). M. Martelli, 'Schede sulla cultura di Machiavelli', *Interpres*, VI (1986) 283–330. W. A. Rebhorn, *Foxes and Lions: Machiavelli's Confidence Men* (Ithaca, NY, 1988). P. Godman, *From Poliziano to Machiavelli: Florentine Humanism in the High Renaissance* (Princeton, 1998). J. M. Najemy, *Between Friends: Discourses of Power and Desire in the Machiavelli–Vettori Letters of 1513–1515* (Princeton, 1993).

74. H. F. Pitkin, *Fortune Is a Woman: Gender and Politics in the Thought of Niccolò Machiavelli* (Berkeley, 1984; reprint with a 'New Afterword', Chicago, 1999).

75. S. H. Jed, *Chaste Thinking: The Rape of Lucretia and the Birth of Humanism* (Bloomington, 1989). C. Jordan, *Renaissance Feminism: Literary Texts and Political Models* (Ithaca, NY, 1990). P. Benson, *The Invention of the Renaissance Woman* (University Park, PA, 1992).

76. For example, D. Romano's *Household and Statecraft: Domestic Service in Renaissance Venice, 1400–1600* (Baltimore, 1996), whose first chapter is devoted to the political theorists of the household; and Chojnacki, *Women and Men in Renaissance Venice*.

# select bibliography

Abulafia, David, ed. *The French Descent into Renaissance Italy 1494–95: Antecedents and Effects*. Aldershot, 1995

Bailey, Gauvin A. *The Jesuits and the Great Mogul: Renaissance Art at the Imperial Court of India, 1580–1630*. Washington DC, 1998

Bailey, Gauvin A. *Art on the Jesuit Missions in Asia and Latin America, 1542–1773*. Toronto, 1999

Baron, Hans. *The Crisis of the Early Italian Renaissance: Civic Humanism and Republican Liberty in an Age of Classicism and Tyranny*. 2 vols. Princeton, 1955

Baron, Hans. *In Search of Florentine Civic Humanism: Essays in the Transition from Medieval to Modern Thought*. 2 vols. Princeton, 1988

Bassani, Ezio, and Fagg, William B. *Africa and the Renaissance: Art in Ivory*. New York, 1988

Baxandall, Michael. *Painting and Experience in Fifteenth Century Italy: A Primer in the Social History of Pictorial Style*. Oxford and New York, 1972

Beltrán, Antonio. 'El Renacimiento en la historiografía de la ciencia'. In *Filosofía y ciencia en el Renacimiento: Actas del simposio celebrado en Santiago de Compostela, del 31 de octubre al 2 de noviembre de 1985*. Santiago de Compostela, 1988, pp. 141–9

Benjamin, Walter. *The Origin of German Tragic Drama*, trans. John Osborne. London, 1998

Bentley, Jerry H. *Politics and Culture in Renaissance Naples*. Princeton, 1987

Bertelli, Sergio, ed. *Florence and Milan: Comparisons and Relations*. Florence, 1989

Black, Christopher. *Italian Confraternities in the Sixteenth Century*. Cambridge, 1989

Black, Robert. *Benedetto Accolti and the Florentine Renaissance*. Cambridge, 1985

Black, Robert. *Humanism and Education in Medieval and Renaissance Italy: Tradition and Innovation in Latin Schools from the Twelfth to the Fifteenth Century*. Cambridge, 2001

Black, Robert. 'The Origins of Humanism, its Educational Context and its Early Development: A Review of Ronald Witt's *In the Footsteps of the Ancients*'. *Vivarium*, XL (2002) 272–97

Boas, Marie. *The Scientific Renaissance, 1450–1630*. New York, 1962

Bouwsma, William J. *Venice and the Defense of Republican Liberty: Renaissance Values in the Age of the Counter-Reformation*. Berkeley, 1968

Bouwsma, William. 'The Renaissance and the Drama of Western History'. *American Historical Review*, LXXXIV (1979) 1–15

Bouwsma, William. *The Waning of the Renaissance, 1550–1600*. New Haven and London, 2000

Boxer, Charles. 'Some Aspects of Western Historical Writing on the Far East, 1500–1800'. In W. G. Beasley and E. G. Pulleyblank, eds, *Historians of China and Japan*. London, 1961, pp. 307–21

Brading, David. 'The Incas and the Renaissance: The Royal Commentaries of Inca Garcilaso de la Vega'. *Journal of Latin American Studies*, XVIII (1986) 1–23

Brotton, Jerry. *The Renaissance Bazaar*. Oxford, 2002

Brown, Alison. *Bartolomeo Scala, 1430–1497, Chancellor of Florence: The Humanist as Bureaucrat*. Princeton, 1979

Brown, Alison. 'Jacob Burckhardt's Renaissance'. *History Today*, XXXVIII (October 1988) 20–6

Brown, Alison, ed. *Language and Images of Renaissance Italy*. Oxford, 1995

Brown, Judith C. 'Prosperity or Hard Times in Renaissance Italy?' *Renaissance Quarterly*, XLII (1989) 761–80

Brown, Judith C., and Davis, Robert C., eds. *Gender and Society in Renaissance Italy*. London and New York, 1998

Brucker, Gene. *The Civic World of Early Renaissance Florence*. Princeton, 1977

Bullen, J. B. *The Myth of the Renaissance in Nineteenth-Century Writing*. Oxford, 1994

Burckhardt, Jacob. *The Civilization of the Renaissance in Italy*, trans. S. G. C. Middlemore. New York, 1958

Burke, Peter. *The Renaissance Sense of the Past*. London, 1969

Burke, Peter. *Popular Culture in Early Modern Europe*. London, 1978

Burke, Peter. *The Renaissance*. Houndmills and London, 1987

Burke, Peter. *The Fortunes of the Courtier*. Cambridge, 1995

Burke, Peter. *The European Renaissance: Centres and Peripheries*. Oxford, 1998

Burke, Peter. *The Italian Renaissance: Culture and Society in Italy*, revised edn. Cambridge, 1999

Burnett, Charles, and Contadini, Anna, eds. *Islam and the Italian Renaissance*. London, 1999

Camporeale, Salvatore I. *Lorenzo Valla: Umanesimo e teologia*. Florence, 1972

Cantimori, Delio. 'La periodizzazione dell'età del Rinascimento'. In Delio Cantimori, *Storici e storia. Metodo, caratteristiche e significato del lavoro storiografico*. Turin, 1971, pp. 553–77

Cassirer, Ernst. *The Individual and the Cosmos in Renaissance Philosophy*. Oxford, 1963

Chastel, André. *The Golden Age of the Renaissance*. London, 1965

Chittolini, G., Molho, A., and Schiera, P., eds. *Origini dello Stato. Processi di formazione statale in Italia fra Medioevo ed Età moderna*. Bologna, 1994

Chojnacka, Monica. *Working Women of Early Modern Venice*. Baltimore, 2001

Chojnacki, Stanley. *Women and Men in Renaissance Venice: Twelve Essays on Patrician Society*. Baltimore, 2000

Clunas, Craig. *Superfluous Things*. Cambridge, 1991

Cochrane, Eric. 'Science and Humanism in the Italian Renaissance'. *American Historical Review*, LXXXI (1976) 1039–57

Cochrane, Eric. *Historians and Historiography in the Italian Renaissance*. Chicago, 1981

Cohn Jr, Samuel Kline. *The Laboring Classes in Renaissance Florence*. New York, 1980

Concina, Ennio. *Arabesco*. Venice, 1994

Connell, W. J., and Zorzi, A., eds. *Florentine Tuscany: Structures and Practices of Power*. Cambridge, 2000

Contadini, Anna. 'Artistic Contacts: Current Scholarship and Future Tasks'. In Burnett and Contadini, *Islam and the Italian Renaissance*, pp. 1–16

Copenhaver, Brian P. 'Did Science have a Renaissance?' *Isis*, LXXXIII (1992) 387–407

Cox, Virginia. 'Ciceronian Rhetoric in Italy, 1260–1350'. *Rhetorica*, XVII (1999) 239–88

D'Amico, John F. *Renaissance Humanists in Papal Rome: Humanists and Churchmen on the Eve of the Reformation*. Baltimore and London, 1983

Farago, Claire, ed. *Reframing the Renaissance*. New Haven, 1995

Ferguson, Wallace Klippert. *The Renaissance in Historical Thought: Five Centuries of Interpretation*. Boston, 1948

Ferraro, J. M. 'Family and Clan in the Renaissance World'. In Ruggiero, *A Companion*, pp. 172–87

Findlen, Paula. *Possessing Nature: Museums, Collecting, and Scientific Culture in Early Modern Italy*. Berkeley, 1994

Findlen, Paula. 'The Renaissance in the Museum'. In Grieco, Rocke and Gioffredi Superbi, *Italian Renaissance in the Twentieth Century*, pp. 93–116

Foucault, Michel. *The Order of Things: An Archaeology of the Human Sciences*. New York, 1970

Fubini, Riccardo. 'Renaissance Historian: The Career of Hans Baron'. *Journal of Modern History*, LXIV (1992) 541–74

Fubini, Riccardo. 'Prestito ebraico e Monte di Pietà a Firenze (1471–1473)'. In R. Fubini, *Quattrocento fiorentino. Politica, diplomazia, cultura*. Ospedaletto, Pisa, 1996, pp. 159–216

Fubini, Riccardo. *L'umanesimo italiano e i suoi storici: Origini rinascimentali – critica moderna*. Milan, 2001

Fubini, Riccardo. 'La "Dialectica" di Lorenzo Valla. Saggio di interpretazione'. In Fubini, *L'umanesimo italiano*, pp. 184–207

Fubini, Riccardo. 'Origini e significato del "Die Kultur der Renaissance in Italien" di Jacob Burckhardt'. In Fubini, *L'umanesimo italiano*, pp. 211–29

Fubini, Riccardo. 'Rinascimento riscoperto? Studi recenti su Jacob Burckhardt'. In Fubini, *L'umanesimo italiano*, pp. 256–64

Fubini, Riccardo. *Humanism and Secularization, from Petrarch to Valla*. Durham, 2003

Fubini, Riccardo. *Storiografia dell'umanesimo in Italia da Leonardo Bruni ad Annio da Viterbo*. Rome, 2003

Fubini, Riccardo. 'Pubblicità e controllo del libro nella cultura del Rinascimento. Censura palese e condizionamenti coperti dell'opera letteraria dal tempo del Petrarca a quello del Valla'. In *L'Humanisme et l'Eglise du XVe siècle au milieu du XVIe siècle (l'Italie et la France méridionale)*, ed. P. Gilli. Rome, 2004, pp. 201–37

Garfagnini, G. C., ed. *Savonarola: Democrazia, tirannide, profezia*. Florence, 1998

Garin, Eugenio. *La filosofia come sapere storico*. Rome and Bari, 1959

Garin, Eugenio. *Italian Humanism: Philosophy and Civic Life in the Renaissance*, trans. P. Munz. Oxford, 1965

Garin, Eugenio. *Ritratti di umanisti*. Florence, 1967

Gay, Peter. *Style in History*. New York and London, 1974

Gilbert, Felix. *Machiavelli and Guicciardini: Politics and History in Sixteenth-Century Florence*. Princeton, 1965

Gilbert, Felix. *History: Politics or Culture? Reflections on Ranke and Burckhardt*. Princeton, 1990

Ginzburg, Carlo. *No Island is an Island: Four Glances at English Literature in a World Perspective*, trans. John Tedeschi. New York, 2000

Godman, Peter. *From Poliziano to Machiavelli: Florentine Humanism in the High Renaissance*. Princeton, 1998

Goldthwaite, Richard. *Private Wealth in Renaissance Florence: A Study of Four Families*. Princeton, 1968

Goldthwaite, Richard. *The Building of Renaissance Florence: An Economic and Social History*. Baltimore, 1980

Gombrich, Ernst H. *In Search of Cultural History*. Oxford, 1969

Goodman, Anthony and MacKay, Angus, eds. *The Impact of Humanism on Western Europe*. London, 1990

Gossman, Lionel. *Basel in the Age of Burckhardt: A Study in Unseasonable Ideas*. Chicago and London, 2000

Gossman, Lionel. 'Burckhardt in the Twentieth Century: Sketch of a *Rezeptiongeschichte*'. In *Jacob Burckhardt: Storia della cultura, storia dell'arte*, ed. M. Ghelardi and M. Seidel. Venice, 2002, pp. 17–40

Grafton, Anthony. *Defenders of the Text: The Traditions of Scholarship in an Age of Science, 1450–1800*. Cambridge, MA, 1991

Grafton, Anthony, and Jardine, Lisa. 'Humanism and the School of Guarino'. *Past and Present*, XCVI (1982) 51–80

Grafton, Anthony, and Jardine, Lisa. *From Humanism to the Humanities: Education and the Liberal Arts in Fifteenth- and Sixteenth-Century Europe*. London, 1986

Greenblatt, Stephen J. *Renaissance Self-Fashioning, from More to Shakespeare*. Chicago and London, 1980

Grieco, A. J., Rocke, M., and Gioffredi Superbi, F., eds. *The Italian Renaissance in the Twentieth Century*. Florence, 2002

Gruzinski, Serge. *La pensée métisse*. Paris, 1999

Gschwend, Annemarie Jordan. 'Curiosities and Exotica in the Kunsthammer of Catherine of Austria'. *Bulletin of the Society for Renaissance Studies*, XIII (1995) 1–9

Gundersheimer, Werner L. *Ferrara: The Style of a Renaissance Despotism*. Princeton, 1973

Hale, John R. ed. *Renaissance Venice*. London, 1973

Hale, John R. *The Civilization of Europe in the Renaissance*. London, 1993

Hankins, James. *Plato in the Italian Renaissance*. 2 vols. Leiden, 1990

Hankins, James. 'The Baron Thesis after Forty Years'. *Journal of the History of Ideas*, LVI (1995) 309–38

Hankins, James, ed. *Renaissance Civic Humanism: Reappraisals and Reflections*. Cambridge, 2000

Hankins, James. *Humanism and Platonism in the Italian Renaissance* I. Rome, 2003

Hannay, David. *The Later Renaissance*. Periods of European Literature, VI. Edinburgh and London, 1911

Heikamp, Detlef. *Mexico and the Medici*. Florence, 1972

Helgerson, Richard. *Forms of Nationhood: The Elizabethan Writing of England*. Chicago, 1992

Herlihy, David, and Klapisch-Zuber, Christiane. *Tuscans and Their Families: A Study of the Florentine Catasto of 1427*. New Haven, 1985.

Hersey, George. *The Aragonese Arch at Naples, 1443–75*. New Haven, 1973

Hinde, John. *Jacob Burckhardt and the Crisis of Modernity*. Montreal and London, 2000

Howard, Deborah. *Venice and the East*. New Haven, 2000

Howard, Thomas A. *Religion and the Rise of Historicism: W. M. L. de Wette, Jacob Burckhardt and the Theological Origins of Nineteenth-Century Historical Consciousness*. Cambridge, 2000

Huizinga, Johan. *The Waning of the Middle Ages*. London, 1924.

Hyde, J. K. *Padua in the Age of Dante*. Manchester, 1966

Ianziti, Gary. *Humanistic Historiography under the Sforzas: Politics and Propaganda in Fifteenth-Century Milan*. Oxford, 1988

Jacobson Schutte, Anne, Kuehn, Thomas, and Seidel Menchi, Silvana, eds. *Time, Space, and Women's Lives in Early Modern Europe*. Kirksville, MO, 2001

Jardine, Lisa. *Worldly Goods*. London, 1996

Jones, William M., ed. *The Present State of Scholarship in Sixteenth-Century Literature*. Columbia, 1978

Kelley, Donald R. *Foundations of Modern Historical Scholarship: Language, Law and History in the French Renaissance*. New York, 1970

Kelly, Joan. 'Did Women have a Renaissance?' In *Women, History, and Theory: The Essays of Joan Kelly*. Chicago, 1984, pp. 19–50

Kelly, Samantha. *The New Solomon: Robert of Naples, 1309–43, and Fourteenth-Century Kingship*. Leiden, 2003

Ker, W. P. *The Dark Ages*. Periods of European Literature, I. Edinburgh and London, 1923

Kerrigan, William, and Braden, Gordon. *The Idea of the Renaissance*. Baltimore and London, 1989

Kirkpatrick, Robin. *The European Renaissance, 1400–1600*. Harlow, 2002

Kirshner, Julius. *Pursuing Honor While Avoiding Sin: The Monte delle doti of Florence*. Milan, 1977

Kirshner, Julius, ed. *Origins of the State in Italy, 1300–1600*. Chicago, 1995

Kirshner, Julius, and Molho, Anthony. 'The Dowry Fund and the Marriage Market in Early Quattrocento Florence'. *Journal of Modern History*, L (1978) 403–38

Klapisch-Zuber, Christiane. *Women, Family, and Ritual in Renaissance Italy*, trans. L. Cochrane. Chicago, 1985

Kovesi Killerby, Catherine. *Sumptuary Law in Italy 1200–1500*. Oxford, 2002

Kristeller, Paul Oskar. *Eight Philosophers of the Italian Renaissance*. Stanford, 1964

Kristeller, Paul Oskar. *Medieval Aspects of Renaissance Learning: Three Essays by Paul Oskar Kristeller*, ed. and trans. Edward P. Mahoney. Durham, 1974

Kristeller, Paul Oskar. *Renaissance Thought and its Sources*. New York, 1979

Kristeller, Paul Oskar. 'Humanism and Scholasticism in the Italian Renaissance'. In Kristeller, *Renaissance Thought and its Sources*, pp. 85–105

Kuehn, Thomas. *Law, Family, and Women: Toward a Legal Anthropology of Renaissance Italy*. Chicago, 1991

Levenson, Jay A., ed. *Circa 1492: Art in the Age of Exploration*. New Haven and Washington, DC, 1991

Loewenstein, David, and Mueller, Janel, eds. *The Cambridge History of Early Modern English Literature*. Cambridge, 2002

Maclean, Ian. *The Renaissance Notion of Woman: A Study in the Fortunes of Scholasticism and Medical Science in European Intellectual Life*. Cambridge, 1980

Mansfield, Bruce. *Erasmus in the Twentieth Century*. Toronto and London, 2003

Marcus, Leah S. 'Renaissance/Early Modern Studies'. In *Redrawing the Boundaries: The Transformation of English and American Literary Studies*, ed. Stephen Greenblatt and Giles Gunn. New York, 1992, pp. 41–63

Martin, John Jeffries. 'The Myth of Renaissance Individualism'. In Ruggiero, *A Companion*, pp. 208–24

Martines, Lauro. *The Social World of the Florentine Humanists, 1390–1460*. Princeton, 1963

Martines, Lauro. *Lawyers and Statecraft in Renaissance Florence*. Princeton, 1968

Martines, Lauro. *Power and Imagination: City-States in Renaissance Italy*. London, 2002

McLaughlin, Martin L. 'Humanist Concepts of Renaissance and Middle Ages in the Tre- and Quattrocento'. *Renaissance Studies*, II (1988) 131–42

Michelet, Jules *Œuvres complètes*, ed. Paul Viallaneix, VII: *Histoire de France au seizième siècle: Renaissance et Reforme*, ed. Robert Casanova. Paris, 1978

Milner, Stephen J. 'Partial Readings: Addressing a Renaissance Archive', *History of the Human Sciences*, XII (1999) 89–105

Molho, Anthony. *Marriage Alliance in Late Medieval Florence*. Cambridge, MA, 1994

Molho, Anthony. 'The Italian Renaissance, Made in the USA'. In *Imagined Histories: American Historians Interpret the Past*, ed. A. Molho and G. S. Wood. Princeton, 1998, pp. 263–94

Molho, Anthony, and Tedeschi, John, eds. *Renaissance Studies in Honor of Hans Baron*. Florence, 1971

Muir, Edward. *Civic Ritual in Renaissance Venice*. Princeton, 1981

Muir, Edward. 'The Italian Renaissance in America', *American Historical Review*, C (1995) 1095–118

Najemy, John M. 'Politics: Class and Patronage'. In Grieco, Rocke, Gioffredi Superbi, *Italian Renaissance in the Twentieth Century*, pp. 119–36

Nichols, John. *The Progresses, Processions, and Magnificent Festivities of King James the First, His Royal Consort, Family, and Court*. 4 vols. London, 1828

Norbrook, David. 'Life and Death of Renaissance Man'. *Raritan*, VIII.4 (1989) 89–110

O'Malley, J. W. *Praise and Blame in Renaissance Rome: Rhetoric, Doctrine and Reform in the Sacred Orators of the Papal Court*. Durham, NC, 1979

O'Malley, J. W., et al., eds. *The Jesuits*. Toronto, 1999

Ogilvie, Brian W. *The Science of Describing: Natural History in Renaissance Europe, 1490–1620*. Chicago, forthcoming, 2005

Pane, Roberto. *Il Rinascimento nell'Italia meridionale*. 2 vols. Milan, 1975–77

Panofsky, Erwin. 'Artist, Scientist, Genius: Notes on the "Renaissance-Dämmerung"'. In *The Renaissance: Six Essays*. New York, 1962, pp. 123–84

Panofsky, Erwin. *Renaissance and Renascences in Western Art*. New York, 1969

Parry, V. J. 'Renaissance Historical Literature in Relation to the Near and Middle East. with Special Reference to Paolo Giovio'. In Bernard Lewis and P. M. Holt, eds, *Historians of the Middle East*. London, 1962, pp. 277–89

Patterson, Lee. 'On the Margin: Postmodernism, Ironic History and Medieval Studies'. *Speculum*, LXV (1990) 87–108

Peterson, David S. 'Out of the Margins: Religion and the Church in Renaissance Italy'. *Renaissance Quarterly*, LIII (2000) 835–79

Porter, Roy, and Teich, Mikulás, eds. *The Renaissance in National Context*. Cambridge, 1992

Pullan, Brian. '"Three Orders of Inhabitants": Social Hierarchies in the Republic of Venice'. In *Orders and Hierarchies in Late Medieval and Renaissance Europe*, ed. J. Denton. Basingstoke, 1999, pp. 147–68

Quint, David. *Epic and Empire*. Princeton, 1993

Rabil, Albert, ed. *Renaissance Humanism: Foundations, Forms and Legacy*. 3 vols. Philadelphia, 1988

Reeds, Karen M. 'Renaissance Humanism and Botany'. *Annals of Science*, XXXIII (1976) 519–42

Rocke, Michael. *Forbidden Friendships: Homosexuality and Male Culture in Renaissance Florence*. New York and Oxford, 1996

Rowland, Ingrid D. *The Culture of the High Renaissance: Ancients and Moderns in Sixteenth-Century Rome*. Cambridge, 1998

Rubiés, Joan-Pau. *Travel and Ethnology in the Renaissance*. Cambridge, 2000

Rubinstein, Nicolai, ed. *Florentine Studies: Politics and Society in Renaissance Florence*. Evanston, IL, 1968

Ruggiero, Guido, ed. *A Companion to the Worlds of the Renaissance*. Oxford, 2002

Rüsen, J. 'Jacob Burckhardt: Political Standpoint and Historical Insight on the Border of Postmodernism'. *History and Theory*, XXIV (1985) 235–46

Ryder, Alan. *The Kingdom of Naples under Alfonso the Magnanimous: The Making of a Modern State*. Oxford, 1976

Said, Edward W. *Orientalism*. 3rd edn, London, 2003

Saintsbury, George. *The Earlier Renaissance*. Periods of European Literature, V. Edinburgh and London, 1901

Scaraffia, Lucetta, and Zarri, Gabriella, eds. *Women and Faith: Catholic Religious Life in Italy from Late Antiquity to the Present*. Cambridge, MA, 1999

Schiller, K. *Gelehrte Gegenwelten: über humanistische Leitbilder im 20. Jahrhundert*. Frankfurt am Main, 2000

Sheehan, J. J. 'The German Renaissance in America'. In Grieco, Rocke and Gioffredi Superbi, *Italian Renaissance in the Twentieth Century*, pp. 47–64

Shelton, Alan A. 'Cabinets of Transgression: Renaissance Collections and the Incorporation of the New World'. In John Elsner and Roger Cardinal, eds, *The Cultures of Collecting*. London, 1994, pp. 175–203

Skinner, Quentin. *The Foundations of Modern Political Thought*. 2 vols. Cambridge, 1978

Smith, George Gregory. *The Transition Period*. Periods of European Literature, IV. Edinburgh and London, 1900

Smith, George Gregory, ed. *Elizabethan Critical Essays*. 2 vols. London, 1904

Soussloff, Catherine M. *The Absolute Artist: The Historiography of a Concept*. Minneapolis, 1997

Sperling, Jutta Gisela. *Convents and the Body Politic in Late Renaissance Venice*. Chicago, 1999

Starn, Randolph. 'Who's Afraid of the Renaissance?' In *The Past and Future of Medieval Studies*, ed. John Van Engen. Notre Dame, IN and London, 1994, pp. 129–47.

Stinger, Charles L. *Humanism and the Church Fathers: Ambrogio Traversari (1386–1439) and Christian Antiquity in the Italian Renaissance*. Albany, NY, 1977

Stinger, Charles L. *The Renaissance in Rome*. Bloomington, IN, 1985

Strocchia, Sharon. *Death and Ritual in Renaissance Florence*. Baltimore, 1992

Symonds, John Addington. *Renaissance in Italy*. 7 vols. London, 1875–86

*The Renaissance in Europe*. 5 vols. New Haven and London, 2000.

Trevor-Roper, Hugh. 'Jacob Burckhardt'. *Proceedings of the British Academy*, LXX (1984) 359–78

Trexler, Richard. *Public Life in Renaissance Florence*. New York, 1980

Trinkaus, Charles. *In Our Image and Likeness: Humanity and Divinity in Italian Renaissance Thought*. 2 vols. Chicago, 1970

Vasoli, Cesare. *Umanesimo e rinascimento*, 2nd edn. Palermo, 1976

Ward, John O. 'Rhetorical Theory and the Rise and Decline of *dictamen* in the Middle Ages and Early Renaissance'. *Rhetorica*, XIX (2001) 175–223

Weinstein, Donald. *Savonarola and Florence: Prophecy and Patriotism in the Renaissance*. Princeton, 1970

Weisinger, Herbert. 'Who Began the Revival of Learning? The Renaissance Point of View'. *Papers of the Michigan Academy of Science, Arts and Letters*, XXX (1944) 625–38

Weissman, Ronald F. E. *Ritual Brotherhood in Renaissance Florence*. New York, 1982

White, Hayden. *Metahistory: The Historical Imagination in Nineteenth-Century Europe*. Baltimore and London, 1974

Witt, Ronald G. *Hercules at the Crossroads: The Life, Works and Thought of Coluccio Salutati*. Durham, NC, 1983

Witt, Ronald G. 'Medieval Italian Culture and the Origins of Humanism as a Stylistic Ideal'. In Rabil, *Renaissance Humanism*, I, pp. 44–50

Witt, Ronald G. *'In the Footsteps of the Ancients': The Origins of Humanism from Lovato to Bruni*. Leiden, 2000

Zamora, Margaret. *Language, Authority and Indigenous History in the* Comentarios reales. Cambridge, 1988

Zemon Davis, Natalie. *Society and Culture in Early Modern France*. Stanford, 1975

Zemon Davis, Natalie. *Fiction in the Archives: Pardon Tales and their Tellers in Sixteenth-Century France*. Oxford, 1987

Zerner, Henri, ed. *Le stampe e la diffusione delle immagini e degli stili*. Bologna, 1983

# index